# FOXFIRE 12

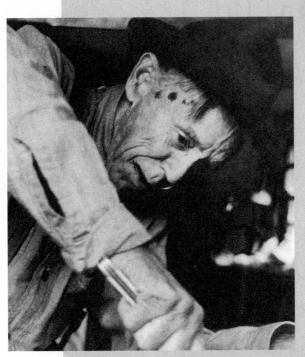

# FOXFIRE 12

WAR STORIES, CHEROKEE TRADITIONS,

SUMMER CAMPS, SQUARE DANCING,

CRAFTS, AND MORE AFFAIRS

OF PLAIN LIVING

Edited by KAYE CARVER COLLINS, ANGIE CHEEK,

and FORMER FOXFIRE STUDENTS

ANCHOR BOOKS

A Division of Random House, Inc.

New York

AN ANCHOR BOOKS ORIGINAL, SEPTEMBER 2004

The Foxfire Fund, Inc.
P.O. Box 541
Mountain City, GA 30562-0541
706-746-5828
www.foxfire.org

All material in this book originally appeared in *Foxfire Magazine*.

Library of Congress Cataloging-in-Publication Data
Foxfire 12 : war stories, Cherokee traditions, summer camps, square
dancing, crafts, and more affairs of plain living /
edited by Kaye Carver Collins, Angie Cheek, and
Foxfire students.
p.  cm.
ISBN 1-4000-3261-X
1. Rabun County (Ga.)—Social life and customs.   2. Appalachian Region,
Southern—Social life and customs.   3. Country life—Georgia—Rabun County.
4. Country life—Appalachian Region, Southern.   5. Folklore—Georgia—Rabun County.
6. Folklore—Appalachian Region, Southern.   7. Handicraft—Georgia—Rabun County.
8. Handicraft—Appalachian Region, Southern.   9. Rabun County (Ga.)—Biography.
I. Title: Foxfire twelve.   II. Collins, Kaye Carver.   III. Cheek, Angie.
F292.R3F715 2004
975.8'123—dc22
2004045136

Book design by JoAnne Metsch

www.anchorbooks.com

Printed in the United States of America
10

*We dedicate this book to our heroes: our elders, men and women, those living and those already gone, whose hearths and hearts provided warmth and solace to family, friends, and neighbors, both young and old. We recognize them and honor them as sentinels of true strength and courage, fierce warriors who faced the battles of life with a steely resolve. They have left an enduring legacy for those of us who follow: wisdom, personal integrity, and true honor, as well as love and respect for self, for others, for our country, and for the land. "Clothed with strength and dignity," they are "worth more than rubies." We arise to call them blessed.*

# CONTENTS

# ACKNOWLEDGMENTS

Writing the thank-yous is supposed to be the easiest part of any book; however, when you have as many people involved in the process of completing a book as Foxfire does, the task can be daunting! First, we are grateful to all of our contacts who have graciously opened their homes, hearts, and lives to thirty-seven-plus years of Foxfire students and have shared their old family photos for this and our other publications. Second, we need to thank the students. Their enthusiasm, exuberance, and energy are contagious! Their zest for learning keeps us all going! We also need to recognize the Rabun County Board of Education, Superintendent Matt Arthur, and Principal Mark Earnest, who have espoused the Foxfire program. Without their unfailing support, we wouldn't have easy access to the students in our community or to the well-equipped computer laboratory at Rabun County High School.

As always, the Foxfire staff and part-time employees have provided unwavering aid in countless ways. Last summer, Margie Bennett, supervising a crew of current students (Maggie Whitmire, Heather Woods, Ivy Garland, and Kasie Hicks), conducted extra interviews for this book, and Ann Moore has spent countless hours proofreading all the articles and editing drafts. Robert Murray and Lee Carpenter, handymen extraordinaire, have done everything from computer troubleshooting to maneuvering dance formations for the square dance photos. Volunteers such as Ernie Holt gave us words of encouragement and provided needed humor to break the tension of deadline blues.

Lois Nations, who works for the Habersham County Board of Education, and Estelle Brown, a longtime friend of Foxfire, helped us track down deceased contacts' relatives in order to obtain the necessary permission to publish their stories. Mary Elizabeth Law, a member of the Rabun County Historical Society, provided invaluable information for our research. The assistance provided by the Folkways Center at North Georgia and its supporters made the square dancing chapter complete. Helen Wall, wife of the late Lester J. Wall, provided a wonderful photo of her husband, and Mark Warren aided in research on "The Trail of Tears."

Many friends worked together to give you *Foxfire 12*. We thank you, our readers, for your interest and your unfailing support. Without you, our work could not continue.

# INTRODUCTION

A s my husband and I have traveled to various world destinations, strangers have come up to me and said confidently, "You must be from Georgia." I wonder how they know. Is *Georgia* stamped indelibly on my forehead? Is the secret detected by some other defining feature or fashion? Or is it that Georgia mountain drawl?

I'm proud to call Clayton, Rabun County, Georgia, my hometown. It's a small, rural mountain community in the northeast corner of the state, a few miles from both the North Carolina and South Carolina state lines. We have our own way of talking; various dialects become apparent as visitors travel to different parts of the Peach State. For example, I don't talk anything like those folks at home at Tara: "Ahm gonna set ayut own the verayundah an' siyup mah mi-yunt tay." Mine is a Northeast Georgia mountain accent—not quite so "drawly" but soft and flat and apparently marked. "Georgia mountain girl," however, is more than dialect.

My roots are in this place, 377 square miles of blue mountains, green lakes, ancient hardwoods and tall pines, and heritage. Our county, nestled in the foothills of the Appalachians, boasts five lakes; three state parks; Tallulah Gorge, a chasm that geologists have called the Grand Canyon of the East; the southernmost ski resort in the United States; hundreds of hiking and biking trails (the Appalachian Trail forms our western boundary); and a population of fifteen thousand that doubles during tourist seasons. Rabun Bald (the highest undeveloped mountain in Georgia), Screamer Mountain, and Black Rock rise thousands of feet above sea level and offer beautiful vistas of a patchwork of fields and streams, as well as of other mounts. Trillium, lady slippers, jack-in-the-pulpits, and other wildflowers are colorful pools on the dark palette of the cool forest floors. Deer, black bears, red foxes, wild turkeys, bobcats, and of course a host of squirrels and birds inhabit National Forest lands, and dozens of waterfalls (Bridal Veil, L'eau d'Or, Estatoah, Stekoa, Hurricane, Tempesta, Oceana . . .) cascade into our wild and scenic rivers: the Chattooga, the Tallulah, the Little Tennessee. Kayakers and rafters brave the torrents and hydraulics of class 4 and 5 rapids: Bull Sluice, Sock 'em Dog, and Corkscrew. With a quick flick, trout fishermen cast their flies into our mountain streams and angle for hours. Folks park themselves in wooden rockers on front porches and watch their children and grandchildren bathe in a shower of fall leaves or glory in a southern sun as it sets behind the purple mountain. Ours is an area unparalleled for recreation and grandeur.

When I return from a trip, driving north on Highway 441 back into Rabun County, I top that hill in Tallulah Falls and feel my stomach unknot. I pass the sign that touts our slogan: "Rabun County, Georgia, 'where spring spends the summer.' " I take a deep breath and know an indescribable peace. I am home.

I went to high school in the old building in "downtown" Clayton (the school's gone now, doomed by fire and "progress"). The floors were of dark wood, which the janitors cleaned with a reddish, oily, grainy compound and a push broom. Halls were lined with open wooden lockers and filled with students who respected their teachers and elders and knew that if they got a whippin' at school, they'd get a worse one at home. Best friends, driver's licenses, first dates, proms, sock hops, senior plays—many of us share some of the same memories.

A baby boomer, I left for college in 1965. The times were the turbulent sixties, but I never got caught up in the maelstrom of "revolution." *Groovy?* Grooves are in the sides of boards found in cabins and well-made furniture— tongue and groove. *Far out?* Those folks who live in the Satolah community live far out on the edge of Rabun County. Burn my bra? Nice girls wear underwear! *Free love?* Love of God, love for your mama, daddy, siblings, grandma, and grandpa—they loved you freely, and you freely reciprocated. That *other* love? Oh, no. Nice girls didn't do that—no Christian boy would marry you. My roots grounded me. Besides, your mama always found out any and every indiscretion, and you could bet consequences would ensue!

No, I was "raised in the way I should go," and my raising grounds me. My roots run deep. Clayton is Daddy's hometown, too. He graduated from the University of Georgia, served in the Army in World War II, and returned here to practice law. My grandfather and my father practiced law together, and folks around here called them both Colonel Davis because that's just what they called lawyers in the old days. The Davises are in the local history book: *A History of Rabun County and Its People.* My parents and grandparents are buried here in the old Roane Cemetery on Old Highway 441 between Clayton and Tiger. My nurturing came not only from my immediate family but also from my community, a community that seemed to be connected, a huge, extended family. So I am a part of these people and these hills.

When I married, I married an "outsider" from Toccoa, a town about thirty miles from here, and I moved away—you know, whither thou goest, I will go (a principle which, by the way, I espouse); however, as fate would have it, fickle as it is, the company for which my husband works relocated him to . . . guess where? My hometown! So I came back home in 1992 and became chair of the English department and facilitator for the *Foxfire Magazine* class, and now I am honored to have had a hand in *Foxfire 12*. I feel very fortunate to have become a part of the Foxfire endeavor, for not only did I become a better teacher through my involvement with the Foxfire Approach to Teaching and Learning, but I have also had a small part in recording and preserving the language, culture, and heritage of the people of Appalachia, my people.

The colors, smells, and sounds of home fill me, lift me. The red clay sucks at my shoes; the green lake waters lap the rhythm of the past and the future; the purple mountains stretch to the heavens. Tree frogs trill; bobwhites babble their own names; katydids call. The wind whispers the secrets of kindness, joy, peace, wisdom, and an enduring strength, the secrets many of my elders already know. I strain to hear.

—*Angie Cheek*

I'M ONE of those people who love a good challenge, so when an opportunity presented itself recently, I said yes! I'm starting a new job in August, a new chapter in my life. I'll be teaching math to fourth and fifth graders. As my friends and acquaintances hear the news, they often call and say, "I hear you're leaving Foxfire." My answer is always, "No, I'm not leaving Foxfire." Even though I won't be here every day, as I have been over the last thirteen years, I truly believe that once you see students making real connections with the community around them and with their own lives, when you experience firsthand those connections from having been a Foxfire student, and when you are entering the teaching profession with the knowledge of how important those connections are to learning, you can never leave Foxfire!

On a dark, dreary, rain-soaked afternoon, as I sit in Foxfire's archives room writing this introduction, I am overwhelmed to think of all that surrounds me and what it represents. The negatives, the photographs, the transcripts of interviews, the file of past articles all document not only a way of life but also a community: relatives, neighbors, and friends. The treasures in this room are much more valuable than gold, not only because of their being my people, but because of the impact those people, this community, and a bunch of teenagers have had on both educational philosophy and people around the world. However, the greatest treasure by far is the impact those old-timers and the kids have had on each other.

As I look back on all I have experienced here, the moments that moved me most happened with the people I've met over the years. My first interview as a sixteen-year-old was with Aunt Arie Carpenter. Her kindness, graciousness, and friendliness hooked me on Foxfire. Over the succeeding years I've met and grown to know many more of the elders in our community. Each added to my sense of self, community, and belonging and affected me in a very personal way. Lawton Brooks, Kenny Runion, Max Woody, Flora Youngblood, Nanny Ramey, and countless others have all greatly influenced who I am and what I believe. And through Foxfire, I was able to understand and value my own parents, both of whom were Foxfire contacts, in a new way.

The experiences I've had are certainly atypical for a young girl from the mountains. I've traveled to Chicago; Washington, D.C.; Colorado; Alabama; and Louisiana to give speeches and workshops to teachers, students, and community groups. As a seventeen-year-old, I had my photograph in *People* magazine. As an eighteen-year-old, I brushed elbows with then vice president Gerald Ford. As an adult, on the Foxfire staff, I have had the opportunity to meet numerous people who have been affected by *The Foxfire Magazine* and Foxfire books, as well as the teaching approach. Most important, I was given the opportunity to work with the teachers and students at Rabun County High School in the *Foxfire Magazine* class and thus was able to pass on knowledge and skills to a new generation of Foxfire students. Because of that experience, I discovered how much I love working with students and decided I needed to become a teacher.

The skills I've gained over the years are innumerable. I've learned interviewing, editing, photography, and computer skills, as well as people and life skills, and more. My fervent hope is that all students who come through the *Foxfire Magazine* class can have similar experiences that affect them on a personal level and can develop skills that will help them throughout their lives.

The students, staff, and volunteers with whom I have worked have been extraordinary. They are hardworking, dedicated, industrious folks who care passionately about Foxfire and about the people in our community, both young and old. They are willing to do whatever they can, including spending countless hours working, to ensure Foxfire's success. The Foxfire Fund is extremely lucky to have such devoted leaders, associates, and volunteers.

I have often been accused of being the world's number one pessimist, but as I look ahead, I'm excited about my new vocation and about Foxfire's future, too. Even though Foxfire's endowment has taken a huge hit from the downturn in the stock market, as I sit here and gaze at the Foxfire Center, it's difficult to be pessimistic. Foxfire students and staff have restored or built twenty-eight cabins. The Foxfire Center, nestled among a hundred and thirty acres of mountainside land, is a true learning laboratory. Everything that Foxfire is today grew out of that center or the Rabun County classroom: *The Foxfire Magazine,* the Foxfire book series, the Foxfire Museum, and the

Foxfire Approach to Teaching were dreams that were begun and realized at the Foxfire Center.

Very few places like the Foxfire Center exist where you can visit and say, "Students did this!" The buildings have historical and educational significance. Students helped build those cabins and documented the entire process, and in the course of doing so, they learned more about curriculum mandates (math, English, spelling, writing, and so forth), local history, their community, and their elders; and most important, they learned more about themselves and what they were capable of doing. In addition to all that, each student could find some way to be successful at the Foxfire Center. All those skills and opportunities are assets students will carry with them the rest of their lives.

At the same time, the center gives students and community members a sense of place and belonging often missing today. Nowadays, we are so involved in our own lives that we rarely think about others and our connections to them. A large part of what the center gives people is that notion of connectedness: to our lives, other people, books, or the past. Almost all visitors sense that strong connection at the center, where students, teachers, parents, community elders, and visitors all become investigators. They may be investigating for different reasons and in different ways, but each comes away with a learning experience that is enduring. These memorable experiences are touchstones that change each person's way of thinking, way of doing, and/or way of living. What happens at the center is what makes Foxfire unique and what gives me optimism about Foxfire's future.

As I write this, the mountains have faded from green to blue and finally to purple. The hues remind me that, even though Foxfire and I are both going through changes, the important possessions are basically the same. The wild turkeys still come out here early in the morning while the dew is still on the leaves. The bears still come down from Black Rock in the dark of night to scavenge for food. The students and teachers still work hard every year to produce quality pieces for *The Foxfire Magazine.* Passionate teachers still care deeply about their students' learning. And there are still people like Aunt Arie and Lawton Brooks, people willing to embrace life and all the changes it brings.

King Whitney, Jr., once said, "Change has considerable psychological impact on the human mind. To the fearful, it is threatening, because it means that things may get worse. To the hopeful, it is encouraging, because things may get better. To the confident, it is inspiring, because the challenge exists to make things better." As Foxfire and I move forward, I am hopeful and confident. We both face new challenges, new opportunities to make things better. I know the best is yet to come!

—*Kaye Carver Collins*

# FOXFIRE 12

# PERSONALITY
# PORTRAITS

"I hear voices from long ago

telling their stories to me."

—*Bob Justus*

M any of the folks who have appeared in the Foxfire magazines and books are folks near and dear. Foxfire students interviewed my mother, Lina Davis, for *Foxfire 7*, and her amazing story appeared in *The Foxfire Magazine*, Spring/Summer 1994; my mother-in-law, Ruby Cheek, demonstrated the making of rose beads in the Spring/Summer 1995 issue. Mom died two summers ago, but having her story chronicled forever in Foxfire publications is important to me—memories preserved.

Many of the folks whose lives we have recorded are familiar friends. Maneuvering through Rabun County with horse-drawn or donkey-drawn covered wagons, Johnny Eller and Frank Rickman were familiar sights on rural roads (and even on Main Street, Clayton, on Saturdays!). Melvin Taylor and his "fish tales," the infamous Ches McCartney (aka the Goat Man) and his strange entourage, Fred Huff and his Top of Georgia Jamboree, and so many others have been a part of the fabric of our lives. Folks enjoyed Saturday night square dancin' with caller Lester J. Wall at the Mountain City Playhouse or going to the Jaycee-sponsored Mountaineer Festival and witnessing old-timey events: catchin' a greased pig; climbin' a greased pole; entering the pie, canned vegetables, quilting, and sewing contests; and various and sundry other forms of mountain mischief and mayhem. One year Mama even made me a dress with a bustle and a matching bonnet, and I won the costume contest. The festival was an opportunity for citizens and civic groups to showcase a bit of our heritage, a heritage others often belittle.

For us at Foxfire, both staff and students, venturing into Appalachia has enriched our lives, for we have met multitalented down-to-earth characters and craftsmen (and women) whose voices have resounded with strength the wisdom of the mountains and echoed lessons learned from the past, lessons we would do well to heed.

Chronicling the poignant stories of those older and wiser than I is what I love most about Foxfire. The sixth Core Practice of the Foxfire Approach to Teaching and Learning reads, "Connections between the classroom work, the surrounding communities, and the world beyond the community are clear. Course content is connected to the community in which the learners live." I like that word *connections*. Why is an initiative like Foxfire's important? Connectedness. In an extended metaphor, metaphysical poet John

Donne, in "Meditation 17," dramatically suggests that all people are connected, just as all clods of dirt form a continent:

> No man is an island, entire of itself; every man is a piece of the continent, a part of the main. If a clod be washed away by the sea, Europe is the less ... any man's death diminishes me, because I am involved in mankind ...

Mankind is less for having lost any of us: a mass of people or a friend; we will be less when you are gone, for we are all connected. Donne also compares humanity to a volume, a book composed of many, many chapters:

> [A]ll mankind is of one author, and is one volume; when one man dies, one chapter is not torn out of the book, but translated into a better language; and every chapter must be so translated.

When each of us has passed from this life, our chapter will not be ripped from the volume. When *The End* appears, our personal story will remain a part of the great work. We have a common humanity. No one is isolated: Each of us is connected to everyone else. An *aha* moment?

As the years have passed and I have grown older, I have come to realize the sacred gift left me by my elders. I have listened to their reminiscences: their tales of surviving seemingly insurmountable hardships; of finding their lifemate; of loving their God, their families, their nation, their land. I grow every day in my understanding and appreciation of my heritage. I begin to sense the presence of those who were here before. I hear the voices of a bygone time whispering from the mists, calling from forests, singing from the rushing rivers and streams, crying out from the red clay, and shouting from the depths of Tallulah Gorge and the heights of the Great Smoky Mountains. Those who are still with us, as those who are gone, are chapters in a great story, the story of humankind. They have much to tell us. My prayer is that we will heed their words.

—*Angie Cheek*

# CHES McCARTNEY:
# THE LEGEND OF THE GOAT MAN

*"The goats have taught me a lot in the past thirty years. They don't, for example, care how I smell or how I look. They trust me and have faith in me, and this is more than I can say for a lot of people."*

—Qtd. in Patton 7

I am not originally from Rabun County. Because I am from the Lone Star State—Texas—I had never heard of the Goat Man. Although I now know that he has been in forty-nine of the fifty states of America (all except Hawaii), he is not as well known in Texas as he is in Georgia. I've lived here in Northeast Georgia for three years, and his name has been mentioned off and on in conversations with home folks. As everybody does, when, as an outsider, you're unfamiliar with a subject, you often tend to pay it no attention because the name means nothing to you. My lack of knowledge on the subject of America's Goat Man was about to change.

After I was chosen to work at Foxfire during the summer program and had completed some unfinished articles, someone mentioned the Goat Man. I was intrigued. This man, for many decades, up to 1987, with and without goats (mostly with), traveled all over the continental United States. At the time, most did not know his real name or where he was from.

I learned that the Goat Man always appeared, along with about twelve to thirty goats—which "he proudly called his maternity ward" (Patton 3) or his babies (Patton 19)—and wagons full of junk, around the time of Clayton, Georgia's Mountaineer Festival, a celebration that used to be an annual event. There are various accounts of Charlie, Chester, better known as Chess or Ches McCartney, aka the Goat Man, that tell of sightings of his strange caravan over the span of thirty-eight to fifty-five years. (For the record, I have found various names and many different spellings of Mr. McCartney's name, but in an effort to remain as historically accurate as possible, the spelling of Ches McCartney's name is the same as his signature.) The sightings became rarer until finally there were none at all. Georgia newspapers began reporting that the Goat Man had retired from the road, and folks began telling tales of his demise. I wanted to meet this national legend, so in trying to find out anything I could, I called local libraries and newspapers. My search ended successfully: Mr. McCartney was in a nursing home in Macon, Georgia. Having fractured his hip, he, at a self-professed one hundred and five years of age (he was probably several years younger), was in a wheelchair. His white hair peeked out from underneath his blue cap, and his blue eyes, set in his weathered face, sparkled and danced as he recounted the tales of the roads he has traveled.

This article represents research from various sources: personal interviews with some eyewitnesses from Rabun County, Georgia, and others who have vivid memories of the Goat Man, and my own interview with Mr. McCartney, as well as quotes from the pamphlets he sold during his traveling years. Darryl Patton's book *America's Goat Man (Mr. Ches McCartney)*, used with permission, was an invaluable resource.

Some who met Ches McCartney thought he was a friendly genius; others thought him filthy and crazed. All, however, remember the Goat Man as a mysterious, eccentric, legendary character, a gypsy mountain man, a folk hero who followed his own way, herding goats from Florida to Maine, from Washington, D.C., to California. "Like a Knight of the Round Table," Mr. McCartney once averred, "I am in search of the Holy Grail" (qtd. in Patton 55).

*—Stephanie Dollar and Angie Cheek*

CHES MCCARTNEY was born in the early 1900s, on the farm of his parents near Van Buren Township, Keokuk County, Iowa, the son of Albert McCartney and Louise E. Russell McCartney. He lived there until he was fourteen years old. He ran off to New York City and, at the age of fourteen, married a twenty-four-year-old Spanish knife thrower who threw knives at him in local bars to make tips. Charlie (Ches) recounted that his wife "threw the knives in his general direction: she would throw a couple to attract attention; then as the coins hit the floor, she would throw all twenty-five. The closer the knives came to Charlie, the bigger the tips. Charlie was unable to grow a long, flowing beard during this time" (qtd. in Patton 73).

The pair discovered they were going to have a child, so Ches invested in a sturdy team of horses, some goats, and a twenty-acre farm near his childhood home in the What Cheer community of Iowa. Albert Gene (Bert/Gene) was born here. McCartney averred that his son thrived "on pure country air, vegetables, spring water, and plenty of goat's milk" (qtd. in Patton 74). Life was good for a time. Ches even became "a devoted reader of the Bible and started expounding the Gospel to his fellow man" (qtd. in Patton 74).

PLATE 1  An early photograph of Ches McCartney

Then came the Depression. No market existed for their abundant crops, and during an extremely hard winter, they lost both their horses. McCartney related the misfortunes that befell him when the Depression of 1929 hit hard: "I lost my life savings in the bank failure and had to take a job on the Works Project [Progress] Administration—the well-known WPA" (qtd. in Patton 6). Most people farmed in that area. You were either a farmer or a log cutter, or you worked for the government in the WPA, CCA, or CCC. "While he was working for the WPA, a tree fell on him and left him with a crushed lung, a crushed left shoulder, a deformed left elbow, and a smashed right hip" (Patton 25). According to Darryl Patton, "He was left for dead for a while before they found him." McCartney said he lay there for hours before anyone came to help: "They thought I was dead and took me to the undertaker. He was sticking the embalming needle in me when I woke up" (qtd. in Patton 14). "Luckily," as McCartney so succinctly put it, "the undertaker was slow" (qtd. in Patton 6). The Goat Man ended up with a permanently mangled arm and shoulder. In fact, his arm was so crushed that he couldn't do heavy work.

After the physical limitations caused by his injuries in the WPA accident and the Depression exacerbated his problems, he came to a realization: He had a family and needed money. He needed a gimmick: He liked Robinson Crusoe and liked preaching. McCartney decided that there "were places to be seen, and a challenge to be met" (qtd. in Patton 74). He had his wife make them goatskin clothes. He hitched a number of billy goats to the front of a ramshackle handcrafted wagon, loaded his wife and son onto it, traveled around locally, and finally decided to hit the roads of America for good. McCartney related that the challenge "proved too harrowing for Mrs. McCartney (a 1984 article in *The Atlanta Journal-Constitution* reported Albert Gene's mother's name as Saddie Smythheart), and [Ches] awakened one morning to find that their party of three was now a party of two" (qtd. in Patton 74–75): himself and Gene. Ches said, "She went away and left me and the boy . . . took up with another man" (qtd. in Patton 33). Some purport that Ches soon returned to Iowa, left his son with grandparents who enrolled him in school, and, thereafter, returned to his travels. Many witnesses, however, testify to having seen his son with him, even as a teenager. In fact, most agree that Gene traveled, off and on, with his father until the age of fifteen. A Fayetteville, North Carolina news reporter commented about one encounter with father and son: "Gene's face clouded with petulance . . . The old man grinned at him. 'He thinks he knows as much as the Lord . . . but he's stupid' . . . Gene crawled out of the wagon. His teeth were rotten. He hummed vacuously to himself . . . crawled out of the top of the wagon and began loosening tubs . . . let them crash to the ground" (qtd. in Patton 33). Ches McCartney, with or without his son, set out across the country to fulfill his wanderlust, and the rest, as they say, is history.

PLATE 2  The Goat Man
coddles one of his "babies."

"His hair and beard were long and shabby and would remind you of a stump full of 'Granddaddy long legs.' "

*—Qtd. in Patton 21*

A writer for *The Atlanta Journal-Constitution* reported that the Goat Man was five feet eleven in height, weighed 190 pounds, and had a beard that reached almost to the hipline (Patton 25). One witness claimed to have a vivid recollection of the Goat Man in the summer or fall of 1948, '49, or '50: "The Goat Man's appearance was pitiful to say the least. His clothes were old, tattered, and soiled beyond belief. His hair and beard were long and shabby and would remind you of a stump full of 'Granddaddy long legs' " (qtd. in Patton 21).

"A lady asked me when I last had a bath, and I told her probably when my parents bathed me sixty-five years ago."

*—Qtd. in Patton 69*

An article that appeared in *The Rome* [Georgia] *News Tribune* described his appearance in 1969: "His skin, stained molasses brown from years of sleeping in fields and forests, and his shaggy, grisly beard give him the appearance of an elderly hippie who forgot to file for Medicare" (qtd. in Patton 83). "His attire consist[ed] of blackened overalls, a dirty, shredded jacket, brogans, and a ball cap that was once some other color" (qtd. in Patton 57). "The smell was so bad that it was hard to get close to him or the wagon" (qtd. in Patton 21). In fact, McCartney himself vowed he hadn't had a bath in "God knows when" (qtd. in Patton 55). "A lady asked me when I last had a bath, and I told her probably when my parents bathed me sixty-five years ago" (qtd. in Patton 69).

"The junk inside the wagon bed was so arranged it looked like a billy goat's stomach all screwed up" (qtd. in Patton 21). The Anniston, Alabama newspaper, *The Anniston Star*, reported that the wagon was "decorated with everything from George Wallace stickers to signs warning 'Prepare to meet thy God' " (qtd. in Patton 104). A *Savannah Morning News* reporter wrote, "It was really a dual wagon—a main vehicle and trailer, six goats pulling, seven hitched to the trailer, and about a dozen spares hitched alongside. The main wagon had four wheels, the trailer two. Both were piled high with pots, pans, lanterns, sleeping gear, and Lord knows what else" (qtd. in Patton 113). Arleen Snow says, "I remember in our crowd we all stood quietly in awe just to survey the whole scene. It was so unusual because here was this man with a long beard and long hair back in the early sixties, and the wagon would literally be covered in pots and pans and trinkets and junk.

PLATE 3  The legendary folk hero and his caravan of goat-drawn
wagons traveled across America.

Barely could you see the wagon itself for all the junk. He would sell his
junk." A reporter for *The Charleston Post Courier* described the strange
sight: "The wagons rest on makeshift wheels and chassis, and the front
wagon is a crude affair, fashioned from pieces of metal. The singletrees were
whittled out by a pocketknife. The harness is handsewn leather, stitched to

PLATE 4  Signs warned folks of the end times when God would return.

fit the various-sized goats. The driver sits in the first wagon and is aided by rearview mirrors on each side. The sides are built up out of boards, tin cans, license plates, glass, wire, bottles, tree branches, straw, pots and pans, rope, tinfoil, canvas, cloth, etc. Kerosene lanterns, used for parking at night and camp illumination, hang from the four corners. The crippled goats ride on a ledge in the first unit. Small windmill ornaments turn merrily in the breeze. Bins of hay and oats for the animals are stored in the wagon. Tubs for watering are also among the equipment" (qtd. in Patton 29).

"He would sell his postcards: one for twenty-five cents, two for fifty cents, and three for a dollar; and the people that would buy three for a dollar would think they had gotten a great deal and would go home and just hit themselves when they realized what they had done. My uncle was one of those."

—*Arleen Snow*

Apparently the Goat Man and his entourage traveled "about 2.5 miles per hour and with time out for camping, milking, and feeding, a total of 12 miles a day would be about a top day's journey" (qtd. in Patton 22). In his travels, Ches McCartney, who now was becoming infamous as the Goat Man, always had a scheme to make money. The curious wanted him to pose for photographs; he heard others express regret at not having brought a camera. In pamphlets, McCartney then compiled answers to the questions he was asked most frequently; he had photographs taken of him and his goats; he made copies in the form of postcards and made them available to anyone interested. He sold these postcards from a large garbage can. Arleen Snow can remember a gimmick: "He never did sell any of his junk expensive. He was a crafty fella; he was a businessman. I consider him an entrepreneur in his own way. For instance, he would sell his postcards: one for twenty-five cents, two for fifty cents, and three for a dollar; and the people that would buy three for a dollar would think they had gotten a great deal and would go home and just hit themselves when they realized what they had done. My uncle was one of those." "The Goat Man would," Darryl Patton recalls, "start a fire out of whatever sticks, pieces of paper, and other trash he could find. The final touch was always an old tire scrounged from the side of the road during his travels . . . Standing in a cloud of thick, acrid black smoke, he would wait for the crowds he knew would come just as surely as moths attracted to a flame . . . The oily black smoke billowing up from his campfire was just one of many ploys he used. This not only worked, but worked well, as people for miles around would see the smoke, and wondering if there had been an automobile accident, would immediately go to investigate. Once they made it to his campsite, they would rarely leave without having parted with a dollar or two for his wares" (Patton 2). Besides selling postcards and booklets, he sold anything he could pick up, anything he could fit on his wagon. "Through the sale of these photographs and this literature, Ches was able to put his son through college, build several churches, and acquire some real estate." He "paid the government in cash" (Patton 75).

People thought that the reason he traveled was because he was homeless, stupid, and broke. Mort Meadors, who grew up in Macon, has his own thoughts on why the nomad traveled: "The Goat Man did not travel because he was homeless or because he had to. I think he traveled because he liked to be around people. He was always nice to me and to everyone else. He was just like an attraction; he just did his own thing." Arleen Snow said, "I believe he was very intelligent; he obviously had a mind for business. He thought through what he could do during the Depression, of all times, to make money, and he did it and took care of his family."

Darryl Patton recalls, "Just because he was dirty and smelly, people thought he was dumb. But he probably had a higher IQ than average. He was very eccentric, but there's a difference between being eccentric and being stupid. I think he was very intelligent: He knew exactly what he was doing." McCartney himself boasted, "I never went to school in my life, but I can read and figure with any man" (qtd. in Patton 83). He added philosophically, "A lot of people think themselves smart and become fools" (qtd. in Patton 83).

PLATE 5  The eccentric wayfarer with one of his beloved goats

Darryl Patton concurs: "I think he was very intelligent; he knew exactly what he was doing. Now, he got taken on a few occasions, fell for some of the jokes that were played on him." A Macon, Georgia citizen who lived in Goat Man territory recalls a story told him by a fraternity brother who later became a county attorney and state legislator: "Once a carnival appeared in Twiggs County [Georgia]. Along with the many attractions was the mummi- fied remains of Ethyl, 'the petrified woman.' Several of the local pranksters decided that Ethyl should join the Goat Man's team. During the night, when all was calm on the Goat Man's estate, the group kidnapped Ethyl and placed her in the covered wagon of the Goat Man. His passenger was not discovered until the group had reached Macon" (qtd. in Patton 70). He didn't see a dead body with him for several miles because of all the junk in there. The story goes that McCartney was very calm and notified the local sheriff that he "would like to relinquish his right to Ethyl and have her reunited with the carnival" (qtd. in Patton 70). Some oglers played tricks on him, and he played tricks on them.

> "Sure, the thirty goats cause a lot of commotion everywhere I go . . . but they mean one thing to me: independence."
> —*Qtd. in Patton 25*

All of the junk on his wagon, not to mention the wagon itself and the goats, caused quite a commotion. Rabun County, Georgia native Sonny Cannon remembers all the commotion the Goat Man caused: "His wagon wasn't that big. Down around Tallulah Gorge, around the old Tallulah Point, that was the little, narrow road [old two-lane Georgia Highway 441] he traveled. Back then it was a major highway. We didn't have these big highways that we have now. All that road that come up through Tiger, that was a major part of it, too. You can imagine what a feller could create with a hundred goats and a wagon. It was a pretty big traffic jam. The law would have to let you go through." Sonny's wife, Becky Cannon, can remember, from her girlhood, the Goat Man: "The wagon was like an old covered wagon, you know, like you see in movies. It was just loaded down with all kinds of stuff. Lanterns would be hanging off his wagon all the time. He had everything in his wagon for his goats and him. At night he would light his lanterns so cars could see where his goats were." Ches McCartney knew that he caused confusion and excitement everywhere he went, but it didn't bother him: "Sure, the thirty goats cause a lot of commotion everywhere I go . . . but they mean one thing to me: independence" (qtd. in Patton 25). He did love those goats of his, his babies. A witness recalled that the "Goat Man had a three-legged goat he carried in a box-like chamber attached to the wagon. The little goat would

PLATE 6 Twenty to thirty goats pulled and accompanied wagons filled with "treasures" collected along the roadsides.

jump onto his lap, and once in doing so, the goat's spiked horn hit the Goat Man in the left brow. I cannot remember if the impact broke the skin or not. The old man would quote Scripture for a while and curse for a while" (qtd. in Patton 58).

The Goat Man's wagon would always be covered. If he came across junk on the road, he would pick it up. Mort Meadors said, "He had so much junk in his wagon. I guess it was a hobby of his. As he would travel, he would find old road signs, bottles of RC Cola, and things that everyone else thought was trash. But to him, these things were not trash: They were valuables. To make a little money, to afford to eat, he would sell all the stuff he would find. He also had postcards for sale. The postcards always had the same picture on it of him and his goats. I have always been told that he did not need to sell junk to live. He just did it as a hobby, like I said before." His expenses were few. Traveling, the Goat Man spent "$62 a month for feeding the goats, $22 for wagon repairs, and $79 on himself" (Patton 25). Arleen Snow recalls, "There was always a rumor that he was quite wealthy. I don't know if it was true, but the rumor was that he had several bank accounts at small banks in different states. He didn't trust bankers." Contrary to the rumors, the Goat Man said, "Me and my goats never been real well off, but we've always managed and I thank God for what we have. And I thank the Good Lord that I never been sick a day of my thirty years on the road" (qtd. in Patton 88).

Arleen Snow remembers, "He would pick up anything he could find and hang it on a wagon, and a lot of people would feel sorry for him and buy junk they didn't need just because they didn't understand him. They didn't know that much about him. He would sell things at a reasonable price but, you would have to remember, he's traveling from the thirties through the seventies, so he had to be reasonable with his prices, considering the people that he was working with. A lot of rural people didn't have extra money. He really didn't have any expenses if you think about it. His animals grazed off the pastures he would camp at. He would have to buy them feed occasionally, which he didn't mind to do. Sometimes he would buy them a bottle of cola. That was a real treat for the goats. He would turn it up, and hold it for them, and they would drink it down. They loved that, especially the lead goat. He loved that one very much. He always kind of gave him special treatment, I think. He was really fond of Old Billy."

"When daylight broke the next morning, Billy was found lying in the bloodstained snow with a hunting arrow protruding from his side."

*—Qtd. in Patton 60*

Though it's difficult to fathom the meanness of some folks, some were indeed cruel to this harmless wanderer and his goats. *The Chattanooga News Free Press* of December 28, 1967, reported that one Christmas night, the Goat Man "had tied his lead goat, Billy, to the rear of the wagon. Billy had traveled some 30,000 miles with Mr. McCartney and he considered the goat his 'companion of companions.' When daylight broke the next morning, Billy was found lying in the bloodstained snow with a hunting arrow protruding from his side. Billy survived the incident, but it left him crippled and weak and he could not pull the wagon again" (qtd. in Patton 60). "One

PLATE 7 McCartney often posed
for the cameras of the curious.

witness in the racetrack business claims that while at the old Attalla race-track, the Goat Man made one loop around the track and set the world speed record for a goat wagon" (qtd. in Patton 50). He claims that while the Goat Man was there, "his old goat Billy died and we buried him at the track" (qtd. in Patton 50). The following is an excerpt from the poem Ches McCartney composed for his beloved companion:

### IN MEMORY OF OLD BILLY

*Old Billy was a friend and a mile post*
*On this rocky road called life—*
*Old Billy was ever at my side.*
*During the lean years*
*When the going was rough and lanky*
*Old Billy brightened the picture*
*As we shared strange roads, hunger,*
*And long toilsome hike.*

*During the nights of sparse days*
*We'd console one another—*
*With thoughts of better grass around the bend*
*Or a few postcard sales on the morrow . . .*

*Billy and I forgive that bowman and others*
*Who seek to maim and be unkind.*

*Old Billy was my mascot of mascots—*
*My companion of companions— . . .*

Ches McCartney loved his goats very much, every one of them. The Goat Man recalled, "The goats have taught me a lot in the past thirty years. They don't, for example, care how I smell or how I look. They trust me and have faith in me, and this is more than I can say for a lot of people" (qtd. in Patton 7).

Larry Cannon of Rabun County remembers seeing love in the Goat Man's eyes for his goats and his travels: "I was eleven or so years old when I first saw the Goat Man. I had a pretty big cut in the back of my head, and I had to get stitches. After I got my stitches put in, my parents took me to see him. I remember talking with him. He was friendly, but I don't remember what we said to each other. Another time I remember seeing the Goat Man is when he spent the night on the side of the road, and I watched him milk his goats. After he finished milking them, he just tipped the jug of milk up and drank it. He didn't strain it or anything. The Goat Man always had attention; people were always around him. If anything was for sure, the Goat Man didn't travel with his goats to get attention from people, and he didn't do it because he didn't have any money or he had nowhere else to go. He did it because he loved his goats and loved to travel."

"On cold winter nights, my goats are the finest electric blanket I can find. The colder it gets, the more goats I cover up with. Thirty degrees is a one-goat night and below zero is a five-goat night."
—*Qtd. in Patton 84*

Mort Meadors remembers his thoughts and encounters with the Goat Man: "When I was growing up, I saw the Goat Man at least four times a year. I guess I saw him so frequently because he owned a piece of property near Gordon, Georgia. I lived in Macon, Georgia. Every time we saw him on the road, we, my brother and I, would make Daddy stop; that is, if he was not in a hurry. Even as a little boy, I always worried about him because I wondered what happened to this man after the sun went down and it got dark. Where would he sleep?"

In the winter, nights got pretty cold, but Ches McCartney said he made it through: "On cold winter nights, my goats are the finest electric blanket I can find. The colder it gets, the more goats I cover up with. Thirty degrees is a one-goat night and below zero is a five-goat night" (qtd. in Patton 84).

As a young girl, Arleen Snow also worried about the Goat Man: "I was twelve years old when I first remember the Goat Man. My dad came home from work one day, and he had heard that the Goat Man was coming and was going to be camping at Piedmont, which was about twenty miles from our home. During that time, word traveled fast through friends and relatives—through the radio—about that man, because he was like a one-man carnival coming into town. In a rural area there wasn't that much to look forward to, so when someone as unusual as the Goat Man came through, everyone would come out, and everyone would tell their friends and families he was coming. He always had a crowd. I can remember seeing all this stuff and the crowd gathering. That was very unusual. No one really ever explained who he was or what he was doing. It was during a time that children didn't talk too much. They just listened. No one really said who he was, where he was going, where he was from, or what he was doing. I just quietly stood and observed like everyone else, and all of my grown-up years, I have wondered and thought back on those things. I never really thought to ask anyone about him, but I remember seeing him so clear in my mind, even now."

PLATE 8  The Goat Man often let children play on his wagon.

"I got licenses with seals on 'em . . . I can baptize you, marry you, and bury you."

—*Qtd. in Patton 42*

One of the greatest influences on Ches McCartney's life was probably his faith in God. With him, McCartney carried his certificate of ordination from the Universal Pentecostal Church of Jesus Christ and a ministerial license issued by the state of Georgia. Ches never traveled on weekends. On Saturdays he rested; on Sundays he preached, with "phrases more commonly heard in a pub than a pulpit" (Patton 75), to anyone who would listen and did not solicit donations. The pilgrim expounded, "Fellers, the three thousand years is almost up, and we don't have much time left" (qtd. in Patton 14). He quoted avidly, "The Lord is my shepherd. I shall not want." Ches proudly stated, "I got licenses with seals on 'em . . . I can baptize you, marry you, and bury you" (qtd. in Patton 42). "I thank Almighty God for the protection and strength through the years and over the miles of rustic life in His service. In fact, I miss it when I eat in, as no cafés cook with junk tires or lost recaps" (qtd. in Patton 2).

The Goat Man received a variety of reactions from folks in his years of travel. Someone told Arleen Snow a story of folks' reactions: "This was in Uriah, Alabama. He camped with his goats there on the side of the road, and he was going to a general store there, or maybe it was a café. He was approaching the café, and they saw him coming, so they locked the door and turned around the CLOSED sign and would not let him in. It didn't bother him at all. He just turned around and went on. He was blessed because there was so many people that did not know [his] situation and felt sorry for him. He was always brought food. Someone would have dinner and make a plate for him and have a child run it over to the Goat Man. He'd always have several plates at the end of the evening. People thought highly of him—the ones that liked him. The ones who didn't scoffed, but it didn't seem to hurt his feelings. He had been doing this for around forty years. You get used to it and see these reactions, and you don't think anything about it. He always had money on him, and he would find someone to sell him something. He always got enough to eat. He loved his goat milk. Some people would stay around for hours. We'd always stay for a little, buy some postcards, and then leave."

Arleen Snow also recalls how, in the earlier days, people socialized with the Goat Man: "Basically, early on in the evenings, he wouldn't talk that much. He was setting up his camp, and he was busy doing things. He would not take time to talk." Becky Cannon remembers: "When he was building his campfire, then people knew instinctively that they could gather around and begin talking to him, and they would. They would talk and he would talk and there would be a little banter back and forth. Somebody might tease him about not smelling good and the last time he took a bath. He would always make a comment back to the person and get the crowd laughing. He was always quick on his feet. He was very clever, and people loved to listen to him. He could tell some great tales. He had some of the biggest yarns! People didn't know whether to believe him or not." Sonny Cannon knew him as a genial soul: "He never did talk a lot, but he always tried to give you some milk. You would have to talk to him first for him to say anything. He might answer a question or two. He just done his thing. At night when he would camp, people would gather around him and take pictures of him. I'll bet he was one of the most photographed people in this country." Like taking photographs of Santa Claus, folks took pictures of the bearded wanderer dozens of times a day.

"There was always people around him," Becky Cannon recalls. "We would always taste the milk—sometimes he would squirt the milk at us, toward our mouth. All the kids around would have a chance to taste the milk." The Goat Man swore by goat's milk: "The goat milk I drink by the gal-

PLATE 9  Ches McCartney after the 1970s

lon; it's a fine food in itself" (qtd. in Patton 30). In fact, McCartney felt "that by drinking plenty of goat milk and buddying with billy goats, he had become immune to sickness" (qtd. in Patton 56).

> **"The Good Book states that before the end of time, the earth shall be inhabited by seven women to each man . . . If this time is already here, I am not playing this hand. I am leaving four more wives available for some man who needs them more than I do."**
> —*Qtd. in Patton 75*

At one point in time, McCartney wasn't married anymore. He certainly had some definite and unique ideas about marriage. Since the beginning of his journeys, Ches had taken three wives. He divorced the first one for desertion and remarried twice. His second and third wives both died. Ches averred in his booklet *Roads to Rocking Chair* that the Bible talks about men and women in the last days: "The Good Book states that before the end of time, the earth shall be inhabited by seven women to each man." He elaborated on this quotation by further stating, "If this time is already here, I am not playing this hand. I am leaving four more wives available for some man who needs them more than I do" (qtd. in Patton 75). Arleen Snow recalls a story about his third wife: "His third wife, he sold to a farmer for two five-hundred-dollar payments because she was tired of being on the road and he needed money. The farmer had a real liking for her, and she kind of liked him, too. So it all worked out. They all ended up happy. He got money out of it. It is so unusual." Ches McCartney said that his third wife would be his last. "The Good Lord gave me three, which proved to be three too many . . . I'm mighty glad that Leap Year is over for a spell because during the last one I had twenty-five proposals, but sixteen years of single bliss have made me say no to every one of them" (qtd. in Patton 37–38). A story that appeared in the February 11, 1976 issue of *The Macon Telegraph* reports McCartney as saying that he "married Irene Angel, twenty-four, of Davenport, Iowa, sometime last year and is waiting for her to finish college" (qtd. in Patton 91). He said, "She's a beautiful thing . . . Got coal black hair, long enough you can sit on it" (qtd. in Patton 91). Truth? Who knows?

Besides various stories of his wives, varying accounts exist as to McCartney's offspring. Some report that Albert Gene, who oftentimes traveled with his father, was his only child. Others claim there were other children. On October 23, 1969, *The Rome News Tribune* reported that McCartney had children by each of his three wives: "One son, a product of his third marriage, has been missing in action in Vietnam for two years . . . Another son travels with Roy Rogers and Dale Evans, and one is employed with a New York City newspaper" (qtd. in Patton 83). On one of his many trips to Washington, D.C., McCartney himself said, "This is my last trip. I'm on my way . . . to talk to 'Old Mixon' (as he referred to the President). I want him to help me find my boy that's missing in Vietnam" (qtd. in Patton xi). Another witness reported, in 1979, that the Goat Man gave him a picture of the little houses he owned and said, "His daughter came to see him at my restaurant and he introduced me to her. She was from Florida and he had a son, too. I was thinking he told me she taught at a college in Florida. She was fairly tall and a handsome looking person and was driving a Cadillac." (qtd. in Patton 99). The truth of these rumors and reports remains a mystery to this writer.

After his third wife, he was alone on the road most of the time, and times started to change, along with people's attitudes. Sonny Cannon remembers that the Goat Man "always seemed nice, but he would always have an eye on his goats to make sure no one would try to kick or pull them. I remember he got on to a boy for pulling on a goat and kicking at it. Now, if somebody was mean to his goats, it was a different story. Mr. McCartney tried to get along with everyone, but according to him, that was not always possible." McCartney told me, "I love my fellow man, but sometimes they can be pretty mean to me and my goats. I have to be broadminded and grit my teeth sometimes . . . They stole eight of my goats up in Tennessee, and some kids set my wagon afire."

Darryl Patton comments on how the times changed: "Over the years, people's attitudes changed, especially in the sixties, as times got rough and a lot of drugs were going around. The interstates started developing. What happened was that he was tying up traffic, couldn't get out on the interstates, and it was getting harder and harder to travel. During the early years, his protesters were satisfied to overturn his wagons or apply turpentine to his goats, but in time, acts of hatred and intolerance became more violent. A man and his girlfriend were driving from Paxton to Rantoul, Illinois, in the late forties when they passed the Goat Man about two miles south of Paxton. When they stopped to eat at a restaurant, two young men came in and bragged about having poured lighter fluid on one goat and lighting a match to it. They boasted about the old man's getting really angry and running them off. The witness was horrified: "I thought to myself, 'How mean can people be!' " (qtd. in Patton 22). In 1964, a nineteen-year-old Dayton, Tennessee youth faced a larceny hearing on the charge of stealing one of McCartney's goats. Mr. McCartney recounted an incident that depicts pure meanness: "In the summer of 1968, in Chattanooga—now it's a wealthy area, but back then there was a lot of bootleggers—I was coming through, and a local guy tipped my wagon, knocked me out, and slit the throats of eight of my goats." The Goat Man, in *The Man and His Mountain*, one of his booklets published during his travels, relates that he woke up in an area hospital with twenty-seven stitches in his scalp. With eight of his beloved goats dead, he recovered the surviving members of his herd from the local humane society and hired a trucker to haul him to Conyers, Georgia, where he hoped to recuperate in peace. After a short stay near Conyers, Ches awoke one morning to find two of his remaining goats missing. One, the local authorities never found (it was presumed to have been eaten); as for the other, authorities found particles of flesh, animal hair, and a pair of goat horns scattered over a wide area along a nearby railroad track, and a piece of rope was found tied to a crosstie.

An article in *The Macon Telegraph* reported another incident: At around 3:00 A.M., near Macon, Georgia, on a Saturday night in the summer of 1969, three young men in a Mustang overturned and damaged his little covered wagon and killed two of his favorite goats tied to it. McCartney, sleeping inside the wagon, suffered three broken ribs (Patton 76). The men in the Mustang eluded the authorities. Darryl Patton points out that being on the road "was getting rougher and rougher, and the Goat Man was getting meaner to people because of the way he had been treated. He figured when they would come up and see him that they were going to talk ugly to him or hurt him, so he got sort of grouchier, and he pretty much slowed down his traveling."

Even when he had given up the goat caravan and taken up flying in planes, on one excursion to Los Angeles, in 1987, a couple of gunmen mugged him. He ended up in a California hospital. When he seemed to have disappeared for three months, folks back home, friends and relatives, filed a missing persons report on him. Sore feet and the amputation of two toes landed him in a Georgia nursing home in 1987, and he was a resident there until his death in 1998.

Before times changed, the Goat Man could take care of himself. When people were rude to him, Darryl Patton remembers, "He could give, as well as he took, negative responses. If someone came up to him and was critical of him, he would burn them with his tongue. There are several instances of people criticizing him. A woman would come up to him and say, 'You stink!' Or she would say, 'I can't see how you could sleep with goats—they stink.' Or she might ask, 'How long has it been since you have taken a bath?' He would say, 'I haven't had a bath in three years. How long has it been since you have had a bath?' And the lady would say, 'I had a bath this morning.' He would say, as he was pointing out two hundred people around him, 'Lady, I've got two hundred people to see me today. How many are here to see you?' And he would leave it at that, and she would skulk on off. He said, 'I may stink, but they are here to see me.' He was very fast on his feet, but, you see, he was a preacher. He was used to speaking in front of people. He actually didn't care what people said about him. I would think he was actually a borderline genius in his time. He may have lived a dirty, grungy life, but he lived the life that he wanted to live, and he chose what he did."

Arleen Snow concurs: "He was his own man. He made his own decisions. He traveled where he wanted to. No one told him what to do. He was happy. I would think of his way of living as a miserable existence, but he got into this, and he was happy. He didn't like taking baths anyway, so it didn't bother him not to take a bath. He also loved his goats and got to meet as many people as he wanted to in a day's time. He could draw three hundred people in a day, and all those three hundred people had money in their pockets of some kind."

About 1931, McCartney went to the little town of Jeffersonville, Georgia, in Twiggs County, and bought four acres of land just off Highway 80. He lived in a ramshackle two-room shack—boxes, lean-tos, hubcaps up in trees, and goats. McCartney's home also served as a chapel. It had a small metal steeple and several small crosses tacked to the front of it. He called the church he founded the Free-Thinking Christian Mission. His mother and stepfather, Mr. and Mrs. John Shellard, are buried in a vault in the rear.

Ches McCartney once confided, "I made this back in the forties. It's a tomb. My mother and stepfather are in there. When I die, I'll be in there, too" (qtd. in Patton xii). While he was living, however, the wanderlust would strike often; Ches set out on many a journey from that shack in Jeffersonville. While at home, in 1978, McCartney was awakened in the night by the sound of timber crackling. His house was ablaze. He jumped through the flames and stumbled out the door. A moment later, the roof caved in. McCartney swore, "Another second in there and I'd been a goner . . . I was darn near cremated" (qtd. in Patton 96). His long white beard caught fire, and much of his hair was singed. He suffered first- and second-degree burns on his face and right shoulder. Apparently, after preparing and eating pork chops and fried eggs, he decided to take a nap and forgot to douse the flames in his makeshift stove.

Albert and his dad needed a new home. Hope came in the form of Twiggs County School Superintendent Charles Keily. Used school buses would soon be up for bid. Albert (Gene) made the highest bid on three buses and chose bus number 8: sunshine yellow, large, and clean (after a scrubbing by some concerned folks). Though it had no electricity or modern conveniences, it was a dream home. By 1984, Ches McCartney had only one goat, Barbara, but said he had no use for goats anymore. Though he was slowing down, the wanderlust did not diminish; however, now he was traveling by bus, train, and plane. One *Macon Telegraph* reporter encountered McCartney at the Macon Municipal Airport. The old man confided, "I'm on the go all the time. When I get home, I'll stay a few days, then get going again" (qtd. in Patton 115).

Though his birth records do not exist, in 1990, McCartney purported that he was a hundred and four, but his records and his own book indicate he was much younger, perhaps ninety. Nursing home records indicate that he was eighty-seven in 1988. Who knows the truth? Yes, people told their tales about what had become of this wayfarer (the most popular tale is the one about his being struck and killed by an eighteen-wheeler), but I had the pleasure of meeting Ches McCartney at the Eastview Nursing Home in Macon, Georgia. Some folks there told me he had had a girlfriend, another nursing home resident: Virginia Tanner, a retired nurse who was purportedly two years younger than McCartney—if records are correct. When I met him in June 1995, he was still spunky, still entertaining visitors to the home, and he was happy to regale me with stories of his glory days on the open road. He enjoyed being with strangers. He liked being an attraction.

I had heard so much about this legend. Some told me he was friendly and gentle, an eccentric genius. Others averred he was filthy and rude, a crazed

PLATE 10  An elderly but spunky McCartney in the
Eastview Nursing Home in Macon,
Georgia, June 28, 1995

lunatic. That men such as he die is difficult to comprehend. Ches McCartney, America's Goat Man, passed away in December 1998, but he remains a
part of American folklore, a kind of Johnny Appleseed, roaming the nation's
highways and byways with twenty to thirty goats in tow, selling his postcards,
and preaching the Word. Though he will not be remembered in historical
accounts with some of the great men in our nation's history, he has certainly
won a place in our legends, for he was certainly a curiosity, a marvel, a spec-
tacle that fired the imaginations of young and old alike. And the legend lives
vividly in the memories of those whom he encountered, those who were
lucky enough to see the Goat Man, an American folk hero, and his strange
entourage.

*References*

Cannon, Becky. Personal interview. Summer 1995.
Cannon, Larry. Personal interview. Summer 1995.
Cannon, Sonny. Personal interview. Summer 1995.
McCartney, Ches. Personal interview. 28 June 1995.
Meadors, Mort. Personal interview. Summer 1995.
Patton, Darryl. *America's Goat Man (Mr. Ches McCartney)*. Gadsden, AL: Little
River Press, 1994.

Patton, Darryl. Personal interview. Summer 1995.
Snow, Arleen. Personal interview. Summer 1995.
Photos: Darryl Patton and Ches McCartney.

***Editor's note:*** Darryl Patton's book *America's Goat Man (Mr. Ches McCartney)* may be ordered in paperback with check or money order for $12.95, including shipping, from the Foxfire Museum, P.O. Box 541, Mountain City, Georgia 30562 or www.foxfire.org. You may call 706-746-5828 for more information.

# BOB DANIEL:
# IT'S BEEN A GREAT LIFE

*"I worried my poor mama to death, I know, but she finally
realized, I guess, that I was goin' to be a rambler."*

When I was looking for a personality for my article for *The Foxfire Magazine* and needed some advice on whom to contact, I called one of Foxfire's good friends: Max Woody. Mr. Woody advised that I meet Bob Daniel in Westminster, South Carolina. Max said that Bob was a very interesting character.

A few minutes later, I was talking to Mr. Daniel, and he was willing and excited to share his time with someone from Foxfire. He and I set a time for an interview, and I drove the thirty or so miles to his home the following Sunday. Bob and his wife, Dot, welcomed me into their home as if I were their own grandson. Soon Bob was telling me about his childhood days of romping in the woods by the river, hunting coons and squirrels, and about his mom, a Scot, who married his dad, half Lakota Indian.

I quickly realized that Bob Daniel is an American Renaissance man of sorts. He was a deep-sea diver in Alaska during World War II; he mined and cut precious stones in Franklin, North Carolina, and Toccoa, Georgia; and he is a talented wood-carver and artisan. Most important, however, Bob Daniel is kindhearted and congenial, two qualities that seem to become scarcer with each passing generation.

—*Russell Bauman*

**Editor's note:** Mr. Daniel has in fact become a friend to many of us here at Foxfire. After Russell had graduated and gone to college, Bob came to the high school and visited with me in the Foxfire laboratory and even gave me a piece of his scrimshaw. We saw him when he came to the spring celebration. Then, while we were working on this book, some questions arose. Russell called him and left a message on the answering machine. Mr. Daniel drove over from South Carolina, and he and Miss Dot waltzed in while Russell and I were having lunch. Mr. Daniel succinctly informed us that he hates that answering machine: "Sounds like they're talking through a grate."

His warmth bubbles. The camaraderie is instant. We spent an hour and a half or so just chatting, and Russell told them before they left that he'd be over to visit them soon. We walked them to the truck, but they weren't leaving just yet. He and Dot were going to scour the parking lot with their metal detectors—that's what they do for fun now—and see what treasures they could discover. We at Foxfire have discovered the real treasure: folks like Bob and Dot Daniel.

—*Angie Cheek*

WELL, I guess the best thing to do is show you a picture or two. I have four or five cardboard cartons of old photographs. My family was very fortunate in having my grandfather, Jim Crisler, as a photographer. This made things real good for us for getting family stuff. I been thinkin' very seriously about doing a videotape about all these things in order to be sure that our children know who's who in the family and who the old folks are.

This was my father's headdress and vest. Mama wanted to doll me up a little. This thing is faded pretty bad. That's my great-grandfather, my

PLATE 11  A young Bob Daniel
in his father's headdress

PLATE 12 Bob Daniel right before his teens with family members
(from left: great-grandfather John Henry Bruce; grandmother
Adora Bruce Crisler; mother Vara Crisler; and Bob)

grandmother, my mom, and myself just before I hit my teens. My grandpa
Bruce dug his wife's grave. He got down to rock and had to dynamite it. He
blasted his own while he was at it 'cause he didn't want to disturb her. My
grandpa Crisler, Herbert, and my mother's daddy lived in Elberton, Georgia, and the western edge of South Carolina. His father and four brothers,
I believe it was, joined in the Civil War. They'd be my great-great-uncles,
my grandfather's uncles. (One of the Bruces walked from Comer to Athens
trying to enlist, too; but he was only thirteen or fourteen, so they wouldn't
take him. He was madder 'n h——.) Two of the Crisler brothers were killed
on the same day, and a third died in another skirmish. Only one survived.
Their mother, a big woman, used to challenge everybody in the county. I
don't know if there was something the matter with her mind. But somebody took her up on it. They found her dead body in a trash can. Her dis-
position didn't show up in any other family member. There's a story about
Grandpa Crisler. Grandpa Crisler used to oversee prisoners while they
were working. He worked for this guy named Smith, who always had a
bodyguard with him all the time. One time Smith said, "I don't think I'll
pay you." Grandpa took out his pocketknife, said, "Yes, you're gonna pay
me." He got his money.

"My mother married Louis Prairie. Chief, they called him all the time. He was half Lakota, and so that meant I was half of that."

I was born in Jacksonville, Florida, on March 6, 1917. The family moved out. My mother and father separated when I was three years old, and of course we had relatives all over Georgia, so to speak, and Mom came to Athens, which was a closer place. Her father had a photographic studio there, and she came to Athens and worked in the studio awhile. My father folded up and started rambling around here and there. He went out west, and that was about it. We haven't been able to get a line on him. The boys are workin' on it—I had four sons.

You can see by lookin' at the eyes, they kind of wanted to name me Old Iron Eyes, but not my mama. He named me Bright Star, but Mama said my name was Robert Bruce. Her family was Bruces who came over to this country from Scotland, and her mother married a Crisler. The marriage produced some very interesting people. My mother married Louis Prairie. Chief, they called him all the time. He was half Lakota, and so that meant I was half of that. I had only one full brother and sister, and they both died as infants. I was born in 1917, and she had these two babies, one after the other. One lived about a month, and I think the other one lived about two weeks. One was a girl, and one was a boy, but anyway, that was the only full brother and sister that I had. They're buried at Vineyards Creek Church right around Comer, Georgia. That's where the Bruces had a big twelve-hundred-acre farm down there; that's where the family branched out from. Mother worked with my granddad, Jim Crisler, in his studio, and then she later did the same thing as a widow. She worked as a photographer and studio technician for years.

"My father made his living making herb medicine and goin' around with the old, typical medicine show, you know. As a young man, he was with Buffalo Bill's Circus awhile. He was a trick shot and trick rope and all this, that, and the other typical Western type of thing."

Mother was not Native American. She was just dressed. She made her outfit and all. She dressed that way because my father made his living making herb medicine and goin' around with the old, typical medicine show, you know. As a young man, he was with Buffalo Bill's Circus awhile. He was a trick shot and trick rope and all this, that, and the other typical Western type of thing. He'd do a little trick shootin'. Back then, they wasn't as afraid of guns. He'd do a little trick rope work just to attract a crowd of people. I say

PLATE 13 Chief Prairie, Bob Daniel's father

a crowd: I guess if he attracted two dozen, he was happy and would start sellin'. When they got married, Mama dressed the part and went around and helped him with his medicine show. He was married on that, and he wanted to keep movin' all the time. She was a very sensitive type of person, especially about children, and she lost those two babies. He wanted to keep on movin', and she just wouldn't take it anymore. He kept tryin' to come back, but she wouldn't let him. I suppose I was about three years old.

I've talked to several people who knew him, people that were older than I am. I guess they're all gone now. I was eighty-six on the sixth of March 2003. But anyway, I talked to several people. One fellow—I remembered him as a kid—that I talked to, I ran into in a machine shop. I got a job in a machine shop in Athens; he was workin' there, and he was tellin' me that Chief could shoot that ol' .45 pistol better than my friend could shoot a .22 rifle. He referred me to someone else that knew him. I got a chance to talk to several people, you know, and that was a great thing for me. I didn't really know him and wasn't old enough. One of the fellows told me he'd come to visit them out on the farm, you know, out of Athens somewhere. He said that Mama and Chief and myself—they'd bring me along and spend the day maybe—said they could run an old horse or an old mule by him, and he could take his lasso and catch that mule or that horse by any foot they'd name. They'd tell him which foot to catch him by, and he'd catch him. He must have been fairly well accomplished. He supposedly was with Buffalo Bill's Circus as a boy, and he went into traveling around with carnivals and this, that, and the other. What I'm tellin' you is what people have told me, and my mother told me that he said he had been to Carlyle as a kid. Carlyle is an Indian school in Pennsylvania. They sent him to Carlyle. My youngest son checked at Carlyle, and they were in the process of checking and trying to straighten out the real old records.

Carlyle said they had no record of him being there, but now whether the record is not in order or whether Chief was buildin' himself up, I don't know—in other words, fibbin'. But that's the way I get it. Supposedly, according to what he told my mother, his mother was one of Sittin' Bull's daughters—Sittin' Bull's lineage children, according to that. I don't think it would be possible for him to have been a direct descendant of one of his daughters. Sittin' Bull was rather well known for likin' children, and he adopted any kid he had a chance to. He just adopted them, took them in. He liked kids, you know. He was known to have adopted several kids, and I assume that, if this information is correct, it must have been one of the daughters he adopted. I can't swear to it, but that's my analyzing way of arrivin' at the possible truth, you know.

My father was a typical nomad. He was a westerner, and he was born, according to my birth certificate, on the plains of Texas. That's on my birth certificate, and he was. Incidentally, I weighed thirteen pounds or a little better when I was born, so I don't feel bad about wearing a forty-inch waist. He was in his, well, he was up about forty-somethin' or fifty when I was born, somewhere along in there. He was old. My mother was twenty-one at that time, so he was a pretty old codger when I came along. We did find that he had had and divorced a wife out in Kansas. We had a letter from one of his sons out there, but we lost track. I couldn't find them. Mama, my ma, was the one that was in touch with them, found them through the Salvation Army, oddly enough. I kept hassling her about wanting to know more about Chief, you know, and she finally put out an inquiry in *War Cry*.

I think that the Salvation Army published it. This half brother of mine answered, but we lost contact. I tried to get in touch with him after I went in the service in World War II, and a letter came back with no forwarding address, you know, and this sort of thing. I just lost contact there, but my sons have made efforts, my youngest one especially, and he hasn't given up yet. So we don't know. It's just a case of a ragamuffin growin' up, I guess, in my case, you might say.

I can remember sellin' papers on the streets in Athens, Georgia. That's where Mom went to. The papers were a cent and a half each, which meant you had to buy enough to make your cents come out, your money come out right. I didn't know. I couldn't count money. I was about four years old, or maybe five, hadn't never been to school or anything, and of course there wasn't any kindergarten in those days. I could not count money; I'd hold my pennies in my hand, and my customers would make their change. I usually wound up with either enough or a little more. Mama did all the countin' up of the money, but that was the first earnings that I ever had, and of course my mother was working. It was just two of us, and she had a rather hard time.

I went to school in Athens. I had an awful hard time gettin' through grammar school. I guess you could say I inherited a good bit of that nomadic attitude, you know. I used to carry a flip [slingshot] and a huntin' knife and snitch a quilt from off the bed and a pocketful of matches and quite often go to the woods and stay sometimes as much as two weeks. I like to've run my mother crazy, but I didn't realize it. I was just doin' what I thought was normal. I enjoyed it. I guess I must have eaten a pickup truck full of sparrows, and I'd raid every cornpatch I came by. Whether it was green or dry, it didn't make much difference. I'd parch it if it was dry, and if it was green, I'd roast it.

**"I'd hunt and I'd fish and I'd mess around. I was in hog heaven. There ain't no doubt about it—I just was in heaven."**

I had a hard time getting through grammar school, and that was primarily the reason—I just didn't want to go to school. I didn't like school, and I'd generally get expelled from every one I went to. Anyway, in grammar school, when I'd get disgusted, the next day I didn't show up. In fact, quite a lot of times Mama didn't know. I worried my poor mama to death, I know, but she finally realized, I guess, that I was goin' to be a rambler. I'd get a quilt if it was cold weather; if it wasn't, I wouldn't worry with the quilt. I'd take my flip and get some matches, and I'd make lead slugs for my flip about as big as the end of your little finger. They were very effective on squirrels. I could handle a squirrel pretty good with that thing and those lead slugs. I'd go to the woods and I'd stay a week. Sometimes I'd stay two weeks. I'd swim in the river, and I'd play in the woods. I'd hunt and I'd fish and I'd mess around. I was in hog heaven. There ain't no doubt about it—I just was in heaven. That report card I was tellin' you about, I think I was present about sixty-somethin' days and absent thirty-somethin' days. That was just my life. I think I was expelled from every school in Clarke County [Georgia], which is about four, I think, or five. I got expelled from College Avenue School, from the Normal School, from Chase Street School, and from Chile Street

School. That's four schools. I think that's the only grammar schools in Clarke County, or it was at that time. I got expelled from every one of them.

My mother, some way or the other, met a fine old gentleman, a farmer that lived out in Madison County about three miles from Ila, Georgia. I don't know if you know where Ila is. It's about as big as this house. It had a cotton gin and this, that, and the other. I think they had one fillin' station over there. But she met this fellow, and she also found some people that knew him. He was a wonderful sort of person. It was a farm family. He was a good man, but Mama satisfied herself that it was a good family, you know. She boarded me down there, and I think I was still in the first or second grade. I didn't make much progress the first few years I went to school for some reason, but anyhow, he had one daughter, and that's the only child they had. I believe she was a little older than I was. I'm sure she was . . . well . . . just a few years older, anyway. Anyhow, Mother boarded me down there, and it was just all farmland for three or four miles in either direction you could go. Just farms, that's all there was to it. They had a little settlement over there at Rogers . . . the Rogers community right out of Ila, Georgia, and I went to school at the Rogers School. They's a blacksmith shop and a church and a little country store. It was on a crossroads, dirt roads.

The man was an interesting outdoorsman, and they decided that if they put me down there, where I had plenty of room to ramble, that things might be a little different, and they were. He took me in like I was his own son, and they boarded me down there for about two or three years. His name was Williams, Coyn Williams. The ol' man, he loved to hunt and fish, and he was a gentle, easygoin' kind of a fella, you know. He had a pretty good humor. I liked him very much. In fact, he come close to becomin' the only daddy I knew till I got married—I just felt like he was my daddy after a period of time, but I stayed out there and went to school.

I was lookin' at one of my report cards here the other day. I was in the seventh grade, and I had more Cs than anything else, but I'd passed everything—Bs, a few. As I think about it, I had a hygiene class. I got an A on hygiene, but math was a snap for me. I loved math. In four years of high school, I never took a book home, and I averaged 98 in math for the four years. In all the math they taught, I took every course they taught. The driest part of the whole thing was business arithmetic. I didn't like that worth a durn.

Both the schoolteachers boarded at the Williamses' house. There was a little old two-room schoolhouse 'bout a half a mile, I guess, from his house. They kinda kept pretty good tabs on this ol' boy, and I didn't have as much opportunity to just wander off, so to speak. That put a cramp in my ramblin' 'cause, you know, when they went to school, I had to go. I mean they saw to it that I went, period. I couldn't dodge it; they wasn't no way I could get away from them. I did slip away one time, but I got caught pretty quick. Anyway, I had to go pretty regular out there, and I did all right, I think. I went through second grade or like maybe the third grade. I don't know. But he and I got along real well.

Of course I tried to help on the farm when Mr. Williams needed my help. I admired him, and I liked him very much. He'd take me fishin' and huntin', you know, and that just suited me fine. I did love the woods and the river. See, Athens is built right on the side of Oconee River—matter of fact, in the forks of that thing. It's two miles one way and a mile the other way, and you're on two rivers, you know—typical muddy Piedmont area rivers, but, Lord, it was so interesting out there on the river and in the woods. I wasn't big enough to do much—mostly aggravate him, I reckon.

I know one time I came home to Mother in the summer, and the Barnum & Bailey Circus was coming to Athens. I remember down there on King Street in Athens—it was there where Tom Mix came in with the Barnum & Bailey Circus. He was a movie cowboy. D——, he was a tall boy! I got to shake his hand. When I was a teenager, people thought my mother was my date. She didn't show her age. I was the biggest injustice she ever birthed. I've regretted and prayed about that many times. We lived on Cobb Street, and the house faced King Avenue. We was on the opposite side of Cobb Street, and King Avenue went thataway; on down King Avenue, 'bout half a mile or a little farther, was a big open field, and that's where they had the circus. I got the wild idea that I wanted to sell some hot dogs and Co-colas, so Mom pitched in and bought me some hot dogs and I bought a case of Co-colas. They cost me eighty cents a case. It was two dozen bottles in the case, and I got in my front yard and sold everything I had. I made nine dollars and somethin'. I went to town and bought a single-barrel .410-gauge shotgun, an old Stevens, you know. It was a good little ol' gun.

> **"I had that ol' gun loaded, and that rat came out there. He got about right there, you know, and I blowed him off of that sill, knocked a chunk out of that sill about the size of your fist and blowed a hole in the roof and shingles."**

It 'as a good gun. But anyway, I had enough money to buy that gun and two boxes of shells. So it wasn't long after I got that gun, I had to go back down to Mr. Williams and start school. I stayed with him all winter. The first thing I did when I got down there, out in the smokehouse, they was an old barrel set in the corner of the building. You come in the door and go around. You could shake that barrel, and a rat would run up the side of the wall and then run across a beam, a ceiling joist, you know, up there. So I was bad about huntin' them rats. He had an old redbone hound, and me and that dog tore up all the rats around the country there. I went out there and I shook that barrel and I had that ol' gun loaded and that rat came out there. He got about right there, you know, and I blowed him off of that sill, knocked a chunk out of that sill about the size of your fist and blowed a hole in the roof and shingles, you know, like that. I didn't think nothin' about that. I killed a rat! Boy, I was so proud of that! Ah, man, I went over there and went around the front. He was settin' on the front porch, and I said, "I killed that rat! I killed that rat!" He said, "Let me see," and he come down there, you know. He looked, and there 'as that hole there in the roof. I know what he thought. Later I realized, of course. At that time I was excited, and it didn't mean nothin' to me. He said, "Well, that's all right. That's a good shot." He never did fuss at me about shootin' a hole through the roof. I guess I was about eight years old, maybe nine, somethin' like that. He didn't raise Cain with me about shootin' the hole through the roof, you know. I blowed them shingles every whichaway, but he was just kind enough and gentle enough that he knew how thrilled I was. He didn't fuss at me, not the first word. I thought about that a lot of times since those days. At that time I didn't realize, really, the true emphasis of that. He and I got along real good. He was just that kind of man. When I was about ten, I hunted with an ol' double-barreled L. C. Smith hammer shotgun. I love to hunt, yes, sir, yeah.

We'd go fishin', and he loved to hunt turtles when they'd come up the creeks in the early summer. I'd go with him, drag an old croker sack. He'd hunt the turtles and drag 'em out from under the banks, and I'd drag 'em around in that ol' sack. I killed a squirrel out of season. 'Course the law back then wasn't like it is now, and it wasn't as strict. We was over at a store, and the guy that run the store was the game warden. I didn't know him. Coyn Williams was tellin' him, said, "Yeah, he killed a crow with that old .410 shotgun!" I said, "Yeah, I killed a *squirrel,* too!" It was out of season. I guess they figured they wouldn't bother with that little ol' ragamuffin.

Man, I'd get into some bad spots once in a while. It was one place over there west of Athens off of Epps Road. I found that I could wade the river, the Oconee River, the North Fork, I believe. I found a place where I could wade the river, and I know one time I went ramblin' off over there. It was about four miles from where I lived, and I waded the river in the cold wintertime. There was ice on the edge of the river, and I'd pull my clothes off and wade the river and go off on the other side, you know. Of course I kinda dried off a little, put my clothes on, and I felt hot then. Anyway, I was real interested in the deep, big woods. I was squirrel huntin' and messed around too long, and it got dark on me. I couldn't see to get back across the river 'cause it was just one little place between big rocks where you could go. So I

PLATE 14   Bob with some of his cousins (from left: Bob, Elsie Jones,
Mary Sue Daniel, and Byron and Dot Newton)

wound up hollerin' and whoopin', goin' on, and I had a candle. I took a candle—that saved me—and matches if I wanted to build a fire or whatnot. But
that's the only thing I had to keep me warm, and I didn't want to build a fire
over there in the woods. Some old, old man come over there; he had an old
boat somewhere up the river, and he heard me hollerin'. He come back, and
he hollered and found out where I was. He come over there and brought me
back across the river so I could go home, and it was flat dark then. I had to
walk four miles in the dark gettin' home.

> "I saw what I thought was a white stump, an old bleached pine
> stump right in front of me. I just walked over and straddled it and
> set down. When I did, it jumped up and run off on me, and I just
> knew the ol' devil had me just sure as the world."

I used to go with Mr. Williams possum huntin' in my early teens, and I
enjoyed that. We had an old redbone hound, and I remember one night I
wanted to go possum huntin', and he didn't want to go. He said it 'as a full
moon, the moon too bright, said the possum wouldn't be out, but they
would on a dark night. Well, I wasn't that wise to the way of wildlife, and
twelve o'clock, me and the old dog took off. Well, I rambled around bein' a
kid, so to speak, just a growin' boy. Long up about, I'd say about three or
four o'clock, I got tired and sleepy, staggerin' around, you know. Old dog
hadn't struck no possum, nothin' to keep me excited. I saw what I thought
was a white stump, an old bleached pine stump right in front of me. I just
walked over and straddled it and set down. When I did, it jumped up and

run off on me, and I just knew the ol' devil had me just sure as the world. I
don't remember how I got off. I know I must have just fallen, and I was
layin' on the ground lookin' up at the stars, you know, tryin' to catch my
breath. Come to realize, it was an ol' cow who was layin' down. I had just
walked over and set down on it. And, course, that was the last time I ever
went possum huntin' by myself. I was always gettin' into somethin'. I had to
be doin' somethin' all the time, but like I said, it 'as a good life. It's a wonder
I hadn't been killed as a kid, I guess. I been pretty lucky, I think. I think I
been *real* lucky.

I went back home: My mother got married to a Jones. She married a man
who'd lost his wife. He had a grown son in the Navy and a grown daughter
livin' in Athens. He couldn't get along with those two children of his, and he
and I couldn't get along. It was a personality conflict, is all. It was as much or
more my fault as it was his, and I ran away from home when I was twelve
years old, went back down in the country to Mr. Williams's home and stayed
with him a year or two. My mother had married a Jones. He got acute
appendicitis, and this was before sulfa drugs or anything like that, you know,
but anyway, his appendix ruptured on him, and he came very close to dying.
I went back home, and I worked in machine shops and kept the family fed.
I guess he was off of his feet for two years, but he finally overcame it. In the
meantime, I was in high school there.

After my stepfather, Mr. Jones, got able to be up and around, I moved to
Toccoa and got a job as a tool and die maker. I served an apprenticeship all
those high school years and even before. I lost my first job because I wasn't
quite old enough to work. When Franklin Roosevelt started that National
Recovery Act, I was makin' three dollars a week, and when I went back to
work, I got a little more on account of that federal law.

Well, after I got into high school, I was absorbed in sports: football. I had
five scholarships, and I just didn't want to go to school. I didn't lack but
about three, four, five months to graduate, but I just quit. I mean, I was
through. I was too old to play football the next year; I just walked out, and
she [his wife, Dot] walked out with me. No, she graduated. Until I got to
high school, all I wanted to do was stay in the woods on the river somewhere. I was a lifeguard at the American Legion pool for three summers,
and happily, I was able to assist about thirteen people to get out of the emer-
gency situation of drowning. I don't say that I saved their life. I don't think
you can save a person's life. I think the Lord is the only one that decides that.
He may use you as an instrument, but He's the only one that saves you. That
was a playing experience, but it was a working experience, too. It was fun,
you know, workin' around the pool. I enjoyed swimming. I could swim over
a hundred and fifty yards underwater, and I could hold my breath almost

two minutes. Now if I get a handful of water and splash my face, I'm out of breath.

I only had one problem in that particular line. An ex-neighbor called me one day. It was real early in the morning. I was still in bed. He wanted me to come to his house. His wife was in the bathtub, and they thought she'd drowned in the bathtub. We got her out of the tub and got her stretched out and covered up and hot water bottles and everything we could think of. I was workin' for artificial respiration, which is something different from what we use now. The doctors gave her several shots of adrenaline tryin' to get her heart started beatin' again, but it didn't work. I think she just had a heart attack and just died right there in the tub. Oh, Lord, I don't want to see that no more. Things happen, you know. Sometimes it doesn't affect you one bit in the world, and other times it really gets to you. They's nothin' you can do about it. Well, that's about all the war stories I'm gonna tell you. I ain't gonna tell you about some of the things 'cause I ain't never told Mama, and I don't want her to know.

I played football, and Mama played basketball. That's Mama over there. That's the wife. I call her Mama. We both grew up in Athens, Georgia—I moved there from Jacksonville, Florida, when I was two or three years old. She played basketball, and she was just like a banty hen out on the court. Boy, she'd just scoot around under those big gals like you wouldn't believe, and she played a mighty good game of basketball. She was on the regular team, and I got to watchin' her play ball, you know. The first thing you know, we was datin'. You know how that goes. I have to tell you this, though: One time she brought me some of the best homemade fudge I'd ever tasted in my life, and just as creamy as Hershey chocolate. She never has made any like that since. We got married, and she can't make it anymore like that. I think she pulled a trick on me there somewhere or the other. I believe what she did, she got some Hershey chocolate and melted it down, you know. She got me hooked, and it was too late then.

We got married on a Saturday night, June 18, 1938, and I had to go to work on Monday. Not long after, I had to have my tonsils out—sat right there, and the doctor took them out right there at the table. Bled. Sewed 'em up. That's when it hit the fan. I was weak as water.

I was a trained diver in the Navy Deep Sea, when it was hard hat. There was no scuba diving back then—old brass hard hat. That was during World War II. I spent three years in the Pacific during World War II. I got qualified as a deep-sea diver, and I finally got out of the South Pacific and up to the North Pacific and went on out there to doin' salvage work. I commissioned a salvage barge. They called it a derrick. It was a salvage derrick—had a boat that was about a hundred feet long; had a sixty-foot clear workin' deck in the

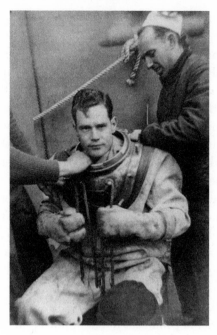

PLATE 15  Bob suits up for a dive.

forward section, thirty foot wide; and had a derrick on there that would lift thirty-two tons. Well, our primary job was aircraft. There was a naval air station at Shemya, Alaska, and also one at Attu, Alaska, but when they lost a plane at sea, if it was in water that was shallow enough for us to salvage, we'd go pick up the plane and put it on deck and bring it in, net it up on dock for the corps of engineers to take the bodies out of it. That's all they wanted, was to take the bodies out of the plane. In fact, one of the last planes I salvaged was a privateer bomber, a Navy privateer twin-engine bomber, light bomber, kind of like *The Mitchell,* and those engines were over a hundred yards apart on the bottom of the ocean. That plane was just one big ball of scrap metal and wire cables, you know, and there were six boys in there.

When the war broke out, my son, my first son, was born January 5. Pearl Harbor was December 7, '41. He was born January 5, '42, a month later. I nicknamed him Spike. His real name is Robert Lewis. He lives in New Orleans now and goes by Bob. I'm flattered, but it does get kind of confusing when he comes home. That was our first kid, and man, I tell you, they's just nothin' like it. But anyway, I stayed home; Mama got up an' stirrin' good. Everything was goin' fine, and I decided I'd tell Mama. I said, "Mama, I cannot stay home with that war goin' on. I just got to get in it." I said, "I feel I got as much or more to protect than anybody with that boy and everything." I didn't realize how it was goin' to be. In other words, I just had that drive, you know. Anyway, when he was five months old, I believe it was, I went and enlisted in the Navy. I went to Norfolk to "boot"—basic trainin', they call it in the Army, I think. I got a chance to come home, and he was nine months old. Then I went and reported back to duty, and I was transferred to Navy Pier at Chicago. They put me in a diesel school up there, which I didn't know anything about diesel engines, you know. Most of the new construction they was doin' in those days, especially any of the lightships, was all driven by diesel engines. They needed diesel engineers bad. I was in a class of two thousand. I graduated fifty-eighth, I think it was, in the class.

The PC586 come to Miami, and they needed more crew. I had just gotten down there, hadn't been down there very long. They looked at our records and they said, "Well, you got all that we can teach you. We don't need to put you in school here and hold you up." Said, "You want to volunteer for this ship?" I said, "Sure, that's what I came for." So I went aboard the PC586. We convoyed a troop ship over to British Nassau. We got there about twenty-four hours after the troop ship did. It beat us all to pieces. It was a little outfit, you know. It wouldn't ride the seas like them bigger ships would. We had a boy in the crow's nest forty foot above the water, and he said he could have done his laundry while he was there, the way the thing was rollin'. I stayed at my duty station seventy-two hours. I couldn't get out.

"We got in a fight with a submarine one night at Midway and dropped, between us and our sister ship, I think we dropped eighty-somethin' depth charges and never did get that thing."

We operated out of Pearl Harbor, convoying and hunting submarines and you name it. The primary job for that vessel was submarine warfare, but we did a lot of convoy work, just protecting the larger ships from submarines, you know. We went on down at Midway. We went to . . . Christmas Island, all 'round, takin' these troop ships, supply ships, convoying for them. We got in a fight with a submarine one night at Midway and dropped, between us and our sister ship, I think we dropped eighty-somethin' depth charges and never did get that thing. They got a radar contact on it up in the wee hours in the mornin'. I guess it was a periscope, but they got a contact, and it was halfway in between us and our sister ship. We were cruisin' a parallel course, and here's this thing cruisin' right in between us. We'd dropped so many depth charges, the water, the silt in the water, was so turbulent that the sonar system just wasn't worth a durn. You have to wait for that to settle, and the sub had time to do what he wants to do, you know. At that time, that's the way it was. It's different now. The equipment is so much better.

I stayed down there and caught this durn jungle rot, we called it. Both my feet swelled up like two ten-pound hams. I couldn't wear shoes. I spent a month at the naval hospital out of Honolulu. They didn't know how to doctor the stuff, but they got it down to at least where I could get my shoes on, and then they transferred me back to Vallejo, California, commissioned a salvage barge. Actually, the proper name for it was yard derrick, but anyway, I commissioned it and took it to Seattle, Washington. I had to put in at Seattle. We had one hatch leakin' water into one of the compartments, and we had to refuel and this and that. Then we went from there to Sitka, Alaska. I stayed at Sitka three months workin'. I took shore batteries off of the beach there. They originally started to build a sub base at Sitka, and when we run the Japanese off of Attu, they didn't try to follow up the invasion of the Aleutians. They were goin' to come on up the chain and get into Alaska proper, mainland, you know, but we run them off of Attu, and the action down in the South Pacific was such that they couldn't maintain an offensive up in the North Pacific. After they got the Japanese off of Attu, they didn't have a chance to invade that far east, so they abandoned the plans to make a submarine base. The Navy decided they didn't need to build a sub station up at Sitka, so I was takin' shore guns off of the beach. I think the barrels and actions were somewhere around twelve tons, and the bases were around fourteen tons or better. I'd go and take the bases off the beach and haul 'em off at Sitka. The transport ships, the cargo ships, I'd let 'em down on the cargo ships. I just picked that thing up and put it on deck or in the hold if they needed it. We had a twenty-foot tide at Sitka, and we had to work according to the tide. To me it was just hard work. We always did a lot of other things, too. We'd move anchor buoys around the harbor where the ships could come in and tie to them, you know, and things of that nature, heavy lifting. Any heavy lifting, I took. It's been a real interesting life. I've enjoyed it.

"[T]hose things rolled out of that net and fell 'bout one deck. Boy, you talk about a bunch of people ridin' on tiptoes! Whoo! That scared us all! Those things were rumblin' down there in the hold of that ship, *a-bloombiadabloombiada*! I guarantee you, buddy, there was some tight hide walkin' around that deck."

One time I was transferring depth charges in a cargo net. 'Course, they didn't have any detonators in them, and I think they were three hundred pounds, *ash cans,* we called them. Just a metal drum full of TNT is what it was. In one end they had a place to put the detonator, and I had six of them in a cargo net, a rope-woven cargo net. I guess it was kind of old and frayed or whatnot; I was goin' to pick 'em up off of the dock and put them over on the cargo ship and lower them down in the hold. I got it in the cargo ship and started down with those things. That dang net tore, and every one of those things rolled out of that net and fell 'bout one deck. Boy, you talk about a bunch of people ridin' on tiptoes! Whoo! That scared us all! Those things were rumblin' down there in the hold of that ship, *a-bloombiadabloombiada!* I guarantee you, buddy, there was some tight hide walkin' around that deck, everybody drawed up, but we didn't have any problem. All the detonators were out, which, I guess, was a darn good thing.

I had a cook (we lived up on that barge) from Colorado. Name was Wilson. He lived at Grand Junction, Colorado, when he enlisted in the Navy. I'd go out and catch fish, and when I was divin', every once in a while I'd catch a codfish or somethin', you know. I'd go out and look for scallops along the rocks and whatnot and bring 'em in for him to cook, and he'd holler and whine and went on about that. He wasn't used to that sort of thing, but after he got kinda settled and into it, the crew enjoyed fresh fish. Mama sent me these packages of gingerbread mix. I tried to bake a pan of them, and that thing didn't rise. It was just about a quarter of an inch thick, just like a piece of leather. In fact I beat that pan on the table just tryin' to get it out of there. I pried and scraped and everything else, and then when you got it out of the pan, you couldn't eat it. But it was a big treat anyway. I got ol' Wilson to work on it. He cooked us a bunch of gingerbread; we enjoyed that.

I'd catch a lot of Japanese perch up there along the docks. It wasn't a large fish—oh, maybe a foot long, you know, and built kind of like a bass but didn't have quite as big a mouth, you know, and they was turquoise blue. When you cleaned them, the flesh was turquoise blue, beautiful color, but it made you wonder if you oughta eat it or not, you know. You'd put 'em in the 'frigerator, and there they'd be, just shinin' blue. Ol' Wilson, boy, we had a terrible argument about that. He didn't want to cook 'em at all. He didn't want to deal with those fish. I said, "You cook me some of those fish. *I'll* eat them. Then if it's all right, we'll all have fish," and they were pretty good. I enjoyed them. It was the oddest thing to see them things when you clean 'em. That flesh was just turquoise blue, just as pretty as it could be, but it was so odd that you were a little bit gun-shy of the things.

The war ended when I was on Attu. The base commander told me: "I'll give you a commission if you'll stay here three more months and help us shut down and secure the base." Boy, I'd been overseas so long. I wanted to, but I just couldn't do it. I saw my firstborn son at nine months old when I got out of boot camp; the next time I saw him, he was two years old, and then when I got home, he was four years old.

He was the perkiest, prettiest little ol' boy you ever laid your eyes on, smart as he could be, and Mama had made him a little Navy uniform and

everything. She went to live in Athens with her parents while I was overseas. They had a Navy school down there, and of course he saw those boys
marchin' all the time, trainin' and whatnot, while I was gone. When I got
back, boy, that's all he wanted to do. He wanted me to march. We had a
time walkin' up and down the street, marchin'. He'd hup-hup, that little ol'
duster.

Other than him, I had all my boys swimmin' before they could get out of
diapers. I had one boy, the one that's livin' up the road here, would go off of
a ten-foot board and swim. He was still wearin' diapers. I'd get down under
the water, you know, and watch for him to come off. He had them little ol'
hands and feet just a-goin'. I'd just be sure he was makin' it back to the top.

In 1939, Dot and I moved to Toccoa, Georgia, from Athens. She and I
worked in a plant. She went to work at seven in the morning, and I went in
at three in the afternoon. After seventeen years, I went into business for
myself thirty days after I left the plant. We had always been interested in
collecting arrowheads and walkin' the fields in the woods, you know, and we
had collected a good many interestin' minerals and got interested in that. In
1955, I decided we'd go into the gem and mineral business, and we had the
handsome sum of a hundred and fifty dollars to operate on. I paid a month's
rent on the building there in Toccoa, bought a safe, took our personal collection of stones, and opened shop. I'd been cuttin' stones for a long time. I
had already built my own equipment and learned to cut gemstones—taught
myself. I was cutting faceted stones. We started our shop down here in Toccoa, and Mama kept workin' at the plant. She was makin' about forty-
somethin' dollars a week, which kept us fed. In '47, I had gone to Cowee
Valley, in Franklin, North Carolina, and got that ruby mine started. A Mr.
Brady wrote an article—I believe it was for *Woman's Day*—about my mine,
and it caught fire like prairie grass. I met Weaver Gibson and Will Holbrooks. Their farms were right up there in the middle of Cowee Valley in
the same area where the old original ruby mines used to be. So I went up
there visitin', lookin' around, and I talked to them. We got to be pretty good
friends with them, and I talked to them. I told them, I said, "You oughta quit
plantin' corn. You're gettin' too old to be farmin'. Let the public come in
here and dig these stones and charge them so much a day, you know." I said,
"You sit over here under a shade tree and take the money in. Your land will
produce more money, more income for you, and you won't have to work so
hard." And they did, both of them.

Weaver was an old mica miner. He had scoliosis, so he wasn't able to work
anyway to amount to anything. He got his brother Carroll to come over
there and manage, you know. Of course, I think Carroll finally bought the
property. Weaver died, and Carroll inherited or somethin' or bought the

property. We enjoyed goin' up there once in a while, made good friends out
of the whole bunch, and they dug that whole area up there.

Anyway, I built my machinery and went into business. It was touch-and-
go. I kept that youngest boy for, I believe, a year or two in the playpen, and
every day Mama'd have me some clean diapers and bottles already mixed. I'd
take the boy or the two youngest boys to work with me and keep 'em during
the day and try to do what I could to operate the business. Of course I wasn't
crowded or anything like today, maybe three or four or five customers a day,
and that was it, but we pinched and finally shuffled along till we got fairly successful, so to speak, but when that thing got goin', like it did up in Franklin,
we moved our shop up there. That was in the winter of '58 and '59. We
moved up to Franklin. I thought it was right funny when we first went up
there—Mama had to take those boys in school, you know. She had to go
down to get some dungarees and clothes and stuff for them to go to school
decent lookin'. She bought fifty-somethin' dollars worth of dungarees. Of
course, back then that was a whole lot of dungarees. That took care of all four
of the boys. I apologized to the principal of the school for dumpin' four
rowdy boys into the school system. I said, "I know I've sure put a burden on
you." But I said, "If you make them behave there, I'll make 'em behave at
home." I made a paddle and sent it with them. I marked it THE BOARD OF
EDUCATION and sent it to the principal of the school. We stayed up there in
Franklin for twenty years and sold out, bought this place in Westminster, and
moved here in '78. Since we were twenty-one years old when we were married, we been twenty years everywhere we went. We were twenty-one years
in Athens, twenty years in Toccoa, twenty years in Franklin, and we been
here since '78, so I don't know where we gonna go the next twenty years.

We got along real well, and 'course we were hassled up there in Franklin
like we weren't used to being. In other words, a lot of times they'd keep me
up till twelve or one o'clock at night, people just wanting to pick your brains,
you know, about stones and whatnot, cuttin' stones. Well, I taught lapidary
at Haywood Tech over at Waynesville, North Carolina. I taught lapidary
there in the winter for twelve years, and that was fair income for the
winter—not a lot, but a fair income. I had little or no business in the winter.
I also served as the deputy sheriff up there with Harry Thomas and Brice
Roland. I put twelve years there free—no charge, in other words. I just
helped them because they were both friends, and they were covering a
county 'bout twenty by twenty miles with one man, you know. It wasn't all
that easy for them, and it was just somethin' for me to do to keep occupied
in the winter. I didn't work all the time anyway. I just worked when they
needed me to fill in to give 'em a chance to rest or whatnot. I really enjoyed
it in a way, and in another way, I learned more than I should have about

some people. I guess that's all just part of livin'. In 1976, we bought the shop in Westminster, South Carolina, and moved there in '78. I'll operate six months, starting in May, and close six months—after leaf season.

> "My craft was primarily gemstones, and I've survived on craft work since 1955. 'Course, I did a lot of wood carvin' and handmade jewelry. I can make arrowheads, can chip arrowheads. In fact, all my brains are in my fingers."

We had an organization called the Village of Yesteryear, and we did all kinds of crafts that were practiced and produced in the old days. It was in Raleigh, North Carolina. Each person had their own thing. We had one boy makin' muzzle-loadin' rifles and another one doin' wood carvin' and another basket workin'—you name it. You know we had a hundred craftsmen and all of them doin' different things. Maybe two or three of them would be repetitive, but not much. I did my gem work. My craft was primarily gemstones, and I've survived on craft work since 1955. 'Course, I did a lot of wood carvin' and handmade jewelry. I can make arrowheads, can chip arrowheads. In fact, all my brains are in my fingers. We went over there to Raleigh twenty-one years. Here's [a gold medallion] what they gave me in 1978, fourteen-karat gold. It was for being named Craftsman of the Year for the whole state of North Carolina. They give it to one man and one woman. It was really touching. It really got to me, the ol' boy. We had a friend, Jimmy Burns, that was the bandmaster down in Cary, North Carolina, not far away, at the high school. He had been to the Rose Bowl twice and took that high school band to the Rose Bowl out in California. By golly, he came up there to the Village of Yesteryear and invited Mama and I out. We went outside, and he had the band out there and serenaded us. I stood there and cried like a baby. When he got through, he gave me the baton, and I still treasure that. That was great. I enjoyed that.

Oh, yeah, I've got a stone in the Smithsonian. I cut a cat's-eye semonite—didn't know what it was. Found a bunch of it, but it was all trash except that one piece that was solid. I got Dr. Furcron, the state of Georgia geologist, to identify it for me. I didn't know what it was. Anyway, I cut it, and it was the prettiest bronze cat's-eye you ever saw. To the best of my knowledge, I've never seen or heard of it occurring like that before. We got pounds and pounds of crystal out of that mine. We leased that thing, and I advertised it in *The Lapidary Journal,* a national magazine. The only sale I ever made was that one I cut for the Smithsonian. It paid for the other expenses, and that was about it. That's the only one now, and it's on display in the Smithsonian. I sold one to the North Dakota School of Mines. I did one for them, but it was flawed so bad I was ashamed to do it, but I sent it on to them and charged them practically nothin', just mostly postage and packaging, but they had one anyway.

When I was doin' gems and jewelry, I did scrimshaw for a diversion. It was a hobby. Then when I sold the gem business, I did scrimshaw at all the craft shows. I used to go to Raleigh, North Carolina, every year, went to Raleigh twenty-somethin' years, I think, and went to Rockingham a lot in North Carolina, that craft show up there. I went to the Anderson Fair. Down here they started a craft building, and I went down there. We were charter members of all this except Raleigh. I just got tired of going to craft shows. Years were building up, and another thing, my eyes weren't as good for doing scrimshaw. I started doing woodwork before I stopped going to craft shows. That was my diversion. I got to doing woodwork and did whatever I took a notion to do. It kept me busy. It's been about two years since I quit makin' this stuff. Doctors don't want me in that dust anymore.

I had bypass surgery in the VA hospital in Asheville, North Carolina. I held out pretty good for ten or twelve years and had another one and went back to Emory over here in Atlanta. They did angioplasty work, and I did real well for about a year and a half. I went back, and they put in stents— that's been a few years ago—and I held up pretty good for a time. The doc-

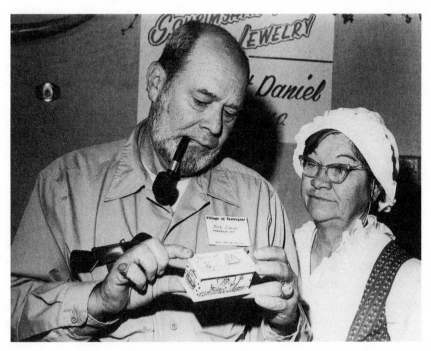

PLATE 16 Bob and his wife, Dot, with one of Bob's scrimshaw
boxes at a craft show

tor told me after that, "Your heart sounds good." I said, "Great! Put a good flutter valve in that thing and a choke so I can choke it and crank it if it starts givin' me trouble." I think now, though, they might have to put in a pace-maker, and I hope it has two speeds. I'd like to have High so I could get out there and dance.

We went over to Memphis to visit that oldest boy. He was in his early years of being in the Navy. They put him in the electronics school over in Memphis, and we went over to visit him. It was sometime about the mid-sixties, I guess, and comin' on back, we decided we wanted to go see the Hermitage. We had never been over there. We went over and looked that over, and we noticed a pile of old lumber layin' out there that was pretty well rotted. I told Mama, I said, "When that was first put over there in the weather, that would have been good for somethin'." Anyway, we went through the building, the home, Andrew Jackson's home, and we couldn't go into the kitchen area. They had some bad sills under the kitchen floor, some bad floor joists. They had to tear the floorin' out. That floorin' was about an inch or an inch and an eighth thick yellow poplar. It was tongue and groove, and you don't see that type of material, nowadays anyway. They were splittin' out that tongue-and-groove area and takin' it out. They couldn't get it out any other way without damaging the edges of the boards. I told Mama, "You know, I'd like to have that wood," so we went to the director's office and asked him: "You know what you are gonna do with that wood?" He said, "I don't know. We'll put it out there somewhere." I said, "Well, you don't want to set it out there and let it rot like that other pile is out there." He said, "Well, I don't know anything to do with it." I said, "Well, look, I'd like to have it." He said, "What in the world do you want with it?" I said, "I'd like to have it to make my first grand-child's baby cradle. We're expecting our first grandchild before too long, and I'd like to have it to make her a baby cradle and maybe a few other things for the rest of the family." He said, "Well, that sounds all right. I don't know any other thing to do with it. Just go ahead and get it." He wouldn't let us drive the van back around inside the gate so we could get it. Mom and I . . . I passed the lumber out over the fence to her. She took it and laid it down by the van, and then later I loaded it all in the van. There we were in dress clothes, just shufflin' that lumber like you wouldn't believe. People come and look. I guess they thought we were about half nuts. We got the lumber and made a lot of things for the family out of it—of course, sentimental types of things—and everybody was happy with it.

**"I get worn out now. I'm much better at sittin' in a La-Z-Boy chair and exercising that table muscle than anything else right now."**

Dorothy Frances Daniel—I call her Mama all the time. The grandchildren usually call her Dotty. They all call her Dotty. She was a Bryant before I married her. She's a tough little girl. In fact she's tougher than I am—I reckon she is—'cause she's managed to make me do what she wants done. Oh, yeah, she's my social secretary. She tells me who I'm goin' to see and who I'm not. She's also the president of the financial side of the family—got me on an allowance. Naw, it's been a great life. We been married sixty-five years in June. [Dot adds, "After sixty-five years, we're still friends."] We've never struck each other, but I did kick her off the bed once. I was lying in bed, and I had a great big ol' Washington apple. I polished it on the blanket. It was perfect. I told Mama, "Look at it. Just look at it." ["He kept telling me that over and over," Dot amends.] I stuck that shiny apple over there to show it to her. She had those long fingernails, and she poked holes all over that apple—ruined my apple! [Dot confides that he apologized to her for

PLATE 17 The Daniels, with Dot in a cast, celebrate their fiftieth wedding anniversary.

the incident years later when he was away in the Navy.] I did it from far away
'cause I didn't know what she'd do. [They both laugh.]

I firmly believe, always have, in fact, believed, that if it hadn't been for
her, I'da been dead a long time ago. Somebody'd killed me when I was
about twenty-five or thirty years old. She's nine days older than me. She was
born February 25, 1917. I get her and her mother goin' when I say she's a
year and nine days older. They get to carryin' on, and I just leave the room.

We got four fine sons. Two of them belong to the AARP. Our oldest son is
sixty-one years old. He's retired from the Navy. He's an aviation electronics
engineer. He does repair estimates for Lockheed. He's the contact between
Lockheed and the Navy. My second son is Jimmy. He's on the hill with me.
He works over in Seneca, South Carolina, and makes golf balls, Dunlop golf
balls. My third son is Chris. He's named after an uncle: Herbert Crisler.
Chris is a commercial artist. My youngest one is about forty-somethin'. Idn't
he about forty-eight? Jody's about forty-eight, and he's a commercial security supervisor out of Smyrna, Tennessee. They're all settled and have nice
families. Jody's twelve years younger than Spike. We got seven granddaughters and one grandson. We raised four sons, and we got seven granddaughters. We got one grandson, and we got three great-granddaughters.

It's been a great life. I've done a lot of very interesting things. I can just
about do anything that I want to do, or I used to before I got so old, you
know. I get so frustrated sometimes I don't know whether to scratch my
watch and wind my fanny or what. We like to metal detect. We don't go for
long. I get in trouble with her. She mistrusts me. [Dot interjects, "He wants
to tell me how to do it."] I just don't want to find more than she does. [He
laughs.] I get worn out now. I'm much better at sittin' in a La-Z-Boy chair
and exercising that table muscle than anything else right now. We already
found our spot. We're plantin' wildflowers right down here, and when the
time comes, we're gonna be cremated and our ashes put right down there in
our little flower garden down by the picnic shed, so when the kids have a
party, we're gonna be present.

# HARVEY J. MILLER
# OF PIGEON ROOST

*"That writing, though, I enjoy that . . . I took this writing up when
I was twelve years old and been at it ever since."*

Nearly every community that has a weekly newspaper also has neighborhood correspondents whose job it is to report the neighborhood news through their weekly columns. Most of these columns are pretty dismal affairs confining themselves to a roll call of visitors, illnesses, births, and deaths.

Occasionally, however, a blessed columnist here and there goes light-years beyond that tired formula and fills the columns with sunlight. Harvey J. Miller, who was born in a log home in Pigeon Roost, North Carolina, and who went only through the sixth grade, is one such person. His first offering appeared over eighty-five years ago when he was twelve, and he wrote a column regularly. His last contributions appeared in *The Tri-County News* out of Spruce Pine, North Carolina.

And what a column! Every edition was filled with odd events, stories he had heard during the previous week, pieces of his own philosophy, and observations made by a mind intensely curious about, and awed by, all he saw around him. A sampling of past headlines hints at the richness of the work: "Ravenous Coon Stages Midnight Henhouse Raid on Pate Creek," "Sabbath Gnat Storm Plagues Pigeon Roost," "Helicopter Scares Cattle; Train Kills 3 Head," and " 'Falling' Racer Snake Misses Preacher; Fox Chases Dog out of Woods."

The stories are even better. Take this one, for example, of November 14, 1963: "Reverend Harrison Street of the Pate Creek section of Pigeon Roost told me this one: He said the other day he cut down a maple tree on his farm and the tree was very knotty, and when he was trimming one of the large knots off the tree with an axe, he cut into a hollow place of the knot, and out rolled a black snake like a ball. But as the snake went down the hill, it stretched out by degrees and then crawled away. He said that he didn't know how long the snake had been embedded under the knot—there had been a hole in the knot, but it had completely growed over on the outside with a new piece of bark. It is believed that the snake had went into the rotten knothole to hibernate for the winter, and the knothole on the outside had growed up. But it does not seem possible that it could do that in one winter's time. So the snake had a permanent home; in fact, it was in prison, as there was no other way for the snake to get under the knot but by only through the growed-up knothole."

Here's another memory, one of hundreds parceled out over the weeks: "A way back 'yander' ever' mother had certain ways to kill the first louse found on their children's head. The way the first louse was cracked could shape her kid's destiny: crack it on a song book, and he would become a singer; on a Bible, he would be a preacher; or on a tin cup and he would become a great professor."

We learned about Harvey through one of our subscribers, went to meet him, and were so impressed with his work that the Winter 1974 issue of *Foxfire* was devoted to excerpts from the columns he wrote between 1950 and 1973. We called it *News from Pigeon Roost.*

During subsequent visits, we tape-recorded Mr. Miller and compiled the stories from those tapes. The following is an article that appeared in the Spring 1978 issue of *Foxfire.*

PLATE 18  Hannah Hunnicutt Barnett, Harvey Miller's grandmother

PLATE 19  Reverend Spencer Barnett, Harvey Miller's grandfather

MY GRANDFATHER came in here from Cherokee, near Tennessee. He was part Indian. He took up land here—homesteading. They built a big two-room log house. My father was Dave Miller. I was born and raised on Pigeon Roost Creek. I was raised in a log cabin. My parents farmed. You know I was sick till I was about thirty years old. Never did work on a public job. All I done was farm.

There was a bunch of us kids, but by the time they was gone, I was still at home. I didn't marry until my mother died. I stayed there with her. That's one reason I know so much of this old stuff. I lived with it so long.

You know, old people back then paid attention to things that young people today don't even know about—like if you sweep with a broom under your feet, why, you'll never get married. Now you boys better not let nobody sweep under your feet! And now if you sleep under a new quilt, why, the one you dream of, you'll marry her. People back then—well, it worked out, they said.

Like when you get a new dog? Cut the hair off the end of his tail and put that hair under the doorstep and the dog won't leave—stay right with you. Then you've got you a dog there.

"Now to keep your nose from bleedin', get lead from a bullet that killed a hog, beat it out round, and put you a hole in it and put a common red string to it and wear it around your neck."

And I know you've heared of this one: Never start a job on Wednesday that you can't finish the same day. Sometimes bad luck'll happen. Now, my

PLATE 20  The Dave Miller family—Harvey,
age three, sits in his father's lap.

PLATE 21  Harvey as a teenager
astride his pony, June

mother, you know, she'd never let us start on a big field of corn on Wednesday. Little one was okay 'cause she knowed we could get it done.

   And if you get your hair cut, don't never throw it out outside. A bird'll get
it and put it in a nest, and you'll 'bout die with a headache. Now I used to cut
hair, you know, and an old man come and he had a little poke [paper sack].
He'd get all that hair up when I'd get his hair cut and put it in his pocket.
And I said, "What's that for?" And he said, "I'm not gonna let you throw my
hair out here on the outside and let the birds get it and," said, "me with a
headache." Said, "I don't never have a headache." He'd take and turn a rock
up. I'd see him and watch him, you know, go down the road. He'd come to a
flat rock and put that hair under there and put dirt over it and go on. And I
got checkin' on that, and you know, all them old people believed that.

   I had a lot of those things wrote down here in this notebook, but I can't
find them. Yeah, here now. You ever hear about cattle havin' a holler [hol-
low] tail? My remedy is slit their tail and put salt in that and tie it up. And if
cattle has a holler head, put turpentine around that soft place on their head.
Let that sink in. And cattle, when they got a bloat . . . you know, eat some-

thing that bloats them up? Put turpentine to her navel. Pour that turpentine. Put it in a little pan or something, or jar cap, and hold it up there, and it'll soak in there in a minute. I've tried that. That helps the cow.

Now to keep your nose from bleedin', get lead from a bullet that killed a hog, beat it out round, and put you a hole in it and put a common red string to it and wear it around your neck. Keep that around your neck all the time. Has to be where it killed a hog. We had one here. My daughter, Ethel, lost her'n one time in the third grade, and her nose went to bleedin'. We got it replaced with another bullet.

I guess you've heared of this: If anybody springs their foot or arm—gets a sprain—why, make a poultice out of apple pummies [squashed apple pulp]. When they grind apples to make cider, you know, to make vinegar, they'd have pummies left. Get that out. You know, with a sprain, you take a fever in that, and those pummies are cool. Vinegar and salt poultice is good, too. You can use those pummies to make apple brandy, too.

And sometimes, certain places, you get milk sick or milk poison. There's a place back here on the head of Pigeon Roost they keep fenced in all the time because what causes that grows there. They call it white snakeweed, I think. And when you get it, it has a place it settles—might settle in the leg. They say that there apple brandy, if that don't cure it, nothing will.

My mother kept a little bag hanging on the wall, and when someone'd get sick, had all kinds of herbs tied up in paper. Get them out and she'd know what to do, you know. My brother one night come in from the sawmill and coughin' every breath, and oh, he was bad off. And she went in there and grabbed that little poke off the wall and went to gettin' it out. She said, "He's got pneumonia fever." But next morning, she had that broke, but he 'as so weak he couldn't set up. Yeah, now, he had it. She used boneset tea for that.

She was a good doctor, but I saw her scared one time. Our daddy took the croup, and I reckon she was afraid she couldn't doctor anymore like she did before, since she was old then. She got me and my brother out way at midnight and sent us after my sister who lived way up on the mountain—told us we had to go after her. Sick Daddy, and she [Mother] hadn't done a thing. He'd took the croup. He'd choke to death. Said, "You hurry and go get them."

We went, and she hadn't done a thing. We lit the kerosene lantern. That's all the light we had. Oh, it was way back on the mountain. It was, I guess, three miles we walked. But now we went up that mountain, and she told us, "Now, don't fool no time." When we got back, why, he had got all right. I said, "What happened there?" She said, "I doctored him at last." She said, "It cured him." She had him up when we went in. She built a fire and had him up there at the old fireplace. She built a fire and had him baking his

PLATE 22  Mr. and Mrs. Dave Miller,
Harvey Miller's parents

feet. I didn't ask her, but she greased his feet with somethin'. She told me
the next day that she was nervous. But back when I was young, it seemed
like I never did see her get scared much.

One night there was a storm, and she was gettin' pretty old then. One
night it come a heavy storm and rain, and we lived right up over the creek.
We heard that creek. She come and called for us—wanted to take to the
hills, but I wouldn't let her. Next day I told her, I said, "I never . . ." (It was a
bad time, you know—the water around the door.) I told her, I said, "I never
seen you do that way before." She said, "I was scared." She said, "That was
good you begged us not to go to the hill." I said, "There's no place there—no
shelter." She said, "I guess we could have gone up there in that broomsage
field on up higher on the hill, but we sure would have got wet."

Back then we didn't have any clocks, and they had sun marks to tell what
time it was. My grandma and grandpa, where they lived, when it was light at
the edge of the porch, it was twelve o'clock. My uncle and aunt live there
now, and it still works. And when a shadow fell across a certain place on the
back door sill, it was six o'clock. The evening, six o'clock, was behind the
house. And that worked out. Where I lived with my mother, there was a sun
mark on the hill. It's there yet. We called it the rye field. This land was
cleared up, this here wooded place. When the sun would get down there
where the clearin' started, it was six o'clock. We could see it way off the
mountain where we were working in the fields. When the shadow of the
mountain hit the edge of the clearin', we'd start off the mountain. We

watched that. We'd say, "Oh, it's six o'clock. Now let's go in." We called that sun mark time.

We raised some feed on that hill—had to "shock it up." Have to take and cut the top of the corn and pull them blades and tie the tops and blades together and shock it up till it dries and then haul it in and stack it up in them stacks—big, high stacks. There is somebody up on the stacks, and they throw it up to them—bunch of men. It goes up fast. I've seen them take a piece of wood and set it in the middle of the stack like a pole and make them stacks higher—go on up 'em. Then to get down, somebody would put a pitchfork in there to step on or get on somebody's shoulders. One time I was stackin' a stack of fodder way up high, and they was a bullet. I heard that bullet a-singin' in the air. It went like it was close to me. I was tellin' a man about it, and he said, "Why, I guess it was a long ways off." Said, "You can hear them singin' that way." But now I heard it go through! I never did hear the fire of the gun. I heard the bullet, though.

> "Then the rats would gnaw and eat that dough. Mother put bluestone in that, and that kept the rats away. It's a kind of poison. It's good to give dogs—worm a dog, that bluestone."

But we had to raise everything. No money. Didn't have much. Everybody in them old log houses papered the walls with catalogs and newspapers. Sometimes they would do it over and over and over, three times. They'd change that when it got yeller and aged—redo that. Not long ago I seen that in a house: put up with wheat paste. Then the rats would gnaw and eat that dough. Mother put bluestone in that, and that kept the rats away. It's a kind of poison. It's good to give dogs—worm a dog, that bluestone.

Another thing we used them catalogs for was fly flaps [swatters]. They would take and trim them. Back when I was a boy, somebody had to stand over the table all the time with a fly flap—keep the flies off. They was like a bee swarm. Everybody was that way here.

> "Now we got one pair of shoes a year, and we went barefoot except for on Sunday."

To show you how poor people was, you know how we got our brass kettle? My mother bought it. People would go broke and sell out. They would put the word out they were selling out. When people moved off, they'd sell things. So these people moved down in Crossville, Tennessee—went on a train. They sold their things for what they could get for them. People didn't have much money, so that kettle didn't cost us over three or four dollars. We

PLATE 23  Taking a breather and swapping stories—Harvey wrote
about life in Pigeon Roost.

was offered forty dollars for it. Then another man said that he'd give me a
hundred. I said, "I've been offered forty already, but I won't sell it." We still
make apple butter in it. We take the apples and peel them the night before.
For a quick run, you sugar them down the night before, twenty-five or thirty
pounds for a twelve-gallon kettle—depends on the thickness you want.
Then the next morning, you boil them off. Stir it with what they call an apple
butter stirrer. Boil it four to five hours if you want it thin. If you want it thick,
you do it longer. Back then, we sweetened it with molasses. Keep stirring
that in, and it would be way in the night before it was done. I've seen my
mother take and slice it out, and it would be red apple butter. Now you put
that sugar in, and it's clear. Then she'd put it in crocks. It'd mold over the top
of them crocks, but that wouldn't hurt it. They can it now. That's good eatin'.

Then we had gardens. I still have one. We saved seeds. With things like
mustard and turnips, we'd just go out, and what you didn't use, gather the
seeds to plant next year. Now tomatoes, you take them and dry the seed. Put
it on a paper or pasteboard and dry them and keep them until next year. And
cucumber seeds, you know, save them. And that was all right back then, but
now it seems like it don't do so good. They just knowed how, and they done
good. There's still some people on Pigeon Roost that does that now, but back
then everyone done it.

And most people through here now still plant by the signs. Man yesterday
told me not to sow my tobacco seed till next week. It wasn't a good time this

PLATE 24  Harvey Miller and Harvey Garland wend their
way up the long path to the Garland cabin.

week. He goes by the signs of the moon, you know. He said it wasn't a good time, said to wait till next week. A lot of boys I know about even wait till a certain time to get their hair cut. One boy raised on Pigeon Roost—now, he'd fight anybody 'fore he'd have his hair cut, he'd wait till a certain time, you know [see *The Foxfire Book,* pages 212–227]. My aunt always told me if I wanted my hair to grow, to cut it on the new of the moon, and then it would grow as the moon grows. Yeah, that made me think of it. When I was a boy, what would you say I made my hair tonic out of? Grapevines—these here wild grapes. Go and tap them and set you something under them. Get the juice out. That would help now. Make it grow better. Just cut the vine and set me a jar down and let it drip—same way with maples. That was where you got your maple sugar. We didn't make none ourselves, but there

PLATE 25  Two mules hitched to a sled help in gathering tobacco.

was people right around did. They done it mostly in the home there. They didn't go into it in a big way. But storekeepers would buy that from you in a store. It brought high. That was good sweetenin'.

And honey, lots used that. People kept bees. Sometimes they'd swarm. Noon was when they come out. Some of them would go wild and go to the mountains. Have a tree cleaned out. They'd take off to the mountains. People'd hunt them bee trees and then cut them. Or you can catch the swarms. Beat on a plow point with a rock to make them settle. I've heard of men grabbin' an old shotgun and shootin' in them, but that there tears them up, they say—gets them confused, scattered. And some beat on dishpans with a spoon to make them settle. I've heard of that. The noise of that ring, I reckon, is what does it. You ever heard bees go over in the air? There is a noise, ain't they? Now one time I was at the graveyard. Man lived right down in the holler below there had a lot of bee gums, and we seen a bee swarm a-comin'. It looked like it was a-comin' to that gatherin' on the little hilltop. Before it got there, it turned. They was down low, you know. I don't know why they turned. Everybody said it scared them. If they'd got there to them people, somebody might've been hurt, but when they got there, they turned, just rolled on over and over.

But that maple sugar was one way of gettin' a little money—and ginseng, yeah, and that goldenseal. It brought a good price. It was scarcer than that ginseng was. Ginseng now is high. But that cultivated 'sang, it don't bring much. They can tell the difference by the fiber of that root. Now, they was an old man who is still livin' down here. He told me last summer about his boy. His boy bought a lot of 'sang to resell to a dealer. Said when he brought it to him, the old man said, "Son, you're ruint. That's *cultivated* 'sang. You know what that brings." The boy said, "No, I know it isn't." But when he took it to sell it, it was. If he'd knowed, he said that he wouldn't have bought it, but he didn't know no better.

We gathered all kind of raw herbs. We'd pull pennyroyal and put it in a tub and take and run that off, just like making moonshine. They bought that pennyroyal spirits at the store—so much a gallon. You get the root off and put the whole plant in there in water; put a little fire under that tub, and you have that straight pipe comin' out of the top of the sealed tub. It runs out that pipe strong.

And we used to get balsam. Take and get that; that was good kidney medicine—spirits of balsam. And now them bam buds [balm of Gilead buds]—you know about that, don't you? Boil them down and use that for a salve. They went one year for a dollar a pound. They're eighty-five cents now down here at North Wilkesboro.

And there's a man that took a load of hides down there Monday. That was another way to make money. He took eighty-five. He called them rat hides— muskrat hides. He said, "Hides this year, it just ain't been cold enough, so their fur's not thick." He said they was bringing a good price, though. He made money by taking them down there. He just called them rat hides.

Now we got one pair of shoes a year, and we went barefoot except for on Sunday. Mother would make soup [pinto] beans. Back then, soup beans brought a good price. You've heard talk of what they call brogans? Buy those. Sell them soup beans. Take a big sack full—a bushel. Go and buy shoes and other things. Fall of the year, they would thrash those beans out. Set them [on] a cloth on the porch—or a bedsheet or something—and thrash them out when they got dry. Took them and beat them out with a frail [flail]. They didn't bring the price they bring now. Now two pounds of beans are $1.40!

Some people made their own shoes since there wasn't much money. We didn't, but we made our own cloth. Mother had a little spinnin' wheel. My sister took it off. Now where we lived—you've heard talk of flax breaks, ain't you? In that old log house, there was holes in there on the outside, and that was for flax breaks. And then she'd dye that. She used walnut hulls, and she used pokeberries. They called it pokeberry red. Put them in a pot and pour in a little water to cook it, you know. Dipped that in there. And she used eggshells. That give a kind of yellow color. Then make coverlets to go on them big old corded beds. And then have trundle beds under them. Pull them out, and somebody sleep in them. And in the mornin', push them back under them big old high beds. They was a pretty little ol' thing.

Then we kept geese to pluck for pillows and bed ticks [mattresses]. My mother would take ahold of them by their feet and turn them over there and pull that down off. Talk about squalling and letting on like it was a-hurtin' losin' them feathers. But it wouldn't take long till that growed back—grow back prettier than it ever was. You know, one would turn off a whole lot of feathers. She had her a big old gourd. It would hold over half a bushel—had the neck cut off. She called that her feather gourd. Put feathers down in there. That was the dandiest thing. We didn't have to clean that down. The geese kept clean in the branch.

One time Mother had three geese gone, and we hunted for them everywhere and couldn't find them. Some of them heard an old man talkin'. His son-in-law lived way up in the holler from us, and he said there was three geese come over and come there. Mother said for me to come with her, and we would go up and see if that was my geese. We went up there, and that man, he said, "Yeah, them geese come here," and he didn't know where from. "Them is my geese," my mother told that man. He said, "How do you know?" She told me to catch one of them, and she said, "I'll show him." I grabbed one and handed it to her, and she had that toenail cut off. Said, "Right here." She said, "I cut that off there." He said, "Is the others that way?" She said, "Sure." I catched them, and she said, "See there!" He said, "Huh." He said, "Them is yours. You know." Said, "Take them on."

I had my geese fenced in—had a rail pen. That kept them from bothering people's crops. I'd go to school in the mornin' and cut up apples and take stuff and feed them on the way. I went one mornin'. I had acid wood piled up there right down below where they was. I heard somethin' or other. They had been tellin' bear tales and I heard somethin' a-growlin' and I took off. You know, it scared me. I was pretty small. I heard somethin' growl. I went out and got way up toward the house, and, why, a man poked his head up over that acid woodpile. He went to laughin'. He was a one-armed man. He said he was afraid I'd get gone and get somebody and afraid he might get shot!

> **"Be sorta like that old woman I wrote about in one of my columns, but she was a witch . . . 'Get you a silver bullet and shoot. You'll kill the witch, or 'bout kill it.' "**

Be sorta like that old woman I wrote about in one of my columns, but she was a witch. She'd turn into a turkey hen. There's a place called Turkey Cove where wild turkeys would stay. One of my kinfolks would go in there early of a mornin', and he got to goin' in there, and an old turkey hen was pickin' around. He got to shootin' at it. He couldn't kill it. He hit all around. He'd shoot that old hog rifle—load that; pull down. Somebody told him, "You're shootin' at an old turkey witch. Get you a silver bullet and shoot. You'll kill the witch, or 'bout kill it."

He did, you know, melt him a silver bullet and one morning went in there at the same place and here come that old turkey hen walkin' around, and he pulled down and shot. And it fell over, you know, flopped, rolled down hard. Gone. Disappearin'. And it never come back that time. He went on home, and somebody told him that that old lady was down with rheumatism and couldn't get out of bed. In a few days, she was out of bed and limped, always limped. He changed back to his old kind of bullets and never was bothered with a turkey witch no more. That was a true story. He died in Georgia. He was some of my kinfolks. My dad and mother tell me that was facts.

Them witches . . . we put witch marks over the door—keep them away. They'll come and ask to borrow different things. You let them have a certain thing—somethin' sharp, like a knife or somethin'—and that breaks the spell.

I had an uncle that was said to be a witch doctor. My daddy had a heifer. They found her rolled in a ditch. They rolled her out, and she'd roll back in there. She couldn't stand up, and they couldn't find nothin' wrong with her. She hadn't hurt herself. And they sent for my uncle. He come, and he went and looked at her and examined her. He said, "She's bewitched." And he told Daddy, said, "Do you want me to doctor her?" And Daddy said, "Law, yeah, drive that witch off." They said he took his pocketknife. He built him up a little fire and took his pocketknife and cut the ends of her ears a little off and threw them in the fire. When that burnt up, she jumped up and run off.

A man saw a cow, and she was pourin' milk. He asked to borrow some, and they wouldn't give him none. He got mad at them and come down. This old lady was milkin' the cow. He said, "You gettin' a lot of milk?" She said, "Gettin' a peck bucketful." He looked and looked at that cow and walked around and went on down the road, and next mornin' that cow was dry— never did give. And she went to nothin'. I remember that. That old lady said that man put a spell—he bewitched her, you know. Put a spell on her. That used to happen. And they wasn't much they could do. Find out, and then you could accuse certain people of bein' witches by the way they was actin'. Nothin' they could do about it, though.

I believe we've got them yet. Now I seen an old woman not too long ago. She lived in the holler below me. I had an old cow went crazy. I went down there and told her about that and told that woman about the way that cow would do. She said, "Harvey, I'll go up there and doctor her." She went up, and she done what I told you my uncle done—had her knife and cut a little dab off the ear, and she put that in a poke and took it to the house. We had a fire in the cookstove, and she burned it in there. That evening we went back, and that old cow was all right. She said, "Don't you talk about it. Don't tell nobody nothin'." Said, "Somebody's going to be a-hurtin'." She claims she's a witch doctor. That ain't been too long ago—'bout eight, ten year ago.

Now there's a place on Pigeon Roost called Hatterock Hill. An old man come there making fur hats and caps. That's the reason it's called Hatterock Hill. Somebody said he was a wanted man. Come a big bunch of men. You know, back then if a hundred men wanted to take a man out of jail, the law couldn't do nothin'. A hundred men ruled the law. So a bunch of men came there to where that man was livin' under that rock cliff and got that old man and hanged him to a tree. After that, that place was hainted. This man and me went up there one day, and he told me to climb up on that rock, "I'll take your picture." Said, "I don't reckon there are any ghosts around." I'd been tellin' him that ghost story comin' up the road. Well, when he got the picture back, he said, "Harvey, I got your picture back took on the Hatterock Hill, and it looks like there's something—a shadow or something—up over you." I said, "That's that ghost." They say these here ghosts was the meanest people they is when they were alive. They don't believe in God or nothin'. Certain people can drive them away. Drive a spike, a nail, in a tree. You can kill them ghosts—drive them away.

Now they say if you see somebody comin' . . . I heard of a woman that lives back in the holler and she seen her brother comin' up the holler and she went back in the house, went to doin' other things, and waited a while. She went back and looked and never did see him no more. He never did get there, and he lived a way off. She was anxious to see him. In a few days she got word he was dead. Now they say if you see them a-comin' and they don't get there, that's a bad luck sign.

> "There's some way you can be bewitched by a frog. I've heard of girls, they claim, puttin' spells on boys. Take a frog, put it in a box, and let it die in there, and then there's a certain bone pulled out of that frog and hooked to that boy and not let him know, and he'll go crazy as a lunatic about that girl."

Or a hen a-crowin'. Now this place where I'm wantin' to go today, that old lady? I said, "You'uns got any chickens?" She said, "I ain't got a chicken." Said, "We had one old hen and she went to crowin' one day. This boy, he was out there with his little gun to shoot her. You know, he had to shoot seven times before he killed that old hen—throwed it down the hill. Throwed it away. That man with me, he said, "What was that?" I said, "That was a bad luck sign for her for a hen to go crowin' like a rooster." Yeah, now some people, they'll kill them there old roosters if they crow at night. Well, now if a rooster comes to the steps and crows, that's a sign company's comin'—yeah, comes up on the steps and crows. However many times he crows, it'll be that many people comin'. People bank on it. They look to that. A lot of that's fadin' out, though. But now, like me, raised up with a lot of that, it'll still be in; but the children, they believe in some of that, and some they don't. It's fadin' out, fading away.

Like, let's see. There's something about a frog. I forget now. There's some way you can be bewitched by a frog. I've heard of girls, they claim, puttin' spells on boys. Take a frog, put it in a box, and let it die in there, and then there's a certain bone pulled out of that frog and hooked to that boy and not let him know, and he'll go crazy as a lunatic about that girl. Now that's a story I've heard: certain bone from that frog hooked up there on his shirt. You'll fall now! Some girl will hook you now!

Another thing I want to get across to you is about horseshoes. You've seen horseshoes tacked up around. Back when I was young, hawks were awful bad to catch chickens. Put that horseshoe up there. That warned the hawks off from catchin' little chickens. Put the horseshoes anywhere around where the chickens were.

You know, I had me a little old bantam hen setting in that cold weather the other day. She hatched out seven pretty little banty chickens. I kept puttin' them back in the nest every night for a couple of nights, afraid they'd get cold—kept them in a box where that good nest was. Went out there, and something or 'nother had killed every one of them. We thought it was a black rat, but couldn't see no sign. But, they say, though, them old big black rats, that's what's bloodthirsty. A cat can't handle them. They say if one of them, them old black ones, bites you, that's it—poison.

> "And them black snakes. I've heard of them milkin' cows . . .
> See'd that old big black snake come out, come out there and get her
> milk. She'd let him do it."

And them black snakes. I've heard of them milkin' cows. They'll do that. There's a story about that. A man had a fine cow. She didn't give any milk, but her tits, when she came in, were wet. And he didn't know what was wrong. He said he kept watchin' that old cow. She'd go to a stump and stand at that stump. See'd that old big black snake come out, come out there and get her milk. She'd let him do it. She'd go to that old stump. She'd know where that was.

A snake can charm anybody. And you know a cat can charm a snake? And birds. Now we have a cat here'll bring in a lot of snakes. Cats eat certain kinds of snakes. They can charm a bird. That tail a-goin'. They keep comin' on up. That's the way snakes do a young'un. Mean! That's boogerman, them snakes is. They say it'll get around your neck, and that's it. But there's people that will let a snake wrap around their arm. This here Florida boy come over here. He found a big old black snake up over there, and he wasn't a bit more afraid of that—got it wrapped around his arm goin' up there. Oh, that looks scary gettin' toward his neck. He wasn't afraid.

Now, you know them snakes get in the woods where people is ridin', you know, people ridin' in the woods. They'll come right down and get around anybody's neck—fall there, drop off the branch. They know when to do it, time to do it. One day I was goin' up the road here, goin' along. Heard something thud—come down. Looked at my feet. I stopped. There was a snake fell out of a bush, fell right at my feet. It was an old racer.

But now people got pet snakes. I'm afraid of a snake. After we moved over here, we rented some land from an old man over on the mountain over here; and he had a pet snake, and it stayed in an apple tree—hollow place in the apple tree—and he said, "If you see my pet snake around here, don't you'uns hurt it. I wouldn't take nothin' for it. That's a pet." Said, "It won't bother you." Now my wife, we was there one day sittin' under there. It poked its head out. My wife, she got her a rock, and I told her, "Don't throw it. That's a pet snake." Well, she throwed that rock, and it liked to 've come out of there. But it went back in, hurt bad. We looked for that snake every day. We never did see it no more. That old man told us, "My pet snake is gone. I didn't want that snake killed." We didn't tell him. He said, "I ain't seen it." Said, "It's gone." We never did see it no more.

Garther Barnett's killed more than anybody. He'd kill every snake he seen. Had a rifle. He lives over there on a creek bank. He'd see a snake out on a limb—ker-bang! He'd know when he'd get one. That'd be it. The others, you know, they'd run a race with him. Keep a record. I lived over there, and he run a store. He said, "I've got a hundred and forty snakes this year so far." Yeah, he went up to three hundred snakes. He cleaned them out over there. You never see no more snakes. He had so far he patrolled. His wife would tend the store. He'd go up the road. You'd hear him shoot, come back, put it on the record. He'd put down "killed so many snakes"— champion snake killer of Pigeon Roost.

But the old people on Pigeon Roost believed a lot of that stuff I was tellin' you. That was way back in the mountains—no cars, telephones, radios. But now, back then they was a lot of people on the road. The road goin' up Pigeon Roost Creek was the road that led to Tennessee. There was a lot of different people come through there travelin' on horseback and walkin'. There'd be families. Some of them didn't have any money, and my brother—that was back before I can remember, but he remembered—he said one night they was a family of eleven. The man had lost his wife, and he was movin' them into Tennessee somewheres. He had a big family, and he told my daddy, he said, "I tried all the way up the creek. It's getting late, and I can't get nowhere to stay all night." He told my daddy he was a widower. And my daddy told them, "Well, we'll have to try to keep you some way. Might fare a little." We just had two rooms, and see, they was a big family of us. But Mother made beds on the floor. She had some extra bed ticks, you know. And they said they fared all right. Bedded 'em all down. That man said he didn't have no money at all. The next morning, why, they went on up across the mountain, walkin'. They had some things with them a-carryin' them.

There was one old man come down across from Tennessee. It was a pretty cold time. He built him a fire in an old tree, and that tree stood there for years. People would say, "There is where the old man set the tree on fire." Burnt the inside out, you know. He stayed out on the ground around that.

But they was all movin'—like what we call today "transient." They was changin' places. I remember about one time I was up on the hill, and I could see way up the road half a mile, and seen what looked like three old women comin', and I went and told my mother. And it was up in the evenin' about two o'clock, and she said, "Yeah, they'll come on through here."

And we kept watchin' for them, and we seen them comin'. They was goin' to Huntdale. They went on down the creek, them old women. They didn't stop and talk. They just went on through like they was in a hurry.

Some went in wagons, but most walked. I can't remember, but they said there was a boy went through. He was a kind of a queer boy. Said he had a big old dog right with 'im, and he went through, oh, in a hurry. And the next day they was some people come through a-huntin' for 'im, you know, a-tracin' after 'im, said there was somethin' wrong with 'im. He wasn't right. We told them we seen 'im go up the road. Had a dog. Said, "Yeah." Said, "He left with a big dog." Went on. We never heard. See, like that, you never would hear no more.

And there was peddlers on the road. We called them Irish peddlers. They carried it on their back, you know, sorta like a five-and-ten, little things. Tablecloths and all kinds of little things: needles and stuff like that—what you used at home. Anybody could buy some good stuff from them: ribbons.

Them peddlers, the way they worked that . . . they had a house below me. The people in the house kept boarders. They would be two or three of them Irish peddlers, and they'd go in different directions. Like one would go across Bean Creek, and one to Cherry Gap. Come Saturday, they'd stay there over the weekend. You'd see them sittin' out under shade trees. They knew where to come to. On Monday morning, they would take off a differ- ent way. You had to pay money to them peddlers mostly. I know about one, one time, come to our home. My sister, we was out in the field and he come about dinnertime. He was a new one, you know. He got her to get dinner for him. He didn't pay no money, but he give her things to pay for the dinner. Said, "I'll give you this and give you that for my dinner."

And back then we had what we called a wheel store. Did you ever hear talk of a wheel store? They would come and have like a certain time on like Monday mornin'. Everybody in the community would gather up to a certain place and wait for the wheel store. Now they done good tradin', too. It was a big old truck and what we call now a trailer. He had his stuff in there like a store. You go in there and get what you wanted. He come from back in Yancey County. He would buy roots and herbs, too.

There was a man down one time. He wouldn't get up there where I lived, up over Hatterock Hill. He would come down there as far as the mail come. Mail come down there on the creek where Ike Lewis lived, and people would meet out there and wait for him. He'd be on horseback. But one mornin', I guess they was twenty people there. We seen the old man what run that store that was in competition with the wheel store most of them dealt with. And he come up there where people had roots and herbs and eggs and everything ready to sell to that wheel store, and he said, "What do you get for this stuff?" And we wouldn't tell him, you know. And he said, "Take it down to *my* store, and," he said, "I'll give you more money than that." Said, "I want your people's trade up here." And some of them went and talked with him—were goin' down there—and come to me and asked me, and I said no. I had a bunch of stuff, you know, eggs and chickens. And I said, "No, I'm not goin'." They said, "Why?" I said, "Well, you've got a special day on prices from this new man." I said, "If we all go, this regular man may won't come back here no more if he sees us goin' down there." I said, "We'd better keep our regular man here." I said, "This new man is goin' to give us a special day, but next week he might not give us as much as our regular man does." I said, "We better hold to it." Some of them said, "You're right about that." You know he had a list. He handed it around—had a list of what he'd give. He went on back, said, "Come on down." He went on back. They's some went. Just a few went.

That Hatterock Hill is fixed now. Back then it was rough—had more trouble there than anyplace on Pigeon Roost Road. When we got our road fixed there, why, that mail come right past home. And that held up for years. That there was WPA work. Fixed it, and we got our mail through. People ordered more stuff again than they do now. There was a dozen big mail-order houses. When he went on horseback, he'd have that horse loaded down with packages tied, swingin'.

After I married, me and my wife had three children: two girls and a boy. After we had the first two, we moved down off Pigeon Roost on account of them goin' to school. It was too hard for them to get there from our old home. They all went through high school. That's their graduation pictures over there.

They got more of an education than I got. Do you know how I learned to write? With my finger thataway [making letters with his finger in the air]. I never could do no good with a chalk on account of that hand or somethin'. I never could do no good, and I got out and got interested in writin' doin' that. My folks all thought I was goin' crazy. They kept watchin' me. My mother said, "Harvey, what are you doin' out there," said, "with your finger?" I said, "I'm a-writin'." Said, "You are?" It wadn't long till I had learnt me how to do a good handwritin'. That's right.

> "We took our dinner in a little syrup bucket. I'd take milk and cornbread. That was good eatin'. That was it."

My parents wanted me to go to school, but I was sick a lot and couldn't go much. I did get to go some, though. We had one teacher, paid from fifty cents a day to sometimes thirty dollars a month. If they went through school and had four months of trainin', they was allowed to teach. We'd go from eight to four, and they'd be about twenty-eight to thirty of us in the whole school. The teachers was hired by committees [the equivalent of our community school boards today]. If they liked them pretty good, then they'd keep them. I've known them to stay three years. Most of the time, they lived in Spruce Pine and walked. One lived across the river. She rode a little old pony from where she boarded. Come evenin', you know, get on that pony and ride home.

One time, they was a woman teacher lived over here on Brummet's Creek. Her parents or somebody'd come after her every Friday evenin', and bring her dog along. She would go home for the weekend. One Friday, her dog got there and come in. That dog come runnin' in the schoolhouse. It scared that teacher, and she thought somethin' had happened to her mother. She told some of them to watch the children, and she said she was goin' down the road and look. She was gone a few minutes, and they come. That dog was just ahead of them. But her mother was comin' so they could walk back across the mountain together.

Then there was one, he lived down on the creek. I'd come up in the mornin' and holler for him, and I'd walk to school with him. Wadn't no ridin' to that! They didn't have too many grades. They had a primer, a first grade, a second; then they had a speller, and on the last they had what they call geography and history and health. The last I went to school, I had a load of books. Books didn't cost much. We'd buy them in Huntdale. We had to buy them. And if you wanted to go every year in the same book, why, they would take you in. When I went to school, there was men and women there who were twenty-two years old.

We'd have a spelling match every Friday. I was just a little feller. You know how these spelling matches work: two groups. They'll all pick on one to be a leader. They was one teacher and his sister was a lot older than I was and I got up beside of her and in a few minutes I had her spelled down. That teacher, boy, he shamed his sister. Said, "I'd be ashamed. That little Harvey Miller turned you down." Me and my cousin, when we got up there, we stayed there a long time spelling. She would be on the other side. I'd dread when she'd get up. She was hard.

Then on the blackboard we done our problems. We'd stand up there and do them. And slates, we had slates. Never done much on the writing paper.

And then we had a country doctor that'd come around once a year. He'd examine your tonsils. Boy, them children was skittish. He'd come in and sit down, have an old stool and look down your throat. Examine you. I was pretty big then. That teacher come in, and she said, "Harvey, you lead the way. You start off." Said, "Go on up." I'd go up, and he set down and looked at me: "You all right."

One time they got a dentist. That was a long time after I quit, though. They got to fillin' teeth. He come on horseback. The local doctors done that from Relief, North Carolina. If somethin' happened, you know, he would go sorta check on you. And he would hold inquests, you know—when they found somebody dead, decide what killed 'em.

We took our dinner in a little syrup bucket. I'd take milk and cornbread. That was good eatin'. That was it. When my sister went, why, we would take enough for the both of us. When corn got full enough, now, that was big eatin'. They'd boil that corn, take roastin' ears. That was good.

Then during recess our biggest game was dog and fox. We had somebody appoint somebody to be the fox. The rest of us was dogs. See, we was right in the woods—get up there in them woods. Sometimes we would get way back in the mountains there and makin' so much noise barkin' like dogs, you know, that we couldn't hear that bell ring, and we'd come in late. But the dogs would have to catch the fox and bring him in. When they caught 'im, they'd have a dogfight. You could hear them. Somebody would catch him— you could tell. You could hear them and go see what was takin' place.

When we started a new term, the new teacher didn't know the children. They would send a certain boy to go out to cut them a switch. Them boys got to wringin' them before they brought 'em in; so the teacher would give a strike, and it'd fly all into pieces. That teacher, she come to me one day and asked if I'd go and cut her some ironwood switches. She said, "Now, I don't believe you'll do what they been a-doin'." I went and found some good ones and brought them in, and talk about some boys gettin' it—they did. But the teachers didn't keep order much. It was pretty noisy in there. That hurts about studyin'. They didn't keep much order. Some did, but about all of them was women teachers, and them big old boys, you know, wouldn't mind. About the biggest thing we got punished for was writing letters. Like a boy would write a girl a letter. One time me and a boy was sittin' together. We oughtn't to have done it, but we did. We didn't like a certain boy. We wrote a love letter. That boy I was sittin' with said, "You write it. Write a good love letter, and when we are out, I'll slip in and put it in a girl's book." I wrote it, and when we come back in, we keep watchin' and we seen her read and read and she took it up there and give it to the teacher. She read it and looked everywhere. And when we had another recess, she told that boy, said, "I want you to stay in here." He stayed, you know, and she shut the door. Boy, that boy told me that he was gonna get it now. He come out, and he said, "Boy, somebody played a trick on me." He said, "I never wrote her no letter. Somebody played a trick." He said, "She beat me to death about it. I couldn't tell her." He said, "She don't like me nohow." She had had trouble with 'im. He was pretty rowdy. I told that boy I was sitting with that we done wrong there. He said, "Don't ever tell that boy or we will have a fight with him." I never would pull a trick like that again.

One day we got a new sheriff back in there, and he went to makin' raids on them moonshine stills. They'd get men in there to go a-still-huntin'. One day they come down. They had an old still and some of them drunk, you know. Me and the boys were settin' at the window, and we went and poked our heads out to look and see, and oh, they come slappin' their hats, you know. Teacher said, "What they doin'?" I hollered over, said, "They out here at this window slappin' us with their hats!" Had them old high seats, and we'd poke our heads out. They were hollerin', "Poke your heads back in there!"

One day I disturbed the whole class. We was sittin' around that old long woodstove. It was one of them potbellies. It was three or four feet long. We was all settin' around there, and a boy got that poker hot there at the front of it—got it red hot—and he poked my leg through a hole in my overalls. Lord, talk about . . . see, I didn't know. I was studyin'. I didn't know what had taken place. Law, I screamed and jumped up. Now that teacher—talk about him with a limb—he hit him with a hickory switch! I seen a man teacher one day strike a boy. He struck him; he jumped plumb across the seat—big high seat, now. He went right over the top. The teacher went around to 'im and kept on beating 'im. That evenin', his folks come in. He did beat him up, you know. The teacher come told me, he said, "Harvey, you and me are friends. Now you stay with me." They didn't come in, and he wouldn't go out: 'fraid they'd come in and beat up on him. He said, "Stay with me if they come in." But they didn't come in, though. I have went many a day—just be me and the teacher. Students didn't like him, and back then, they didn't have any law. If you didn't go, then they didn't do nothin' about it. No law. Parents wouldn't make them go.

We had two schools at the last on Pigeon Roost. Sometimes the teacher would get hurt or somethin', and the students would walk and come to the other one. They had committees. Them committees had to sign them vouchers so the teachers could get their pay every month. This teacher I was tellin' you about where everybody got mad at him, he went and called on one of the committees, and they wouldn't sign that voucher. Said he wasn't no good. Nobody wouldn't go to his school. He come back and told me that if I talked good to the committee, he believed they would sign it. Said, "I'll give you a dollar." I went over there and told them he was down sick with the rheumatism. They said, "Well, hasn't done nobody no good." And I said, "He done *me* some good"; said, "He was good to me." I said, "Sign it. This is the last of school. He won't bother no more nohow."

I kept on beggin', and they said, "Bring it around here." Said, "I'll sign it." I took and give it to 'im. He lived way over across the mountain. He promised me a dollar, but I never did get a dime. But that committee told me, "If it wadn't for you, we wouldn't have signed it."

There was one teacher, they said he was the best teacher. He had taught for four or five years. He often begged me to come to him. He said, "Harv, now I'll learn you somethin'. You goin' to them up there . . ." Said, "You won't learn nothin'." Said, "Now if you'll come, I'll really learn you somethin'." But I never did go. It was a mile further, and I didn't want to take that extra mile. But they said he was one that tried to learn you somethin'. Some of them, if you had a lesson today: "Well, I ain't got no time. We'll wait till tomorrow to go over it." A lot of them teachers just set, but this one never did. He'd come to you to see what help you wanted. Where I first went to school, teacher set up there, and if you needed help, you had to go up to her and ask, but that other one, he'd go to you.

**"Now that one schoolteacher I was tellin' you about, they found him dead out in the mountains in the snow. He had nineteen steel traps in his clothes and stuff. He had been killed."**

There was one teacher . . . we had the answers in the back of our arithmetic. I would go up there and tell that teacher that I couldn't get the answer. She said, "Right there is a problem that I never could get the answer to." See, didn't get no help there. In arithmetic, I never did do no good, but in spelling and pronouncing words, that was my biggest.

PLATE 26 Harvey meanders toward Conway and Parks Hughes as
they take a break from working in their tobacco.

Now that one schoolteacher I was tellin' you about, they found him dead
out in the mountains in the snow. He had nineteen steel traps in his clothes
and stuff. He had been killed, but it was all in kinfolks. All the kinfolks was
on the jury. Everybody was kin to this boy they said done it, and the man
who was dead was this boy's uncle. It was all mixed up. They didn't want to
charge him—found where he'd been choked to death. The jury said that he
froze to death.

I wrote stories on that. I was sittin' right there. When they had the main
trial, I was there. They locked the jury up in a room. This man that was in
there, I walked up the road with him afterwards. I said, "What did you find
out?" He said, "We know he was killed, but we didn't tell." Kinfolks, you
know. Didn't want to get everybody into it. They said he had got bad to
drink, and they said he was mean to fight. So they killed him.

There was another man, a schoolteacher, over here at Rock Creek that
they found him dead. They never could find out nothin', or they didn't,
you know. Back then, if they didn't crack the case, they just let it off by
mysteries—mystery to it.

We had a place on the head of Pigeon Roost where there was bootleggers,
and they said they was gettin' a lot of men killed in there. They is a place
back in there; they call it Dead Man's Hollow. They was a man come out of
college, and his people was rich people. Said he was goin' to Africa. Wanted
him to go to the mountains of North Carolina and stay and train for the trip.
He was found there at Cherry Gap Mountain. That was it. They said he was

killed in there. They know he got to Cherry Gap Mountain. He was swallowed up there.

That moonshine whiskey, they would bring it out in wagonloads. They was bad men connected with that. One, they claim he had so many notches on his gun that he'd pull a smokin' gun! He was the one they claimed killed so many people. A long time after they come down off Pigeon Roost, a man come down with a bunch of clothes. He said he found them back there, all bloody, you know, and then somebody found some bones one time and brought them out. It was a bad place.

PLATE 27  Harvey at the Barnett Cemetery on Grove Byrd's farm.
His grandparents are buried there.

I'm gonna come out with some more stories. But you have to be careful. If you bring somethin' out in the papers, a lot of people livin' get hurt: "Oh, you told a lot of things not true." I got a lot of stuff wrote and laid back because that is embarrassing when you bring somethin' like that out. They say, "Oh, that's *my* people!"

That writing, though, I enjoy that. The first typewriter I ever owned, I dug this spignet root [Also called spikenard; Latin: *Aralia racemosa*]. It was a good price, you know. I sold it and ordered me a typewriter. I done my stories by hand till I dug them roots. I just peck. I've got a bad hand: fell in the fire when I was a baby and hurt them fingers there—crooked. If it hadn't been for that, I could have done better.

**"I get letters from everywhere tellin' me to keep on writing. Now I'm connected up with it—keep on it."**

I took this writing up when I was twelve years old and been at it ever since. The first piece was about my dog. I called him Mack. Me and my daddy was out clearin' new ground one fall, and Mack went up a holler chestnut after a squirrel and come out a limb way up. It was thirty, thirty-five feet high out there. And I told my daddy, I said, "What we gonna do?"

I called to him, and he come down just twistin', you know, over and over. When he struck the ground, struck on his feet. And I studied about that, and I hadn't never read no papers much. My sister, she lived in Irvin, and she brought me a daily paper from Johnson City, Tennessee. I wrote to them. I was studyin' about that dog, and I sent the story. They printed it on the front page in block letters. And they wrote me a letter and wanted me to send the community news then. So I did that a long time. They just told me to write all the news. And then I wrote these special stories, and that got people interested in my writing. These personal items don't amount to much. People like the other stories better. Now I write every week for the Irvin, North Carolina paper, and irregularly for the Johnson City *Tri-County News*.

I've had some difficulty. One time somebody told a lot of stuff that wasn't even in my column. One man I saw in church, and he told me—he hadn't spoke to me in a long time—he told me what was the matter. A man had told him that I had written a slanderous talk about him, and he wouldn't speak to me for a long time. I met up with him over here at the top of the hill at the church, and he come to me, told me, "Harvey," said, "I've been hurt at you a long time." And I said, "Yeah, I noticed you wouldn't speak to me." He said, "What you wrote in part of the paper," and he wouldn't tell me what it was. I said, "Did you read it?" He said, "A man told me *he* did." And I said, "That's a mistake." He said, "I studied it all over the other day, and I thought you wouldn't be allowed to put that in the paper just that way." I said, "No, that'd be a-slanderin' you. I didn't do it." He begged me to forgive him. I said, "Well, you wouldn't say anything. You wouldn't speak, so I didn't say anything to you." He said, "I feel better." I said, "I do, too."

Lot of people can't read, and other people tell them, "I seen it in the paper." "Well," they say, "that's bound to be Harvey Miller. He's the only one writes." I tell them to get it out of the paper and come with it, and then anything I have put in the paper, I can't deny it then. But it's just now and then. I get letters from everywhere tellin' me to keep on writin'. Now I'm connected up with it—keep on it. I quit it one time—not hardly a year. I was sick, you know, but I got back and been at it ever since. I like it. Seems like I get down and out and get to studyin' and writin', and it picks me up.

Sometimes, back then, them daily papers would edit my columns. Sometimes I wouldn't hardly know I'd wrote it. I didn't like that. That's about the reason I almost quit. A whole lot of people said, "Somebody's helpin' you." Said, "You're losin' your style." So I got hooked up a long time ago with *The Tri-County News,* and that lady down there, she told them not to do a thing, that my writing was too good to fool with!

# FRED HUFF: TEACHER AND COUNTRY MUSIC BUFF

*"I have seen a lot of kids grow up. It was all fun. I wouldn't take a thing in the world for it. I think one of the greatest jobs anyone can have is to teach."*

Mrs. Cheek, our Foxfire facilitator, told me about someone with whom she had worked in the past, a man who had taught school for over forty years: Fred Huff. She told me he was quite a character. I set up an interview, and after meeting him, I became very intrigued by his life story.

In Eastanollee, in Stephens County, Georgia, his present home where he has lived since 1948, Mr. Huff has been very active in his community and the surrounding area. One of his favorite subjects to discuss, besides school, is country music and the Top of Georgia Jamboree, a live show he helped produce each Saturday night through the summer months, a jamboree that featured some of the area's top country music talent and clogging teams.

Mr. Huff also talks about how he became a teacher and how he met his wife, Marguerite. In his long career of teaching, forty-six years, Mr. Huff received many awards: Presidential Recognition for Contributions to Education, 1980; Who's Who in Georgia, 1982; Stephens County STAR Teacher, 1959, 1964, 1967, and 1968, just to name a few.

Fred Huff is now retired, but he still works at the local radio station and does special shows. He has one of the biggest collections of country music from the past in the state of Georgia. In 1999, his collection included 2,512 33⅓ rpm records; 5,560 45 rpm single records; 1,437 78 rpm singles; 140 reel-to-reel tapes; and 370 cassettes.

His love of his chosen profession and the students he taught, as well as his love of country music, defines Fred Huff. I discovered, as will you, that he is truly quite a character!

—*Dee Jay Wall*

I GREW up in Jasper County down in Central Georgia about thirty-five miles north of Macon. Monticello was known for farming and peach growing. My father was thirty-one years older than my mother. He was sixty-two years old when I was born, and my mother was thirty-one. At the time my father was born, during the Civil War, 1864, his father was in the Confederate Army. I was nine years old when my father passed away.

"Fred, I saw a sign in Monticello that said HOME OF TRISHA YEARWOOD but I didn't see the sign that said HOME OF FRED HUFF. I told him that they were so glad to see me go that they wouldn't put up a sign for me."

Monticello is a small town. I left there about fifty years ago, and it hasn't grown much since then. I don't guess the population of the whole town is much bigger than it was at the time I left. Monticello has a lot of antebellum homes, kind of like Madison, Georgia, which is just above it. Monticello is also the home of Trisha Yearwood. They got a little sign as you go into Monticello that reads HOME OF TRISHA YEARWOOD. My ex-preacher came back here to preach a funeral a couple of years ago, and he said, "Fred, I saw a sign in Monticello that said HOME OF TRISHA YEARWOOD, but I didn't see the sign that said HOME OF FRED HUFF." I told him that they were so glad to see me go that they wouldn't put up a sign for me. I lived in Monticello until about 1938.

I was involved in sports. I played football and basketball, and ran track. I didn't play baseball; I didn't even know what a tennis ball was back then. The big deal was football. That is what I was crazy about when I was growing up. I jumped on the track team. The year that we were seniors, our track team won the state championship in our classification. Back then, instead of having classifications 4A, 3A, 2A, and A, they had a AA, A, B, and C, and we was class C. We didn't have but about thirty-eight in my graduating class, the 1944 class. Our football team, my senior year, had the best record for our school. We played for the region play-off: district. It wasn't regions then—it was district. We played Dublin at Dublin on a cold night and got beat in the play-off game 33 to 6.

I enjoyed growing up in Monticello. It was a pretty good little town to grow up in. In the summertime we all, everybody from age nine to ninety, tried to get a job workin' with peaches. They was eight peach-packin' sheds in the county at the time. I started workin' for my granddaddy—my uncle, after my granddaddy got killed. My uncle ran the peach shed there, and I worked for them for a while. I started off makin' a nickel an hour stampin' baskets with a little stamp that put the brand of peach and the size on. I did that for a nickel an hour, and then they sold the peach business. I started workin' out in the peach orchards with another fellow by the name of Mr.

Brazy who lived in Monticello. He had a big orchard there, and I worked with him in the orchard. I didn't pick peaches. I was water boy for a while; then I was promoted to a liner. A liner is where you pick up the buckets of peaches and line them up and put them up on the wagon. You could pick up about thirty buckets on a wagon. Then I got a job workin' in the shed after that. I did everything in the peach shed back then.

We were consumed with a lot of work and everything, but we dated when we wanted to. When I was in high school, I was too interested in sports and athletics and workin' on the farm and that kind of stuff that I didn't have a whole lot of time to date.

My grandmother, grandfather, two aunts, and an uncle died in a wreck on April 11, 1937. They had been down to Vidalia to visit one of my uncles who was a doctor there. On the way back, they were killed instantly in a car wreck. My grandfather was a farmer. At one time he had 30,000 peach trees. He had a peach-packing shed there, and he owned quite a bit of property down in the lower part of a county called Agateville. After he died, his estate was settled between the children. My mother got ninety acres of land there, along with a home. So we moved from Monticello to the little community of Agateville. My mother remarried after my father died, and we moved there and started farming.

> "Me and this boy used to put on a boxing match for them every Saturday afternoon there for three or four weeks till we could find something to sell. We would go in there and beat the daylights out of each other, and they would give us some money."

I was always trying to find some way to make a little spendin' money. Before we moved to Agateville, my brother, a couple of years older than me, we liked to go to Western movies on Saturday afternoon. They didn't have a theater in Monticello, but they had a tent show. They had a tent and a projector and everything in there. My mother told me that I could go to the movies all I wanted, but I had to pay my way. I used to save all the glass medicine bottles, and I'd get them from anybody that would give them to me. I would wash those things up real clean and sell them to a druggist. They had a fellow by the name of Dr. Jim Pittard who ran the Pittard's Drugstore; he lived next door to me. When I was living in Monticello, I sold those medicine bottles to him for two cents apiece. When I couldn't get medicine bottles, if they was any scuppernongs in the fall of the year, I would pick those things and sell those. So I always paid my way to the movies. When I couldn't find anything to sell, there were some older boys there at the Royal Theater. Those older boys used to bring boxing gloves in an alley behind the theater. Me and this boy used to put on a boxing match for them every Saturday afternoon there for three or four weeks till we could find something to sell. We would go in there and beat the daylights out of each other, and they would give us some money. I think the admission to the theater was fifteen cents, and Cokes were a nickel. They would give us a quarter apiece for fightin', and we would go in there and eat that popcorn. Where you went and got your mouth busted, that salt in the popcorn would burn the heck out of your lip there, but we would go in there and sit together and watch the movie. We were good friends, but both of us wanted a way to get into that theater.

I went to the high school prom. Back then, we had a meal with the prom. We went to the meal, and then we took off and went to Indian Springs State Park, which is only about seventeen or eighteen miles from Monticello, and piddled around.

I used to trap rabbits to sell to make a little extra money. At one time I had twenty-six rabbit boxes distributed over the four-mile area. I used to get out about four-thirty or five in the morning, carryin' my croker sack. Y'all would call it a burlap sack now, but we called it a croker sack back then. I would go around to my rabbit boxes, and if I got any rabbits, I would put them in a sack and bring them home. I had a pen there, where they couldn't get out, and I would put them in that. When I got several, we would dress them, and I would send them to Macon to the Mulberry Market run by a guy that ran a little truck from Monticello to Macon, which was about thirty-five miles. I got twenty cents apiece for the dressed ones, and I would get fifteen cents for the live ones.

**"I knew I was going to school somewhere because I didn't want to farm the rest of my life: I never did like anything about the farm."**

When I got ready to go to school, I knew I was going to school somewhere because I didn't want to farm the rest of my life: I never did like anything about the farm. We ran a little ol' country store on the side, down there with the farming. I had learned how to do everything you do on a farm, but I didn't like any of it. We raised cotton and corn and pimiento peppers primarily. Every time I used to go by a cotton patch, my back would start hurtin' 'cause I remember how it hurt when I picked that cotton. I knew I was goin' to college somewhere, but back then it wasn't as hard to get in college. Back during the war, World War II, I had a second cousin that was graduating high school. I didn't know where I was going to school. I hadn't even applied anywhere when school was out. He came to see me about the last of June, and he said, "Fred, I'm going to go to Gordon Military College to school over at Barnesville, Georgia. Why don't you go over there with me?" Well, I got to thinkin' about it, and I said, "By golly, here I am." (I was seventeen then, and I was gettin' pretty close to the draft age.) So I decided, "Well, if I get into military school and take that ROTC and get a couple of years of that, if they do call me into the service, I may get in OCS, Officer Candidate School." So I checked with them and went to goin'.

I loved it. I played football over there and enjoyed it. I went there when I first went to college. I didn't know how I was going to go after I was accepted. I didn't know how I was going to get the money to go. My mother had eleven acres of nothin' but big pines, and she said, "Fred, I'll give you that pulpwood. If you will cut that pulpwood and sell it, you might get enough money to go. What you can't make with the pulpwood, I'll see if we can't get some money for it." So, anyway, the summer before I went to school, I cut pulpwood with a Swedish bow saw. I cut that pulpwood and got enough money from that and what my mother paid to go for my first year. I went to school. My mother wanted me to be a doctor because I had an uncle that was a doctor in Vidalia. Well, I wanted to study prelaw, so I got there and ended up changing my mind right quick. I had a zoology class under a fellow by the name of Captain Hanes. I thought he was the smartest man I had ever seen in my life. I thought I had some pretty decent teachers in high school, but when I got under him, the way he taught and everything, it was easy for me to learn, and everything came pretty easy for me. I was always pretty good at math and science. English was my worst of the whole business, but the science and math I never had a whole lot of trouble with.

I decided right then and there, "Shoot, I'm going to see if I can't be a teacher." So I did, and I also, since I was involved in athletics so much, wanted to get in the coaching business, too. So I finished two years goin' to military college; then I transferred from there and went down to what is now Georgia Southern at Statesboro. It was Georgia Teachers College at that time. Well, I went down there and stayed a quarter. I didn't like it at all, so I came back and cut more pulpwood and then enrolled at Piedmont College at Demorest.

I went to Piedmont and finished up my degree. I got a major in science and a minor in history and physical education. I had applied for a job with the State Health Department, and I had also applied for some teaching jobs. There was also a boy up there from Stephens County that was going to college at Piedmont. He was a freshman when I was a senior. He came up to me one day and said, "Fred, they got an opening for a science teacher over at Stephens County High School. I'll go over there with you if you want to apply for the job and introduce you to the principal." So I came over, and it sat on a little hill right over here within walking distance of this house. I talked to the principal, and he sounded pretty favorable. He said, "I'll talk to the superintendent and get back in touch with you." Well, he waited so long I went to summer school that summer to finish up. One day, as I was coming out of class, I saw Mr. Watson and a fellow with him, and they motioned for me to come over. I went over to them, and they asked me if I was still interested in the job. I told 'em yeah. He told me to come to Toccoa and sign a contract, so I went and signed a contract the following week.

> "The first day that I went to class to teach was my twenty-first birthday. I had a pretty blond-headed girl in one of my classes . . . She invited me to her home to eat Sunday lunch with the family."

When I started teaching in 1948, I taught two classes in physics and three classes in chemistry. The first day that I went to class to teach was my twenty-first birthday. I had a pretty blond-headed girl in one of my classes. She was always smilin' and everything, you know. After class I would talk to her a little. At Christmas I sent little Christmas cards, you know, and as the year progressed, she invited me to her home to eat Sunday lunch with the family. After school was out, we started datin', and we got married the following December. That was in December of 1949.

As a teacher and coach, I coached many sports. I was an assistant football coach for the first year or so. I coached boys' basketball for three years and

PLATE 28  Fred Huff early in his teaching career

PLATE 29  Marguerite as she appeared when she first knew Fred

coached girls' basketball for two years. I coached track for nine years and coached tennis for three years. I had a boy on the track team that won the state 100-yard and 220-yard dashes. He won All-State. Then we went to Alabama and had a meet with the best from Alabama. He won the 220-yard dash over there and came in second in the 100-yard. He went on to become a state patrolman and died just a few months ago from cancer. I enjoyed coaching track very much. I led the boys' basketball team to seven straight wins the beginning of the season. We went down to Colbert. We lost our first game and ended up 19–6. That was the best season I had. Girls' basketball, back then they had such crazy rules. It was the most boring thing you have ever seen in your life. They couldn't take but two dribbles. They would take the ball; they played three in the front end and three in the back. There were six girls: three forwards and three guards. The guards would get the ball, and they couldn't cross the centerline. They had to put it up there, and I've seen 22 points win several ball games. I remember one game we got beat 20 to 16.

Girls' basketball has progressed quite a bit since those days. They have changed the rules and got them playing like boys now. After you scored a basket, the other team took the ball out at center. It was crazy rules.

PLATE 30 Fred clowns with his students.

I enjoyed it. I have always had a good time. I had a pretty good time with the kids. I used to carry on a lot of foolishness with them. They liked that, and they always talked about my being hard. I said, "Hard will be easy tomorrow."

I taught night class at Truett-McConnell College for twenty-three years. While I was teaching at the high school, I also was teaching at Truett-McConnell through a satellite. They had a satellite school here in the county. I taught Biology 101 and 102. Then I taught physical science two or three years for them. I went with them through the spring quarter of 1996. I quit with them. I retired from the high school in 1994, after teaching for forty-six years.

I have seen a lot of kids grow up. I was teaching third-generation kids when I quit. It was all fun. I wouldn't take a thing in the world for it. I think one of the greatest jobs anybody can have is to teach. I had some real good students; I had some poor ones.

**"Listen, suppose you get here runnin' a hundred-yard dash, and you run as hard as you can go and come in last. You ain't got a thing in the world to be ashamed of. But suppose the boy that won that thing had so much more ability than you did, and he just loped around on the last twenty yards. He's the one that's failed because he failed to do what he could."**

But I'll tell you what, I had a theory. My theory was that you always tried to treat everybody fair. It didn't make any difference whether they were black or white, whether they were from someone with plenty of money or from someone who had nothin'. It didn't make a bit of difference to me. I tried to teach them all the same. I tried to encourage them. Any time that any kid ever did anything good in my class, I said, "I appreciate you doing that." If anybody had any problems in the classes, I stayed after school with them sometimes.

I never will forget one night just before we had semester tests over chemistry class. I told them, "Y'all meet me down there at seven o'clock. We'll go over this chemistry test." So they came down, and they stayed down there from seven till nine-thirty one night, going over, just reviewing for the semester test. I had very few failures. I probably passed some that didn't need to pass, but my theory was this: As long as you are doing the very best you are capable of doing, you ought to pass. I used to tell them, "Listen, suppose you get here runnin' a hundred-yard dash, and you run as hard as you can go and come in last. You ain't got a thing in the world to be ashamed of. But suppose the boy that won that thing had so much more ability than you did, and he just loped around on the last twenty yards. He's the one that's failed because he failed to do what he could." So I always expected a lot of the kids, and I pushed them. I pushed them to try to get the most out of them I possibly could, but, realizing the fact that all kids haven't got the same IQ and can't learn the same way, I always tried to rate 'em according to how they performed according to their ability; that is the way I graded them. Sometimes I had a lot of seventies on them final grades. I had this guy lookin' over my final grades one time, and he asked me, "How in the world did you get so many sixty-fives and so many seventies?" I told him, "I don't ever give anybody anywhere between a sixty-five and a seventy because if they are going to fail, I am not going to fail anybody with a sixty-nine or a sixty-eight. I'm not that good to tell two or three points difference or not. If I fail anybody, it's going to be a sixty-five, and if they absolutely refuse to do anything, I'll give them a sixty, but I never gave anybody an average below a sixty because most of them are going to drop out anyway, so it didn't matter." I always felt like you can't judge that close on stuff. They used to get on to me on the way I gave tests. In biology I used to have a lot of blanks. I put in a lot of fill-in-the-blank questions. On chemistry and physics I had a lot of problems to work, a lot of equations to work there.

> "She was backing up her car. I walked up behind it, took my hand, and smacked up against the fender and hollered, 'Oh!' like that, and I started limpin' around . . . I started laughin' and put my leg down, and she said, 'You devil, you. If you ever do that again, I'm going to try my best to run over you!' "

I got along with the teachers. Well, I thought I did anyway. I used to pull some tricks sometimes. We had an English teacher teaching down here one time. I was out gettin' the buses off down at the road. We alternated bus duty, stopping traffic and letting the buses out. When I came back, she was backing up her car. I walked up behind it, took my hand, and smacked up against the fender and hollered, "Oh!" like that, and I started limpin' around, and she jumped out of the car and said, "Oh, Mr. Huff! I am so sorry that I hurt you!" Then I started laughin' and put my leg down, and she said, "You devil, you. If you ever do that again, I'm going to try my best to run over you!"

Another trick that I pulled on several teachers was back when George Busby was governor of Georgia. The teachers didn't get a raise that year. That was one year we didn't get a raise. Well, we got our checks at the end of September—that was the first checks we got. The teachers were out there in the lobby looking at their checks and everything. They were talkin' about how they didn't get a raise. They knew they wasn't goin' to get one—I thought they did, anyway. They said, "We got the same thing that we got last check." I said, "I don't see why they didn't give you a raise. I got a good raise on mine." They asked me how much my raise was. I pulled out a piece of paper and acted like I was tryin' to figure it out. They said, "Well, how did you get that raise?" I said, "Well, the state give us a raise." I thought they knew better, but they believed everything that I told them. I told them to go up there and talk to Ed Stowe, the superintendent, and tell him that they made a mistake on their checks. I thought they knew that I was kiddin'. They went up there and told him that he made a mistake on their checks. He said, "Who told you to come up here and told you that you got a raise?" They said, "Fred Huff did." He called me that night. He said, "Fred, don't you ever tell them teachers anything like that anymore. They, two of them, came up here wantin' to know why they didn't get a raise." I told him that I thought they knew better, but evidently they didn't.

When I was in high school, I stayed in the principal's office a good bit. But my problem, what I did, wasn't nothin' serious, or that I would consider serious. It was more or less just aggravatin' the teacher or throwin' spitballs or paper at one another. It was never anything like stealin' or cussin' somebody out. We didn't have that many fights when I was in high school. Everything was pretty calm. Up until the early seventies, late sixties or early seventies, we never did have much of a problem with teenagers like we do today. I'll tell you what started most of it, what got a lot of it started. You didn't hear much about drugs until the Vietnam War. The soldiers got involved with marijuana and other drugs, which was the culture in Vietnam and other . . . countries. Our GIs went over there, and they took up some of their habits. I am not sayin' that they caused anybody else to do it. The pressure and the torture that they went through during that period of time, they needed something that they felt would calm them down and so forth, so they started usin' drugs. Well, when they got back, everybody had read about it and wanted to try it. So you had a lot of young people that got started on it. I never did. I drank a beer or two when I was in high school, and that was about it. I would say that you could take all the liquor that I have ever drank and put it in a pint bottle. The beer, you could take about twenty-four bottles of beer, is about all that I have drank. I drank a little wine occasionally, but I never did fool with it. The reason that I didn't was that I was so crazy about athletics that I figured that it was hurtin' me to do it. I think that alcohol and drugs have caused a lot of discipline problems. All the stealin' and robbin' and things were because people needed money to buy drugs. Today we have people that get in fights and everything and want to pull knives and all that kind of stuff. They don't know how to get along.

**"I think that drugs have done more to corrupt and cause more discipline problems than anything the school has ever had."**

One of the stupidest things that they want to fight about is when a boy is dating a girl and another boy speaks to them. They want to fight over that. All they had to do was just speak to them. The girls were just as bad. I've broke up girl fights. Good golly, I mean some of them girls, you wouldn't believe how they fought. I think that drugs have done more to corrupt and cause more discipline problems than anything the school has ever had. I really never had many discipline problems in my classroom. I had to break up some fights on the playground and in the halls and things like that, but most of them always respected me pretty well.

When they took the paddle out of the teachers' hands and wouldn't let you paddle the kids, that was the worst thing that ever happened 'cause the thing about it is this: I always said if you got a paddle and let them see it, a lot of the time, that is all you have to do.

When we moved up in this new building in '71, they had a lot of kids smokin' in the bathrooms. They told us that we could handle it ourselves or send them to the office. I caught two boys with cigarettes in their mouths in the bathroom. Another little boy had already gotten rid of his. I didn't catch him. I told them, "Well, y'all can take three licks from me or go to the office and argue." So they took three licks from me. A week later I caught them again. I said, "You can get three licks or go to the office." They decided they would go to the office. The same little boy was in there that time, and he told me, "Mr. Huff, you'll never catch me. I'm too slick for you." I didn't say anything, but it stuck in the back of my mind: "I'll get you. You said the wrong thing. I'll get you. You said the wrong thing. I'll get you." About three weeks later I was in chemistry class, and about the middle of the class, I saw him walkin' in the hall goin' toward the bathroom next to the library. I thought to myself, "That bird has got out of class to go smoke." I waited about two or three minutes and walked in there, and he was leanin' up against the wall, had a cigarette in his hand. When I walked in, he drew a fist around the cigarette. I could see the smoke comin' up through his fingers. I started talkin' with him. I taught his mother back years before, and I started talkin' to him about his family, his mother, and how she was doin', and all that stuff. Finally he opened his hand and said, "Mr. Huff, you caught me. Are you going to give me three licks?" I said, "Let me see your hand." He had a size of a quarter blister in there, and I said, "No, you have had your punishment for today."

"There was a guy called Lew Childre, the Boy from Alabam. He later became a member of the Grand Ole Opry. That was the first stage show that I ever saw."

I have been a country music fan ever since I was a little kid. We had an old Grafonola. Back then, the only thing that they played was old 78s, old 78 rpm records. The people that you could buy records of at that time were Jimmie Rodgers and the Carter Family. So we had some of those records around. My mother's first name was Ida. Gil Tanner had an old record called "Ida Red." I used to get up in a chair and wind that thing up and play that record. I got to listenin' to those old country songs back then and country music. I just love it. The first country show that I ever saw was in Monticello School in 1935. There was a guy called Lew Childre, the Boy from Alabam. He later became a member of the Grand Ole Opry. That was the first stage show that I ever saw. Then every time any would come around there anywhere, I would try to go. I started collectin' country music in about 1958. I got a little money, and I started buyin' a few records and collectin' country music. I started to work part-time at WLET, the radio station here in Toccoa. Billy Dillworth was doin' a radio show at that time, and me and Billy got to be friends. I started workin' with him; then I had my own show for eight and a half years called *Saturday in the Country.* I played country records. Then I started doin' this thing up in Dillard, Georgia, called the Top of Georgia Jamboree. We—Billy, me, and Marguerite—started that up in Dillard in 1975. We did that every Saturday night through 1992. Billy dropped out after about ten or twelve years. Me and Marguerite finished the last five

PLATE 31 Fred's vast collection of records, tapes, and cassettes

PLATE 32 Fred Huff with George Hamilton IV

or six years, just the two of us. We used talent from Greenville, South Carolina, and other places. Mr. Oscar Cook was principal up at the community school there, right there next to the Dillard House. [See *The Foxfire Magazine,* volume 31, issues 121 and 122.] We did that every Saturday night during the summer for thirteen Saturday nights. I know a lot of people from Rabun County, especially around Dillard and Mountain City.

We used to raise money for senior trips with all kinds of projects to go on trips to Washington and things. In 1964, there was a fellow in the senior class came to me and said, "Mr. Huff, we ain't got much money, haven't got much way of makin' any money to go to Washington this year. I know you like country music and everything. Do you think you can promote a show for us?" I said it would be no problem at all. So I got with him, and we set a date for March 12, 1965. This was in the fall of the year, and I told him to talk with the principal and see what he said about it and everything. So he did, and we decided to have a show. I got on the telephone and started callin'. I had been goin' to Nashville since 1962 to the Country Music Association. They had a disc jockey convention up there every year, so I knew some people. I called a few agencies, and at that time, Sonny James was real, real hot.

We got him and a girl by the name of Connie Smith. Connie had two hits: "Once a Day" and "Little Tiny Blue Transistor Radio." Sonny James had "Going Through the Motions of Living." We packed that place out. We had it in the gym. The bleachers were full, and we had chairs on the floor that were full. We had it packed, and I only scheduled one show. So I told them to send the overflow to the lunchroom, and we would have another show. I didn't have two shows on the contract. I told Sonny and Connie that the gym was packed and asked if they could do another show, and they said yes. So we worked out a deal to pay them more, and they did two shows. We cleared, well, almost $3,000 after paying for the bands. We done so good that year that we had Loretta Lynn, Roy Drusky, Ray Pillow, and George Hamilton IV later on. Then we moved up to the new school, and school officials said the school was too big and we couldn't go to Washington. I thought that I had a good thing goin', so I asked them to give me permission to go ahead and do this project and use the money for senior scholarships to deserving seniors. They said it would be okay, and over the years we gave $82,000 in scholarships to about two hundred and some odd students. After I retired, they said, "Well, why don't we just keep this thing goin'?" I told them I was not able to organize the show and assign things for kids to do to help the shows. But I said, "I'll tell you what, we had put back a little money each year, so we had $27,000 saved back; on top of that, we had about $12,000 or $13,000 donated without any solicitation at all." We are still givin' scholarships. We will have given over $90,000 in scholarships this year. We are able to give $2,500 worth. We split it up into $500 increments, and we give kids $500 apiece. It is set up now that we use the interest off the money each year, so it is a continuous thing. When I retired, I told everyone that I didn't want a gift like we had done for others. Well, the last day I worked, Charlie Morris, the basketball coach, went around that morning and collected money for the scholarship. That night he gave me a check for $700, just from the teachers there at school. The next day I got $45 more from teachers that didn't have money the day before.

> "She said, 'I want to tell you how much I appreciate you. I was dyslexic and didn't know it, and you were always very kind to me and helped me read the test.' She told me about how she had two kids that were dyslexic . . . She went out there and came back with a check written for $3,000, and she gave that to the scholarship fund."

We had a contribution as high as $3,000. It happened about two or three years ago. I was in there watchin' basketball, and somebody knocked on the door. This lady said, "Mr. Huff, you don't remember me, do you?" I told her that I had no idea. She told me that I had taught her back in the 1950s, and she asked me what I had been doin'. I told her about the scholarship and everything. She said, "I want to tell you how much I appreciate you. I was dyslexic and didn't know it, and you were always very kind to me and helped me read the test." She told me about how she had two kids that were dyslexic and wanted to thank me for helping her. She told me that she had done well and wanted to know if she could make a donation. I told her that she could make a donation if she wanted to. She went out there and came back with a check written for $3,000, and she gave that to the scholarship fund.

I had a good career of teaching. I really did. I got many awards, including STAR Teacher for four years, a recommendation thing from the Georgia Senate for my work with kids, and a presidential thing from Jimmy Carter. I was selected Teacher of the Year for three or four different years, but I got more awards than I deserved.

# BOB JUSTUS:
# IT'S A GREAT ADVENTURE

*"I really believe that I had a wonderful upbringing. Lot o' people wouldn't look at it that way. I mean, who would want to be raised in a house without insulation, without running water?"*

Even before I was in the Foxfire class, I knew who Bob Justus was because I had read his articles in the local newspaper. He had written about hunting, tornadoes, childhood memories, Colorado, and countless other adventures, so, knowing that he would have some tales to recount for *The Foxfire Magazine*, I arranged an interview.

One week later, I was standing in Mr. Justus's house and listening to him tell me the stories behind old letters, photographs, rock collections, arrowheads, and other remarkable collectibles. He told me stories about an old one-room schoolhouse, corn shuckings, life in the Philippines, and even a story about a rescue that took place in an outhouse! As I, laughing one minute and shedding tears the next, sat on the edge of my seat, Mr. Justus, with youthful excitement, told story after story of his "great adventure."

Bob Justus's love of family and his reverence for his heritage and the beautiful mountains that he calls home are obvious. His words echo his love of America, and his voice reverberates with a prophetic warning to all of us.

—*Austin Bauman*

ONE OF the first things I remember was—well, I really can't remember this, but the first three years, my parents lived in my grandparents' home till Dad built a house. They had the bedroom upstairs, and the tornado in 1932 blew the house and bed away. Luckily, Mother was with her parents on Liberty Mountain. Mother said from the very earliest that she had to watch me every minute, or I would be off to the barn. She got down there one time looking for me, and I was sitting behind the hind feet of a horse, pulling on its tail. That horse had enough sense not to step on me. When I was twelve, and probably my brother Norris—he was a year younger than me—but anyway, we were playing in some sand in the front yard, and my grandmother

Lela, she looked out and said, "Go get those kids and bring 'em in here." They didn't really know why, but Jessemae, I believe it was, or one of my aunts run out and brought us in, and right after that, someone happened to look and saw a big rattlesnake crawlin' right across the spot where we was playing.

I remember—I couldn't have been over three or maybe four years old—helping my grandfather Dock Dickerson split shingles. Grandfather was a sawmiller, and he split these shingles for roofing houses. He had a sawmill that you just load on the back of a flatbed truck and take it to where you want to saw your timber. They did not have clear-cutting back then. They just marked off the biggest timber and what they were supposed to cut, cut it, and then they'd move on somewhere else. I remember stacking those shingles so they'd dry, crisscrossing 'em and that sort of thing. I remember in the spring of the year when we kept milk and butter in the spring [a place where water issues from the ground], and in the fall some of the men would make grape wine and have it in these churns. The spring was a wonderful place in the hot summertime with big poplar trees around it, and they say the spring went back to Indian days 'cause right where we lived, all my young life, we'd find arrowheads and pieces of pottery. Indians lived around that spring. I always had an interest in Indians—plus in my family is Indian blood that goes way back, I guess, three generations. I just have an affinity for 'em, and I love to do the things that I'm sure they did—walked around, looked for signs, always looking for signs and looking for things. That's why I love the trips to Wyoming. It's just unbelievable for someone like me, a country boy, to get out there where these unbelievable mountains are so vast. In Wyoming, there's less people livin' in the whole state than live in many cities. I don't think there's a million people, not even a million people living in the whole state of Wyoming!

> "Some of the early memories I wrote about . . . were wakin' up and findin' snow on the foot of my bed . . . I can remember it being so cold that as [Mother] hung the diapers and clothes, they'd freeze."

To me, it's a great blessin' to be born and raised in the mountains of Rabun County, no matter if we were poor. Some of the early memories I wrote about in *The Clayton Tribune*—anyways, a recent one—were wakin' up and findin' snow on the foot of my bed. But I remember that so clearly, and it was the first house we built. It didn't have insulation when it was built, and little by little, we added amenities like wallpaper. To show you how things were, when the little room was built for me, I was older and had more brothers. I was the oldest. Brother Norris was born, and after him there was

PLATE 33  Bob; his mother, Durell; sister, Virginia; and
dad, Neal Justus

Dick and Jack and then Glen. I called him my baby brother, and he was just
a tiny little thing when I left home. Anyway, we had to get more room, and
they built a little room off to the side of my room. I helped Mother put
newspaper on the wall—pasted it with flour paste, just mixed paste with
water—and I'd say, "Make sure you turn it up where I can read the comics."
I could lie in bed and read the comics on the wall.

I can remember helping Mother. She was trying to make a girl out of me
too, I think. I'd wash dishes and do stuff like that, and my brothers and sister, Virginia, would not admit it now, but I would have to change diapers and
hold one kid in my arm and churn butter. Mother claimed she'd come in and
find both of us sleepin', and I'd be holding on to that kid. Virginia came late,
and I had grown up and left home when she was born. That was life.
'Course, all of the chores, some of 'em, I didn't like. You know, it's like anything in life. But one of our main chores all our life, till running water came
in, was carryin' water, carryin' water. You had to carry water to take a bath,
and you can understand why people don't take but two a week. You have to

fill up the tub, and if it 'as summertime, we'd let the sun warm it up, and you'd just jump in and hang your feet over and take a bath. In the wintertime, you put it behind the stove. Mother was always after us to wash our feet before we went to bed. I guess we felt like we was clean if we'd washed our feet. Anyway, I had to help with all the chores—being the oldest—and take care of the kids and wash 'em. It was somethin'. How women coped is beyond me. I can remember bitter cold days when Mother would be washing clothes right below the stream, and there'd be a big ol' black pot boilin', and kids would have to "feed" it; I'd help hang out clothes and stuff like that. I can remember it being so cold that as she hung the diapers and clothes, they'd freeze. Mother would be washing 'em in that boiling water and then cold water, and we used lye soap, and it made her hands red and raw. That used to get to me even though I was a kid.

Our early house—our first house—we had a dirt yard. You didn't plow your yard and sow grass and fertilize. Mama'd have walkways lined with rock, and to beautify it, she'd have flowers everywhere. She loved flowers. There would be flowers that bloomed from early spring to late fall, and she had beds all around the house, pots in rows on the porch, on the windowsill. I'd have to help water 'em. I can remember taking a twig broom and sweeping our walk, which was dirt, and smoothin' the sand out. 'Course we had to feed the chickens, and slop the hogs, we called it, 'cause we had leftovers from the kitchen—plus we'd feed 'em leftovers after we'd picked beans and shelled 'em and all that. Hogs eat just about everything. Before my time— and some did when I was a kid—they would run hogs loose in the woods. Back then, of course, we had a lot more acorns because they had a lot more oak trees. Too, they had more acorns 'cause they burned off when they burned the woods. I mean, they did it on purpose. I can remember, it was kinda scary lookin' around the valley at night: You'd see a ring of fire, maybe about this time or probably a little later, before the buds came out, while it was damp, to help prevent the chance of getting out of hand. 'Course, when they burned the forest floor leaves off every year, it didn't build up to where the fire would kill the timber.

My grandfather Jesse said that when he was young, the great American chestnuts were still livin'. You could ride through rows of those chestnuts with a wagon right between the trees. The forest floor under those giant trees was clear, more or less. He said they would just gather chestnuts by the bushels. I've eaten 'em. I have found they still sprout out in Georgia up in certain sites, and I've found 'em huntin' in the woods up till recent times. They're far better to eat than any other type. I have read somewhere that 15 or 20 percent of the forest at one time around here were the chestnuts, and it's wonderful wood to build with and last. My grandfather said that they—

he and his dad, Jim—would go out and stay all day and fill wagons up with split rails, and that grain was straight. They'd go and put up those rail fences, some people call 'em. When I was a kid, many of our fences were still the old way of fencin'. Many of 'em were chestnut, and they lasted for years and years. I brought a few pieces home, when I first moved here, from an old fence up there. I put them out there, and it seemed like after I moved 'em, they rotted. They were many, many years old, so that was life.

Mother would always be having a baby, seemed like, and she'd go out in this big garden—she always had a big garden—and she'd throw out an old blanket or old quilt and put a kid in the middle of it. She'd say to the older ones, "Now you watch every once and a while, and if he gets to the edge of the quilt, yank 'im back," and we'd go to work. We'd carry water and water the tomato plants or the cabbage plants, and we'd do other things. What we didn't grow, nature would provide. Like that burnin' the woods off, that really improved the food supply for the wildlife and everything 'cause blueberries would grow. Oh! A couple years after a fire went through, you could go and just pick them by the handfuls. Mother used to get on to us for putting too many leaves in the bucket. She said, "You're trying to fill the bucket up." But I hated blackberry pickin' more. I shouldn't say hate it, but I didn't like it much. I'd always end up with a bunch of chiggers and gettin' scratched. It just wasn't as much fun as blueberries, but it took longer to fill the bucket up with blueberries. One of my cousins—I believe it was Robert Dickerson—was pickin' blackberries one time, and he got struck by a rattlesnake. I heard this. He started runnin' down the mountain, and his dad ran and caught up with him and sucked the wound. It's a wonder he didn't catch something—I mean get poison in his mouth—but now they tell you not to do that.

Now, talking about people that lived in that day, here's a list of taxpayers in the 636 district of Rabun County, Georgia, 1902, that I got from the courthouse. Back then, either you paid taxes to maintain that road or you worked on it. Looking through these records, though, you can see that we're related to nearly every family in Rabun County. It's tremendously interesting, for that reason, to get into the history. In a small way, I helped with that *History of Rabun County.* It was a green book. I loved the life and getting back to keeping the land and keeping it from washing away and keeping it from erosion. My grandfather led the way. They learned terracin', and they put terracin' in all those upland pastures and hillsides. Rotating the crops and all that, he jumped right on that, and like I said, because of the way he farmed and kept cattle out of the creek, he had a healthy farm. In the bottomlands was the corn and beans and potatoes and the crops we had to have for the cattle and the sheep. There were, on some of the branches or side

streams that run down the mountainside, an opening where the cow cross-
ing was. And also, 'course, by gravity, they ran a pipe down to the barn, and
for a long time, behind that barn we had this huge bowl-shaped rock that
my great-grandfather found thrown in a stream, probably hidden by the
Indians when they were driven out, probably used to pound corn, but I
mean, it was big! One person could no way lift it. We used it to water the
stock 'cause you could put water in there. It wasn't too many years ago it
laid there, and weeds grew up around it. I got it in my mind: I'll bet that
thing, nobody wants it. If they don't want it, I'm gonna go ask if I can get it.
And lo and behold, somebody stole it, hauled it off—probably got a few
dollars for it.

So, anyway, the old barn has got great memories for me, good and bad
too, I guess. For instance, we would haul hay up and fork it up to the loft
there and fill that up. Then all around the barn, 'cept on the front side, was
stables. There's a row of stables all the way around three sides of that barn,
and I always remember the horses' stables were on the left side there. For a
long time, we had a shepherd dog that knew where every cow, exactly what
stall they were supposed to be in. Back then, you know, you brought 'em in
at night, for one thing to milk them and then, in wintertime, to help protect
'em. But that dog would go out and herd the cattle in, and if that cow went
too far, he brought 'em back.

Anyway, we milked them in there, and we would throw hay and so on
down. Each stable had a hole or passageway to the upper loft; I mean, it was
organized. And of course, each stable had a trough for cows to eat out of.
We'd feed 'em corn and that sort of stuff, cotton meal. That barn was an
activity all the time, but in the wintertime we'd get in what we called the
corn crib and spend days shucking corn. It was beginning to die out then,
but I can remember a few old-fashioned corn shuckin's where the neighbors
all got together. I was at one, and two of the younger men got in a fight.
Some of us kids were sitting on the floor, and these two men come stumblin'
around. One of 'em's hitting the other in the head with an ear of corn. You
very rarely ever saw a fight or anything like that. They'd probably been
drinkin', and, anyway, the older men put a stop to it in a hurry. I remember
someone—I don't know if it was Dad or someone else—hollerin', "You'd
better not step on one of these kids!" But most of the time we were peaceful
people. We really were.

Here's a picture of my family: Bob (that's me); Norris (that's my brother);
my dad, Neal; and my great-uncle, Marion; Jesse (that's my grandfather);
and Bruce Justus, my uncle. There's a couple of probably Dad's foxhounds.
He was a great fox hunter. All of 'em were: Dad, my grandfathers, both sides
of the family. Those traditions of hunting go back, I assume, all the way to

Bob, Norris, Neal, Uncle Marion
Jesse and Bruce Justus - 1938

PLATE 34  Bob, Norris, Neal, Uncle Marion, Jesse, and Bruce Justus—1938

the old country. Back then, we were close-knit, like I say. We'd get together for all these great reunions and at Christmas and affairs like that, and I'd go to spend a lot of time at my grandparents', the Dickersons. Nanny, that's what we called her, Nanny. Her name was Effie Dickerson, and she was one of the first ones to work there in that clinic in Clayton. Anyway, her picture has been in some *Foxfire* editions. [See *Foxfire 2,* page 278.]

She told me one time when I was on vacation from the Air Force, she said, "You like to write, and I like to talk. You ought to write down what I know," and I never did. She knew the Indian herbs, the Cherokee. I mean, she could do it! I don't know how she did it. It was always amazin' to me. She said, "You have to know, and if you don't have it in you, you can't do it." And she said that when she died, it'd die with her.

Well, I'll tell you one thing, we didn't have TV, and we had very few toys. You'd be very fortunate to get one toy, maybe a cap shooter back then like Roy Rogers, Red Ryder, or something. I can remember one time, when I was a little older, I got a BB gun, and I thought that was something. But we usually made our things to play with. We made up our games, and we, for instance, would make wagons. Really, they were go-carts, they call 'em today. We would saw the wheels out of black gum. Anyway, we'd bore a hole or burn a hole through wheels and make axles out of hickory, and we'd make those wagons and grease 'em up good and make a handle out of wood and have ropes leading to the front axle. I'm surprised it didn't kill us 'cause we'd go up on the side of the pasture or even in the woods and make us a racetrack down there. It was a lot of fun. 'Course, I had scrapes and accidents. I remember jumpin' off of a fence and drivin' a rusty nail up in the bottom of my foot. I tell you, it really hurt when they swabbed it out, probably with kerosene.

'Course, we had all these home remedies when we got sick. Mix a little honey and a little whiskey if you were really sick. That was the only time mother let alcohol in the house. You'd take it if you had a terrible cough, bad cold, or flu. 'Course, they would bundle you up till you sweated it out and put you in bed. But going back to playin', we would go to some old bank down there, a clay bank left from where they did the road. We would spend all day out there making roads around there and pushing these little cars, most of 'em homemade. We'd have a little town, and we'd make money out of leaves and stop; and to get gas, you'd have to pay for it.

> **"I'll tell you one thing: They talk about bulls being dangerous, but we never had a bull on our farm that was not afraid of us boys."**

We had hoops—we'd take a stiff wire and make curves in it, and you can guide that hoop and run it along a road or path and see how long you could keep it up. One time we was playin' with a tire, rollin' it down this hill. That sounds like fun, don't it, rollin' a tire down a hill? And we'd roll this tire down this hill. We tried to roll down the hill *in* it, too, but it don't work out. I never did go rollin' down a hill and stay in one. No, sir! But one time, what was funny, well, it wasn't so funny—it could have been tragic—we rolled this big tire down this hill and happened to look down, and Grandfather's prize bull was down there eatin' grass and didn't even notice that tire till it got right on him. He saw it, and that bull—this is hard to believe, but—a barbwire fence, he went through it! Evidently it didn't hurt him enough for no one to notice because no one ever said anything. We was afraid to say anything, but he just stretched that fence as he went through! I think Papa Justus found it in the wrong field.

I'll tell you one thing: They talk about bulls being dangerous, but we never had a bull on our farm that was not afraid of us boys. Now they would fool with the women. You know what I mean? But when they'd see us boys, they'd go to the other end of the pasture. They knew better. We just had a lot of fun.

> **"'Course, back then we'd go skinny-dippin'—no bathing suits. We'd shoot off down through there and hit this big swimmin' hole."**

I guess we kept in shape, too, 'cause we'd play fox and dogs. You know, one'd be the fox, and one, the dog. 'Course, we really made bows and arrows and spears. I mean, we made bows and arrows. We didn't fool around. Luckily, evidently, we didn't shoot at one another much 'cause if we had, we'd o' hurt one another, but we would do this and play all afternoon on Sunday afternoons. Sometimes we'd do things—'course it wasn't safe—like climb Big Face Mountain, they called it, when we got a little older, and it had rock cliffs on it. We'd climb around those things and do all kind of crazy things. One time we was playin' down on another slope. We was playin' on this rock, and one of my good friends, Ted Parker, fell. It was wet for some reason, water seepin' down the rock. He slid all the way down the face of this huge rock. It just scalped the back of his head. Scared us to death. Blood was just a-pourin'. Life was great, boys, I'll tell you what. We'd go swimmin' in what we called an old swimmin' hole. It was the baptizin' place, too.

When I joined the church, I was baptized in that cold creek, but thank goodness, thank the Lord, it was in the summertime! It was still cold. It'd shock you, but you'd get used to it. There was this long, slick rock. The whole creek came over that thing. 'Course, back then we'd go skinny-dippin'—no bathing suits. We'd shoot off down through there and hit this big swimmin' hole. Like I say, I spent many a wonderful day fishin' that creek and even those side streams—Little Creek, we called it—with these little brook trout, and you'd catch a mess up there, especially on a rainy day. They wouldn't be very big, but how good they were to eat!

> **"We'd camp out up on Glassy Mountain by a good spring, and Grandpa would make a big pot of squirrels and dumplin's. Kids with you, you couldn't cook enough!"**

We worked hard and played hard. When we got old enough, my grandfather, Dock Dickerson, he would be wonderful with kids, and he was an outdoorsman. He would take us camping over on Lake Burton, fishin'. Back then—I want to tell you fellas something—that lake and most of those streams had fish, lots of 'em! I can see visions now, no kidding. We'd get over there in the summertime, and he'd make us help set up camp. All we had for shelter was a big tarp, and we'd make a lean-to out of it. If you thought it was gonna rain, you had to put a ditch around it, bring in the wood, and all this stuff. Then he'd say, "Go get us a mess of bream, bluegills"; and we would! Wasn't no problem catchin' fish. You'd catch 'em everywhere. We'd have big fish fries. I can remember sittin' around and eatin' fish; sometimes we'd make hush puppies 'n' pork 'n' beans. 'Course, if corn was ripe, we'd roast ears of that. We'd often run trotlines all night—spend most of the night up—and then we'd go squirrel huntin'. We'd camp out up on Glassy Mountain by a good spring, and Grandpa would make a big pot of squirrels and

PLATE 35 Timpson Creek waterfall, lower end of
Germany Valley, Rabun County, Georgia

dumplin's. Kids with you, you couldn't cook enough! They'd eat everything.
No matter how much you'd cook, we'd eat it. Like I say, work hard and play
hard, too.

School, I went five grades in a one-room school, and I am tellin' you the
honest truth: I learned more good things to help me in life in that five years
than I ever learned since. It was a lot more discipline. I mean, you behaved

or else. Teachers weren't mean, but they just did not put up with no non-sense. It didn't take much to get you a spanking, but the main thing is that we learned obedience. I think that a missing factor in most children is they're growin' up without real discipline. Now I don't mean harsh treat-ment, but firm. You got punished—wasn't no foolin' around. I wasn't that smart, but to show you how big the difference was, when they consolidated schools, I finished fifth grade in that one-room school; I was supposed to go to Clayton and enter the sixth grade. Evidently they did some kind of test because I remember 'em telling me, "We're gonna put you straight in sev-enth grade." I said, "Well, I thought I'm supposed to go to the sixth grade." "You're too advanced. We're gonna put you in the seventh grade." And I missed a grade, and, you know, schools then were only eleven grades, so I only went to school ten grades. I probably shouldn't have missed that year. I must have missed something important, but I can look back. There's two teachers alive today that I know of: One taught me the first year, and I didn't know about her till a couple years ago; and then the other, my second-grade [teacher], was Louise Hill. She lived next door to us there in the community. Anyway, one of the great teachers was James Keener. He lived over the mountain in Wolffork, and he walked. He taught in that one-room school, and he walked to school every day. I can remember me and my friend Elmo Dickerson spent the night with 'im, and boy, that was a big trip! You see, in other words, these teachers meant a lot to us.

We didn't have a care unless we got in trouble. We had this one-room school that was a church. I really do think this separation of church and state is just a big drive to cut out all the influence of church because that building on Sunday and Wednesday nights was a church, or for funerals, but five days a week, it was a school. Nobody thought anything about it—didn't see no wrong in it. The county, to make it legal, held the title to it, and back when school ended there—in other words, they didn't need the school anymore—they turned the title over to the church, and we went right on. But we would go in the morning, in the wintertime, to help get the fire going. (I can't tell you that I had to walk miles through the snow 'cause you go out our door front and you could see the school.) That 'as our heat-ing system, and at night, there were rows of kerosene lamps around the wall with that reflector thing, and the walls of that old church were knotty pine. I remember that, and all the windows were on one side of the buildin'. Those old folks didn't have no mercy. They wouldn't put windows on the road side. They didn't want no one distracted either in worship or in school, and when I first started going, in my early years, you'd go in, and men and boys would sit on one side, and women and girls and babies would sit on the other side.

PLATE 36  Mountain Grove Baptist Church, later destroyed by a
tornado on March 21, 1932

Going back to schools, I really think today they need to get back to basics.
To me, the sole purpose is to prepare you for life. I know it's more complicated
today, but I'd venture that a lot of the courses, they're wasting your time on. I
always believe that some cannot be educated like others, but I believe the
standards ought to be high, and I believe that discipline is education. I believe
that's part of education, and they oughta bring it back. You're learning
together, and you've got these standards of performance, which we had.

One time, to show you a good example, I think Dad went seven grades—
I get it mixed up, five grades or seven grades—but I wrote an article one

time, and I wrote it just like I would say it, but I said we used to go possum hunting. (There's some other stories there.) We'd go possum huntin' and have fun. We'd carry lanterns and sacks—in case you caught a possum—and take off and hunt. But anyway, I said, "We used to go possum hunting," and I spelled it *p-o-s-s-u-m;* and I can't remember Dad writing me a letter before that (Mother always wrote me letters), but anyway, he wrote to me and said, "When I was going through school, you spelled it *o-p-o-s-s-u-m.*" So he corrected me there.

We had games even in that one-room school. I think they called it anty over. I don't even know what it meant, but we'd bounce something like a tennis ball over the school or the church—same thing. Somebody'd be on one side and some on the other and just bounce it back and forth. And then we had a game we played, something like baseball, with three bases out there, and 'course, the boys had a lot of marbles. Back then, everybody had a pocketful of marbles, and you'd go and try and win some and keep from losin' 'em, and you'd swap one for another. We had those popgun things, too, and it was a dangerous thing, too.

We just did with what we had to do with and played with whatever. People back then didn't have all this, you know. Now they talk about gaps—what is it?—gender gaps and all this. I can remember back then. For instance, you know now they try and entertain 'em. What I'm tryin' to say is I remember many a time one of the adults would holler, "Get out o' here and go play!" We didn't have that problem at school. When that bell rang for recess or something, nobody would have to tell us to go. We went.

> **"I dropped that pencil in that outdoor privy, and I looked down in there—I saw it. It was on top of everything; I told him to hold my legs."**

I remember we had the outhouses—one for the ladies and one for the men. Somebody said at one time we only had one, and then you had to watch and all, but I don't remember that. I always thought we had two. But one time, to show you how things are valued differently, I had a new pencil. I can remember that just as clear as a bell. I had a new pencil, and I went up there, and either my cousin was along or I yelled for him. I don't remember now. Anyway, I dropped that pencil in that outdoor privy, and I looked down in there—I saw it. It was on top of everything; I told him to hold my legs, and I reached down there. Boy, I either was very dumb or was trusting. He must've been a very trustworthy fella. He held my legs and I got that pencil out. Saved that pencil, I did! Life was something goin' on all the time.

Back then, see, almost everything was done by hand. I guess it was after the Second World War before we ever saw any electricity and runnin' water. I'll never forget when Mother got her first washin' machine, and it had that roller. You'd squeeze your clothes out on top through that roller. When they moved that thing in, she cried. You know it was just like slavery to go out and wash clothes in a boiling pot and beat 'em out on a bench there, cold wind and drizzly rain or whatever. It was just terrible. So that was a wonderful thing, and why it didn't come earlier? You know, the towns had it many, many years before the country did. My grandfather Jesse used to say, once these modern things came along, like automobiles—for us today it's absolute; you gotta have 'em—he said, "It's gonna be a breakdown of the family." He said, "It's gonna ruin the young people's morals and discipline," and all that went about the same time. And not long after people started getting automobiles, my age group, the roadsides began to be littered with beer cans and that sort of thing. It never happened, you see, before. 'Course, you had your alcoholics like any time in history. But they say, "Well, there's always been violence." I want to tell you something: I cannot remember anytime I went to school—from the first grade through all of it—I cannot remember anyone getting killed by a young person or anyone ever bringing a gun to school. Of course I'm sure a lot of those older boys probably had deer or squirrel guns.

Not many had cars even in high school. I didn't have a car. Most of my friends did not have a car till they were through high school—had to go to work. And I'm not sure it wouldn't be a good idea now. Anyway, very little violence, and I don't know about you, but I've talked to a lot of older people—women older than me, I'm talkin' about—and very few of 'em will tell you they had a terrible life or an abused life. I just believe that most people respected one another more. I know boys and girls respected one another more. We were taught to. That was part of that discipline. We just did not get familiar like today. They lump you all together and try to treat you as—I don't know what—being the same, maybe. It may work out, but it's alien to me. For women, for instance, to be the same, like in the Army now, sleep in the same tents, and go marching through the mud, and all that stuff, why, it's just unreal to me that all that kinda thing goes on today. And yet I was raised to respect all women. They say, "Well, they did not teach you sex education." Listen, Mother would put the burden on us boys. She'd say, "You have to protect girls." She'd tell us, "You'll get those girls in trouble, and it's up to you not to, see?" And there ought to be more of that going on today. Now, since everybody's gonna do it, just let 'em do it. Back then, families were more united. There was this discipline, and I do not regret any of the punishment I got. Today, some of it might be called "child abuse," but I do not look at it like that at all. I believe it shows that my parents loved me 'cause they would not beat me or strike me when they was drunk 'cause they weren't drunk. They didn't get drunk. Thing is, the schools and parents worked together. For instance, you couldn't get away with nothin' at school if your parents found out about it. If you got a whippin' at school, you'd get one at home. There 'as no mercy. But today, see, there's so much outside influence, and my grandfather talked about it: the corruption that you get on television. You can get on this computer here—you can get anything you want on this computer, more than you want. I get advertisements all the time to go to look at this web. But it's corruption, and you ruin your mind, I believe.

It just grieves me that they're downgrading all the great people like George Washington and the early forefathers who brought freedom to this country and now try to find something bad that they've done throughout the years. How is it that the United States is looked upon as a haven for the whole world? In every country in the world, there's people yearnin' to come to this great nation, and we were taught that way. George Washington, we were taught (and I believe), he was a great man. I believe he was a God-fearing man, and he sacrificed years upon years fighting for the freedom of this country. He deliberately chose. He coulda almost been king, and he made sure that the office of President was what it was supposed to be: an executive position balanced by the judicial branch and legislative branch. It set the mold for the whole thing, and we ought to be teaching that. We used to salute the flag every morning. Kids were chosen to carry the flag up there in the front when we was pledging allegiance to the flag. That was a great honor. It's funny, isn't it? We would almost fight over who got that and also who cleaned the chalkboard with those old erasers. Boy, we'd volunteer to do that job, and we got picked. We'd go out there and beat them things, get powder all over us. Now they don't use stuff like that.

Most kids got computers now. That's another thing. I don't think a kid in a classroom ought to see a computer for about three years—use his head. That's why I skipped a year. Too, they had to have discipline. We had five or six grades. It could have been seven grades. It depends on your age, see? You'd fluctuate. I might be in a class with just three or four kids, and we would have our assignment—teacher'd work with us. The other grades'd be working on homework or working on their spelling, and that's another thing, see? You would maybe be learning to write, and you'd have these sheets of paper, ruled paper. They don't do that anymore, I'm sure. I don't write that well anymore either, and I used to write well when I was a kid. You would learn to shape your words, and you would go down through "a-a-a," "b-b-b," you know, and do it by rote. They say that's bad for you now, that you shouldn't do that now, you see.

Anyway, while the teacher worked with one class, you would be working on some other phase of your studies that didn't need a teacher. Maybe it was shaping your letters or it was learning to spell. Whatever it was, you'd learn to add and subtract, and she'd give you work to do while she was working with another class, but anyway, you was bound to listen to what the other class was working on. You wouldn't really mean to learn about what the other kids were doing, actually, but you would. So I had learned enough, evidently, when they gave me that test to see where I stood. It could have been that some one-room schools would have not done that good, but I had good teachers. Many of 'em, like Louise Hill [Louise Parker Hill], I think, at that time, you only had to have two years of teacher training; she got her two-year certificate, and so she began to teach. Wouldn't that be something, teaching right next door to your house? They could do this because the parents backed 'em. Discipline was important back then, and children, they did behave better. There were always a few bullies around and that sort of thing, but boy, listen, teachers ever caught a bully, he'd get a tannin', see!

All in all, I really believe that I had a wonderful upbringing. Lot o' people wouldn't look at it that way. I mean, who would want to be raised in a house without insulation, without running water, without a good hot, warm bath, no radio? Well, we finally did get a radio, but kerosene lamps and no TV to entertain. Poor kids get bored today. Can you imagine what you'd do if suddenly you were transported back? You know what I think you'd start doing, though? You'd start usin' your imagination like I did.

One reason I believe that I loved the outdoors so much was because it's all around. You can just go out there and observe the animals and the birds, and like I say, I'd look for signs. The older hunters taught you all this stuff. I did move away and go to places like Colorado, and all that background, see, done me so much good. Like Colorado, a glorious moving feast, was it Hemingway called it? Anyway, I'd explore the rugged mountains and look up the old gold-mining towns and go far back in there and fish all these wild creeks and get on top of these mountains and see things like that because of how I was raised here in Rabun County.

I went two years to Truett-McConnell Junior College, and there I met my wife, Florine. She is from Banks County. She comes from an old family of pioneer Kelleys. Anyway, we didn't get married then, but we met then. At the end of the two years, the Korean War broke out. I wanted to volunteer. I was going to join the Navy, but I ended up joining the Air Force, and I went to Korea in August 1952, and remained there till the Armistice was signed—never had any intention to stay in the Air Force, but to make a long story short, I stayed twenty years. That's why I told you when you first came in about making friends with this guy [Fred Barrington] I served with in the

Philippines. Also, in 1967, I went to Vietnam. I was in the highlands in the 2nd Corps headquarters, which was the Army. I was in the Air Force, but I worked for the Army, believe it or not. I had a life. I've even got a map showing my journey.

I landed in a ship at Yokohama, processed there, and rode this little Japanese train. It was made on a scale of Japanese people. It was an old Japanese troop train, and they fixed it up and hauled us down across through the islands here. It was a funny thing, anyway. You'd have to stoop, or you'd bust your head on the door; and you'd go where the john was, the toilet, and it was a hole in the floor. You could look down and see the tracks, and they say that people would go along and pick the waste up and put it on the fields. So I learned a lot; now I'm actually getting stories off the Internet about my old outfit in Korea. I was in the Third Bomb Group, which had three squadrons (8th, 13th, and 90th). The veterans put together a website, see, and I'm learning some stuff. For instance, an accident near me occurred on that base when bombs blew up, and among other things, it says here it blew an armorer's legs off. Well, I was very near there, see, and it scared me half to death. I thought I was gonna get blown up, but after I run out of the danger zone, I got a camera and I took lots of pictures. I've had good and bad assignments. I saved, through the years, a lot of old notes.

I wrote this in Korea: "A Day in Korea." The title of my article says "Echoes from the Hills." When I lived in Rabun County, every day that old choo-choo train, the old steam engine, used to go up to Clayton, and on certain days you could hear that whistle. It echoed off those mountains, and you knew the train was coming through. 'Course, we used to yell, and you'd hear an echo come back at you. That's why I called it "Echoes from the Hills," see. But I got to Korea, and one bitter cold winter day, there was a group of us walking around the side of this snowy hillside above a little village, and I heard this whistle way off. We turned around and looked. Coming out of the valley into the mountains was this steam engine, and it sounded just like the one that used to run in Rabun County. I'll never forget how that old mournful whistle just brought tears to my eyes 'cause I'd never been away from home before. I was just young—eighteen, nineteen years old; there I was in Korea, and it sounded like home.

> "I'd just like to see more people wake up and see what they're doing. It's amazing what you can do with just common sense."

These mountains are just not the way they were when I was a kid, though. It's been trashed. I don't understand. My grandparents, my dad, when I began high school, they were teaching us, in school, to preserve the land: row crop-ping and the terracing and maintaining trees and foliage along streams and all that good stuff. And years before that, they had farmed badly. That erosion ruined a lot of the land, and the early cutting of the forest ruined a lot of the streams early on. But anyway, we're doing worse today than we did fifty years ago. If you talk to an individual, they say they care. I never was much of a joiner, but I've joined the Smart Growth Coalition and the Soque River Watershed Association. Now, home, by the way, when I say it, is always Rabun County. I mean, really, this is my home with my wife and the children nearby, but what I mean is, to me, the ancestral home, the childhood home. That's always there. Now it grieves me: like that lovely valley where I was raised. It's been trashed. Those beautiful mountainsides have been scalped and the beautiful, wonderful trout stream we had with the deep dark holes and the grapevines growing over the stream and the ferns along the banks and snakes and frogs and turtles, all the insect life in summertime just swarming with all different kinds of water life, see. Now you walk down there, and it's full of sand and mud and the banks caving in and cattle everywhere. A recent report I read was where they took a test somewhere on the creek. It had too much *E. coli* and very few fish anymore and very few frogs. It's that way on the lakes, too. We used to go to Lake Burton. 'Course, there 'as very few houses then—mostly woods. I have fished over there as a boy and met a moonshiner with a boatload of moonshine in the daylight— jumped out on the bank to get a plug loose from a tree, and there at my feet would be moonshine behind a log. That's how remote it was, you know. Then the lake was full of fish, and sometimes we'd cook 'em for breakfast or midnight or whenever we got done. And we began to cook all the little frog legs and whatever we had to go with it. Fifteen years before Dad died, we was over there fishin', and I said, "I don't hear no frogs." He said, "They're gone." He said, "They're almost all gone." That's the way it is now. 'Course, it's probably pollution and too much wave action. Frog eggs and most fish are in shallow water, and that's where they lay their eggs.

But that's life now. There's just too many people living that close to the lake, but it's a nationwide, and even gettin' to be a worldwide, problem. The frogs and lizards, spring lizards are the first ones to be affected by poison. I don't know. I'd just like to see more people wake up and see what they're doing. It's amazing what you can do with just common sense. Maintain a border on all your streams; keep your land from erosion whether you got a farm or whether you just got a lot. I tried here on this place to keep every tree I could possibly keep and had to cut some 'cause every time I had a ice storm, there'd be limbs on top of the house. But that's the way we was raised. I'm not saying we were perfect. We were far from perfect, but overall, we took care of the land. I remember that time when the government came along and said, "Well, there's too much erosion. We're goin' to spend millions of dollars and bring rock in here and put 'em on the stream banks to stop this erosion." My dad and grandfather, Neal and Jesse Justus, told 'em, "We don't need any." "What do you mean?" "Well, we're takin' care of our land," and they were. They had all that growth along the stream banks. They didn't need no rocks, and they didn't take any. I read not long ago that most of that was a failure. You just cannot dump a bunch of rocks, especially if the cause is continuing on. I just believe that I learned a lot of respect about it, and I think it's common sense. I don't care what anybody says.

I've got friends in the Forest Service, but I never, and Dad didn't either, agreed with the clear-cut, not on the scale that they're doing it. Here's what I believe: Nature or God or whatever had the right things growin' where they should be growin', and for man to come along and say, "Ahh, we don't need none of this," and whack it all out, you know, especially with many, many acres over steep hillsides, is just not necessary. So as a result, I think it's caused a lot of harm. But now the great harm is development. Everybody wants to come to these lovely mountains. If they keep developing, they won't be lovely, see? Here's the thing: A lot of the people that appreciate it the most—the mountains and what we have here, and join, like, the Smart Coalition, or up in Rabun County, I guess it's the Chattooga River Coalition, or whatever you call it—is the people who move here from somewhere else and see what's still here and what is gonna happen. There's no question in my mind. These four-lanes, see, they're gonna build another one east to west. Habersham County is fixin' to turn into a giant bedroom community of Atlanta. Just in one year, a hundred new subdivisions was approved, last twelve months. It just eats my heart out.

> "There's so many people that's shortsighted. They just don't think ahead. A lot of people that mean well, they don't want no kind of rules or no kind of laws to govern what they do with their land, but it's all being destroyed."

Go back to how I felt when I came back. When I come back, since Dad—Dad was what I call the last one to go. What I mean is, he's the last of the old way of life, the old way. Anyway, go back and see how everything around here is deteriorating, and it just grieves my heart. Now you know why it was so wonderful in Wyoming. It's because of the far mountains and the high mountains. It's so remote back in there people can't live year-round. Part of that is it's so inaccessible, but where they have built good roads, where any kind of camper can go in there, it's bein' ruined. If you can take a four-wheel-drive truck and you know these old roads that you can get on, you can go through the forest and down some of them steep, steep places and get down there on the river like we did by ourselves. It's just almost like you was carried back to the day of the trapper and the Indians, and these fish come out of that water and tear your line all to pieces. Boy, some of 'em, I think, want to pump out and tear into me! But, anyway, see the eagles and the hawks flyin'. There's so many people that's shortsighted. They just don't think ahead. A lot of people that mean well, they don't want no kind of rules or no kind of laws to govern what they do with their land, but it's all being destroyed. I don't know the answer. I just hope that they can work out some things, save some things for guys your age, your family. I mean, where you gonna go? I just hope and pray that people will wake up.

During and after the Great Depression, they began to use CCC [Civilian Conservation Corps] camps. They corrected a lot of things like that. They began to bring the land back then. They restored watersheds; they began to practice terracing so all the water doesn't rush downhill at one time in great force. I notice a lot of farms now. They're bulldozing away those terraces. They want it all smooth, see. They don't think. You got grass, thick enough sod; they hold most of your land together, but on these slopes, the water's gonna shoot off. It's not gonna stay, and it's gonna hit down there on the stream with a great force and undermine it. Trees are gonna topple in. That's why anywhere you go, any of these streams and rivers, you'll see trees toppling in on great bodies of water.

The mountains were more precious than ever when I got back from those wars—not only the mountains but the whole United States. When I came back on the ship was early one morning, and fog was on the water outside the California coast there; then the sun broke through. We were approaching the Golden Gate Bridge, and the sun was shining on that golden color, that Golden Gate, and not just me, but several on that ship, tears were flowing down their face. I always trusted my country and its leaders. Well, I started to have doubts in some places in Korea, but Vietnam, really, the way they fought Vietnam, was a terrible, terrible blunder. But, anyway, each time I come back, actually I start driving and climbing these mountains, and it all comes back to me, you know, the way I was raised and the life I lived, and it was just a rush of great feeling.

War's terrible. You know, it's always terrible. But I believe, like Korea, well, let's face it, there is a free country, though they may not do everything the way we do. South Korea was saved at great cost. They were afraid to go all out and win the whole country. That country, at the end of World War II, was supposed to be reunited. 'Course, Russia wouldn't do it and so on, and that led to that war. The Korean War was even more political and was led so horribly by our leaders and so on. Here's the thing: I served, and I'd serve again. That's the way I feel. It's my country, but what we're doing today in a lot of these countries is, we're becoming a police force. I mean we have. We've stood on street corners and directed traffic like Haiti. I do not believe in getting more and more to be part of the United Nations. I remember the old leaders saying, "Our troops will never serve under foreign leadership." Well, that's been thrown out the window. I'm still struggling over that Kosovo thing, where they bombed it to smithereens. Months and months, they seemed to be idle threats. They said that we were gonna do this or that. Anyway, that guy did take over a land that, I guess, legally was Serbia. I've just struggled with that thing. Now, you know, both our military and our civilian police went over there. We're in a torn country. We're doing things that we wouldn't dare let nobody do here, or at least we say that.

I believe in the integrity of keeping our own sovereignty. I don't believe in selling out to the United Nations. I don't believe in one-world government, is what I'm tryin' to say. I believe that if we become a one-world government, we're gonna lose our freedom and gonna lose our identity. I don't care. That's why I was opposed to that World Trade Organization. These people you'll never see in these back rooms are gonna be making decisions about what we buy and sell, and eventually it will drag down just like the school systems have done, in my opinion, and drag down everybody to a lower level, and we're gonna be turned into a third-rate country like some others. See, I've been over in other countries, and American people'd better wake up. There's never been on the face of the earth a nation blessed with more than we've got, includin' freedom, even the poorest, and I'll say I think most street people are there because of drugs, alcohol, and that sort of thing. Almost anyone in America can make a living and have decent shelter. I mean, look at what a lot of us lived in when I was a kid and the hard, hard work we used to have to do. Did you know in the middle of the Depression, most of these big cities even were safe? You didn't have all that rape and breakin' in and robbing. I was reading where a congressman walked into his what-was-supposed-to-be protected apartment, a high-class apartment there in Washington, D.C.—found a woman murdered there at the foot of the stairs. He had been robbed once at gunpoint, I believe he said, and something else. He said, "I'm not gonna run again." He said, "I'm gonna go back to Indiana where it's safe." So you ask me, and I tell you: I really believe it was an honor to serve the United States.

"It boils down to fighting, and I think what carries most all men in war is your home, your family; and America is your home, your family. You think about that."

There were countries that had more people in uniform than we did in World War II. It was somethin' like seven, eight million citizens went in uniform and got trained and went to war with Germans and Japanese soldiers that'd been fighting for years. They can say what they want to about all this—well, that we had the material. We didn't even have the guns and tanks and planes until after the war was under way. If it wasn't for the great oceans, I guess we'da been gone. See, it goes back to it was still being taught when I was in school: patriotism. It wasn't what the government owes you or the country owes you, but it taught us to appreciate our country and to do what we could for it. I don't agree with everything in Kennedy's life, but you know what his statement was: "Don't ask what your country can do for you but what you can do for your country." That's what makes countries great. But it boils down to fighting, and I think what carries most all men in war is your home, your family; and America is your home, your family. You think about that.

I used to have dreams about these beautiful mountains. I've written an article about this dream I had in Korea. More than once that dream'd pop up, and I'd walk down out of the cove—and this is a true story—I'd walk down out of the cove on Big Face Mountain, and there a little stream came out of that cove and flattened out, went among these great oak trees, and I think near the creek was poplar. There was an open kind of glade there surrounded by trees, and there were ferns high as my head, ferns growing along the stream. And I walked out. I'd been squirrel hunting. All along the

PLATE 37   Beautiful Big Face Mountain, Germany Valley,
Rabun County, Georgia

sandbar there among those ferns were thousands, I guess, of beautiful white
butterflies; and when I'd walk, they'd all come up in a great swarm; and the
sun was shining down. It's just like a picture of paradise, and I would dream
that in Korea. So when I got back home, I went back up there. 'Course, it
wasn't the same time o' year, but, you know, it was still there. The beautiful
little glade was still there. And so help me, I never dreamed that again till I
went to Vietnam years later, over a decade later. I had the same dream two
or three times. Anyways, I was back home, and it was some time 'fore I got
around to gettin' back up there. Used to go up there hunting. At the headwaters we'd catch a lot of brook trout. So I went up in there, and—I'm not
sayin' this to resent 'em; in fact, I think they're a nice couple from Florida—
this couple had the back part of this land and built 'em a house there. Right
where that glade used to be with all those marvelous butterflies and ferns
growin' up high as your head was this house, and they'd cut those trees and
made a pond.

> **"Every day of your life is a new adventure. You all hopefully have
> a lot of time left, and when you get discouraged and upset or things
> go bad for you, you just remember that you've got a new opportunity
> every day."**

Someone asked me, "How can you write so much?" I'll be honest with you. I
could write every day. I could put out an article every day about some fact in
my life, you know, something that impacted my life in a meaningful way. I
just wish I could impart that to children growing up: to get this out of life
because you only go 'round one time. It's a great adventure, and no matter
what they say, you can't explain where you come from. You either believe that
God created you or [that] some random evolution got you here. Every day of
your life is a new adventure. You all hopefully have a lot of time left, and
when you get discouraged and upset or things go bad for you, you just
remember that you've got a new opportunity every day, and every time that
sun comes up and you see something beautiful . . . That's another thing that
has changed since I was a kid (you wouldn't even notice): far more air pollution than used to be. The sky's not as clear as it used to be. It really came
home to me on that first trip to Wyoming. 'Course, I lived four years in Colorado, but the sky out west there in those great mountains is fresh and clear.
In Wyoming, I noticed all the stars are just right down on you. I mean, you
just see a multitude of stars. Those little mountain lakes are unreal. They just
look purple-blue. The colors there are so enhanced more, and it used to be
that way here. It's not that way anymore. All the pollution is floating around
in the air, and I hate to see it. Anyway, I hope I'm making sense to you.

"I can walk by the streams now and just sense the presence of those who were there before."

I hope I can put a book together sometime. I should've done it. Everybody says I can. I have over four hundred poems. I want to take these, and I've got a bunch more that haven't even been put in here. Then my writings, I've got all of this and then all that upstairs. It's unreal what I've kept. For many years I carried notes, written down and put aside, and these poems. I didn't even start puttin' 'em together until the last few years. There's one about North Luzon when I was over there in the Philippines. Poems, to me, bring out life.

I was in Korea, and we were flyin' in. It 'as burned. You've heard of Fuji-yama, Fuji—"the perfect mountain":

> Come Korea on the run
> into Japan for a week,
> I saw the newly risen sun
> shining on the perfect peak.
> Fresh from the warm, mangled hills
> of Korea's long night of war,
> I felt one of life's great thrills,
> When Fuji loomed from afar.
> When I saw that shining crown
> all covered with ice and snow,
> An emotion so profound
> filled my heart and made it glow,
> The reason I carry still
> Mt. Fuji in my mind,
> Which through time
> there's awe and thrill,
> Nor any equal can I find.

That's just one glimpse I had of that great mountain. This next poem shows how much my mother had a great meanin' to me:

> Mother, your hand that pieced the quilt
>   held me unto thy breast,
> That hand, raw and red from washing,
>   reached out in love for me and blessed.
> Mother, your hand that helped to heal
>   held up the flowers to admire.
> That hand which kneaded the warm dough
>   was quick to pluck me from the fire.

*Mother, your hand that knitted socks*
*reached out to touch my fevered brow.*
*That hand which warded off the knocks of*
*young life is sorely missed now.*

I tell you, I get carried away in some of this stuff. I realize a lot of that is old-fashioned. There's one about Papa, you know, Jesse Justus:

*He walks through soft meadow grass*
*Hearing the larks a-trilling*
*In tune with the Earth and sky*
*Knowing life's fulfilling.*

That's how he come through to me, see. That's how I used to know him.

*His sweat mingles with the Earth*
*There on the valley floor.*
*Where the stream captures his voice,*
*It echoes forevermore.*

Some people said it'd be silly—it'd be trite or something—but I can walk by the streams now and just sense the presence of those who were there before. It's just amazing how you can almost hear the voices and just see the faces. You can tell how I love water and I love streams.

But what I appreciate about life is the wonderful folks I had, and you can't judge folks by the amount of money they had. They were good, decent people. They feared the Lord and saw that we went to church and that we minded our manners.

# FANNIE RUTH MARTIN:
# STILL A-DANCIN'

*"Now I've been through it, and I've had a lot of hardships and suf-*
*ferin', but I'm still hangin' in there. I'm ready to see what's gonna*
*happen next."*

Born and raised in Banks County, Georgia, Fannie Ruth Martin, at
eighty-one, still has spunk. Her young years weren't easy ones, but she met
every challenge with spirit, and those challenges have made her the strong
character she is today.

Although I myself have not had the privilege of meeting Miss Fannie
Ruth, I feel as if I have known her all my life. As I worked on this article,
Mrs. Martin's stories enabled me to be a witness to her triumphs and
tragedies. I was privy to many tales: "catching a sucker" at the lake, racing a
Greyhound bus to Commerce, and being attacked by a cow. Some tales
evoked hilarity, but some were of trials and sorrows: walking miles to school,
working from dawn till dusk, and losing her husband and two of her children. Miss Fannie Ruth is truly a remarkable woman, a strong spirit whose
staunch belief that God is going to take care of her has enabled her to continue "a-dancin'."

—*Alicia Nicholson*

I'M FANNIE RUTH MARTIN, and I'm eighty-one years old. I was born
April 25, 1921. I can tell y' a thing or two about my younger years, and then
we'll just keep goin' from there. I was born and raised in Banks County. I
was born in a little four-room house. It was not a very good-built house, but
we lived there anyway. It was very cold in that little house. I lived there till I
was ten years old, and then we moved just one house down below us in a big
two-story house, which was not a well-built house, but it was livable. It was
still open. I'll tell y' 'bout that house. The floors, we could look under the
house through the floor and find a hen nest with eggs in it. We'd pick up the
plank to get our eggs. That house wasn't a warm house at all. The only heat
we had was an open fireplace. We'd stand in front of the fire when it was real

PLATE 38   Spunky eighty-one-year-old Fannie Ruth Martin
recounts tales of her life.

cold, and our legs would burn on one side, and on the other side they were
a-freezin'. I helped cut wood 'cause we had a woodstove and a wood heater.
That was the only heatin' we had unless we had an open fireplace. I sawed
wood with my daddy all day long, and it's tough a-sawin'. We lived there
thirty-somethin' years. I can't remember the exact amount of years, but it
was thirty-somethin' in Banks County.

> "The first time we ever got a rug in our house, it was in the
> kitchen. We put the rug down, and when the wind would blow really
> hard up through them cracks, our rug would just stand up."

Our houses had open fireplaces. We would dig up what we called white mud
and put it in a bucket and pour water over it; that mud would dissolve, and
you'd have what looked like white paint in a bucket. That's what we painted
our houses and around our open fireplaces with. It looked just like it was
painted white. We did it with white mud. I don't know where you could find
any this day and time.

The first time we ever got a rug in our house, it was in the kitchen. We put
the rug down, and when the wind would blow really hard up through them
cracks, our rug would just stand up. We didn't have refrigerators. We put our
food in a bucket and took it to the well. We didn't have runnin' water, mind y'.
We drew our water from the well. We would put our jug of milk and other
food in the water bucket and let it down in the well. That kept our stuff cool.

We finally got an old icebox, and the iceman run twice a week, and listen to this, he hauled his ice in a wagon. We got a little ol' block for twenty-five cents. We put it in our icebox; we'd put our butter in that, and sometimes we'd put our milk in it. Sometimes we'd just draw fresh water, and we'd set our milk down in that. We had to change the water four or five times a day.

I went to school in a little school called Beaver Dam Baptist. Beaver Dam Baptist School went through the sixth grade. Now, I had to walk two and a half miles from my house to the school grounds. I'll never forget my first schoolteacher. She was a Lord lady, Mrs. Blanche Lord, and she taught me from the first grade to the fourth grade. She was a very sweet Christian lady. My hair is natural curly, and the curls hung down just like Shirley Temple curls. She always would sit beside me and put her fingers up through the curls in my hair, and she'd let me read. She didn't let me read sittin' in my desk. She always called me up to her desk so she could play with my hair while I was a-readin'.

When I was in the fourth grade, my daddy bought a T-model Ford car, and he would take us to school in that car when it was a-rainin', with no top on it, but at least you didn't have to walk in the rain. You could get there faster even if it was in the open car. We got wet, but we managed to make it.

When I was a child, I picked cotton and I hoed the crops. We farmed, and I began pickin' cotton in a pick sack made out of a five-pound flour sack. It drug the ground, I was that little. I managed to pick cotton with it even when I was very, very small. I started off bein' the one that carried the water to the field. I took the water to the people that was a-workin'. They all called me the water boy. During the day, everybody worked far from the house. I'd take water down to the field, and I'd go around to each person and give 'em some water. I was busy all day long goin' to the house and back. It was about half a mile. By the time I got back and got another gallon of water, they was thirsty again.

We had to walk the cotton rows during the day, all day long a-pickin' bo' weevils outta the blooms in the cotton so they wouldn't puncture the bolls of cotton. We had to do that, and we would also poison the bo' weevils. We had a little ol' half-a-gallon bucket; we mixed poison in that bucket, and we had a little ol' paddle. It was a stick with a cloth ball stuck on the end of it, and you'd dip it down in that poison and dab it on them cotton blooms and on the cotton stalks. I've done that till I'd be white all over when I'd go to the house at night from poisonin' the cotton. I worked as long as you could see, till the moon come up. You pulled your fodder durin' the day and hauled your fodder in by the moonlight.

We worked from daylight—I mean daylight, not sunup—daylight until sundown and then had to sweep the yard by the moonlight. We had to cut brush brooms and tie 'em up with strings and make a big brush broom to sweep our yards. Sometimes it would be eleven or twelve o'clock at night when I'd get the yard swept good. They'd look like they had been mani- cured after you had swept them good with them brush brooms.

I'd work all day on Saturdays in the field and gettin' the ironin' done, and then I'd sweep the yards by the moonlight on Saturday night. We didn't have to cut grass, but we had to dig taters and we had to pick cotton. We used to dig up our taters, and when we baked the taters, we baked them in the ashes from our open fireplace. We'd wash our p'taters and put 'em down there, nice and clean, and then cover 'em up with hot ashes, and they'd bake. They were just as juicy.

"I heard my mother say, 'Fanny Ruth!' I looked around, and she said, 'You best start movin' that hoe around, or that handle is gonna sunburn!' "

I hoed and I pulled fodder and I walked behind my daddy in the field. He had a cradle that he would sling wheat up onto, and he would reach and pull it. It's a big ol' wooden thing with wooden handles, and that's what he would put the wheat on and oats and all that stuff. We got behind him and picked it up and piled and burned it.

I also helped make syrup. We used mules to make syrup. They'd just walk around in a circle, grindin' the juice outta the syrup cane. Then we had this long vat thing. It was sectioned off, and you pour your juice in at the top and let it cook so long in the first vat. The next vat had little holes in between it, but you corked that off and let that run down into the next one; then go three vats down. When it got to the last vat, your syrup was done, and you poured it in jars. After, you was so sticky. When night come, you could touch your clothes, and you'd get stuck to 'em. That's just how sticky you was.

We took our straw from our wheat and oats and made our mattresses. I can't remember what they call the striped material we made our mattress out of. It was called something started with a *c*. You would make the mat- tress outta that material, and then you stuffed it with straw. Where you packed it, you'd leave a hole about a foot long to pack that straw through till you got it packed real tight. Then you lay on it, and that was our bed. We called it bed tickin'. We had to change that straw, now, 'cause a-sleepin' on it would cause it to just crumble up. The mattresses would just lay down flat, and you'd have to refill it. You'd refill it lots of times so the bed would be so high up that I'd tell 'em that we was a-sleepin' up in the ceilin'.

I stayed at home all the time unless I was a-workin' in the fields. I was still at home after my sisters and brother left home. I was the baby, and I was the only one left at home. My daddy started plantin' some cotton closer to the house 'cause I had to do the hoein', and he didn't want me off way over there by myself. One day I was so tired. I was out a-hoein', and it was so hot. I was just a-burnin' up, and I stopped and propped up on my hoe handle to rest and feel the breeze a little bit. I heard my mother say, "Fanny Ruth!" I looked around and she said, "You best start movin' that hoe around, or that handle is gonna sunburn!"

> "He grabbed that casin', and he whipped me so hard till my mother said, 'If you're gonna kill her, take her outdoors. Don't kill her in the house!' "

I'll tell you somethin' else that I've done in my life. When somebody died in the community, my daddy, I reckon, had to dig the grave. They would come to my daddy to make the casket. I'd help my daddy make caskets, and my mother would make the linings for it. Daddy would pad 'em with cotton, and then he would put linin' over it.

We had to walk a chalk line when I was growin' up. They didn't tell us but one time, and if they had to tell us a second time, we got a whippin'! My daddy never hit me but one time my entire life that I can remember. He whipped me with the canvas out of a tire casing. You know, the tires that go on cars, that ol' rough stuff inside of it? That's what he hit me with. I remember what I did. We got one pair of shoes a year, and that was from the first bales of cotton that was sold. We had to wait till the next year to get another pair. My daddy had got him a pair of new shoes, and he was takin' his shoes off that night. I picked his shoe up by the shoestring, and I was just a-swingin' it, entertainin' myself. We had a big open fireplace. He said, "You throw my shoe in that fire, and you'll get a whippin'!" About that time, it slipped outta my hand, and in that fireplace it went! He grabbed that casin', and he whipped me so hard till my mother said, "If you're gonna kill her, take her outdoors. Don't kill her in the house!" That's the only time I remember Daddy hittin' me. My mother would hit me 'bout every day.

One time my mother thought that I was a-sassin' her, and I wasn't sassin' her. We had wood floors on our houses. We didn't have carpet and stuff like that. We had an ol' shuck mop made out of corn shucks. The mop was a big ol' block of wood that had holes bored in it. It was about twelve by twelve inches. We'd ram those shucks up and poke 'em in the holes and fill them holes up with corn shucks, and that's what we scrubbed our floors with. We also went out and got white sand and put on our floors and scrubbed them with those mops and scalded our walls. We'd take all of our furniture outdoors and do our spring cleanin' by takin' our furniture out of the house and settin' it in the yard. We'd get boilin' water and take it inside and splash it up and scald down the walls and then scrub our floors. That's the way we done our house cleanin'. Me and my [sisters] took all the furniture out of the kitchen and dinin' room, and we'd do all that scaldin' down till late in the evenin'. Before sundown, we had to get that furniture back in. Bertha was the oldest, and I was the youngest. Evelyn was the middle child.

My older sister would also whip us. One time I called her—now, listen to this—I called her a fool. Me and her was makin' up the bed; she pulled it outta my hand, and I said, "You pulled that outta my hand, fool!" She said, "I'll whip y' when we get this bed made up." My grandpa lived with us, and he had one of those old-timey army coats. They was heavy. This was in the summertime, and it was hot in June. That coat was hangin' on our back porch, and I ran out there and got that coat and put it on 'cause I knew she was gonna whip me. I wore that thing all day long, burnin' myself up so that when she whipped me, it wouldn't hurt. She just went off and didn't even bother me. She just let me alone like I wasn't even there! Late that evenin' the sweat was just pourin' off me, and I took that old coat off and hung it up. I never even got it hung up on the rack till she reached, grabbed me, and tore me up! I thought she was gonna beat me to death.

Let me tell y' this, too, 'bout my brother. We was pickin' cotton, and there used to be some people that lived by us. The woman's name was Fannie, and mine was Fannie. We was pickin' cotton, and my brother said, "I ain't doin'

PLATE 39  Fannie Ruth in her younger years

no more! I'm tired!" Bertha said, "Keep on, or I'm gonna pull up a cotton stalk and whip y'!" She would whip the younger ones if we didn't mind. My brother told her again that he wudn't doin' no more, and she pulled up a stalk of cotton and picked the cotton off of it. It had bolls on it, and she grabbed him and beat the fire outta him. He said, "Bertha, Bertha, quit! I see lightnin' over the ol' Fannie house!" I'll never forget that: "I see lightnin' over the ol' Fannie house." Bertha was allowed to whip us when we didn't do what she said. We had to mind her, too! You better believe we did! Bertha was nine years older than me, and they was the four of us: Bertha was oldest, Homer, and my sister Evelyn. She was five years older than me. Younger ones got whipped by the older ones if we didn't mind them, if my mother and daddy wudn't around. If they was around, they wouldn't.

When my brother was pretty young, my mother used to run him down to whip him. He would climb trees. My mom would say he'd done somethin' and she was gonna whip 'im. She'd run 'im and run 'im, and up a tree he'd go. Mother would say, "Now, that's all right 'cause when your daddy gets here, he'll getcha!" Every night he'd get in trouble, and one of us would catch him. He wouldn't get by. You could run your legs off, but you never got by 'cause they would never forget it.

**"We didn't have no slack time to play like children do this day and time. We were raised to work from the cradle on up."**

We had our own cows, and me and my brother had to milk 'em. We milked our cows and we churned our butter; that's the way we had home-churned buttermilk. One day we had to go down and milk the cows. My brother gave me the gentlest cow that we had, and he took the one that would kick a lot. Our job was to milk. We had to milk every mornin' and every night. We went out to milk. He was givin' feed to the cows, and I was out in the pasture. This cow that I had milked all these years, she took a notion to pick me up. She went down with her horns and a-picked me up. I was just a-lyin' between her horns, and she was runnin' and about to toss me across the fence. My brother came runnin' over and grabbed me and took me off 'cause she was gonna throw me over that fence! She was just a-carryin' me awhile just a-laid up between her horns!

We didn't have spare time. Even when it was a-rainin', we had to pick off peanuts and we had to shuck corn. There was somethin' we had to do all the time. We didn't have no slack time to play like children do this day and time. We were raised to work from the cradle on up. A lot of times, I would help Daddy dig wells. He was a well-digger too. I worked all day long drawin' dirt out of the well. We would draw up a big ol' bucket of dirt with the well windlass, empty out the dirt, then let it down, and he would dig and fill up that bucket with dirt again. I helped him with many a well. We did it all by hand. We'd first blow it out with dynamite. He would set off the dynamite at night, late in the evenin'; and when it went off, it would blow the dirt and the rocks loose, and then we'd go down in there the next mornin' and get just a whole lot of the dirt out. I went down in a well one time my whole life. I wanted to go in there and help dig some, and I decided to go in one. My daddy let me down in there late that evenin', and that's the weirdest feelin' you've ever had in your life.

As far as playin', there wudn't a lot of that goin' on 'cause you had to work so hard, but when we did play, we'd play ball; we'd play hopscotch and hide-and-seek. That was the only entertainment we had. We didn't have the movies and all of those things and stuff. What we had is what we had, and that's all we had. That was in 1938.

We got very little for Christmas. We always got a little somethin', but we didn't get toys or nothin'. I'll never forget what our Christmas was like. We got an orange, an apple, a banana, some raisins, and a little piece of candy. My daddy wouldn't have enough money to get us a lot. We got a little piece of candy. You've seen that peanut brittle and peppermint in a long roll, and we had to share. One Christmas I got a pencil box with pencils in it, and it was the best Christmas I remember ever havin'. We looked forward to Mother's cooked pies and cakes and stuff like that, but we didn't have presents like people get now.

One time, though, I went to town with my daddy in the wagon with a load of cotton. He was sellin' the cotton. Daddy, he bought a dozen bananas. Only time we got 'em was when we sold the first bales of cotton. We bought cheese and bananas, and we had to share it. So we was goin' home from town, and I seen my brother in the back of the wagon throw out a banana peel. I told Daddy that Homer was eatin' the bananas. He said, "You better not eat those bananas there." He said, "Y' got to give Bertha and Evelyn and Fannie Ruth some when we get home." When we got home, we had one banana left for the three of us. He had already eat eleven!

We didn't have a lot of fun childhood memories. We had to work all the time. I guess about the best time that we had was at our family reunion every year. I looked forward to that. We had to work so hard that, when night come, we didn't feel like doin' nothin' but goin' to bed. I had to come in from school and change my clothes and go straight to the field and work till slap dark. Then we'd go home and have milk and bread for supper. That was pretty much what we had unless we had a little left from dinner. We just didn't have a whole lot to really have a good time with, but I guess we had better times then than we do now. People visited each other back then.

PLATE 40 Rachel Koch listens to Miss Fannie Ruth tell of cryin' times and dancin' times.

"There was no sound comin' from the thing. It was just a-floatin' through the air. Everybody ran outta their houses to see that. It was an amazin' thing to see, but it scared us. We thought the end of time was comin'."

We walked to church and everywhere most of the time, unless we went in the wagon. The churchyard was filled up with wagons, buggies, horses, and vehicles, except for them who walked. Some that was fortunate enough, now very few were, but if they were, they had a car. They would not let you ride. They felt better than you. I'd be a-walkin' home from church; they would go by me, and I'd say, "That's all right. One day I'll have a car!" We walked to school and we walked to church. There was a bunch of us teenagers, and we would all walk to church. It looked like a big crowd on the road just a-walkin' to church. Once in a while, Daddy would take us in the wagon at night.

Sunday morning I was sittin' out on the back porch a-churnin'. Before I went to church that Sunday mornin', I had to churn the milk so we could have buttermilk and butter. Then I looked up and saw somethin' in the sky. It frightened me and I screamed. It was a dirigible. A dirigible is kinda like the Goodyear blimp, just about four times bigger. It was a huge thing. There was no sound comin' from the thing. It was just a-floatin' through the air. Everybody ran outta their houses to see that. It was an amazin' thing to see, but it scared us. We thought the end of time was comin'. If I hadn'ta been on the porch churnin', we probably wouldn't have seen it.

I always wanted to dance all my life. I still dance just a little bit, but I can't hold out much. I used to dance for hours at a time. The way I learned how to dance was, I got two sisters (well, I had two sisters—one of 'em's gone) and one brother. He passed away, too. They would sit down and pop their fingers, and I would dance. Just about anywhere I could dance, I would. I never went to a dance my entire life. We had family reunions once a year, and they would come to the family reunion to watch me dance. I had three uncles that made music. One of 'em played the fiddle; one of 'em, the guitar; and one of 'em, the bow harp. They would play that, and I would dance for hours at a time. That was all our family reunion entertainment was: me a-dancin'! They'll never forget it! They always looked forward to me a-dancin'. They would all play their instruments, and I'd just be a-dancin'. I still dance, but I just can't hold out.

My parents never told us no stories. They did tell us about mad dogs. My daddy was a very gentle man. He didn't want us children to know about dangerous things like that, and they just didn't talk to us much about it. He just told us that if we seen a strange-lookin' dog, don't let it get close to you. He said to get in the house. We had this little ol' bitty dog, and it had fits. It was runnin' fits. It would always have runnin' fits and fallin' fits, too. That little ol' dog would be out in the yard. One of them fits would hit him, and he'd just fly all through the house! We didn't have no such thing as a lock on the doors, and the door was standin' open. That little ol' dog come flyin' through the house when he was havin' a fit. I'd jump up on the bench and up on the table, and I'd stand on that table till he got through with that fit. They never talked to us much about the mad dogs—just to watch it. Don't get around 'em, and get in the house if you can. It's a disease that the dogs have—like rabies. It would get so bad that they would run just as hard as they could, run and slobber. Slobber would just a-pour outta their mouths. If they bit you, you had rabies, too! It was very contagious, and that's what a mad dog is. The mad dogs, they say, don't see nothin' on the sides. If they see you, they come to you, and that's when they bite you. They don't have side vision—it's just straight vision. They was a lot of that when I was growin' up. I remember a mad dog bit one lady, and she went mad. That was the pitifulest lookin' woman you'd ever seen in your life. If somethin' mad saw water, that's when they would slobber more, and that poor ol' lady . . . they had to strap her to the bed, and they had to take a spoon and just give her a little bit of water at a time. She'd just look and just slobber, and you had to be careful around her, too. She'd bite you if you got close to her. They had to tie her, and when they tried to feed her, they had to keep a distance to where they could just reach it to her. It happened very often. Things would bite the dogs and they would go mad and bite other people's dogs and they'd go mad, too. They didn't have no vaccination for 'em back then. I seen mad cows 'cause the dogs had bit 'em. They'd go mad, and it'd be the same thing. They'd be just like a mad dog. You tried to be very careful, and our parents would send us to check up on our animals. If the cows did show any symptoms of being mad or somethin', we didn't drink their milk.

> "Yeah, this is what I tell everybody: 'I went a-fishin' and caught a sucker!' We were married forty-three and a half years."

Oh, and my husband, bless his heart . . . I got to tell y' how I met my husband. Would that be interesting? I was eighteen years old. No, I guess I was seventeen, and this friend of ours was goin' to take some young people fishin'. We were real good friends, so she asked me to go fishin' with her. So I went over to go a-fishin'. Her name was Miss Lily Ritchie. All the young people was out in the yard, and we was gettin' stuff up to go a-fishin'. They all got in the cars and left to go down to the river except this boy and girl. I knew the girl. She was sittin' in the car with this boy, so we got in the car with them. She told me who the boy was on the way down to the river. Well, he wound up to be my husband! The first time he saw me, he told the girl he was with, he said, "That'll be my wife someday!" We went to the river; none of the girls would go out and help with settin' the hooks and things, and he said, "Who's goin' with me?" I said, "I'll go with y'!" We went down to the creek and back, and he wound up to be my husband. Now that's how I met my husband. Yeah, this is what I tell everybody: "I went a-fishin' and caught a sucker!" We were married forty-three and a half years. When we were datin', you couldn't go by yourself, so my brother had to go with me. Every time I had a date, he had to go with me. He was my bodyguard.

The first car that we had after I married was a A-model. My husband had that car, and we went to get married in that A-model Ford. It had a rumble seat in the car. It was December, December 4, 1938, and it was a-sleetin' and a-rainin' and a-sleetin' and a-freezin', and me and him rode in that rumble seat to get married. My brother was drivin' it, and a friend of ours went with us to get married. We rode in that rumble seat. We didn't have a cover over us in the rumble seat. We was sittin' out in the open, and that's the way we went to get married.

Then we got another car. It was a '34 Ford, and this is when I learned to drive. I wanted to go to town one Saturday afternoon. My husband was busy workin' on a car, and he said he couldn't go. I said, "Well, I've got to go." He said, "Well, the car's sittin' there. Go!" You had to have your license then, but I didn't have any. I remember when we drove and we didn't have to have

PLATE 41 Fannie Ruth Martin and her husband of forty-three
and a half years, Wilmer

a license, but at that time you was supposed to have a license. I went out there and cranked that car up. I'd never been under the steering wheel, but I went to Commerce. I got to Commerce, and I pulled in to park. When I was comin' outta the store, I thought, "Oh, Lord, how am I gonna get this thing backed up?" I finally backed that car up, and I went home. My husband's mother said he'd nearly walked the road a hundred miles just a-waitin' for me to come back. That's how I learned how to drive—by myself—and I didn't know what to do!

Me and my husband had four girls, and two of 'em was twins. Martha Jean was born in 1940, and Doris Wilma was born in 1942. Now my husband always said we was gonna have a boy if we had to cover the hill up with girls, but when the twins came along, he said, "When they start comin' two at a time, it's time to quit!" We quit with four girls, and I have two girls left. The Good Lord has taken two of 'em and my husband.

When my twins was born, food was rationed. We was just allowed so much flour and so much sugar. You had to have stamps to get it with. My twins, Sandra Geraldine and Brenda Myrtle, was born in '46; there was a shortage on milk, and I had to put the babies on a bottle. I couldn't hardly get milk to feed 'em, but Mr. Fowler in Commerce fixed it where I could get milk for my babies, but it was very hard to get anything. When you got stuff, maybe you got five pounds of flour, and it had to do you a month. There was six of us in our family, and it was hard to get that 'cause you had to have stamps. You couldn't just go to the store and buy what you wanted 'cause it was rationed, and they was just allowin' so much. I have eaten corn fritters—that's what we called 'em—and milk and bread. We lived on that.

When we was raisin' our family, we played with our children. Parents don't play with their children this day and time, but we played with ours. We had to entertain 'em and make them happy.

**"I outrun him all the way to Commerce. It was a Greyhound bus. The woman that was a-ridin' with me just kept a-slidin' down and a-slidin' down, and by the time I got to Commerce, she was all the way on the floorboard!"**

I thought when I first started to drive that you had to drive wide open. I went to work in '42, my first public job. I went to work at a sewin' plant (quit at thirty years). I was goin' to work one mornin', and this lady was a-ridin' with me. I pulled out in the road, and a big bus was comin'! I pulled out in front of it 'cause I had room to get out, and I outrunned him to Commerce in that little '34 Ford. I went around a curve called Pittman's Creek. It was a real bad curve in the road. He was tryin' his best to pass me, and I told the lady next to me, I said, "He wants to pass, but I ain't a-lettin' him get by today!" And I'd step down. Then I outrun him all the way to Commerce. It was a Greyhound bus. The woman that was a-ridin' with me just kept a-slidin' down and a-slidin' down, and by the time I got to Commerce, she was all the way on the floorboard! A girl that worked with us was ridin' that bus to work, and she said the bus driver asked 'em if anybody on the bus knew that little woman in that '34 Ford in front of them. She said, "Yeah, I work with her." The bus driver said, "Well, I may never see her anymore, and I don't know her, but she's gotta be one of the best drivers I've ever seen!" I had outrun him, but I thought you had to drive wide open.

We didn't have washin' machines. We drawed our water and filled up a black pot, and we built a fire under that pot. We had a battlin' block, a big ol' block of wood, settin' there by the cabin. We got our clothes, and we'd put 'em in that pot and boil 'em and take 'em out, battle 'em, and then rinse 'em. We had giant tubs, number 310 tubs, that we rinsed 'em in, and then hung 'em up to dry. That was Monday's work 'cause Monday was wash day, and it took all day long to wash.

My mother made my clothes till I got to where I could sew. When I learned to sew, I made my own clothes and I made my children's clothes. I'd pick blackberries and sell 'em for ten cents a gallon. You could get a yard of cloth for ten cents back then, and that's the way I got my clothes—when I didn't make 'em outta chicken feed sacks. Most of the people had to raise chickens and bought the feed in sacks, and they were big. We made our dresses outta that, and I made sheets for my bed. Those sheets would last forever. They were real thick and heavy, and the more you washed 'em and dried 'em, the prettier they got. I only had two dresses at a time, and I would wear one to school today; then when I'd get home, I'd wash it, and I'd hang it out to dry. I'd wear the other one the next day, and that was all the dresses I had. I told everybody I'd wear this'n today and that'n tomorrow. I only had two dresses and one pair of shoes, and when that pair of shoes give out, you didn't get no more till the next fall.

Back then we didn't have televisions or nothin', so we didn't know about things happening in the world like what's happening today. I bought our first television in the 1950s—1953, I believe, was the first television I ever had in my house. My husband watched Westerns, but I didn't watch television much. I still don't watch it a whole lot. My eye has got so bad, and the other one's a-gettin' bad. I can't watch television too much.

One time, our house burned and burnt up everything we had. We didn't have nothin' left. We had a little insurance policy, farm insurance, and because we were not at home when the house burned, they wouldn't pay it. We lost everything we had, and that's the reason I went to work. I went to work to help us get back on our feet 'cause we had two children. I worked thirty years. I reckon it took thirty years to get back on our feet! After thirty years of workin', my husband got sick. He had emphysema and he had to quit work. I kept on workin', tryin' to make us a livin', make ends meet, which I did as long as I worked. I worked in a sewin' plant for thirty years, and I'd come home at night and get my children settled in. I would, in the summertime, can and freeze vegetables so we could have food to eat.

**"When I got my first raise, I thought I was a rich woman! They raised it up to forty-five cents, and buddy, I was livin' high!"**

I first went to work in '42, and I was a-makin' thirty-two cents an hour! Can you believe it? Thirty-two cents an hour! My bring-home pay for a week's work was eighteen dollars. When I got my first raise, I thought I was a rich woman! They raised it up to forty-five cents, and, buddy, I was livin' high! I finally worked long enough to make seventy-five cents an hour, the most I ever made in my life. Workin' in a sewin' plant is hard, hard work! One week, drew a hundred and fifty dollars. Now I was a rich woman that week, but I never got that much but one week in my life. That week I made production enough, and I worked hard enough to make that much money.

In 1964, I worked all day, went home, done my washin', cooked my supper, cleaned my house, and got me a bath. I even washed my hair that night and started to bed. I fell and broke my leg, and Wilmer, my husband, had done sat down on the side of the bed. He was fixin' to go to bed, too. Sandra and Brenda had done gone to bed. That was my twins. My leg popped. It sounded just like a rifle fired, and I looked at Wilmer and said, "You broke my leg," and he said, "I didn't touch you." He picked me up off the floor and laid me in the bed, and I started havin' a chill. The twins were laughin'. I told the children, "This ain't no laughin' matter! I fell." It was funny to them, but it wasn't funny to me. There wasn't a doctor in town. They were havin' a shower for one of the doctors and his wife or someone, and they was all at that shower. I lay there all night long with my broke leg. I could rub across the bed, and I could feel the bone. Wilmer fed me aspirins all night long. The next mornin', I got up to go to work. I had some crutches. I was on crutches. My leg was swelled up and just as black as it could be, and I was gonna go to work. Wilmer said, "You ain't goin' nowhere but to the doctor!" At six o'clock I called the doctor, and I said, "I hate to bother you at this time of the mornin', but I think I broke my leg!" So I went over there, and he said, "Your leg's broke." After a-lookin' awhile, again he said, "Your leg's broke in two!" He spun me around in that wheelchair, and he said, "I'm gonna have to take y' down there and put it in a cast." He was puttin' the cast on my leg, and I said, "Now ain't this somethin'? An old woman, forty-two years old with a broke leg!" He said, "People older than you breaks a d—— leg!" I set in my wheelchair, and my leg had to be out straight 'cause I had a cast from the top of my knee down. My father was livin' with us, and he would sift my flour and set the bread tray in my lap and give me the dough.

I'd sit there and work up my bread for their breakfast with my broke leg. My oldest daughter, Martha, went to the hospital to have her baby, and I laid on a hospital bed with my broke leg and kept her oldest, my grandbaby, while she was in the hospital.

In 1975, I was at work just a-sewin', and I had a stroke. I ha'n't been able to work since. Don't tell me a sewin' plant won't kill you 'cause they will, and I reckon it got me! It took me thirty years, and I worked nine and ten hours a day and then go home and have to cook supper and clean house.

Now I've been through it, and I've had a lot of hardships and sufferin', but I'm still hangin' in there. I'm ready to see what's gonna happen next! I've lost a husband and two children, and that's the worst thing I've ever done in my life is givin' up my children. Now my husband, that hurt—it hurt. I lost two of my children. That was about the hardest thing I've ever done; I've went through some mighty tough times, but God's been good to me. He sure has been good to me; He took me through all of this.

Kids today have too much! They need to, I think, learn how to work. People these days don't know how to work. That's why there's so many children who get into trouble. Children don't have nothin' to do to keep 'em busy. We were so busy all the time, workin', we didn't have no time to get into no trouble like children do this day and time. If I could tell the youth of today one thing, I would tell them to please stay away from drugs and bad women and live a good Christian life! That's what I'd tell 'em. They need to know what it's like to work, and I'm afraid it's comin' back to us.

It's the fulfillment of the Bible. That's exactly what it is, and in Exodus it tells you about the destruction of the high buildings and that they'll be no blood and turn to dust. That's the fulfillment of the Bible, and I'll tell you it's nothin' but fulfillment of the Bible. It's bad, and I think it's gonna get worse. I'm mighty afraid it is. If you read your Bible, it's right there. The Bible is the greatest love story ever written, and I would tell them to stay with it.

I'm back on the road again! I've been livin' outta a suitcase now for seven years, just visitin' people and stayin' a while with them, and I'm still doin' it, still doin' it at eighty years old 'cause I don't have no place to live. I had a home. I thought it was gonna be my home until I died, but somethin' happened and I lost my home. I'm back on the road again with my suitcase. That's about the end of it, and now I'm just waitin' to see what's gonna happen next. We've been through some hard, hard times, but God's took care of us, and He's still goin' to take care of me.

# LEARNING TO
# SQUARE DANCE

"Once you learn how to dance, it seems like it
just flows like the music through the air."

—*Lester J. Wall*

D ancing? Dancing. Dancing! My emotions concerning this topic did as many flips and turns as the leading lady's skirt tail during the Georgia Rang Tang! What did I know about dancing—especially square dancing— and how in the world could I ever make sense of all the allemandes and promenades, sashays and turns, breaks and holds intrinsic in this mountain tradition?

Aside from the sweaty handholds and mechanical do-si-dos forced upon us grade-schoolers in the stuffy gymnasium (because, outside, the day was too rainy or muddy or cold or . . . surely there was some good reason for this torture), I had no experience with this "mountain movement." When I began preparing this section, God smiled upon me when I got wind of the news that the Folkways Center of North Georgia in Dahlonega was hosting a traditional Mountain Square Dance in an effort to entertain and educate a new generation. Unwilling to miss this golden opportunity, the whole family loaded up the camper and headed to the site.

We arrived to find John Kelley setting up acoustic equipment on the large pickin' porch. As a member of the board of directors for the center, he greeted us, shared some general knowledge about Mountain Square Dancing, introduced me to his fellow band members (Ted Sims on banjo, Doug Singleton on guitar, Ann Whitley on fiddle, and Nick Henders on big bass) and then to the evening's caller: Janet Shepherd. Ms. Shepherd was warm and friendly, and I could immediately discern that she would be the one to shed light on my perplexity.

The evening's dance began with people of all ages—tourists and locals alike—gathering on the porch. Those musicians were a talented group who called themselves the Dog Tags and worked together to fill the hall with lively traditional dance tunes. Ms. Shepherd had the small crowd working together as a family within minutes. That novice danced beside master didn't matter, for this was part of the fun. Everyone welcomed even the smallest dancer—my daughter—and the most clueless dancer—me—to the ring with an outstretched hand and a smile. As is customary with small "party" dances, the caller danced most sets with the group and made certain that every person on the floor coupled with every other person before the dance ended.

From the Virginia Reel to the Shoofly Swing, we danced. We do-si-do'd, wound the ball, swung partners and corners, and listened for those calls! We danced circle dances, two-couple squares, four-couple squares, and running sets, and in the process danced our way to unforgettable fun and made new friends. I know that a single square dance instruction lesson does not an expert make, but I'm certainly proud of the fact that I can do-si-do with the best of them now.

Square dancing takes skill, thought, and energy! A dancer must feel the music, listen to the caller, remember the moves, and keep his mind on position. You can add as much or as little to your movements as you like. Mistakes, if noticed, bring understanding laughs, claps, and helping hands rather than ridicule.

The contacts, especially Lester J. Wall and Melvin Taylor, gladly shared their square dancing expertise with Foxfire. My new friends from the Folkways Center, including dancers Jay Bland and Lori Wilbanks; Bill Martin, of www.bubbaguitar.com; and Thad Byers, an experienced Rabun County square dancer, graciously dispelled my confusion with call executions and provided step-by-step instructions and photo opportunities. Duncan Taylor willingly supplied song names, and Foxfire staff and students "willingly" performed the intricate steps and posed for photographs to enhance an understanding of the maneuvers.

Square dancing, buck dancing, and clogging are traditions around here. People used to move furniture out of several rooms and hold dances in their homes. Home folks spent many a Saturday night at the Mountain City Playhouse during its heyday. Kenny Runion expressed his feelings about dancing: "I used to dance. Reckon it's [a] harm to dance? The Bible speaks of dancin', don't it? Shore does! I don't think it's wrong to dance. I'd jist as soon dance as pick on the git-tar or banjo."

Many believe that heavenly beings dance in heaven; some earthbound dancers begin a square dance with a prayer. I discovered this prayer when I was compiling my research. The following is an excerpt:

*Father in Heaven,*
*Some people wonder why we should open a square dance with a prayer. But that doesn't surprise You, does it? Perhaps, Lord, You even danced now and then Yourself . . . When You have made a new star or painted a perfect sunset . . . Thank You, Lord, for hands and feet and music. Thank You for laughter and friends, for swirling skirts and scuffling feet. Come dance with us, Lord. Help us unwind. Teach us to rejoice in everything that is good. Help us to love each one whose hand we touch tonight. Come dance with us, Lord, among us and with us.*
*Amen.*

To satisfy your toe-tapping urge to learn square dancing, I have included specific delineations of square dance formations, explanatory photos, and sample calls. If you find yourself still unsure of a move or a call discussed herein, I encourage you to seek instruction or to attend a real Mountain Square Dance, because doing is much better than reading. Happy dancing!

*—Teresia Gravley Thomason*

SQUARE DANCING has deep roots in Southern Appalachia. As our ancestors from Europe settled the beautiful mountains, they brought with them a colorful variety of steps, from Scottish reels and Irish jigs to ballroom dancing and waltzes. The cotillion and the quadrille meshed with the rest to influence Appalachian Square Dancing as our fathers and grandfathers know it. Circle dances, running sets, round dances, clogging, and buck dancing are just some of the types of dances that comprise a Mountain Square Dance. People of this previously isolated region can take pride in the fact that, with westward expansion, their ingenuity in social recreation has been the major influence behind today's Western Square Dancing. Sadly, true Appalachian Square Dancing is becoming a rare talent, and skilled callers are ever rarer.

While an exact date of origin is unknown, it is safe to say square dancing has been around for generations. Many of our older contacts remember square dancing as a way of life. The earliest remembrances place square dancing at the end of a hard day's labor as a welcome refreshment for weary farmers. Preacher John Freeman remembers, "They'd gather in the fall of the year when harvest time came. Why, they had to get this corn off the ground as quick as they could to sow it back in the wheat for another crop. They'd gather the corn, and they'd have a corn shuckin'. They'd invite all of the neighbors—boys and girls, men and women. They'd come gather around that thing, y' know, and they'd shuck corn till they give out or till they got done. And then they'd have a dance or somethin' like that, y' know. Oh, that was kindly their manner of entertainment."

"They called them shindigs in them days; that's what they went by the name of: shindigs."

*—Willard Watson*

Willard Watson recalls, "Well, we made up the molasses, and everybody'd gather in and have a good time. Lot o' times, we'd have some old-time string band music. Old man Ben Miller and Smit Church would come over and bring their banjo and fiddle. Old man Ben Miller was as good a fiddler as I ever heard, and he was a good dancer, too. And so when we got the molasses all made up, they'd have one of them old-time square dances. They called them shindigs in them days; that's what they went by the name of: shindigs. They'd move the things out of the house, and here they'd go. And they'd play maybe three or four hours. Have a good time. They always foddered and topped their corn—topped the corn and pulled the fodder to feed their cattle in the wintertime. So we'd get the corn all done up and then we'd have a corn shuckin', you know, and the neighbors would all gather in and have one of the finest times you ever seen. And then, most of the time after the corn was shucked, they'd put it up and put the shucks away and feed the cattle them shucks in the wintertime. Then we'd have an old-time square dance—have a shindig for three or four hours."

Due to limited transportation, folks held square dances in individual homes, not only at harvest time but year-round to provide neighbors with entertainment and the much-needed social interaction we humans crave. Richard Norton recalls, "We used to have dances every two [weeks] or sometimes [once] a week, and we'd maybe have one over at our house. Somebody'd be makin' music, and we always had Bill Lamb play the fiddle and had some banjo and guitar pickers, too, you know. They's a lot of young people around here then."

> "Mr. Ritchie had a square dance every Saturday night because he said there wasn't nothing any better than good, clean, wholesome fun for young people."
>
> —*Margaret Norton*

Richard's wife, Margaret Norton, adds, "They'd get all the furniture out of the room and had somebody a-callin' and somebody a-pickin', y' know. We had the whole place covered up with young people, y' know, because they hadn't got this crave to go up to Atlanta or some big city. They just stayed on and helped farm in the summertime and then go to school in the wintertime and have fun. We walked every place. We went to square dances at the school and ball games and movin' picture shows. Anything they had, y' know. Mr. Ritchie had a square dance every Saturday night because he said there wasn't nothing any better than good, clean, wholesome fun for young people. They didn't have any drinkin', any bad doin's, or anything like that— just plain fun. They'd last about two hours from about eight o'clock to about ten o'clock. Then you got home about eleven o'clock—early enough, that time. We had a long walk, but it was all right. There were several couples along. You had your boyfriend, and maybe you had your brother or sister alongside of you, too, 'cause they had to go and they had to be looked after."

"My daddy was always the fiddler. I've often told people I cut my teeth on a fiddle back."

—*Mrs. E. H. Brown*

Mrs. E. H. Brown remembers, "We didn't have very much for entertainment, y' know, and when we did have some little somethin', we really enjoyed it. An' everything was nice; everybody behaved themselves. I used to go to country dances, too. I never went to a public dance in my life. It was th' same at the neighbor's home. And ever'body had better behave themselves. If they didn't, they was invited t' go home. My daddy was always the fiddler. I've often told people I cut my teeth on a fiddle back."

Lester J. Wall reminisces: "We used to have parties. When they had these house parties, we didn't have automobiles. Most people had to walk back in the thirties. You know, that was in the early thirties. Most people had to walk. Then around maybe fifteen to twenty people would gather in a home. I learned Mountain Square Dancin' back when I was about the age of five or six years old. You can do a lot more with fourteen or fifteen of them than you could two hundred couples at the Mountain City Playhouse [Mountain City, Georgia]. We'd have, say, six or eight couples in the same room at the same time. It doesn't matter if you're crowded a little bit. You can still get away with it.

"Most of the old homes were boxed form. They had two or three doors leadin' into one room; if there wasn't a door, there were windows. You were

PLATE 42   Lester J. Wall *(photo courtesy of his wife, Helen Wall)*

not in the same room all the time. You were maybe in the livin' room forward, and then maybe you were in the kitchen or dinin' room. Usually the kitchens and dining rooms were together. Most of the time they could fold up a bed and clear out and use the bedroom, and if you were involved in the dance, you would be in that room. The rest of the rooms, people were sittin' in them.

"Maybe the parents would have a cake or Kool-Aid or some kind of thing like this. This is what we served for refreshments. They would put refreshments on the table, and you passed through to get you something and go on out. Most of the time, you'd pick up a piece of cake, and if you were lucky, you got a napkin. Then they would maybe have a paper cup with Kool-Aid in it. They would have coffee. Beyond that, those were about the only refreshments you had.

"But these parties ran about, well, I'd say, once a week. We had loads of fun. Most of the time, at the house parties, the caller would be part of the dances. He would have a partner. He would probably be the leader to maybe wind up the ball. He and his partner might be the leader for openin' up the pearly gates. A majority of the time, the caller was involved.

"Everybody in the community took a part. We had people who would come in for our dances with fiddles. Hilliard Taylor used to be one of the most famous fiddlers around. That is Mrs. Laurel's—Mrs. Clyde Laurel's— father. Eula Taylor is the one that named Hellcat Creek. They named it after her because she was quite a character. Hilliard was her husband and he had a fiddle and he'd come and bring his fiddle. Sport Queen, he's as good a guitar picker as back in his younger days. Hump Welch used to play a lot of guitar—Bill Welch's brother. He could make a fiddle; he could play anything. He could take a cigar box and make a fiddle out of it. He had a lot of fun and ability—musical ability. I guess that's what many men do: they play the guitar. At home, Peter Taylor used to bring in a fiddle, and I forgot who brought a banjo. It seems like it was Welch or some of them would bring a guitar, banjo, or mandolin. That is the kind of music we had. They were all very good at playin', and, whenever they had a party, they would just keep playin'. They didn't bother at all. They would come on in and play. It didn't cost you anything at all. They were more than glad to play. See, we didn't have much trouble gettin' people to play. There were several other musicians, but I can't recall all of them. It's been a lot of water over the dam since then.

"But, in these parties, we would play a game like Skip to My Lou, which was one similar to a type of dance, and you'd sing it. It's a circle and a dance just like the others. What you'd do is get a girl, and there'd be one person in the middle that didn't have a girl. What he would do when he was dancin' around is steal your girl, and you'd sing, 'Skip to my Lou. She's gone, so what shall I do?' All this adds up to that. There's a song that everybody sings; and in between the time, you say, 'She's gone again'; and that's when somebody has stolen her. You're out on the floor, and you're lookin' for another one. It's just a choice of goin' around and dancin' with a different one, but you have to pick the right time to steal the girl while the other man's got her and turn loose. It adds up to that, and it's a lot of fun. If you've got your hands on her, he can't get her, but once you've turned her loose, then she's free to be stolen.

"Then we'd play different kinds of games—Please and Displease—and they even played Spin the Bottle. Back when I was young, you know, a nickel would get you into a movie. A nickel would buy you a Coca-Cola. It didn't take much money, but we didn't need much money. We could walk anywhere we wanted to go. When you walked, you had people with you. We played different kinds of games, like I said. Several more games were involved, but I can't recall all of them. They used to have one—but I forgot what it's called—where you had to walk with a girl, games they played where you had to walk outside, but I forgot what the name of it is. They might even send you on a trip by yourself. You had to go out and come back or maybe find somethin'. This was a lot of fun. All the games we played were a lot of fun.

"I can recall that we liked to play Please and Displease. Well, with Please and Displease, you go around the room, and everybody has a chance to do this. They could say they were pleased and you'd stop, but if they said they were displeased, you'd say, 'Okay. What will it take to please you?' Then maybe one would say, 'Okay. This one has to kiss this girl.' Then the person leadin' would say, 'You go kiss the girl.' Of course, if they didn't do it, we would penalize them. Anyway, it came out pretty good and it was clean fun, nothing unusual.

"I remember we used to play and give people 'airplane' rides. Well, what you do is you blindfold people and get a piece of board—a six-inch-wide board, two by four—and you get two people that are pretty strong on each end. They lure a person into a dark room and let them step on that board. Then they pick the board up off the floor and start shakin' it. It may not get that high, but the person feels it. You hold on to the people's shoulders, and you think you're going right up to the ceilin'. It's scary, but the person is never really very high off of the floor. Movin' the board scares them. But goin' back, it's clean fun.

> "Mountain Square Dancin' was taught to all of the small children . . . Everybody participated . . . They took pride in doing this, so this is really how we learned to dance."
>
> —*Lester J. Wall*

"But everybody was involved, even the smaller children, as well as boys and girls eighteen years old. Mountain Square Dancin' was taught to all of the small children. At that time, everybody participated, and this is where we would learn this stuff. As a small kid, maybe a girl eighteen years old would teach me to go through a dance; this was nothing uncommon. They took pride in doin' this, so this is really how we learned to dance. There was no drinkin', no problem with drinkin' at this time. I can't recall ever seeing anyone drunk at one of these parties. Now that sounds funny, but that's true, even when the dance was over. It usually lasted until about ten-thirty—usually started at eight o'clock and lasted till about ten or eleven o'clock. Then the people would walk back home, which was within three or four miles of the area usually. This became about a every weekend habit.

"Bill and Louise Henson, a couple in Clayton [Georgia], used to have a party nearly every week at their house because they enjoyed dancin' when they were young. They had a big room, and we could get six or eight couples in there. Bill Henson used to have a lot of them [dances]. We used to have parties at our house, too. Most people, Hump Giles and folks, had them at their homes. We would have a lot of fun. It was clean fun. There was no drinkin' and there was no cuttin' up."


"Square dances have been out ever since they ain't no tellin' . . . back in the pioneer days."

—*Melvin Taylor*

Sallie Beaty speaks of square dances: "I never did attend 'em. Sometimes, they would have dances inside people's homes or out at the school, you know."

Melvin Taylor echoes Mrs. Beaty's sentiment: "They used to have them at the [Rabun County] high school [gymnasium]. They had square dancin' places on the lakes. Mama and them, they'd go over there on Lake Burton. They had a square dance place on Timpson over there. I was too young to go to the square dances on the lake, but my mother and daddy went. They went back in the thirties. I always heard about the square dances on the lake. Oh, they used to dance down here at Hall's Boat House, Lakemont, Georgia. [See *The Foxfire Magazine*, Fall/Winter 2001.] There used to be a dance hall years back in the thirties over there, but I forget what they called it. They used to hold 'em at people's houses, too—just as long as it 'as a pretty good-size place, as long as people can get lined up. Just natural clothes 'as what they wore. Square dances have been out ever since they ain't no tellin'. I started to say since the beginnin' of time just about. It's been out a long time; there ain't no tellin' how many years—back in the pioneer days."

PLATE 43 Melvin Taylor remembers much about the days
when Mountain Square Dancing was in its prime.

The expansion of travel provided by the invention of the automobile and the creation of the Tallulah Falls Railroad furthered the forming of community dance halls and gathering spots.

"We mingled with the lowlanders and the natives, too. It was like a great big family, and we got acquainted with people we wouldn't've gotten acquainted with if it hadn't been for the square dances held on the hotel porch."

—*Carl Dover*

Carl Dover shares remembrances of a popular dance spot, the Mountain City Hotel in Mountain City, Georgia: "Now the local boys would come in with their fiddles, guitars, banjos, and that sort of thing on the porch—right on the porch. They would make music all night long if they wanted to dance that way. They would pass the hat around to get a few dimes and nickels and whatnot. That's the way people paid them. And they would just play music, just like that, and they would dance ever' Saturday night. They danced all night long sometimes. Everybody went to the Mountain City Hotel for those square dances. I don't know just how long this lasted. I know that it lasted as far as I can remember up until 1927. We used to love to go up there to the dance, I'll tell you! The caller we used to like to get was the sheriff of the county: Luther Rickman. He was a good square dance caller, and he

PLATE 44 Mountain City Hotel (*photo courtesy of Mrs. Rachel Page Bernheim*)

liked to dance, too. Hilliard Taylor, he lived on Hellcat Street in Mountain City. He played the fiddle. His daughter used to be one of the best square dancers in this whole country. Practically everybody did callin' for the square dancin'—the natives of Rabun County. The residents of Rabun County would go there because it was a good place to dance. We mingled with the lowlanders and the natives, too. It was like a great big family, and we got acquainted with people we wouldn't've gotten acquainted with if it hadn't been for the square dances held on the hotel porch.

"Whole families would come up from 1900 on up to about World War II, for as long as the railroad was runnin'. They come up to Tallulah Falls [Georgia] and walk on up from there. Our highways were pretty rough—not as many automobiles as they are today. For other entertainment, people would take walks in the woods and look at the mountains. They probably enjoyed themselves more then than today."

Mrs. Rachel Page Bernheim shared her memories of the hotel. [See *The Foxfire Magazine,* Winter 1979.] She recalled that the hotel was situated on a hill. A big water tank, which is still standing, furnished running water to the hotel. There was no generator. It ran by gravity flow. Each hall of the hotel had indoor bathrooms. Kerosene lamps and acetylene lights provided lighting. The acetylene lamps used a powder that came in big metal tubs. The Johnsons, who owned the hotel, had their own honey and much of their own meat and grew a vegetable garden for the hotel. They kept hams and other perishables in a sunken well, a room-size cellar about ten feet deep. They owned sheep and goats and grazed them about halfway up Black Rock

Mountain. Mr. Johnson planted apple orchards and grape vineyards. The hotel opened for the season in June when the schools closed for the summer, and then closed again when the guests left in September. Most of them came on the Tallulah Falls train. There were very few cars in this area at that time. Most people rode on horseback or in buggies.

For entertainment at the hotel, various people called square dances on the octagon-shaped porch. They would pass the hat around to collect money to pay for the band's performance. Mrs. Bernheim still sounded quite thrilled as she told about dancing with Sheriff Luther Rickman (he often called the dances), though she was very young at the time. She remembers chamber music played at dinner in the large dining room. The hotel brought black porters and waiters from Atlanta, and even black nurses. A lot of local people also worked there as cooks, maids, and cleaning people. The guests and the people from the community working there enjoyed one another and socialized together.

The hotel had tennis courts and a frog pond (for gigging) and also provided skeet shooting at a skeet tower on the hotel property. A livery stable stood nearby where hotel guests could rent horses for rides and impromptu races to the railroad water tower in Mountain City.

Mr. Earl Dotson [see *The Foxfire Magazine,* Winter 1979] recalled the square dances held on the veranda. This porch was about forty to fifty feet long and held about thirty to fifty people. Nelson Sexton was a caller he remembered there.

The start of World War II brought a close to the square dance gatherings, but soon after the war ended, the art was revived as young soldiers came home and picked up their lives. Melvin Taylor recalls, "I came back after the war [World War II, 1946] and finished high school. All the boys was gone when I come back home from the war up there to Clayton. Well, Lester Wall, he'd come back, too, but there were only two boys in the senior class at Rabun County High School.

"There was a bunch of us boys from up here goin' to school down there at Piedmont College [Demorest, Georgia] right after the war. We went down there in '47. I was twenty or twenty-one. GI Bill, that was one of the greatest things there ever was, GI Bill.

"I called them [square dances] mostly down at Piedmont College, and I used to call over there at Demorest High School. I called over there several times. On Saturday nights, they had square dances in the gym. I never called for money. They found out that you call, you know, and a lot of people'd ask you—call one night or somethin' like that. They just asked me to call, and I'd go on and call—glad to. Most of these mountain boys did call sometimes when they were needed. I called them down there for two years. That's the only callin' I did. Up here, most of what I did was dancin'. I don't remember what the band was, but you gotta have a good 'un."

Mr. Wall remembers, "I used to take square dancin' when I was in college. We did the Virginia Reel, and we did some other square dancin'. Back on Sadie Hawkins Day, we used to play in Piedmont College. We played Skip to My Lou. Girls chased the boys. If the girl got the boy, they were theirs all day. You had to remain with that girl all day. Of course she had all of that expense. There was a pretty good deal there! Sadie Hawkins Day used to be in a comic strip called *Li'l Abner*, and they had it in *The Atlanta Journal*. We started Sadie Hawkins Day at Piedmont College. They jumped on this, and this was back in the younger times when it was a comic strip. Li'l Abner and Sadie Hawkins had a day where the girls could catch the men and make them marry. When we went to Piedmont College, it was one of their favorite times. All of the students there would play Sadie Hawkins Day. If you don't think some of those girls could run, you're not tryin' to get caught by another! Maybe that's the whole idea: You want to get caught by some girls, and some . . . you don't want to get caught by them. We used to do it in 1948 or '49, but you didn't have to marry or anything. They just kept you for a day. If the girl chased you down into a café, she had to pay for it. The guy didn't have to pay for anything: The girl paid for it all. The girl had to spend her money. So, you see, I've seen some of these boys react when they didn't want a girl to catch them. They'd climb a tree, and then the girl would climb the tree. I've seen a limb break off on one old guy. He got caught anyway. They'd line up on a field. You'd have a twenty-yard front run from the girl, and you had to line up on a football field. So the boys lined up in front, and the girls in back. You had to run to get gone. They could come anywhere at you except the bathroom. That's why most of them would get caught. Usually, there were a few that would chase boys that they knew wouldn't go with them. It's just like an initiation—like in a high school when you get initiated. In college, you would do the same thing. Today, I don't think they have any of that except the clubs. We used to initiate them all into the FFA [Future Farmers of America] down here. I ran into a belt, and they warmed me up between the shorts. They could give pretty good licks!"

"It is important, if you are at a dance or somethin' like that and somebody comes up and asks you to dance, that you dance with them. You may not like them, but you do not have to. You are not there to fall in love. You are there to dance, and you are showin' courtesy."

—*Lester J. Wall*

The efforts of the Rabun County Chapter of the American Legion spurred the popularity of square dancing. The Mountain City Playhouse became the area's hot spot for square dance entertainment. Mr. Wall continues, "After World War II started, a lot of the parties and stuff ceased. About that time, the Mountain City Playhouse was built by Mr. Ramey, Thomas Ramey. Then when we came back after service and formed the American Legion, we purchased the Mountain City Playhouse from Mr. Ramey and turned it into a legion hall. From then it started as Mountain Square Dancin', which got up very much so until several years ago when the legion could not profitably keep the Mountain City Playhouse open. I can remember whenever I used to work at the Mountain City Playhouse after I had come back from World War II. Most of the time I worked skatin' nights, which was two nights a week in Mountain City. I would go to the dance on Saturday night and pay to get in and work the other two nights free for the American Legion. We made a lot of money back then, and of course, all they were chargin' was like two dollars per person. I told them what they ought to do is charge three dollars a person. It would be three stag, five drag. What that means is, if you come by yourself, it costs three dollars a person; if you bring your partner with you, you get in for five, both of you. That is two-fifty apiece; that gives a boy a cut for bringin' his girl.

"Even back then, there were so many girls along the sideline that you could go up and ask any of them to dance with you and they would dance. It is important, if you are at a dance or somethin' like that and somebody comes up and asks you to dance, that you dance with them. You may not like them, but you do not have to. You are not there to fall in love. You are there to dance, and you are showin' courtesy.

"Anyway, goin' back to what we were talkin' about, we went into what we called the big square dancing after World War II at Mountain City. The legion operated it. Every Saturday night, startin' some time in the first of June and lastin' through Labor Day, we'd have square dancin' at the Mountain City Playhouse. As many as two thousand to three thousand people came—boys and girls and so forth. The big dances at the Mountain City Playhouse, in order to be heard, you would have to talk into the mike so everybody could hear you. You must keep your mind on what the caller says. If you get out of whack, everything will get out of sync. Most of the time, when you're goin' through any of the sets, if you listen to the caller very carefully, you can go through this very easy.

"A lot of times, at the bigger dances, before they would start the dance, they might get some of the better couples to demonstrate first. We've even done this in Mountain City. This is a good thing. The only thing is, lookin' at it and actually doing it is two different things. Gettin' somebody out there to carry you through it step by step is the best way to learn it. If I taught Mountain Square Dancin', I could take ten girls and ten boys and in a week's time have them goin' through every one of these calls. Let's say if you teach ten couples, they could teach ten more. See, each girl could get them a boy, and each boy could get them a girl. It's usually easier if the boy teaches the girl. If he knows where to go, it's pretty easy for the girl to follow. You can do a lot more with fourteen or fifteen of them than you could two hundred couples at the Mountain City Playhouse. At the Mountain City Playhouse, we used to have ten or fifteen different calls that you would make. With them, that was all that you could do. In smaller groups, there is many more calls you can make. At Mountain City, we probably did a hundred and fifty to two hundred couples or better on the floor at one time. You're talkin' about a lot of people up there. We used to have a lot of calls. They eliminated some of these calls in square dancin' because they just don't lend theirselves to a big square dance like that.

"They had [different dances] at all square dances in Mountain City. One of the dances they had was the Bunny Hop. We would always have a time for cloggin' or buck dancin'. Those people that wanted to hit the floor and buck dance [see page 152], some could. I think we run buck dancin' in the ground sometimes. We let them buck dance till they wore themselves out in twenty or thirty minutes, which is uncalled for. I think buck dancin' shouldn't last over five minutes at the most, and the Bunny Hop shouldn't last over five minutes. A square dance shouldn't last over fifteen minutes, and a round dance [should be] in between the sets of the other dancin'. This gives people an opportunity to do just about any kind of dancin'. There would be slow dancin', round dancin', and even have some fast dancin'. They could do just about anything with all of the dances they have around now. There are so many I can't think of all of them right now. There's a lot of fast dancin'. We've never had any breakdancin', but maybe somebody might like that. The band would play; the best things were a good piano, banjo, electric guitar, an old steel guitar, and a fiddle. This is about all you would really need, and if you've got the good musicians, they can do it.

"I understand that we made a lot of money in the beginnin', and it was run right. Then it got to where it wasn't; we were probably at fault as legionnaires. We let it get away from us. We let too much drinkin' start to take effect on it. Then people got to where they didn't want to come.

"I'd like to see it revived. I'd like to see the drinkin' stopped, and dope. Say 'Look here' at the gate. 'You're buyin' your ticket here; you don't get inside this gate without buyin' a ticket.' Then the alcoholic beverages wouldn't be allowed inside. If you do it that way, then maybe it would stop."

Melvin Taylor also remembers the playhouse: "After the war, they formed the American Legion post. They wanted to make money, so they had an old wooden buildin'. It had been a dance hall in the thirties, up there at Mountain City, so they rented it. It was always called the Mountain City Playhouse—had that name back in the thirties. They bought the buildin' or rented it from a person: Mr. Ramey. It was a wooden buildin' built back in the thirties. It turned into a real big success, and I'll tell you, it did! That thing was about known all of the state of Georgia. The young people, the older people, and all—there was all people there. I'll tell you what, there was people from Atlanta; they come from all around that place.

"There used to be two hotels there in Mountain City. One was a big green one, just right above Law's store there on top of the hill. The other one over there was Ramey's. People from the hotels went over to the Mountain City Playhouse. Oh, one Labor Day weekend, there was over nineteen hundred people up there. That's a crowd!

"Old Apple Savage, he had a band that played for them square dances for years. Maude Ivey—she's dead now—boy, she was a piano player from way back. She played with them for years, I think—years and years, as long as they had the band. It was a good success, and everybody enjoyed it. It lasted for years. About five or so would be in a band. Let's see . . . there would be fiddles and banjos, piano player, and guitar player. There wouldn't be any horns. There was about five of 'em, I guess. I think Apple Savage played somethin'. I don't remember exactly what it was, but he had that band for years—went on for many years with success up there.

"I went up there about every Saturday night. After me and Janie got married, we was both up there on Saturday night. It was a good place to go—good clean entertainment. Young people and older people really enjoyed it, I'll tell you. They looked forward to Saturday nights. Well, it was just general fun, that's all—enjoyment.

"Well, I'm gonna tell you what happened now. To be honest with you, finally had the law comin' around. Lamon Queen, he was the sheriff or policeman; he kept order up there on Saturday nights. They finally got so much law, they run everybody off. I'll be honest with you, now. That's the honest truth. Well, they even had a feller packin' a gun out in the parkin' lot. Now, I'm gonna tell y', people go up there for enjoyment. They don't go up there fer stuff like that, y' know."

Mr. Taylor asserts that callers, musicians, and fun-loving folks knowledgeable of dance steps were necessary to a good square dance: "Well, now, I'll tell you about square dancin'. Well, it was just regular dancin' music, is all it was—'Down Yonder' and some of those. Well, I can't think of all of 'em, but, anyway, they would start out when the dance started. Well, they'd say, 'Everybody get your partner; find you a partner.' And they'd find them a partner. Then they'd say, 'Make a great big circle to the left.' Then they'd get 'em all circled up, and they'd say, 'Swing that lady on your left all the way around.' You'd swing all the girls in the house; they was lined up in there. And then they'd say, 'Circle four.' They had different calls like 'Put the bird in the cage.' [See explanation on page 165.] The girls go in the cage; they let her out and put the male in and circle four and swing out. Then you hunt you another partner. They'd circle four and swing your partner. They had all kinds of sayin's. They'd open up what they call the London Bridge, and you know, everybody would go through that. Somebody brought down here from Michigan or somewhere—a lot of people from Rabun County lived up in Pontiac and Detroit back then—what they call the Bunny Hop. I never had seen that before. That was something else, I'll tell you, that Bunny Hop was!

"There was a bunch of different calls, y' know. Different callers had different ones. It takes a little while for people down there who were dancin' to catch on to it, you know what I mean. Roy York, he called here in Rabun County. Good Lord, I bet he called for fifty, sixty years. He was callin' back when I was a boy. He called up here at the Mountain City Playhouse for years, too. There was just one caller. They'd take a break ever' so often. That's when the buck dancers'd get out there and buck it in between times, y' know? Durin' sets of square dancin', everybody that's a buck dancer— they'd play that fast music—and they'd get out there and buck dance. There

PLATE 45  Buck dancer Jay Bland
strutting his stuff

was a big crowd of 'em, too, boy, and some of 'em good! I used to be pretty good at it myself, back when I was a young feller.

"Well, most buck dancers, they got their own style. Well, they get up there and slide them feet. They do all kinds. The buck-and-wing is a real old mountain step. You bring one foot over, and the crowd would laugh and carry on, and oh, mercy! You can get good at it. They had all kinds.

"There 'as a lot of buck dancers up there [at the Mountain City Playhouse]—boys and girls between sets, y' know. They crank up that real fast music and, boy! All of 'em had their own style. They was there separate. They was a lot of 'em tap dancin'. It was real interestin'. I used to stop myself and watch 'em. It was really good. It was good, clean fun. There were contests sometimes with buck dancers. I don't know whether it was a contest or what, but they'd get out there. I think that it was just the prestige—to see who could last the longest.

"Around here, they used to have them cloggers, you know. Them cloggers all got pants and uniforms. I don't know too much about them. North Carolina, somewhere up in there, had a real sharp team. They went all over everywhere cloggin'. Yeah, they was specialists, that cloggin' business. But there's a shuffle a lot of times when you're doin' square dancin'. I don't know what you call that, but you know how. It's almost buck dancin'. Well, we did round dances in between the square dances, too. We had ballroom dancin', and the band would play that type of music. Well, they just had about all kinds of dancin', though."

John Kelley shares his insights on the music commonly played for traditional mountain square dances: "Well, the square dance music that we play—and my favorites—they must have been playin' a hundred years ago, and some of them that they talk about playin' are from Jefferson's time, so

PLATE 46 Cloggers were generally the only dancers
to wear costumes at the mountain dances.

three hundred years ago or two hundred years ago. 'Soldier's Joy' is the classic one and 'Ragtime Annie' is a great dance tune. 'Liberty' was one that I think George Washington probably danced to—a tune called 'Liberty.' It's kind of a tune that came over a long time ago. Oh, there's just a bunch of great tunes. One of the old-time tunes, they kind of have funny names. Some of them are newer songs with funny names. One of the ones that we play a lot is 'Push the Pig's Foot a Little Further in the Fire.' Who ever heard of that tune? But there are 'Soldier's Joy' and 'Liberty,' and 'Arkansas Traveler' is a great tune, and 'Mississippi Sawyer.' Those are kind of classic tunes that you would have heard a hundred years ago or sixty years ago in North Georgia, for sure. We're still playing them, and they are still the best dance tunes."

Mr. Brett Burrell, a young but experienced buck dancer, shares some of the songs used between square dancing sets to give the buck dancers a time to shine: "They play 'Slew Foot' and 'Wildwood Flower.' 'The Foggy Mountain Breakdown' is by far my favorite song to dance to. I like it because it just has the right beat where you can try new stuff if you want to while you're dancin' to it. They can speed it up during a certain part. If you're dancin' with somebody and tryin' to outdance them, you sometimes need them to speed it up. I have always liked to dance. The love of music was probably what got me started dancin'. The atmosphere is great, and I really enjoy everything about it. Bluegrass is the music that I dance to. I just love the way the banjo sounds and also the beat. It is more up-tempo, and it's really good to dance to. It is really hard to dance to something slow. I just kind of listen to the music and go with it.

"Square dancin' is also a very similar style of dance because you can buck dance in a pattern with a partner. You have the caller, and you just follow his calls and go into whatever he says to go into. Don't worry about how you look in the beginnin' 'cause everybody looks really goofy when they first start. You just have fun and don't worry about it. That is my advice to beginners."

Duncan Taylor shares several of the tunes played for Mountain Square Dancing. He says, "There may be a few others that I forgot, but these are the most popular ones we played around here":

"Alabama Jubilee"
"Back Up and Push"
"Bully of the Town"
"Cattle Call"
"Corina, Corina"
"Down Yonder"
"Georgia Steel Guitar"

"Going Down the Road Feeling Bad"
"John Henry"
"Just Because"
"Old Gray Bonnet"
"Roll Out the Barrel"
"San Antonio Rose"
"Steel Guitar Rag"
"Take Me Back to Tulsa"

Mr. Wall shares some insights: "At every party that we had, we had what we called Mountain Square Dancin'. We could take in a lot more in small groups than we could in large groups. There's a lot of calls that are never called in large groups. Mountain Square Dancin' originated back many years ago. I don't know exactly where or when. In Mountain Square Dancin', you combine a lot of every type of dancin'—like the Virginia Reel, cloggin', and just goin' through it. Mountain Square Dancin', back in the early times, we had probably two of the best callers you've ever heard. They were Mr. York and Mr. McClure. Both of these people done a lot of callin' in the Mountain City Playhouse in the early times. Most of the younger people were grown with these parties. They grew up learnin' Mountain Square Dancin'. This is about the history that I see, and we had these parties up till about the beginnin' of World War II. Ralph Angel used to do a lot of cloggin'. He had the Mountain City Cloggers.

"Mountain Square Dancin' is adaptive to almost any kind of clothin'. Most people prefer something that is very loose. They like shorts, blue jeans, and any kind of shoes. A lot of people prefer using leather-bottom shoes, but basically, you can dance in any kind of shoes. Everybody can take part even if you make a mistake. It's a large group, and it's not noticeable if you do make a mistake. If you keep going, nobody notices the mistake. You learn from everybody.

"The music is very important. I can tell you some of the songs instead of the lyrics. A lot of the songs that we used to use is 'Down Yonder' and 'Under the Double Eagle,' and you could even square dance to 'Jingle Bells.' That is a good rhythm song, and it works very good. Nobody sings or anything in these songs. It's just the music. They would play different songs like that. I am sure that Duncan Taylor over here in town can tell you nearly all of them, and he plays the steel guitar. I think a lot of the music we used to dance by was like steel guitar, a regular guitar, piano, and a fiddle. Now they throw in drums, a band, and horns. Duncan Taylor is very good on a steel guitar. A steel guitar is one that you lay flat, and you play it with a piece of metal in your hand. You have the metal in your tunin' hand, and you pick it.

A steel guitar has got three necks. You play whichever one fits. Then you have the electric guitar. A lot of people used to take a regular guitar and take one of those pieces of metal and tune it. There used to be a guy that played with Lester Flatt that did that a lot. He made it sound like a steel guitar. He would take a piece of steel and run it on the neck. When I was just a boy, we didn't have any electric guitars. I guess there were some, but we did not know anything about them here. We did not have a piano and other things, but a good organ was really good to dance by. The person who it used to be played by was Mrs. Ivey over here. Maude Ivey used to play the piano in Mountain City with Duncan Taylor and them. She knew how to play this music, and she was really good. They had a good band, and they did not want to charge us much.

"I can give a hand, but when you get somebody in there that wants to take over, that doesn't work out. Drums are all right, but some people like to try to take the whole band over. You kill the interest then. Drums are anywhere you go. People that come up here away from here want to see the mountain stuff. You need something that is goin' to go all over the United States. I think Mountain Square Dancin' is not normal except for right here in this area. I went to a square dance one time that was just about seventy-five miles away from here, and when they said 'Swing your partner,' they let you swing them for five minutes, and you could have a dance with her while you were at it. When you swing a girl here, you turn them around once, and that's it. If a good caller gets up there, he may say, 'Don't get married on the floor. Let's get movin'.' He might say this if they're slowin' down on the floor.

**"I still like to dance, but my wife doesn't like to dance. That's no problem, though. You can always find somebody to dance with."**
*—Lester J. Wall*

"To be a good, good caller, you must know the dancin', and he has to keep his eye out there to keep everybody movin'. He needs to know somebody so he can call on them to open up the pearly gates, so he can call their name and make them do somethin'. Again, he needs to have enough knowledge to understand when people are getting tired. He needs to cut the dance off instead of lettin' people wear themselves out. It needs to be someone who will keep the music and calls goin'. Mountain Square Dancin' is not made to go slow. It's made to go fast. That's the way it ought to be. All of the dancing I've been to moved fast. To be a good caller, you must be able to say, 'Let's rest for ten minutes, and then let's get back up on the floor and dance for ten minutes.' The caller has got to be able to give the people that don't have a partner time to find one. I think that one of the things that we've got to get the young girls to understand is that if a young boy asks a girl to dance and she turns him down several times, the boy's goin' to get discouraged. The girls ought to think, hey, look, how would I feel if I was turned down three or four times? Is it goin' to hurt anybody to get up and dance with someone? You have to be a part of a team or you shouldn't be on the floor. If you can't play with the team, you shouldn't be on the team. Like I said, I learned to square dance when I was about six years old. I never started callin' until I got up teachin' school, and that was after I had been in the Army and come out. My daughter used to go to the Mountain City square dancin', and my son went, too. Both of my children learned square dancin' at the Mountain City Playhouse. They thoroughly enjoyed it. Both of them became pretty good dancers, and he became pretty good at buck dancin', too. He does not dance as much now, but he can buck dance real good.

"We had a square dance last year, but there wasn't hardly many people at it. We did it for Mountain City whenever they were having that festival. We only had about eighty couples, I guess. We had a real good time. There wasn't many people, but we had a lot of good music and everybody enjoyed it. In fact they didn't even want to shut down when we did shut down. I still like to dance, but my wife doesn't like to dance. That's no problem, though. You can always find somebody to dance with.

"I called dances at school. We used to have seventh-grade parties when I was the principal. We usually had the dances at Clayton Elementary School in the gym. I used to call the square dancin' for each of the seventh-grade parties. We would have square dancin' two or three times. I called most of them, but sometimes I got Melvin Taylor to help me. We used to teach Mountain Square Dancin' in a school. I used to be a principal at the South Rabun Elementary School for about twenty-six years. So in our school we taught Mountain Square Dancin' until we were told by the Board of Education that we could not do it anymore, that we were not to teach dance, so we had to eliminate it. Now I understand that they'd like to get it back. I think that brings you back up-to-date on the history of Mountain Square Dancin'.

"Today we are missin' out on a lot if we let Mountain Square Dancin' go down the drain. I think that we will miss out on a lot if we let the games we used to play go down the drain. I would like to see square dancin' come back in this area. Apple Savage, a local radio station deejay, tried to get it up here, but I think it was too high, and the land cost him too much. The people forgot how to dance. Who knows how to square dance? How many high school students down there do you think could go through a square dance? I would like to see us keep this part of our culture that has been carried down or handed down through the years. I would like to keep it alive if possible. I would like to see the younger generation do somethin' like this rather than sit over in town in their automobiles. Teenagers have taken everything away from themselves. I'd like to see the Mountain City Playhouse reopened. It's big enough, and it can provide a lot of interestin' stuff to high school students. If you open up a place like the Mountain City Playhouse, you cannot operate it unless you get people to come. It costs us, and if you do not support the good things, then you are takin' it away from yourself. If you brought back Mountain Square Dancin', everybody could afford two dollars a week, and you could have a dance on Saturday nights in the old gym [the old Rabun County High School gymnasium, which, renovated, is currently the Rabun County Civic Center] out here. You could get a band. If you could get, say, two dollars a person—or two-fifty a person would not hurt anybody—and you could get five hundred people participatin', then you could get a band. You would not make much money, but at least it would give them somethin' to do. We need to provide somethin' for teenagers to do. I would like to see it done. We can't turn it over to high school students because of insurance and other reasons—you just can't do it. You've got to back it, and you've got to control it. If the high school would support it, it would be one of the cheapest entertainments; we could probably do it with about five dollars a couple. Where else can you get three or four hours of entertainment for five bucks? I'm talking about it can be good, clean fun, but we'd have to have the support of everybody who wanted to have good, clean fun. We wouldn't want any drinking, no dope addicts. We say no to dope completely. This would be one of the things that I think would be highly interestin' to pursue, and if I could get some other groups to support me, I could probably do some of the calling.

 "Learn to live with temptation. You cannot let temptation rule you. You have got to rule it. I do not care what you say. You are supposed to be thinkin', but you do not think as good as you do when you are thirty or so. If somebody calls you a chicken, you think you can do anything, and you do not want to be called chicken. Which would you rather be: a live chicken or a dead duck? That is what you have got to look at. Which would you rather be, a live chicken or a dead duck? It takes a lot of effort, and I think it takes a lot of wise decision-makin'. I think you're creating more, but are they better? Sometimes we say we have better weapons. It doesn't take but one bullet to kill you, regardless of what kind of gun it is. If we can get away from drinkin' and drugs, and if we can get the young boys and girls back together in the community, we'll create a very nice spot in Rabun County.

 "There is several different types of what we call square dancin'. Everyone has a different way, but all of them have some calls that are alike. There is a lot of designs that are similar that we go through. You can add anything into a call as long as it can be formulated. You can add to Mountain Square

Dancin' because you can put a call in or you can leave them out. If you dance for fifteen minutes, then you are ready to rest, because you move. I guarantee you will dance for thirty minutes out there, and you will be wet with sweat. It does not take you long. You will not hold out that long. It will work you down pretty fast. Mountain Square Dancin' is nothin' but figurations done on the dance floor by human bein's. When you start with the types of figurations that we go through, there are many of them. You'll have a lead couple, and you'll have another couple. But the lead people can change from one foursome to another. When you get in foursomes, they can change.

> "Once you learn how to dance, it seems like it just flows like the music through the air. Everything just moves smoothly, and you get everyone interested."
>
> —*Lester J. Wall*

"Of course I've got the different calls that are in Mountain Square Dancin'. I can go through them if you would like me to. Are you ready to go through them? Square dancin' is nothing but figures in groups of fours. Most of the figures are calls that are made by a caller who is not participatin' in the dancin'. The caller goes through each one of these figures. Some of the figures are Four-leaf Clover and The Lady Around the Lady and the Gent Also, The Lady Around the Gent, but the Gent Don't Go. There are many more calls that are done at home that you would not do in a square dance with so many people. The man who is doing the callin', he is not dancin'. He stands up there, and he tells you what to do. He can say, 'Circle four'; then you get four people, and you can decide which couple wants to be number one. The four people decide which one will go first. He says, 'Shoot the star,' so you shoot the star. You run through and you turn around and you come right back. Then everybody holds hands, and it follows through. You can get back in the same square. Once you learn how to dance, it seems like it just flows like the music through the air. Everything just moves smoothly, and you get everyone interested.

"When you are square dancin', you can be tap dancin' or buck dancin'—it does not make a difference—or you can just move regular. You still can do all the designs, but you can add to Mountain Square Dancin' by any other kind of dance you want to. A lot of these people at Mountain City are going through the square dance, but they probably would be buck dancin' at the same time or even cloggin'. We used to have a lot of cloggers in Rabun County. In fact, all of these would mix in with the Mountain Square Dancin'. There is no age limit on Mountain Square Dancin'. I think some of the best dancin' and exercisin' that you can get is Mountain Square Dancin'. It has a lot of value to it. If we can get it back, I'd like to see it.

"Like I said, you can add calls to square dancin'. In square dancin', cloggers go through a lot of square dancin' designs that they consider their cloggin'. They do their own thing a lot of times. You do not do your own thing in square dancin'. You can do whatever you want to, but you have got to follow the calls. In buck dancin', you do not. They say, 'We will go out, and you do whatever you want to do.' And you go out and tap-dance and try to do your own thing out there in the middle or whatnot. That is buck dancin'. A lot of this is added to Mountain Square Dancin'. The couple can come through the calls making their taps click if they want to. You can go through and just walk through it. You will not actually walk through it: You will go a little faster than that, but you learn. This here is about the only place you can find Mountain Square Dancin'. I've been to square dances at other places that have some similar calls, but they do not mix them. It is somethin' you can learn fast. It does not take long to learn, and then you can get somebody to call it. Then you go through the steps."

### APPALACHIAN ROUND DANCES
Mountain Square Dancing falls under the category of dance known as Appalachian Round Dancing. Mountain Square Dancing requires several different groupings. Dancers could be configured in a single large circle, two long lines divided by gender, and several small circles or squares of two, three, or four couples. Often, dances start in one of the larger formations, such as a large circle, and then break at the caller's direction into smaller groups. The following are samplings from each of the types of common figures used in Mountain Square Dancing. Where available, sample calls have been added to show how the various moves are intertwined to make an entertaining dance.

### ALLEMANDE
Mr. Kelley explains, "Well, if you give the person you're dancing with your left hand and walk all the way around them, that would be an allemande left. And if you give them your right hand and walk all the way around, that would be an allemande right."

### BREAK
Although most figures use moves in which partners, squares, or groups hold hands, some moves require that handholds be broken.

Mr. Kelley clarifies, "When you're doing a square dance, and you're doing those visiting dances, that would be considered a break part. A visiting square dance is one where the first couple 'visits' couple number two and does a fig-

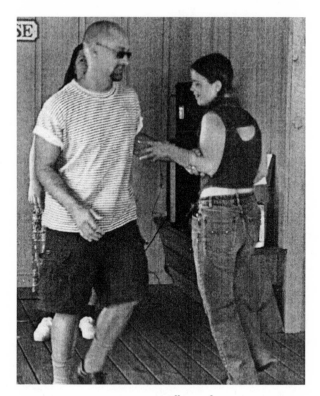

PLATE 47 Allemande

ure with them, then moves on to couple number three and then number four. After that, couple number two visits the other couples; everyone does a break, running it till couples number three and four move on to 'visit' other couples."

## CORNER

Mr. Kelley explains, "If you're in a square dance position, your partner—if you're a gentleman—is going to be to your right; then if you turn to the left, you'll face the next lady, and that's your corner lady. Kind of the classic one that they worked and worked and worked on in third grade is that you face your corner, and you would allemande left your corner with your left hand. So you'd give your left hand to your corner, walk all the way around your corner, and you're walking back and you're facing your partner."

Janet Shepherd echoes, "Now, in your little foursomes, there's someone next to you who is not your partner. That's your neighbor or your opposite or your corner. We tend to do a swing in a sort of ballroom position here, but anything you want to do is fine. It can be an elbow swing; it can be two-hand turning—anything you want. I'd like you to swing your corner. Now let this person go and swing your own partner."

## GRAND (RIGHT OR LEFT)

Mr. Kelley describes this move: "He [the caller] says, 'Meet your partner with a right and left grand.' So you give your right hand to your partner, and you pull her on by; then you give your left hand to the number two lady and pull her by and give the right hand to the number three lady and pull her by. Give your left hand to the number four lady, who's your corner, and pull her by, and there's your partner. Then you promenade your partner."

### THE CALL

Face your corner;
Left allemande with your left hand.
Go right in to a right and left grand,
Every other girl and every other hand,
Till you meet your partner and you promenade.
Take her home and swing.

## PACK SADDLE

Mr. Kelley instructs, "In the fancier style of dancing, there's a way to put your hand on the wrist of the person in front of you."

Mr. Wall shares, "A pack saddle is like what you form with your hands [and arms] to carry people on."

PLATE 48  Pack saddle hand placement

## SQUARE

Although the term *square* depends on the size of the group and the nature of the dance being executed, squares are most commonly formed with two couples or four couples.

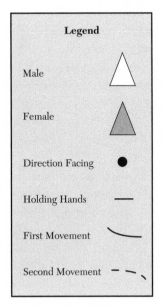

PLATE 49

**Two-Couple Square**

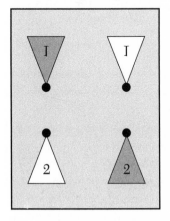

**Four-Couple Square**

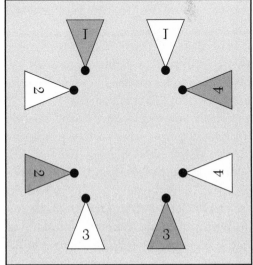

PLATE 50

Mr. Wall shares: "A square is a circle of four. We'd take four people—two couples. Two couples make a square."

Mr. Kelley explains a four-couple square: "A square is four couples, and they're set up kind of in a box position. One couple has their back to the band. They'll be couple number one. The couple right across from them is couple number three. The couple to the right of couple number one is couple number two, and the last couple is couple number four. The dance would last about five or six minutes and give everybody a chance to lead and everybody a chance to follow and have those little breaks. Depending on how sophisticated your group is and how sophisticated your caller is, they may add different things or change different things. As the caller gets used to you, they start fooling the dancers a little bit, and they give them other things to do."

## RUNNING SET

Mr. Kelley elaborates: "That's a boy-girl set; one couple is the first couple, and you don't really need a caller because the first couple will kind of lead it. They'll just turn to the couple on the right; they'll say, 'Circle four'—and they'll circle four—'Circle to the left; circle to the right.' Then they'll do a right-hand star and a left-hand star; then do-si-do your partner, swing your corner, swing your partner. Then they'll go to the next couple, the fourth couple. The second couple will follow to the third couple and everybody will move up. So as they move up, eventually, you'll take in the whole circle. Once they go around, then the first couple will start another set of figures. So it's something that you don't need a caller for because the leading couple kind of sets the pace, and then they [the other dancers] have to try to remember to go from there. That was attractive because you didn't need somebody to call."

## SMALL CIRCLE DANCES

As Mr. Wall told us earlier, some calls are better suited for small circle dances or couples grouped in four. He describes some of the more popular moves used for this configuration:

"Usually you would start makin' a large circle of squares. Then you'd break into squares, which is four people in a square. Sometimes, if there's an extra couple, you'd put six. Then you'd get maybe everybody involved. You can do most of these with three couples as well as two, except for the Four-leaf Clover—you can't do that with six people, but nearly everything else can be done with six squares. But generally speakin', you go with four. We start with a large circle. We break it back to four people. Each square then goes through each call. Once you do one call, then you break this square and form another square with the different couples. You start with the next call; then we finish the call. You do this until the end of the dance.

The dance, or that particular dance, ends with either a Full Swing or Swingin' Lady."

Ms. Shepherd starts by counting off couples. She instructs, "What we're going to do now is, we're going to count off couples. Let's make a great big circle if we could, and we want couples all the way around the circle. I hope we end up with an even number of couples. Let's see, we're going to be number one and number two. When you're dancing, you want the lady role to be on the right and whoever is dancing the gentleman's role to be on the left. So, we've got one, two, one, two [counting off couples]. Oh, we are so good I can't stand it! We've got an even number of couples. Give some weight here, some friendly firmness in our whole bodies, some give-and-take. Join hands and circle to the left. Now turn around and go the other way. Now into the middle, and you come back out. What we're going to do now is a series of moves that involve foursomes. So all of us that are numbered number one, we're the odd couples; we're going to move to our right, and we're going to do something with them [the next even couple in the large circle of foursomes]. We've got all these little circles here. What I want you to remember is that if you are an odd couple, you are number one. Odd couples, you're going to move around the room to other couples around the room."

Mr. Kelley instructs, "In those squares, everybody will do something. Often the first couple will go out and visit the second couple for a while, and then they'll go on and visit the third couple and do something and go on and visit the fourth couple and then come home. Then the second couple will do that and so on. So they are very repetitive. You watch, and you see what's going on and get ready when it's your turn to do the dances."

## CIRCLE FOUR

Mr. Kelley explains, "The simplest move is to hold hands in a circle, and everybody go to the left or circle to the right. Those are, like, the two first things you do. And then, in a circle, everybody would go to the center and come back out. Those are the next two steps that people do. Then people will get a partner—boy, girl, boy, girl—all the way 'round; and the partner, the man, has the lady on his right."

## THE BIRDIE IN THE CAGE

Mr. Wall explains, "The Birdie in the Cage is where, in a square of four, one of the girls gets in the circle. The other three people join hands and start circlin' to the left around this person. Then when you say, 'The bird out and the buzzard in,' then she switches places with her partner. Then you swing your opposite lady; then swing your own partner and go to finish that particular call in a square with another couple."

Ms. Shepherd continues, "One nice, fun move is called the Birdie in the Cage. That means that one of the ladies jumps in the middle, and the other three people circle to the left around her. Now the birdie hop out and the crow hop in. That would be her partner, and we circle around this person. Now, everybody, swing your corner and let this one go and swing your partner. Now, odd couples, move on to another couple."

Mr. Kelley adds, "So they would circle four, and then you may say, 'The birdie hop in the cage.' So the number one lady would get in the center of those three people circling. Birdie hop in and then the birdie hop out and then the crow would hop in. Man number one would get in the center, and they'd circle. Then 'Crow hop out, and everybody swing.' So then all the couples would swing. Then the first couple would go to the second couple, and they'd circle up four. Then the birdie would hop in, birdie hop out, crow hop in, crow hop out, everybody swing. That first couple goes on to number four and they do it. Then they go back home, and it'll be couple number two's time; then you'd take another little break."

## FOUR-LEAF CLOVER

Mr. Wall discusses an intricate maneuver: "The next call I will talk about is the Four-leaf Clover. What you would say when beginnin' this call is 'One to one, let's do the Four-leaf Clover.' What you would do is say, 'Number one, let's do the Four-leaf Clover.' He and his partner will go under the arms of the opposite couple. Without changin' your arms, let your hands [you and your partner's hands] go over your head [and come back down over the opposite couple's arms], where you'll form a four-leaf clover—with, like, a clover in the middle. Then you say, 'The next call will be number two. You turn the clover back over.' The number two couple go under your and your partner's hands. This will put you back in the original square without ever breakin' your hands. You don't ever take your hands apart. After that, you swing your opposite lady; then you swing your own. Then you form another square."

Bill Martin clarifies, "Join in a circle; keep hands held throughout the figure. Odds duck through the evens' arch. As they emerge, the odds turn away from each other to face the evens, odd gent turning counterclockwise and lady turning clockwise. As they turn, the odds lift their joined hands overhead and down to rest on the evens' joined arms to make the clover. Roll the clover clockwise. To finish, odds raise an arch and pull the evens through it. As they pass through, the evens turn away from each other, gent turning clockwise and lady counterclockwise to re-form the circle."

PLATE 51 The Four-leaf Clover
begins by holding hands in the
square formation with the lady on
the right of her partner.

PLATE 52 The lead couple ducks under
the raised arms of the number two couple.

PLATE 53 The lead couple turns back
to inside to form the clover.

PLATE 54 To turn the clover back over, the number two couple ducks under the arms of the number one couple.

PLATE 55 Finally, the number two couple turns back to face center. This completes the move without ever breaking handholds.

THE CALL

Circle left and back to the right.
Odd, duck right under for a four-leaf clover
And turn on over.
Odd, arch; and even go under.
Circle left.

Proficient square dancers might hear the caller say, "Four-leaf Clover . . . Turn it back over."

## FOUR HANDS OVER

Mr. Wall describes this formation: "The third call I will tell you about is the Four Hands Over. The ladies put their hands over first. Then men put their hands over the ladies' hands. Then hold the men's hands. Then the ladies bow their heads and go under the arms of the men. The arms of the men will be behind the ladies. Then the men go under the ladies' arms. Then you break and swing the opposite lady. Then you swing your own partner. You get another circle, and then you form another square [to get ready for another step]."

Ms. Shepherd describes this same move as Two Hands Across. She says, "We're going to do something called Two Hands Across. It's a way of doing something called the Basket Swing. It starts with the ladies taking two hands across; gentlemen take two hands across on top of them. [The ladies bow and go under the men's hands so that the men's arms are behind the ladies' backs. Then the men duck and go under the ladies' arms so that the ladies' arms are behind the men's backs. This maneuver results in a basket weave of the arms so that dancers are in position to do a Basket Swing.] My personal favorite is still that Basket Swing, so ladies bow; gents know how, oh, yeah! Come on out and circle to the left."

Mr. Martin shares his own description of this move: "Gents join both hands, left in right. Ladies join both hands under the gents', and all move clockwise [sometimes called Turn Like Thunder]. Gents raise joined hands

PLATE 56  Final hand position for the Basket Swing

up over ladies and down behind. Ladies then raise joined hands over gents and down behind to form the basket. The basket continues to circle left. All drop hands and swing corner, then partner."

### THE CALL, PART 1

Circle left.
Four hands across.
Ladies bow;
Gents know how.
Corner swing—
And now your own,
And on to the next.

### THE CALL, PART 2

Circle four around the floor.
Four hands across; eight hands over
Ladies bow;
Gents know how.
Raise from under and swing like thunder.
Now swing your own and move along.

### LEFT-HAND SHAKE/RIGHT-HAND SHAKE/TWO-HANDS SHAKE

Mr. Wall begins, "You form a square; then you [the number one lady] start with taking your opposite lady's left hand. It's called a left-hand shake. [Men do the same.] Then you [lady to lady and man to man] take the right hand, and you shake their right hands to complete the right-hand shake. Then you take both of their hands; then drop hands and go straight out, and it's called the two-hands shake. Then you swing your opposite lady, and then you swing your arms and circle four. We always say, 'Circle four.' It could be called 'square four,' but the call says 'circle four.' "

### SHOOT THE STAR

Mr. Wall continues with an explanation of Shoot the Star: "You say, 'Number one, shoot the star.' This is the number one designated couple. A man will go between the man and the lady of the opposite couple—under the arms—and he, with his partner following in hand, will go around the man. Then he will come back to his original position. At that time, the man will have to let his arms go over his head to keep from breakin' his couple and spin. They will tie up pretty good. Then the number two couple, they will turn it back over. He [the number two gent] will repeat the move the same way between

PLATE 57 To begin to Shoot the Star, the number one man breaks handhold
with his corner lady and leads his partner to duck under the
arms of the number two couple.

PLATE 58 The lead man then turns to the right. His partner and the
number two couple follow without breaking hands to return to home
position and end the formation. The move is then repeated with the
number two man taking the lead.

the other two [the number one couple] and then go behind the number one gent and back to the original position. The gent's partner follows him during this configuration.

"In all of these squares, you're startin' out with everybody holdin' hands. When the gent shoots the star, he lets go only of his opposite partner's hands; he goes between the other couple. He still has ahold on his partner. His partner follows him all the way 'round. She still has ahold of her opposite's hands. They don't break hands. The only person that breaks hands is the one doing the shootin' [the male of each couple]; the one doing the shootin' will break hands with the opposite lady. It's really easy to do because you can walk through it. As a matter of fact, it's easier to show than to describe. When you get back, you swing your opposite lady again."

Mr. Kelley's version of this call is a bit different but is most likely a preliminary step to Mr. Wall's figure. Mr. Kelley explains, "If you have four people in a small group, dancing, they'll put their right hands into the center and shake hands with the people across; and if it's two couples, the men will hold right hands across and the ladies will hold right hands across and you'll all walk that direction. That's called making a star. For a right-hand star, put your right hand in. Then the caller will say, 'Shoot the star the other way thar,' which means to put your left hand in and walk the other direction. So that would be one way of doing that. Depending on how fancy the caller is,

PLATE 59  Right-hand Star

these dances will have a little pattern that goes with them. So then it depends on what your caller says, but they will in this style—the old-time style of dancing—walk through that and tell you what you're going to do. The caller may change the jingles, but the moves are the same."

Ms. Shepherd adds, "[In small squares of two couples,] join hands and circle to the left and the other way back to the right. Put your right hand in and shake right hands with the person across from you. Give some weight here; hold on to this person and turn this right-hand star—this is right hands across to make a right-hand star. Now do a left-hand star the other way back."

### LADY AROUND THE LADY/LADY AROUND THE LADY BUT THE GENT DON'T GO/FIGURE EIGHT

Mr. Wall explains, "We say, 'Lady around the lady, and the gentle old soul and the lady around the lady, but the gent don't go.' The lady goes between

**Lady Around the Lady and the Gent Also**

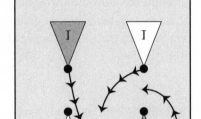

**Lady Around the Lady but the Gent Don't Go**

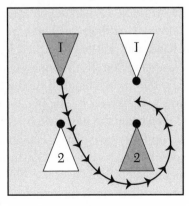

PLATE 60

the man and woman of the opposite couple. Then you just follow what it says. That lady goes all 'round the lady, and the gentle old soul [her partner] follows his partner on the left. After he gets around the lady, the gent stops [in his original position]. Then the lady goes around the gent, but the gent don't go. The girl goes all the way around the other man. So, really, the girl goes through like a figure eight, and she's then back in position. This position brings you back to your original circle of four. You swing your opposite lady; then you circle four; then you shy." [See following instructions of *shy*.]

Ms. Shepherd adds, "Lady around the lady and the gent also and the lady around the gent but the gent don't go—that's still done in foursomes. The lady is going to walk around the lady, and the gent is going to follow her. Now the lady is going to walk around the gent [of the opposite couple], but the gent don't go. So you've done a little figure eight, and we come back and swing our partner. Let's all try that! Lady, walk around the lady and the gent follows. Now the lady around the gent, but the gent don't go. And swing your partner. Lady go around the lady (you split the other couple—you go between 'em). Lady go 'round the lady and the gent, your partner, follows. Now the lady splits that same couple again and goes around the gent, but her partner doesn't follow her this time and she goes back and swings him [her partner]. Oh, yeah!"

## SHY
Mr. Wall explains, "*Shy* means when your lady spins around one time in position. Really everybody shys and spins around in position. If just the men shy, they spin around in position. When you get done, you swing your opposite lady, you swing your partner, and then you circle four."

## DO-SA-DO/DO-SI-DO
Mr. Wall resumes, "The next thing I will talk about is do-sa-do. This is where you break hands—you've got one call where you actually break hands. You take your partner's hand, which is their left hand, in your right hand. You catch it with your left hand and pull her over and let her turn back. She breaks hands with the opposite team. Both couples do this. They hold on to their own girls' hands, and they switch hands from the right to the left hand. Then their left hand turns to their back by steppin' through. They pass each other in the middle and then when the men switch, they drop their partner's hand and hold on to the opposite girl's hand. They make her turn back in; then, when she spins around, she goes through. She turns back around, faced to the inside, and the men face outside. By walkin' through, you can do this. You don't turn around. You walk through the middle. The men switch shoulders over in the middle. Then you break and do the Georgia Rang Tang."

Mr. Kelley gives his version: "You'll face your partner, and you'll pass back to back and come back to where you started; that's called a do-si-do. Pass right shoulders, go past your partner, come back around, and you're facing your partner again. That's do-si-do. Seesaw is like a backwards do-si-do,

**Both dancers move forward until you are back to back.**

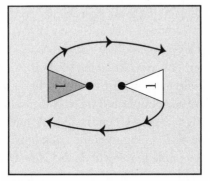

**Stay facing as you are and step around each other.**

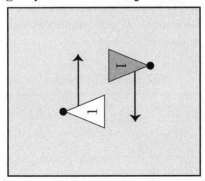

**Pass back to back again and return to your home position.**

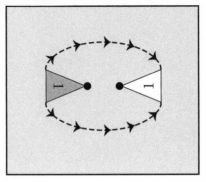

PLATE 61  Do-si-do

where you pass left shoulders. Sometimes it feels more natural to pass left shoulders instead of right shoulders in the course of a dance, so the caller will use the seesaw instead of the do-si-do. So there's 'Circle left, circle right, go to the center, come back out, do-si-do.'"

Ms. Shepherd adds, "Do-si-do and do-sa-do are the same thing here [in this area]. Now with your partner, do-si-do. You pass each other by the right shoulder, you go back to back, you pass by the left shoulder and come back to where you started. Dang, that looks pretty!"

## TAKE A LITTLE PEEK

Ms. Shepherd explains, "What we're going to do is we [the caller and her partner] are going to circle up with these guys here, and we're going to demonstrate. We're the odd couple and we're going to break and go around this couple [the number two couple] on the outside and we're going to take a little peek, and then we're going to come back here and swing our own partner. Now the other couple is going to do the same thing. They are going to go around us [the odd couple] and take a little peek, back to the other side and swing your sweet. Now join hands and circle to the left and whatever else we decide to do. You guys decide amongst yourselves who'll be together. Let's everybody circle up with another couple and practice that. You pick who's going to go first."

## Take a Little Peek

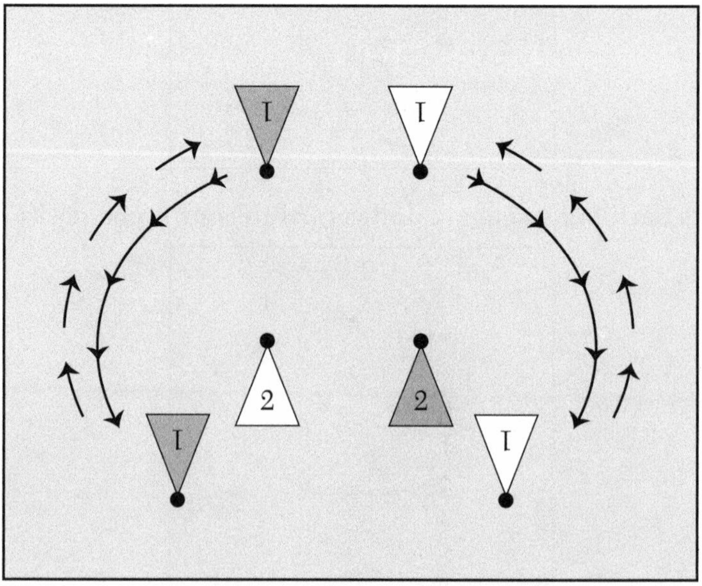

PLATE 62

## THE CALL

Go around that couple and take a little peek.
Come back to your partner; swing your sweet.
Now the other couple, step around and take a little peek.
Run back home and swing your sweet.
With the lady on the right, circle to the left.
Very nice.

## GEORGIA RANG TANG

Mr. Wall shares, "When you do the Georgia Rang Tang, you do it with the opposite lady first. You go around her by holdin' her hand, and you twist her or go all the way around her. Then you come back and meet your partner in the middle. You'll get your partner's hand. You get your partner's left hand in yours with your left hand. Then you go around your partner the same way and come back and meet the opposite lady in the middle; you swing her, and then you swing your partner."

Ms. Shepherd explains further, "To start, you turn your left hand [your corner lady] once. Gentlemen, pass by the right shoulder till you're back to back; turn your partner by the right hand 'round. Gentlemen, pass each other back to back again and turn your corner by the left. Now you could keep doing this again and again. Notice the guys sort of slide back to back each time, and the women stay where they are and keep shooting the guys back in. Typically, it's just a corner-partner-corner, and then you end up with the guys facing out and the women facing in and circling. I don't like it this way so much. I'd rather just have a regular circle and circle and swing our partner, swing our corner, or whatever. Let's go back to our partner's right. We'll roll away with a half sashay to get there. Okay. Again, the Georgia Rang Tang starts like this. We start it off in a circle. We turn our corner by the left; the guys will pass back to back in the middle to reach their partner and turn her by the right. They slide back to back again to turn their corner by the left and then they swing their corner, swing their partner, whatever I tell them to do."

## LARGE CIRCLE DANCES

Sometimes dancers formed a large circle with what Mr. Wall refers to as long calls.

## SWING THE LADY ON YOUR LEFT ALL THE WAY AROUND

Mr. Wall continues, "One of the long calls would be 'Swing the lady on your left all the way around.' This would be done in a big ring. That means you

PLATE 63  For the Georgia Rang Tang, everyone in the square does the movement simultaneously. The man takes his corner lady by her left hand with his left hand . . .

PLATE 64  and turns once.

PLATE 65  Then he takes his partner's right hand with his right hand and turns . . .

PLATE 66  to return to home position to prepare to repeat the move.

[the gent] take the opposite lady [your partner's on the right]. You start swingin' your opposite lady. The men will go on to their left, and the ladies will keep goin' to their right. You swing everybody in the circle until you meet your partner. After you meet your partner, you promenade."

PROMENADE

Mr. Wall explains, "Promenade means that you hold your partner's hands. You hold with two hands overlappin'. You hold them and walk side by side. You know, like when you see people walkin' down the aisle—only they're not holdin' hands, they are side by side. This is about the same way, only you're holdin' the girl's hands. Then you form another big circle."

Mr. Kelley adds, "Promenade is the man will take his partner and walk side by side and hold hands in front like you're promenading down the promenade—the sidewalk—and you'll go around the circle counterclockwise. That's promenade."

Ms. Shepherd continues, "It can be done this way [two hands held in front], this way which is really common in some places [woman's right hand is up to hold the man's right hand, which comes around behind her shoulder, and both partners' left hands hold in front], or it can be done with the gent's right hand on the lady's waist. The lady's left hand is always in front of the gentleman, her hand in his left hand, and the right hand can be in any of three places—the waist, the shoulder, or in front—and you walk around like this together wherever the caller tells you."

PLATE 67 Janet Shepherd and Jay Bland demonstrate
the three common promenade positions.
Ms. Shepherd says, "It can be done this way . . .

PLATE 68  this way . . .

PLATE 69  or this way."

## ELBOW SWING

Mr. Wall describes this type of swing: "The same [forming a big circle] is
true during an elbow swing. You can do this in a pretty small space and in a
small room. The elbow is when you move somebody all the way around. You
start with the opposite lady and you swing only the elbows. You run your
arm through their arm and lock elbows and go opposite; turn one and then
go with another one. When you're in the elbow swing, you hold them in.
The only elbow you keep out is the one you are usin' at the time. If you keep

PLATE 70  Elbow Swing

your elbows out, you're goin' to crack somebody in the head. If you don't hold your elbow in, you'll take somebody up the side of the head, and this is somethin' that's happened to me. You learn to keep your arm down, and you keep the elbows inside. That sounds kind of funny, but it's a good way to do this. Then you swing all the way around, and you meet your partner. Then you promenade again."

## OPEN UP THOSE PEARLY GATES

Mr. Wall delineates the configuration: "Now another call used—and this is a long call—is called Open Up Those Pearly Gates. This is where the lead couple will take their hands together and form a bridge. Then all the other couples have to promenade underneath these. Then as they go under and they form a bridge, you do this till you run out of couples. They, the lead couple, will bend over and go under the whole group. Then everybody else follows them till it's unwound. This takes a good while. It's real beautiful when you get it done. When the lead couple goes underneath the whole bridge, they come out on the other end. The ladies will go to the right, and the gents will go to the left; they cross over. The lady crosses in front of the gent, then you come back up to the original start. You meet your partner, swing her and promenade behind the foldin' gates as it's unfolded. You do

PLATE 71 Arch formed to execute Open Up Those Pearly Gates

this until everybody is done swingin'. Then you start formin' a big circle again."

Mr. Taylor calls this move London Bridge, while Mr. Burrell calls this move Building the Bridge. He explains that in "Buildin' the Bridge [the callers] usually choose the lead couple. The couples will join hands and raise them up. Everyone will go under and join the first couple [to add to the bridge]. This continues until all couples have had an opportunity to go under the bridge."

## TYING THE KNOT/WINDING UP THE BALL

Mr. Wall describes, "The next is to tie the knot. This is where the lead couple goes around inside [the large circle—like a spiral] and keeps tightenin' it up. It will go up about as tight as it can get. Then they start comin' out of this, you know [the leader, now in the center of the tight spiral, 'unwinds' the knot]. By goin' the other way, they can come out of the knot. It looks like you've got people goin' in two different directions. This happens in a circle at one time. This is one of the things that fascinates people who have never seen Mountain-Style Square Dancin'. You call this formation Tying the Knot."

Ms. Shepherd "called" this formation at the Folkways Center square dance. She calls it Winding Up the Clock. In this move, the lead couple breaks from the circle and begins to wind into the circle with everyone following, holding hands. Once the group is in a fairly tight formation, the leader begins to dance back the other way so that, to the viewer, the group looks like a large snake winding in and out. The procedure is similar to playing crack the whip.

Mr. Wall continues, "The other one I was talking about is Windin' Up the Ball, and that's where you hug a girl in the middle. This one is very seldom ever called. It was called a lot at small parties, though."

Mr. Kelley adds, "Well, Tying the Knot, Winding the Ball, that's a kind of a play party thing. When people are in a long line—when you were a kid you used to play crack the whip—one of the things that you do is the leader takes people in a big circle. They'll make a big circle, and they'll make a big spiral and get tighter and tighter and tighter and kind of wind everybody up. Then the leader will go backwards and unwind that circle, so that would be tying people up. You go the other way, and you weave in and out—you tie people in a big knot. That often ends that kind of play party with them having people just in a big knot."

Mr. Burrell adds, "Wind the Clock is a move you can do while square dancin'. You get everybody in a long line or circle holdin' hands, and the caller will choose the front person on the end to start goin' in a circle. They just go right inside the next person, so the spiral will get tighter and tighter as they go in. Then you have to undo it."

## THE LADIES IN THE CENTER, AND THE GENTS GO AROUND TO THE RIGHT

Mr. Wall recalls, "This is somethin' called at parties. I've never seen it called at a big square dance. As for all of the ladies, they put their backs to the center. The gents pull to the right and drop back so many people in the party. You'd drop back one, then another, and another. You'd go all the way around the circle. In the meantime, you'd stop in front of these girls; their partners would either say, 'Look them in the eye, swing her, or fool her.' If the caller said, 'Swing the girl,' then you'd swing her. If they said, 'Promenade,' then you place her in the center again, and you go around. If he says, 'Fool her,' then you place her back right then; you don't swing her or nothin'. You just keep goin' to the right till he [the caller] tells how many to drop back the next time."

## LEFTS AND RIGHTS ALL AROUND

Mr. Wall resumes, "Rights and lefts are all the way around the circle. That's what they have in a big dance. Sometimes the caller will say, 'Put your right hand and left hand in the hands of all the girls around the room,' so you do this. This is called Lefts and Rights All Around."

This dance can be done in a large circle or a small circle. The lead man begins by moving around the circle taking the left hand of the first person he meets, the right hand of the second person, the left hand of the third, and so on until he reaches his original position.

## SWING YOUR PARTNER

Mr. Wall contends, "There is a right and a wrong way to swing your partner. You've got to get them back to a certain position in a circle. You've got to turn them loose so they won't be on the opposite side from their partner. You should be close to your partner when you turn your other partner loose to where she'll be close to her partner, when you swing her. This is true for even when you do the Georgia Rang Tang. You come right back to where there is no distance between the two couples. Your partner should be right next to you; then you turn your corner partner loose, and she'll be next to her partner. If you swing right, it will end up right. All it takes is learnin' to swing your partner the right way."

Mr. Kelley describes various swings: "The other thing that we do all the time is swing. When you swing your partner, you can swing by the elbows—hook right elbows and swing. You can swing in a ballroom position: The man puts his left hand out with his right hand around her waist, and the lady does the opposite. Then you just walk around the circle. Kind of the old-fashioned Georgia way is to join both hands out in front of you and hold them down low [and close to the body]; then you kind of lean back a little bit and go around the circle like when you were a kid."

PLATE 72 The ballroom position commonly
used to swing your partner

PLATE 73 The old-fashioned Georgia way to swing your partner

## THE VIRGINIA REEL

The Virginia Reel is actually an old contra dance that originated in the New England area and drifted down to the Appalachian Mountains with the expansion of transportation and the need for many of the mountain people to head north in search of work during the Depression. Ms. Shepherd leads a crowd through this relatively simple dance done with a large group in two lines. She calls, "We may do what we call a contra dance later on tonight. That's something that moved down this way from New England a number of decades ago. In contra dancing, you're supposed to switch partners each time you dance. I think we're going to start off tonight with a nice old-fashioned Virginia Reel. So everybody who feels like it—and that means everybody—come on out here and grab a partner. It doesn't matter if it's a lady or a gentleman. It can be the same gender, can be opposite gender, can be whatever you want. I need one couple right here. I need other couples lining up right below them. Gent over on this side [on the right of the caller] and the lady over on that side [the left of the caller]. All the gents in a line on this side over here and all the ladies in a line right here. We're going to start off with a nice old-fashioned Virginia Reel that you may have done when you were in grade school long ago. To begin this dance, we're going to shake hands along our lines and know that you

PLATE 74  The Virginia Reel starts in with couples in two long lines.

are connected with a bunch of other folks and not just boogying around by yourself. As you're shaking hands, I preach a lot about what we call 'giving good weight.' What that means is keeping your arms bent, having some connections, some give-and-take, some friendly firmness in your whole bodies so that you know that you're dancing with a bunch of other people and that you are not just floppin' around in outer space. So in these nice long lines, I want you to go forward and back. Very nice, now your partner is straight across from you. Give your partner your right hand, palm to palm, thumbs up allemande style, sort of like you're going to arm wrestle, only don't hurt each other. You want some friendly firmness in your whole bodies there. You want some tension there to help each other move around. I want you to turn your partner by the right one time 'round and go back where you started—end up where you started. Now give them the left hand; go the other way back. Now with your partner do-si-do. You pass each other by the right shoulder, you go back to back, you pass by the left shoulder and come back to where you started. Dang, that looks pretty! That's enough things to start off with. Now, these folks up here, they get to be the active couple, and they get to do all kinds of cool stuff to start off with. They are going to start by turning each other by the right elbow one and a half times around so that they trade places. And when they do, look—they've each got somebody of the opposite gender to go to. So you're each going to turn someone of the opposite gender by the left elbow. Come back, you two [the lead couple], and turn each other by the right elbow.

PLATE 75  Turn your partner by the right hand 'round.

Same active couple, work your way down the line. Turn your partner by the right elbow, somebody else [of your opposite gender] by the left elbow, and work it down. Keep on going till you get all the way down to the bottom. And when you get down to the bottom, you turn each other halfway or once and a half—whatever floats your boat—till you get back on the side where you started. Take two hands with each other and sashay right on back. You've done this before! The gent goes off to the left, the lady goes off to the right, and y'all play follow the leader and follow 'em on down till you get down to the bottom there. Peel off. Now, when you two [lead couple] get down there, you make an arch. Everybody else, scoot up under the arch and come all the way up front, and lookie . . . we've got a new head couple. Now, the nice thing about this kind of dancing is that it doesn't necessarily have to take as long as some of the phrases of the music might. It's just a good way to get some rhythmic action going and have some fun at it. Since they've [the lead couple] already done it once before, we're going to start the dance with you two. You get to be the guinea pigs, but everybody will get the chance to do it at least one time, maybe more than that. This is a good old-fashioned Virginia Reel, and these [the band] are the Dog Tags. I may tell you everything to do, or I may reach a point where I stop telling you what to do and you will know what to do because you've already done it. We're going to go forward and back, allemande right, allemande left; we're gonna do-si-do, and then we get to do that elbow stuff that's way fun; so let's do it!" [Music starts, and Ms. Shepherd begins.]

PLATE 76  Sashay back to the top of the line.

PLATE 77  The top couple makes an arch for the
other couples to duck under.

PLATE 78  When all couples have ducked under,
there is a new top couple to start the figure again.

## THE CALL

Take hands in your long lines.
We're going to go forward and back.
With your partner, allemande right
And back by the left.
Now do-si-do your partner.
Top couple, take right arms.
Come on back now out to the side—
Partner by the right; friend by the left.
Move it on down; work it on down.
Scoot on back home.
Now follow the leader.
Make an arch and come on through.
Now long lines and swing your partner.
[Repeat this process until every couple has had a chance to take the lead.]

## THE SHOOFLY SWING

Ms. Shepherd shares a dance that was common to the Appalachian region but that may have gone by another name or names in earlier times: "Now the old tradition up in the Appalachian Mountains is that they would do these kind of dances all night long, and they would add more complex figures to them and do some really cool stuff throughout the course of the evening. I learned a move that I thought was one of the wildest, craziest things I ever saw, and so I'd like to try that with you guys. Everybody join hands in a great big ring and circle to the left and the other way back to the right. Now, we're gonna start off with this lady right here [the lead lady]. I want you to turn your partner by the left hand like this—allemande style. Turn him by the left hand around. Now go to that man [the next man in the ring] and turn him by the right, and you [her gent] follow her but don't turn anybody. Come back to your partner and turn him by the left and then go on to the next guy around the circle and turn him by the right. So you're [the gent] going to escort her all the way around the circle, taking her to every other man. Turn your partner by the left. This is very much like what we did in the Virginia Reel. Now then, when you get back home, now you [the next couple] get to start. This is called the Shoofly Swing. Now what we may do is, once one couple gets about three or four couples along, the next couple can start. In a group this small, we may not want to have more than one couple going at once. So you turn your partner by the left—left-hand 'round—and he's going to send you off to that man and you're going to turn him by the right. Now you're going to go back to your partner. You go left to your partner each time 'round and then go to the nice man on the side. Go back to your partner by the left, and then he'll let you go on to the next guy—back to your partner with the left hand and to the next guy with your right hand over here. Come back home and give your partner a great big hug. So all the ladies will get a chance to do this, and, then, as they say in Lakemont [Georgia], where I was last week, 'Turnabout is fair play.' They get kind of rough with some of these turns. I mean, those guys would sling 'em on to the next one and sling 'em back out! I'll just tell you to be as gentle or as exuberant as you care to be."

### THE CALL

Join hands! Circle to the left and back to the right.
Go in to the middle and come back out.
Do that again.
Now, starting with the lady who had practice, Shoofly Swing!
Partner by the left and side by the right.
Back to your partner and someone on the side.
Partner and then a gent on the outside.
Partner and back to the outside.
[Repeat to home position.]
Now, your [next couple] turn.
Partner by the left and side by the right.
[Repeat through all the couples.]
Promenade your partner back home.
Partner by the right,
Lady by the left.
[Repeat all the way around.]
While they're going home, you two [next couple] get started.
While they're working their way home, you [next couple] go for it.
[After all couples have taken a turn at this around the circle,]
Promenade your partner.
Okay. Are y'all ready for turnabout is fair play?
Join hands and circle to the left with the lady on the right.
Back to the right.
Into the middle and do it again.
Gentlemen, are you ready?
Swing your partner by the right;
Swing the lady [outside lady] by the left.
Next couple, go!
Take your partner and promenade on out.
Promenade up this way!

## OVER AND UNDER

When Ms. Shepherd shared this dance with the square dancers at the Folkways Center, I had the opportunity to partner with a nice young fellow and my young daughter. The dance starts in two long lines divided, like the Virginia Reel, by gender. After performing various common moves, ladies and gents peel off in lines to get ready to form an arch as in the Virginia Reel. Rather than forming an arch, each couple moves to the sides while still holding hands in the middle. Couples move alternately by raising their hands over the heads of another couple and then passing under the hands of the next and so on to the end of the line. This repeats several times so that every couple has a chance to be the top or lead couple.

## THE BUNNY HOP

Mr. Wall recounts, "The Bunny Hop got introduced to this region when Mr. Ramey had the Mountain City Playhouse. We used to have the Bunny Hop and maypole dancin' in school. Back in the 1930s, we had some Bunny Hops in school. They would get faster and faster."

To perform the Bunny Hop, dancers formed a long line with hands on the hips or shoulders of the preceding person. Once the Bunny Hop music started, dancers put their right heels out and in two times while slightly hopping on the opposite foot. Repeat this move with the left heel. Then on both feet hop forward once, back once, and forward three times. The dance would then repeat as the music became faster and faster.

## SAMPLE CALLS

Mr. Kelley shares one of his favorite calls to get dancers started:

Everybody jump up and never come down.
Circle left around the town.
Circle right, and everybody go home
And settle down.
Face your corner; left allemande.
Go right in to a right and left grand.
Every other girl, every other hand,
Meet your partner, promenade.
Take her home and swing.
Couple number one, bow and swing.
Lead on out to the right of the ring.
Couple number two, visit couple number three
Couple number two, move on to four.

[Then it would be couple number three's turn and then couple number four's turn, and then you take a break to end.]

You'll promenade your partner right off the floor.
That's all there is.
There is no more.

Ms. Shepherd shared a couple of calls that she commonly uses:

### Call 1

Circle to the left.
Now left-hand star
Swing your corner.
Swing your own partner.
Odd couple, move on to another couple and get ready to start.
Birdie in the cage.
Bird hop out; crow hop in.
Swing your corner.
And a right-hand star.
Now turn it to the right.
Swing your partner.
Odd couples, move on off.
[Repeats this several more times.]
Now's the time,
Swing your corner.
Swing your partner.
Everyone, swing your own.

### Call 2

Circle to the left, back to the right.
Now with your partner, promenade.
Odd couples, move up to a couple and circle to the left.
Left hand star,
The other way back,
Two hands across,
Ladies bow,
Gents know how,
And basket swing!
Break out to a ring and circle to the left.
Swing your corner,

And swing your partner.
Swing your partner.
Odd couples, move on to the next and circle to the left.
Lady around the lady, and the gent follow.
Odd couples, move on to another and circle to the left.
[Call repeats.]
Run around and take a little peek,
Come back on home and swing your sweet.
Now, the other couple, step on 'round, take a little peek,
Come back home, and swing your sweet.
Lady on the right and circle to the left.
Swing your corner and swing your own.
Move on to the next and circle to the left.
Put the birdie in the cage.
Bird hop out, and crow hop in.
Swing your corner.
Now lady around the lady, but the gent don't go!
Swing your partner.
Now break that swing.
[Repeat to end of dance.]

---

*References*

Casey, Betty. *The Complete Book of Square Dancing [and Round Dancing]*. Garden City, NY: Doubleday and Company, 1976.

Martin, Bill. www.bubbaguitar.com. 7 July 2003.

# CRAFTS

"Workin' my own business . . . is just like a vacation year 'round."

*—Arthur Speed*

There was a time in our nation's history when instrument makers, wood-carvers, and potters were an integral part of most communities. While most considered those people artisans, their works were also utilitarian. Without them there would have been no music for dancing, beds for sleeping, or crocks for storing food. The major difference in the artisans of old and their modern-day equivalents is that the current artisans do what they do because they want to, not because they have to or because the community needs their creations to continue functioning.

Steve Turpin began his trade as a production potter, turning out row upon row of identical pots. He found this work monotonous and in his heart longed to be more creative. He courageously chose to follow his heart's desire, and although he got off to a less-than-stellar start, he has since become acclaimed as a unique and creative potter, as well as a kind and generous person.

Arthur Speed is a man who whittled all his life. After years of toil in a factory and a few other tedious positions, Mr. Speed chose to pursue his vision of having his weekend hobby, wood carving, become his profession. He said, "I'm really interested in what I've got goin' and just can't wait to get back to it. Now that's the way to make a livin' . . . You can force yourself to do something, but you're not enjoyin' it until you stir up some inspiration." His finesse at taking an ordinary object and creating an exquisite wooden likeness of it is inspiring!

John Huron is another craftsman who came to his chosen profession later in life. What started out as an attempt to be an authentic Civil War reenactor turned into a career change for him, and along the way he met and was tutored by some of the best instrument makers around—Robert Mize and Ellis Wolfe. John told us, "I feel I've been given a level of mountain instrument-building knowledge equivalent to a Yale law degree." When John discusses his instrument making, his eyes light up, his voice becomes animated, and his love for his craft becomes immediately obvious. John builds banjos, dulcimers, mouth-bows, and other traditional mountain instruments. His love for his craft and his skilled artisanship has placed him at the forefront of modern-day instrument makers.

Dwayne Thompson became interested in furniture building while in high school. He pursued more knowledge about the subject in trade school. For a while he worked for a furniture company designing furniture and building prototypes. Eventually he decided to start his own business, the Timpson Creek Gallery. Today he is a recognized and respected artisan who professes, "I can pretty well do it like I want to do it." He attributes his success to the fact that he keeps learning and improving on his craft.

Tubby Brown began producing artwork late in life, after his retirement from the grocery store business. He looked for something to do, started making "stuff," and liked what he was doing. Then he discovered that galleries and customers appreciated his art also. With no formal training, Mr. Brown is a folk artist. Many collect his inspiring, creative, and whimsical pieces, not only for their value but also for their charm.

These craftspeople share numerous traits. They are unique, ingenious, inspiring artists. They are creative visionaries whose talent, workmanship, and genuine dedication to excellence are evident in every piece they create. Most important, they are willing to share their knowledge so that their craft and their artistry will continue long after them.

*—Kaye Carver Collins*

# A DEVILISHLY CREATIVE POTTER—
# STEVE TURPIN

*"To be a potter, you have to have two things:*
*a strong back and a weak mind."*

Pottery is a very popular craft. It has been featured previously in *Foxfire 8* and *Foxfire 10*. In fact, some form of pottery works exists in almost every small town in North Georgia. The pottery created ranges from large pieces to little mugs. Many pieces are unique because of their mediums, forms, or decorations; therefore, each individual artifact is a representation of each artist's individuality.

Steve Turpin represents a newer generation of potters. While Steve Turpin's work is based on the traditions and customs passed from one generation of folk potters to the next, his is a unique and creative pursuit. While he does traditional dinnerware and other popular pieces, he is neither afraid of change nor hesitant to create new pieces. Though his pottery-making is a business, his passion for his work and his creativity have inspired unusual examples of pottery as art. Turpin has become well known for his face jugs, especially his Siamese Devil Jug. He has also created pieces commemorating the tragedy of September 11.

Foxfire first met Steve at a local craft show. We found him to be an extremely warm and hospitable man whose work and personality are inspiring. After meeting Steve Turpin, perhaps you too will feel inspired to try your hand at the wheel or to possess your own devil jug.

—*Jared Weber*

I'M STEVE TURPIN and I'll be forty-four years old this year. I grew up in the town of Gillsville. My family background? Well, they's just farmin' people. When I came to Homer, I met my wife, Kathy, in high school. One thing led to another, and we got married. She lived *here* so I had to get away from *there*. I could not stand bein' there anymore. It just worked out that her folks gave us this land here, and that's how I got over here.

I didn't know what pottery was. When I graduated from high school, I

PLATE 79  Steve Turpin and his daughter, Abby,
display some of their creations.

thought I was going to go to college, but college wasn't for me. While I was
in high school, I worked with Craven Pottery over in Gillsville as a laborer.
He wanted to expand his business in the handmade pottery division. So
when I graduated from high school, the opportunity came up, and my two
brothers tried it. He asked me if I'd like to, and in the first week he had me
makin' production. As far as my background goes, it is in production pottery.
I'm not an art potter. I'm a production potter. I was a member of the management team over there for seventeen years. I always dreamed of doin' the
folk pottery.

I managed Craven's handmade division for seventeen years. I got out of
management with him in 1992. I did continue to work for him until 2000
and then I left and I came home. During my time as manager of the handmade division, the University of Georgia, once a quarter or semester, would
bring their art classes up to our pottery. My job was to show 'em around;
now I'm a potter too. You get all these kids in there; and when Jerry Shapel
was the professor down there, his famous sayin' was—at least I think it's
famous—he'd bring 'em in and they'd see what we had done, you know, in
two or three hours of work, and they'd be sittin' there and say, "We can't do
that in a month," and he'd tell 'em: "That's production." What would take
them ten minutes to do, we made ten in that ten minutes. Not sayin' that
ours was better or theirs, we were right or they were right—we're not sayin'

that. You know, it's just the techniques. So everybody has their own form—
how they do things. There's nothin' wrong with formal training if that's what
you want to call it, but as far as I'm concerned, I don't want it. I don't want
to do your work. And that's what I would be doin' because they're training
me to do their work. I'm trainin' to do what I want to do. I'm showin' my
expression. Sure, a lot of the time, now, I'd be a lot better off if I would
watch somebody. I wouldn't lose as much stuff, mixing glazes. Glaze is an
art. In order to get one glaze, I worked on it for nine months before I got it
to where I was satisfied with it, but experience is the best teacher.

In 1974, I met Lanier Meaders [see *Foxfire 8*, pages 81–209]. Lanier
Meaders was a gentleman who had a very dry sense of humor. He walked in
over at Craven's one day, and I hadn't been makin' pottery long, and his
sense of humor is, oh gosh, he'd cut you in half. But that was Lanier Meaders. After I got to know him, I cherished being around him. But in 1974, I
could've bought a face jug for twenty dollars at the most. That's if you come
in in a Cadillac and he wanted to stick it to y'. If you come in in an old beat-
up truck and he felt sorry for you, you could probably buy it for eight or ten
dollars. But now if you come in in a Cadillac or a Mercedes, one or the
other, you'd better be ready to open the billfold up. But now, that was
Lanier Meaders. That's the way he was.

> "Oh, I started makin' a bunch of face jugs, and they was some of
> the god-awfulest things you'd ever seen in your life."

I always liked what the Meaders did. At work they wouldn't let us do anything like that, especially me bein' in management. In September 1992, I
resigned my position as manager. In July 1993, I came home and bought me
a little wheel and a little kiln and started in my basement. That's when I
started makin' pottery. Makin' the pot was boring. I was going to be the next
Lanier Meaders! Oh, I started makin' a bunch of face jugs, and they was
some of the god-awfulest things you'd ever seen in your life. I can't believe I
made 'em, but I went to a show. Oh, I was gonna get thirty dollars apiece,
which thirty dollars was a good price then. I brought every one of 'em home.

But I didn't realize one thing. I had went from a flowerpot to art. So that's
when I started making bowls and pitchers. I wanted to make pottery—that's
the only thing I could sell. I said, "Well, I priced my face jugs too high."
Well, everybody else was getting fifty and seventy-five dollars for one, and I
couldn't even get thirty. About four years ago, there 'as a gentleman come in
here, and he said, "I like your work. I want to know if you'll let me help you."
I said, "Sure." You talking about a deal on face jugs, now that man got a deal
on some face jugs! I sold him some face jugs for ten dollars apiece just to get

rid of 'em 'cause they'd been here two years. Well, about eight months ago, I went to a little auction right up in Mountain City [Georgia] . . . those face jugs I sold for ten dollars sold for three hundred and eighty-five dollars! The gentleman asked me how I felt about that. I told him I hated it. He said, "Why do you hate it?" I said, "Man, I got ten dollars for the dern things!" But see, it helps you build a name and a reputation. Ever' one of my pieces are signed. This piece here, older pieces like this one, I sell 'em for a hundred dollars now. These pieces will bring a hundred and fifty to a hundred and seventy-five dollars now. That's two to three years old. Thanks to folks that have taken and helped me, I have built my name and reputation.

It has grown from there, and it has not been easy. Making the pieces is easy for me with my background in the production pot. The decoratin' and all is somethin' that has taken, right now, a little over six years to get where I am, and I'm nowhere near where I want to be yet. I have not made a piece at home, since I've started, that I've been satisfied with yet. I always see somethin' wrong with it. It started as a hobby in my basement; then I moved into a little ol' shed that I had behind my house. I've had to build onto it twice.

I enjoy working with my hands. When I first started at home, I wanted to be the next Lanier Meaders. Well, that didn't work. I made some items and went to some shows, and I couldn't sell 'em. So I got in the dinnerware line of pottery. I started makin' bowls and pitchers and things like that, then made churns and just kept makin' 'em. And then when I was doin' the draws to pull the churn up, I'd start seein' things. I'd see a face on it and know exactly how to put it on. Well, the next one I'd make, I'd see it again. Then I made a little thing called a Rebecca pitcher, and the way it closed up, I said, "Wait a minute!" Y' know, you put the spout on it, and y' put the handle on it. I said, "I'll make a chicken." It's hard to explain. It's really, really weird. I don't do it because I have to. I do it because I want to. What I do here is stress relief. I can be stressed out, and I can come down here and turn on the potter's wheel, make a few pieces, and sit down and start decorating. You can give me thirty minutes to an hour, and I'm at ease again. It's just somethin' that I really love.

A lot of people do face jugs, and a lot of people will put two faces on the jug. What they do is, they take and put one face on one side and a face on the other side. They call them the politician jugs. Well, for probably a couple of years, I made a piece I called the boss's jug. I called him Bossy. I'd put a frown on one side, and on the other side I would put a smiley face. And you know what everybody says? "That's not a bossy. That's a politician jug," because that's what everybody calls it. I said, "Okay, well, we need to do somethin' a little different." So one day I was down here, and I was puttin' the eyes and nose and all on the jug and was about to put the mouth on it. I said, "Wait a minute! I need to do somethin' different." I had made an upside-down jug, and I had made a regular face jug, and they were sittin' side by side. The idea just came from looking at those two pieces to make a face jug with one on the top and one on the bottom and put a mouth in between and let the mouth join the piece. So I made one of those and got to sittin' back; the more I looked at it, the more I liked it. I kept wonderin' what to call it. So I finally came up with a name, and I called it my Siamese jug. I make a regular face jug where you just got a regular face on the top and bottom. The one I really like to make is one I call the Siamese Good Me. On the top I make a devil and put little horns on. Now I don't attach the horns separately. I let the eyebrows run around the eyes, and then I curl the horns up on the end of the eyebrows and try to put sort of a pointed eye on him. On the bottom I try to put a face, a regular face that, you know, you'd like to look at. A lot of people don't like looking at the devil, but when you put the two together and get to thinkin' about good and evil, it'd be in a Siamese jug. It brings out a little bit of the good and bad in all of us. You know, all of us got good and bad. So, personally, that devil's a reflection of me bein' bad. But on the bottom here, hey, I know I got good in me, too. The Siamese is my prized one. The next one is . . . I make a one-piece rooster. I put a foot on him, bring him up, and put the tail on him. The rooster is the second favorite piece that I make.

If I get any spare time, I do school groups. Boy Scouts come every year, and I teach them their pottery merit thing. They have to slow me down because I get into this and think everybody knows all that I know, or think I know. I get to talkin' too fast, and they don't understand me. They have to say, "Now, wait a minute. What do you mean by that?"

The working dynamics of a potter's wheel includes a head block. On that shaft, this is the top part where you take and you throw the clay down. The head block is the very top of a potter's wheel. Then there is a potter's rib. All it is is a flat piece of metal with a hole in it. I'll show you the purpose of that in a little while. For college-educated potters, they take and they throw the clay. For us, we turn. The actual process we use while we're makin' the pot, we call it turnin'. They call it throwin', but now we do throw also. When we take and mess that thing up, we take and grab that, and we'll slam it somewhere and let it hit somethin'. That's our throwin'. Now, it is the same process. We use the same process that they do; we just call it a different thing.

To make one of those pieces, I will need about five pounds of clay. It comes processed in twenty-five-pound bags. I don't have the room to take and mix my own clay. If I had the money to buy the equipment to mix my own clay, I wouldn't make pottery. If you're gonna do it right, you're talkin' probably $40,000 a machine for quite a few machines. That should be about five or six pounds.

This clay comes de-aired, meanin' that it's been run through a pump mill that has a vacuum on it that gets all the air out of it. If you don't get the air out of the clay, when you take some and try to make a piece you're gonna have a hole somewhere. Now, to get this ready, I'm gonna knead dough. If you took this piece right here and you tried to put it on the wheel the way it is, you will get an air bubble in the bottom of the pot. To take and keep that from doin' that, all I take and do is just put a little mound right on the bottom of the pot. Now, this serves a purpose. When you throw it down on the head block, the mound hits first and all air is dispersed out. If you don't do that, if you threw this down, all these little holes, there's gonna be an air pocket. Everywhere there's an air pocket, it's just like a little bubble in the clay. You get an air bubble in the clay; if you don't get it out, it will explode in the firing process.

I buy my clay out of California and the other comes out of Pennsylvania. Well, the difference is the processing, and a lot of the clay that the Meaders use is Lizella. Lizella is what that jug's made out of right there. It's a terra-cotta clay, meaning that once that piece in there, if you didn't know it, when that piece is fired, it's gonna be terra-cotta. It's gonna be orange.

I wanna show you how to make a pot. I want you to pay real close attention. I will tell you every step, and then I'm gonna let you make one. I'm gonna see how good you are, and when you take and get mad and don't wanna do it anymore, I'll show you how to do it. Have you ever made a pot before?

I've got my piece of clay now, and all I'm going to do is start pushing down on the clay and kneading it just like you would if you were making biscuits. If you've ever seen your mama make biscuits, or maybe you have yourself, when you get the dough mixed up, you have to knead the dough. Kneading the clay like you do the dough, it helps work the air out of it. You have to work it up. When you get the air out of it, you round it up, and the rounder you get the clay here, the easier it is when you start on the wheel, and you want to try to get it as round as possible. You just cannot throw a flat piece of clay down on a potter's wheel and hope it'll stick. You have to put a little hump on the bottom of it.

Now we're ready to get on the wheel. I turn on a vat. A vat is just a piece of plastic that we cut around. When I get done making the piece, I never touch it until it comes loose. You throw the clay down on the wheel and use the secret ingredient, water. If you don't keep water on the clay, it will slide through your hands and grab, and you'll tear it apart. A lot of people watch potters make pottery. We make it look pretty easy. It's sort of like riding a bicycle. Once you learn, you know. The secret to making a piece of pottery is bracing your cutoff while you're centering the piece of clay. You want to get the clay centered on the head block of the potter's wheel, and you want to start pushing the clay down on the inside. The way I do it, I take the heel of my hand and push it down to put my bottom in the piece. When I get it good and smooth, I will do what I call a pull-up. I take and trim this little ledge off down at the bottom. If you don't, the bottom will be really thick on it. You have to settle the top down. The way you settle the top down is, you let the clay run between your fingers. All you're doin' is just pushin' back down on the clay to seal it up. Now I'm going to do what we call a knuckle draw. I take my knuckles and start on the outside and pull in clay, and I put my other hand inside. Then I run my hand like this. You just start right down there, and now we're doin' a knuckle draw. Now the clay really looks like it has grown. Do it again. Now I'm goin' to take this flat piece of metal here. The proper name for it is a rib, but we call it a chip. With it, I'm going to do the same thing as I do with a knuckle draw, but I'm going to do it with my chip. I'm goin' to try to pull more clay off the bottom and then start smoothin' it up with it. When you start at the bottom of a piece with a chip, you use the bottom of the chip. When you start comin' up to the middle of the piece, you use the middle of the chip, and when you get to the top, you should be using the top part of the chip. You don't just use one part of the chip from top to bottom.

**"If you know the steps and will pay attention, you can do it; but if you don't, all you're gonna make's a mess."**

PLATE 80 Centering the clay on the head block
while pushing down on the inside

PLATE 81  Performing a knuckle draw
to form the shape of the jug

Settle the clay down and add a little more water; then take the chip again
and do the same thing. Basically, what I'm doin' now is just smoothin' the
piece up real good. Then I'm goin' to take me a sponge and get the water
out of it. There is a lot of things you do that doesn't make sense. I threw all
the water on it; now I'm gettin' all the water off of it. You have to have the
water in order for it to do right. Then I will close the top on it. Take the chip
and trim this top end here. I want to get the excess water off the outside
with a sponge. And that's all you do to make a jug. I'm not goin' to touch that
piece again until it's completely dry, and then I will trim the edge off the
bottom and put my name and date on the bottom of it. I will not pick the
piece up by [grasping] the piece. I do it on the vat.

Now, I've just shown you everything I have learned in the past twenty-
nine years. That's how much I've learned. I don't mean to be mean by what
I'm fixin' to do. I want to prove a point to you. It's like ridin' a bicycle or writing an article. If you know the steps and will pay attention, you can do it; but
if you don't, all you're gonna make's a mess. All you're gonna do is make a
mess. What I did was, I took this arm and put it here [on one side of the
wheel], and I took this one and put it here, and I made the clay do the givin'
with my hands. I did not let my hands do this [move with the wheel]. Now,
just get relaxed. It's just like driving a car. You're sittin' behind the wheel.
This is the steering wheel [the head block] . . . your gas pedal. The only dif-

PLATE 82 and PLATE 83
Shaping the piece

PLATE 84  Closing the top of the jug

ference is you're gonna be mashin' it with your left foot. When you take and go down a straight [away], you can fly. When you get to a curve, you'd better slow down. Roundin' the piece up, you're in a straight, but once you quit roundin' it up, you better start slowin' it down because you're hittin' curves.

We've got the piece made; now what I'm goin' to start doin' is decoratin' it. I'm goin' to take the jug and change it from a whiskey jug into a Siamese Devil Jug. Now all we do is get us a hunk of clay, and then I will sit here and just roll it around. Try to get the clay in a round ball. Then I will start with my hands and roll it like this. I'll roll it out to where it looks like a snow cone. It is a funny-lookin' snow cone, but you know it resembles one. Then the water's the secret again. Make the nostrils in it. I take it with my fingers and lay it down. I push in with my finger; then I come here on the top and start makin' it look somethin' like a nose. Now, you don't want to get much water on the back. Anytime you do a 3-D effect on the clay—3-D meanin' a three-dimensional effect where you're takin' and addin' somethin' to a piece—the piece that you're puttin' on can have no little dimples in it. If you leave a spot the size of the head of a pencil in the middle of this, when you get it sealed down good, that little air pocket in there will blow the whole piece off. You have to be very careful not to get that in it. Once you get it to where it's all smooth, you just lay the piece on there

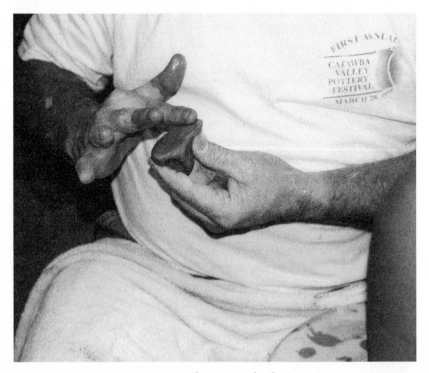

PLATE 85  Making a nose for the jug

PLATE 86  Placing a nose on the evil half of the jug

and push it down. Take your thumbs and just start workin' the clay. Now, what I will do is start at the top of the nose or the bottom of the nose. When you do that, you stick it good and you get it down on both ends all the way down. If there is any air that gets trapped, you push it straight out of the top. Just do the same thing on the other side and get it where it's stickin' good and get it where you've got it smoothed out pretty good. Then we come back and wet our fingers with water and just smooth our finger marks out of the nose. You don't go real hog wild on it, but you try to get it all out to where it's relatively smoothed. And the next step is, once we get that, to take this little stick and make the nostrils. You just put it up in there, and you roll it around. Now for the bottom nose, I don't use as much clay, probably about two-thirds of what you put on the top. Ninety percent of the time, you've got more evil in y' than you've got good. So you try to make that reflect in the piece. The nose, the eyeballs, everything on the top part is normally a little bit larger than the bottom is. You go through the same process on the bottom nose. You then try as good as you can to get the bottom nose where the top nose is. The bottom face is harder to do than the top one because, really, you need to stand on your head to do it. But after you do 'em a little while, you can feel with your hands and your fingers and all till you know when you've got it and when you haven't. Now what

PLATE 87  Positioning the bottom nose on the jug

I will do is, I will come back. Both noses are a little rough, but I am not done with them yet. What I wanted to do is get them smoothed down good and get 'em to where they are gettin' pretty smooth.

Now I take my two thumbs, and I push in the jug. I do the same thing down here, and that's where I'm goin' to put my eyeballs. I have to get a different clay, so I'm usin' white clay for my eyeballs and my teeth. Get a piece of white clay and roll it out in a little tube. I will make two of 'em round, and then I just roll 'em out. I always put the top eyes at an angle to where I can put my eyebrows and eyelashes on it so it looks like it is coming down at that angle. That is on the top. On the bottom I just put these round little pieces and make my eyeballs out of that. The features are smaller on the bottom than they are on the top. Then we will take this clay and roll it into a point, and we'll break it off. Then you just take two pieces of clay, round 'em up, make 'em oblong, take your thumb, and mash 'em down.

I don't go to a lot of trouble of makin' the teeth look like human teeth. They're not human. The more whimsical you can make the teeth and everything on it, the better I like it. Some people will try to make teeth like in a human's mouth. I put the devil's fangs on and curve them around to where they are goin' to the inside of the mouth. Now we're just goin' to put two little flat rounded teeth on the bottom for the good guy. If you want to make 'em buckteeth, you can make 'em buckteeth. Each one, I do a little somethin' different on it. Of all the pieces I have made, there is no two that look the same.

PLATE 88 Creating the eyeballs

Now I am ready to start on the eyeballs. Roll out a piece of clay, probably about an inch and a half to two inches long. Then I will cut it and break it in half. There you start to work it down just like you did the nose. I kinda make a little point at the nose. Put water on it and smooth him down pretty good and then go to the other side and do the same thing. I always try and finish the top part before I finish the bottom. Then I put my horns on the top. We got 'em stuck down, and I'm rubbin' them down with water to smooth them out. Then I take my finger, right around the eyeball, and push up on the clay to where it looks like his eyeballs are kicked up. Then I take the ends that are hangin' over and bend 'em over to make the horns. Then we go to the bottom of the piece. Start workin' on the eyeballs here and just take and round the piece up about the size of a pencil. On the bottom, for the eyebrow, I do the same as the top. The only thing is, I don't make it as long. The bottom face is by far the hardest to take and get it the way you want. It's hard to see, so you do a lot of feelin' about what you're doin'. Basically, everything you do on the jug is just repetitive work. You take and roll the mouth just like you did the eyebrows. And then you just take and stick the mouth on. We'll try to make him like he's smilin' today.

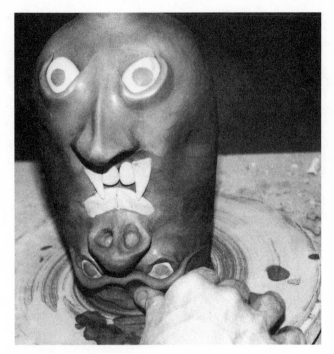

PLATE 89  The teeth

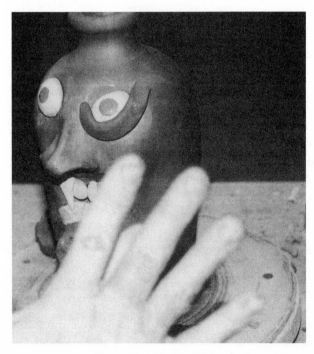

PLATE 90  Placing the clay around the upper eyes

PLATE 91 The horns are positioned on the jug.

Once we get it laid down there, we take our fingers and push it out. Then take our water and smooth it up. I start back at the eyeball and start pushin' the clay in to give him some cheeks on the face jug. Do the same thing for the bottom, and then you just stick it on there and try to make 'em meet. Once you do that, you start at the center of the mouth and start pushin' the clay and stickin' it good to the piece. Start at the center and work out at both sides. Get it roughed and take the water and smooth it up. You have to watch right around the nose where the mouth joins it. If you're not careful, you'll leave a little spot there, and they will come off. As long as you don't let the clay get too hard and don't let air get under the pieces, they should stay on. On the bottom, I do not try to make his cheeks as big as the top.

Now we have the ears. We do the ears the same way as we did the rest. We run one end to a point. I take and tear my clay in half. I start right below its horn and attach the devil's ear. Start workin' the ears to where it looks rounded. Indent the pot a little bit to where it's got a definition in it to where it looks like an ear. Do the same thing for the other ear. You use your finger and thumb on the ear. Then try to get it as smooth as possible without using water. It just makes it easier. Then I start wiggling my thumb in circles and work it out the back of the ear. Now we've got to put the regular ear on the bottom.

PLATE 92  Creating the mouth

As far as this piece goes, we are basically done. There's two other things I do to it. I have to put a handle on it. To put a handle on, just take a big piece of clay. We're going to make a large snow cone this time. Just roll this piece of clay out and put a little water on it. I stick it to the rim of the jug itself, startin' again workin' from one side to the other. Rub it all down on top and bottom. You have to keep the clay wet. Then you just slowly start pullin' the handle. Let it run through your fingers and pull the handle out. When you get it about where you'd think you'd need it, stick it down on the jug. Now the other thing that I do to the jug is what we will see in the finished product. We use really "sophisticated" tools. I use a fork, comb, and even a toothbrush to decorate with. A toothbrush will make a real fine scratch on a piece; a comb is more coarse; a fork is a lot more coarse. I go back and put a mustache on it and stroke it with a comb. The eyebrows, make it look like there's hair on it. Then I scratch the piece to look like it's got hair on it. Some people like what I do, and I hope they continue to.

Then it goes to the kiln. The purpose of a kiln is to take the clay and harden it. The clay in this state is very brittle. When you take and fire the clay in the kiln, this clay will mature around 2200 degrees—meaning that when it gets to that point, it will be in a rocklike substance that makes it hard

PLATE 93  The ears are
attached to the jug.

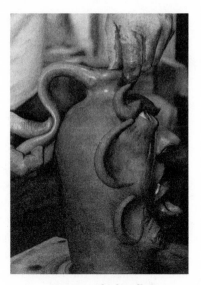

PLATE 94  The handle is
positioned on the top.

PLATE 95  The completed jug

to where you can do whatever you want to with it. You know if you take and drop it on the floor, it is going to break. But the kiln takes the clay, and it fuses all the elements in the clay together and bakes it.

Glaze is no more than I take two to three different chemicals, mix them together, put a coating on this pot when it is fired at maturity, meaning where the glaze melts. Glaze is no more than a glass coating put on a pot. That's all it is.

It waterproofs it. The smooth coating is no more than glass. Oh, I use anything from rust. Rust, seriously. Metal. Rust. All that is, is iron oxide. I use that. You can use different color clays. And then, of course, you can buy [different colors]. One of the most expensive colors is cobalt. Cobalt oxide gives you the blue. That's one of the most expensive ones. The rest of it, you can use green iron oxide. A lot of it's got to do with rust.

I use underglaze. An underglaze is just a matte glaze. And you put it on, like the cones on the roosters, the red. I will paint that, and then glaze on top of it. But this is the glaze. See the blue? See how dark it is?

[Steve mixed up the glaze with a drill that had a really long bit on the end, and the glaze turned kind of smoky looking.] It's ready to dip. Now, that's the color that's on the jug I was holding. That's tobacco spit. Let me mix this one up. What you see is not what you get. That's that bright blue.

I'd always heard of second-generation glazes. I did not know what they were. A second-generation glaze is . . . let me explain it to you this way: We take that color and this color to get that color.

Now if you took and you put cobalt oxide on by itself, you're gonna get that bright blue in yonder. If you took and put this on by itself, you're going to get that color right there. When you take and mix the two together—no, you can't do it here. I can't mix this glaze into that glaze and then do this. It will not turn out like this [streaked]. But if I will take and put this glaze on first, then take and put this glaze on top of it, that's what I will get.

Once I get all these colors that I want painted on, all I do is take and just get the thing down in this glaze and let it coat the whole thing. I get my dark face, I get this color, and I get that color. That is how you get the variations in these colors. You mix two or more glazes together, and the chemical reaction will cause it to do that.

This glaze right here, that is the old-timey tobacco spit glaze. Tobacco spit glaze is not uniform. A tobacco spit looks like somebody spit on it and it run down. That is tobacco spit. To get tobacco spit glaze, you're supposed to have wood ash. You're supposed to fire in a wood kiln. I have neither. I have a tobacco spit glaze without the first drop of wood ash or without it bein' fired in a wood kiln. If you took and compared this with the old-time pottery, you couldn't tell the glaze apart. You could not tell them apart. Just because you have a recipe, there's a lot of people who think no one can copy their recipe, that you can't come up with it. You can. It may not be exactly what they did, but as far as looks go, it will look the same. It's just like this is my creation. The rooster chief is my creation. If this thing starts sellin' like hotcakes, somebody else will be makin' one similar to it.

There is one other thing I'd like to say. To be a potter, I think you have to have two things: a strong back and a weak mind—a strong back to do the work and a weak mind to have no better sense than doin' it.

# PRECISION WOOD—ARTHUR SPEED

*"Anybody is fortunate if they can turn a hobby into a livin'."*

Six years ago, when my grandmother died, I helped my mother inventory the lovely belongings in her home. Among those treasures were several wood carvings by the talented artist Anri. As I handled the beautiful, smooth pieces, I thought about the skill and heart that had created such beauty; I developed a love for wood carving. When I learned about Arthur Speed, a local wood-carver, I was anxious to meet him. My love of wood shaped into something beautiful led me to set up an immediate interview. During the interview I learned that Mr. Speed is one of those rare individuals lucky enough to be able to make his living doing what he loves most: carving wood. From him I learned about the joy of creating art daily, the pride in cherished pieces. Willing to share his talent and gift with all that desire to learn, he is a gift to our community.

—*Andrea Johnson*


MY NAME is Arthur Speed. I was born March 5, 1948, and was raised here in Rabun County. I am a lifelong resident of not just Rabun County but Warwoman [community] as well.

My parents are Richard and Dorothy Seay Speed. I have lots of brothers and sisters. There are seven of us; I am the oldest of four boys and three girls.

Growin' up in Rabun County connects me with my woodwork. My dad was a sawmill man, so by being in the woods all my life, I know woods, trees, and timber. That's been a big help to me when tryin' to go out and locate specific trees to make something out of. Knowing wood is my livin'.

My dad and I didn't make many wooden things when I was a youngster. Back in that time, if me and him were makin' something, it would be building something "important," something necessary. There was no foolishness in woodwork. There was a little bit of woodwork that had nothing artistic about it. Together we would rebuild the carriage on the sawmill or something else along that line.

I am the only one in my family who does woodworkin'. I have a brother who is in the sawmill business, but other than that, no one does any woodwork of any kind. I am the only one in shop work. I used to say I was a shop woodworker, but after going into it full-time, I purposely geared it more to art.

I can't remember how young I was when I became interested in pocketknives and whittlin'. That goes back beyond what I can remember. My parents did let me have a pocketknife, though. They were good to me. They let me carve when I was real small, smaller than I would allow somebody to carve.

One of my earliest memories that I will never forget is that my granddaddy gave me a pocketknife for my birthday when I was five years old. It was a little Case knife. Then I could carve and do whatever I wanted to do. I started off cuttin' myself, but I was really tough. Nobody could take my knife away. It was all mine. Up until then, I'd been borrowin' my dad's and granddad's knives.

**"I knew long before first grade that I had a natural talent. I have never had a lesson before in my life, and I love to be able to say that."**

My mother allowed me to sit in the living room at night while I whittled. It was a problem to have shavin's and stuff in the living room, but I knew I had something goin' for me when it was all right. It had quickly become acceptable.

I did a little bit of what you call Appalachian whittlin'. That's when you just sit and whittle a stick till it's gone. I have a tendency, bein' a sure enough Appalachian, to call it "whittlin'." I'll say I'm whittlin' a boot, but it's carvin' when you are doin' this stuff. You've got to call it carvin'.

I have been doing this all my life, even before first grade. I knew long before first grade that I had a natural talent. I have never had a lesson before in my life, and I love to be able to say that.

I don't remember the first things I made. That would be back when I was really young. I would get a little bit of toys at Christmas, but other than that, I didn't have any. I learned to make my own. I know I made my brothers and sisters things, too, but right now, I don't know of anything in particular. I liked to help 'em make things—makin' anything you can imagine. I didn't have a toy gun to play with, but I made one. If I got a chance to get a broom handle or something like that, I would make a toy. Like the gun I just mentioned, I made my own gun that I could put bullets in. It was a broom handle/shotgun kinda thing. It would break down, and I would put bullets in it. I made the whole works. I still make toys.

PLATE 96 Arthur Speed in his workshop with his tool set,
hamburger and fries, watch, and brogan that he has carved

As a growin' boy, I seldom kept much of what I carved, because back
then, at that young age, I was basically makin' toys. I only made a few things
for myself. The only things I can even locate are things I gave away that people kept. Unlike then, I now have some of the things I've made. My wife
eventually started keeping things. For example, she claimed the deer I did
years ago. Otherwise it would be gone, too.

I do lots of work every year, especially since I have made it a full-time
business. It's an everyday business for me. I don't know, offhand, exactly
how much I do a year. I keep a book of orders and what I have finished, but
some of the pages have been changed. So it doesn't begin to tell you every-

thing I've done. It will only tell you what I have done so far this year and the upcoming orders I have to work on. I keep the book for tax purposes.

It would take me about four months to complete the next ten projects. I am booked through January [2000] as of September 1999. Since starting my business, I have never caught up. I have never advertised to keep my list growin', although that list is my job. Everything stays in the order it was requested. I have just finished a dagger that will be delivered pretty quickly. Right now, I am workin' on a walnut boot. I have a long way to go on it. Something I never do is add color to any of my carvin's. Wood varies in color, depending on the kind of wood it is, so some of my carvin's are made from more than one type of wood.

I have only been doin' this full-time for five years. I spent twenty-five years working at Rabun Mills [Burlington Industries]. Since the mill closed, I have had a few other jobs. I went to work for the county and then at Ace Hardware. I supervised the lumberyard and the men making deliveries. I left that job to begin my own business.

While I was workin' other full-time jobs, I would spend the weekends workin' on my carvin'. I used to work all year long for a week of vacation to do what I wanted to do. I would then spend the whole week whittlin' and carvin'. I have never wanted to go anywhere because I had enough of that in the military. I'd camp a little bit, but I'd spend most of my time woodworkin'.

When I was [called up to serve] in the Persian Gulf, I promised myself that when I got home, I was goin' to have a shop. I should have had one all my life, or at least for the past twenty years. I built it in three or four months, but I did it all by myself while I was workin' another job. I was workin' with the county, in maintenance, at the time I built the shop. I really do wish I had built it years before I did. I would not have been doing all of the other jobs and would have been on my own sooner.

People call me sometimes if a tree or something goes down. Right out there is a lumber shed that's full, and that's how I got most of it. Anywhere I can get a good log, I do. That cedar chest, for example, was made from a tree that was cut where the CVS store is in Clayton. They were about to build the store, and there on the spot stood a monstrous cedar tree. They would have come in and started cuttin' everything down and bulldozin'. I wanted that big tree! After getting it, I had it cut into planks. You see, eight years is how long it has been out here dryin'.

I get wood from anywhere I can find out about it. I found out about a dead walnut tree and went and got it. Well, that's how I try to get wood. It's not easy to deliberately go out and try to find a cedar tree, walnut tree, or any other kinda tree in Rabun County. Here, let me show you another one. That's as yellow gold as it gets. That's an Osage orange tree. I cut that in the parkin' lot of the courthouse. Osage orange doesn't really grow here. That was planted in the courthouse parkin' lot, on the lower side of the lot. It died, so I got it. I've used and used it. I keep and value every little scrap of that stuff. It's a golden color, so that's what I use for my brass and gold colors.

There are two different kinds of wood: domestic and exotic. *Domestic* means they grow around here. Some rare and furniture-grade domestics are walnut, cedar, and things like that. Anything classified as an exotic wood is, for the most part, from South America. Mahogany, bloodwood, and Osage orange are all exotic South American woods. Now, if you want really classy stuff, you use mahogany.

I use all kinds of wood. Everything that I use is natural in color. It's Mother Nature's color. I like to use bloodwood because of its bright red color. And in the tool set, all the yellow wood I used is Osage orange.

There are lots of woods that I haven't used, especially some of the exotic ones from South America. A lot of 'em are too expensive to use. The darkest black ebony is so expensive it is not sold by the foot like other woods are. It is sold by the cubic inch.

You can get into some poisonous woods in my work. You have to know your wood because arsenic is found in some. You cannot breathe the dust of an arsenic wood. I love to use it, though. I love to get the different wood grains, colors, and patterns. I like grain, anyway. I use bird's-eye maple, zebrawood, and rosewood a lot because of their grain. Zebrawood and rosewood are exotic woods, and bird's-eye maple is a domestic wood. The bird's-eye maple is not one of the arsenic woods. When these are unfinished, they look kind of flat.

When workin' with some exotic woods, you're supposed to use a good dust mask, if not a respirator. You're not goin' to just fall over and die by breathing the fumes. It's not that bad. It's breathing the dust you are workin' with. Woodworkers deal with a lot of dust. Handlin' it is not that bad of a thing, but you sure don't wanna breathe it. It gets into your lungs and builds up arsenic in you. Although I work with the exotic woods, they haven't bothered me that much. I keep a mask on when I'm sandin'.

I enjoy a challenge. I have no control over any of the orders I get. People want it done the way they want it done. The pistol is an example of what I wanted to do. I wanted to do one that functioned and was a perfect scale model. I think the pistol could be my favorite. There's no steel, screw, or spring in it. It's 100 percent wood and operates just like the real one. It swivels by going around on a wooden pin that's in it. I broke down the real pistol and used it as a pattern, a model to go by, and reproduced it in wood. I've got a laminated wooden-leaf spring the length of this handle, up inside, that operates it all. I even made bullets to fill the whole thing 'cause the real one had enough to fill it. It's just like the real ones—even looks like real brass and copper. The pistol was modeled after a .44 Magnum. You would think that if a gun squeaked, you should oil it. You don't oil wood—you use wax. It's the best thing in the world—wax or a bar of soap.

I don't sell many pistols. If I did more, I would like for the customer to give me a different model to do. I've done this one, but my doing a different model would give me a new challenge.

I am also proud of a clock I did. It is 100 percent wood except for the cord, which holds the weight, and the glass case around it. It doesn't even have hinges. The dowel pin's hinging the door. There's not a spring, nail, or anything in it. I refused to put a screw or a nail in it. Makin' a clock without a nail, screw, hinge, or spring gave me a challenge. It is accurate, but I don't keep it runnin'. It does have to stay at a perfect balance to run. It will keep time for thirty hours. The weight travels to the floor and stops. You can't get any more travel distance out of it, unless you hang it up higher. It is a real fancy clock. I won a first-place ribbon for it at an art show in Hartwell, Georgia. It got me first place and a hundred-dollar check as well.

My most complicated piece was that wooden clock. I could not have done it without getting in the books to see how a clock is geared. I had to see the ratios, the teeth count, and things like that. From there, you can do it—create an all-wooden clock. That wooden clock was one thing I had always wanted to build. It was fifteen to twenty years till I finally did it. Now there's nothing left hangin' that I can think of.

The hamburger I carved has no color added to any of it. That's a slab of walnut wood that I used as the meat. The cheese is Osage orange. That's my thing—no color. I like to use nature's wood. The toothpick in the hamburger is just to keep 'em in line so they don't slide around as much. The french fries are made out of wild cherry. You see how nothing's been stained. That's what wild cherry is with a little age on it. It looks like it's been stained, but it hasn't.

I'm a woodworker. Everything nowadays is power tools—all electric everything. This is the carpenter's woodworkin' tool set. When I started makin' these tool sets, the idea was kind of like a model. I've got the real tool of each one of these. My scheme in doin' these was to do it all in wood. I added no color, stain, or paint to anything here. I used just Mother Nature's color with a clear finish. All I put on any of it is just a clear finish.

This sixteen-piece tool set takes sixty-seven hours to make. I've done twelve of these sets. They're goin' to people like engineers and architects. Most of 'em are done for people that love woodworkin'. I finished up and delivered the last one I did Friday. It was done for Danny Gillespie's cabinet shop.

Everything in my toolbox is a mix of different woods that are all different colors. The rusty hammerhead is wild cherry, and the handle is ash. Ash is

PLATE 97  100 percent wooden grandfather clock

commonly used. I love curly maple. I use it in a good bit of my stuff, simply because I like it. I can show you everything that I did use metal on. I had to use a screw to keep certain things together. You can't carve the bubble things that are in a level, either, so I robbed 'em out of a plastic level. I made a drill that is a replica used by woodworkers a long time ago. These are what old carpenters called hand tools. I do them with all-natural wood and then add finishes. I use a slick finish that you cannot scratch.

You can't use any of these tools. Some of 'em are functional. Not many of 'em are, but this level is accurate enough to be functional. And that square is square enough. Anywhere you want to try it, it will be a perfect square. Yeah, that's accurate. That's what they call a breast drill, 'cause you can really do some power pushin' against your chest. That's what they had to work with when they didn't have electric drills. Most of these are practical models.

**"I'm really interested in what I've got goin' and just can't wait to get back to it. Now that's the way to make a livin'."**

PLATE 98 An authentic wooden tool set

I like to tell people about my carpenter's pencil. I have a whole drawer full of 'em. They have the flat design. It is a sturdy pencil that is to mark lumber. The lead is big enough that it won't break. You can buy 'em for nearly nothing, so why did I not sand one of 'em off and put it in my toolbox? All you would have to do to pass one off as your own is just sand the paint off of one already made, and you wouldn't know the difference. I had to make it. Otherwise, it would not belong in the toolbox. I spent two hours to make a pencil just to put in the box. I had to split one open and rob the lead to use in mine. It is a saw cut. The lead will lie right in that saw cut. There's two pieces put together, glued together. They all are glued, even regular pencils. You couldn't slide the lead into a really small hole without it breakin'. That lead is really brittle. Even when you are writin' with a pencil, the lead breaks a lot.

The gavels are probably used as gifts. I have done a few that turned out to be gifts to a chairman, a president. People usually monogram 'em on a gold plate with their name and the year that they were in office. It turns out to be a good gift.

Although I get orders from many different parts of the country, it would be misleadin' to tell you that I am that well known. Some of the places I have shipped things to are Maine, Florida, and New Mexico. Those people were here, saw my stuff, and made orders for me to ship to where they came from.

I have a price on everything that I have. I would have to look in my book to see what I have priced things. Everything I do is timed. I keep track of how long it takes me. That way, I don't have to guess the price of an item. I figure out the price of things by timin' how long it takes me to do it, and then I charge 'em by the hour.

I've had people absolutely insist on an estimate. I try tellin' 'em that I can give 'em an estimate if they want it, but I don't want to do that. Let me tell you what I'm doin' when I estimate: I'm tryin' to guess how long it will take me to do the job, and then I practically double it to make sure I come out right. You don't want me doin' that. If I time it out as I do it, then I can charge for materials and time (so much an hour). I'm down on the borderline then and feel safe while I'm doin' the job.

When I saw that I could, I went into this full-time. I am havin' a ball workin' my own business. I love my job. It is just like a vacation year-round. It is what I used to do without it bein' my source of income. Anybody is fortunate if they can turn a hobby into a livin'. I don't care what it is. My work really is just my hobby. I'm not sure how it fits with Appalachian history. I am sure it does, but I am not sure how. It is just my modern job, although you can see that I like to focus on the old style, like the old boot. I like that kinda thing.

I come out here every mornin' with a cup of coffee. I'm really interested in what I've got goin' and just can't wait to get back to it. Now that's the way to make a livin'. If I ever have the opportunity, I'm going to tell people that if they can find something to do on their own, they really do need to pursue it. They can make a livin' at it. I don't care what it is. Let me put it this way: If it's diggin' ditches, go for it. They'll soon own companies where they're sittin' behind a desk and havin' people do the work with machinery. Don't go for some big outfit. I don't care how big they are.

### "You can force yourself to do something, but you're not enjoyin' it until you stir up some inspiration."

I love to get into something. Sometimes I won't take the time to eat. I'll stay out here till after dark 'cause I don't want to quit in the middle of something. I love to stay with it. The thing that does bother me is having these doors stacked up and waitin' on glass or hardware and have to start on another order. I don't like that, but I have to keep it movin'.

You can force yourself to do something, but you're not enjoyin' it until you stir up some inspiration. When you get some inspiration stirred up, that's when you really enjoy it. If somebody orders a cedar chest, I want to do it, but as far as really bein' anxiously inspired and creative, no. They've told me exactly how they want it, how deep they want it, how long they want it, and as much about the style as they can tell me. That's what I'll produce for 'em. I like doin' it, but that's not lookin' for an inspiration before you start. There was inspiration when I did the pistol! When I did the tool set, there was inspiration, and when I did the boot, there was inspiration!

I made a nine-foot entertainment center. It was five feet wide and stood nine feet tall. It wouldn't even stand up in most houses, but it is in a mansion. The entertainment center was made out of yellow pine, step tread, the material you would buy to build steps in a house. Normally, lumber is bought in three-quarters of an inch thick, but I had to have thicker to do the frames of the doors and things like that. It is not pictured in my album because I have just got it delivered.

Goin' through my photo album that I have kept shows a lot of what I have done. I have done a lot of chess sets and tables. Some of 'em are really very fancy. I have tried to show the carvin' detail in these pictures.

That is a chess set I carved before I learned to play chess. It was redesigned to be "hillbilly." I used to call it that, but I'd rather call it an Appalachian chess set. The little carved figures have got lots of attention. Each piece has been redesigned. I don't have any more of these sets; I've not even finished this one. I have all the walnut side finished, but just two or three pieces of the light color is finished. That's what makes up the set. Of course, as you can see, there's more pieces than that. That's a king, a queen, the knight, the bishop, the rook, and the pawn. It's just sort of evolved into an Appalachian set. There's so much carvin' time in those pieces. I don't know how long it took me to make even one of the chess pieces. You can ask me that about anything I do now, and I can tell you. But in this box, I don't know. These were done so long ago, I didn't time them. It wasn't anything but a hobby for me then. The five years I've been in business, though, I've timed everything. These pieces were made way back when I was just sittin' and doin' carvin' as a hobby.

I don't know that I will ever finish the Appalachian chess set. I have come up with something I would like to do with it. I would sacrifice these chess pieces if a company would mold 'em. What I would like to do is hook up with some company and let 'em take the molds and give me royalty off of what they sell.

The orders I work on vary. I have made a few mantels, and lately I have done a lot of doors. I built one door with four-by-twelves—wormy chestnut. I also helped a buddy of mine build a house in thirteen weeks, in Sky Valley. I told him that when the house was finished, I was goin' back to my shop. That's what I did, but I did enjoy the hard work.

I don't usually have photographs of my fireplace mantels because they just don't photograph well. The photos in my album are far from everything that I have done. I have done a little bit of everything. I have mounted my own heads: deer, bear, wild hogs, and things like that.

PLATE 99  Pieces from the Appalachian chess set

I don't know where most of my ideas come from. I won't mislead you. I would want you to know that I'm not carryin' all these ideas all the time. Things do pop up, and an inspiration for each thing does come along somewhere, somehow. No matter what your capability is, you still have to have inspiration from somewhere. I watch all the woodworkin' shows on television, but not to learn. Ideas come along. Sometimes I pick up some techniques. I have a bunch of woodworkin' magazines. I have some things hangin' around in my shop from ideas that came from magazines.

As I said earlier, I have been drawin' most of my life. I will not paint wall-hangin' drawin's. I draw patterns for my work because I don't want to start a complicated project without at least drawin' it. That way I can keep up with what's goin' on.

I tell people about my job every day. Whether it is for an interview or it's just people stoppin' in, I still tell 'em about my work. People come by my shop and sit for thirty minutes or so, and when they leave, I've got another name on the list with something I have to do.

I will make anything someone can dream up. That is the way I make a livin'—by fillin' requests. However, I find repetition borin'. Like that shoe I made, there are no two alike. A lot of my things are machine-shop-produced, not hand-carved, and some things have to be sanded rather than cut. They are not goin' to be the same. I don't want 'em to be the same. A fellow told me that I was honest in tellin' people this, but that I was tellin' 'em things that they didn't want to hear.

When I did this boot, I first did it in one solid piece of wood. The laces became a problem when carvin' 'em, so I just cut the laces and tongue out. I was thinkin' that I could put a tongue in there and then use leather laces in it. People are always asking questions about the laces and tongue. People often ask whether or not the sole has been put on the shoe. I think I have done nine of these; no, I've done ten. Every single one of 'em has different flaws, different problems, and different torn-up places.

Those of us that are old enough can remember wearin' these brogans. When I was a young boy, everyone wore brogans because you could buy them so cheap. You still didn't have but that one pair. You wore 'em till they were gone. I have even cut the sole off and kept wearin' 'em as long as the rest would last. We used to wear these 'cause they were cheap. I kept askin' my mother just how cheap they were. She said she could remember them bein' six dollars a pair. That's why we had brogans while we were growin' up. The style had nothing to do with it. That was just the shoe you could afford to have. If they could find anything like 'em brogans, some of the old-timers, the really old-timers, would want them today.

Wood carvin' is another subject. Wood-carvers are goin' to have all kinds of gauges and chisels. I am a knife carver. I came up as a boy whittlin', and I still do it that way. I avoid things that are easy for others to do. I have people requestin' that I build 'em a set of kitchen cabinets. I tell 'em, "No, I am sorry," and, "There are cabinet shops all over Rabun County." People build kitchen cabinets as a business.

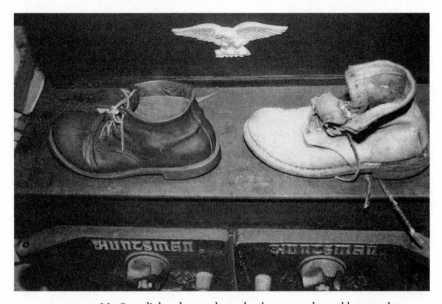

PLATE 100  Mr. Speed's hand-carved wooden brogan and a real brogan shoe

My most prized piece of work has changed a lot. It changes so often that I can't even keep up with it. I don't know. It could be something that somebody has. I can't say that my favorite is a shop-built project because it would have to be a carvin'. I don't know what my trademark piece or my best-sellin' piece is. That's not for me to say. I'll let my orders do the judging. I have done twelve tool sets and ten boots. It looks like the tool set tops the list.

I avoid most shows, but because I'm in the art guild and because this is my full-time business, I do a few. I went to the Celebrate Clayton event they had a couple of weeks ago. The bottom line is that I have done three shows. I don't take things to the shows to sell. I display them and take orders. I couldn't do anything that anyone would want right away, but I don't sell what I've got, 'cause I have to keep enough to show and keep business movin'.

I found myself at one time without a tool set. A lady called me up near Christmas. She had to have a tool set for her husband for Christmas! I said, "Well, I can't do it now. It's too late. Here we are within a month of Christmas, and there's no way I'll break the list of orders I have. It is unfair for everybody for me to do that." After I thought about it, I called her back and told her I'd sell her the set that I kept for shows and make another one for myself later. So I was without a tool set for a while. I did a demonstration at the art guild and referred to the tool set many times. I don't wanna be without things that bring in orders.

Now I brand my name on everything I do. You can't carve something and then take a ballpoint pen and sign it. As for furniture, I usually sign 'em and seal over it. I had a guy from Atlanta who had a signed toolbox, but he wanted to make a trip back up here for me to sign each individual piece. I told him that if he was willin' to drive back up here, I would do it. So, on each one, I had to sand into bare wood—sign it and seal it back over again. I did every piece in his set.

A guy from the Epcot Center at Disney World called Foxfire lookin' for somebody to do an Appalachian carvin'. They referred him to me. He wanted a wagon and a team of mules built as an Appalachian toy. The carvin' is now on display at Disney World in Orlando, Florida. It is displayed at the Epcot Center, in the Appalachian Culture section.

It wasn't my idea at all for Rabun County to have a county seal. They were publishin' a book on the history of the county and realized that other surroundin' counties had a seal, but Rabun did not. Durin' the time they were doin' this publishin', they got the idea that they wanted a seal for the county. So they set up a contest, accepted all the entries possible, and then selected one from these for the county seal. Mine's the one they selected. It is a bell surrounded by symbols. Each one of the symbols has a meaning, so I wrote an explanation for each symbol used. I think I got a fifty-dollar savings bond; that had little meaning. What does mean something is that when I'm dead and gone, I've left a seal in Rabun County, Georgia.

I have given a lot of thought to this: There is no end to the life of things I have made for people. If you are talkin' about wood, I could tear up forever. The county has even named my driveway Precision Lane.

# JOHN HURON:
# INSTRUMENT MAKER

*"Each person that's had it has left his mark on it."*

Coming from a family of musicians, as well as being one myself, I was very interested when I heard about John Huron, who crafts mountain instruments by hand. I couldn't wait to meet this man who preserves a facet of Appalachian culture that we don't often think or hear about—the instruments of Appalachia. John Huron obviously loves his craft. His eyes sparkled and his face lit up with each question I asked about his interest in instrument making. Many times during the interview, he laughed in remembrance of some of his first experiences as he cheerfully related to me the story of how he first became interested in and learned this art. I was surprised to find out how little I knew about many mountain instruments. I had never even heard of several of the instruments Mr. Huron builds, and I certainly had no idea that groundhogs were fit to be used for anything, much less as a part of musical instruments. Meeting Mr. Huron was a memorable experience for me. I'm so glad to know that someone is working to preserve such an important part of our culture.

—*Lacy Hunter*

MY INSTRUMENT building actually started with Civil War reenacting and wanting to do it as authentically as possible. I couldn't understand the reenactors, who for the most part were very authentic during the daytime but at nighttime would kinda let it all slide. To me, sitting around the campfire after dark was a great time because a lot of the places we set up camp had electric poles and modern buildings, and the darkness made all that disappear. I thought this was a really good time to be portraying authentic camp life, music and such, but most of the reenactors seemed content to sit back and talk about modern stuff.

A friend of mine and I decided we were going to do authentic camp life during the evenings. Doug was an old-time banjo player, and I decided I was going to be a fiddle player. I got hold of my uncle's fiddle, which is another long story, and started trying to learn to play it. The banjo that Doug had was old, made in the 1920s, but it was not at all like what was played during the war. Among other things, it had frets on the neck as opposed to the fretless banjos of the Civil War period.

The whole thing that got me started building instruments was that I was up at the visitors' center on the Blue Ridge Parkway up around Asheville, North Carolina, leafing through these books that I had never seen before. They were called Foxfire books. When I came to *Foxfire 3* and it said "fretless banjo," I just went nuts, 'cause from my research I knew this was the kind of banjo that existed during the war, but I didn't have any idea that there was any kind of book that told you how to build one. I bought *Foxfire 3* and went home and began to study it. Soon after that, I was talking to a fellow at work and telling him what I was doing and how thrilled I was to have this book and he said, "I've got this friend that has an uncle that lives up in the mountains and builds those fretless banjos." So I went up on Doe Mountain and met a gentleman named Ellis Wolfe.

PLATE 101 John Huron playing
one of his gourd banjars

"Ellis was more than willing to tell me anything that I wanted to
know, but I had to be smart enough to know what to ask."

Ellis had been a running buddy of Stanley Hicks, who was in the *Foxfire 3*
book I bought. I think Stanley had passed away about a year before all of
this. They had lived only a few miles apart, but Ellis was on the Tennessee
side of the line and Stanley on the North Carolina side. Ellis was a cabinet-
maker by trade, and I'm not sure if Stanley did anything other than farm.

When he became well known for being a banjo builder in *Foxfire 3*, Stanley basically had more business than he could handle, and the way Ellis tells
the story, Stanley much preferred to build "them delcimors," as he called
them, than to build fretless mountain banjos, so he enlisted Ellis's help.
Stanley gave Ellis, who was a skilled woodworker, copies of his patterns, the
old Hicks family patterns, and Ellis commenced to build banjos and banjo
parts to help Stanley out. There are a number of people today who think
they have a Stanley Hicks–built banjo, but it was actually made by Ellis. I
reckon he was kind of like a subcontractor. I believe Ellis started selling banjos on his own after Stanley died. He was very kind and very patient, and my
visits with him were a wonderful time.

After having read a number of the Foxfire books, I thought I had an idea
of how the concept worked, you know, going up and talking to people about
their craft, but because I had grown up totally "citified," this was a whole
new learning experience for me. And Ellis, as I imagine the students who
went out and did the original Foxfire interviews found out, wasn't exactly set
up with lesson plans. It's a good bit different than going to school when you
go visit people. Ellis was more than willing to tell me anything that I wanted
to know, but I had to be smart enough to know what to ask. So it took several
trips. He'd give me all the knowledge I could absorb, and I'd go home and
work until I ran out of smarts, and then I'd go back. Ellis seemed to like that,
too, because it kept me coming back up there to visit him. It turned out to
be very rewarding for both of us.

The rest of the story about the Foxfire connection has to do with how I
came to meet Robert Mize, who's also in *Foxfire 3*. As it turned out, he
didn't live very far from me at all. I was looking for wood down at the local
wood store to build the mountain banjo. They were getting tired of messing
with me because they wanted to sell me a bunch of wood, and I just wanted
a few pieces. Finally they said, "You need to go down and visit Robert Mize,
who builds dulcimers, and see if you can get some wood from him."

So I took their advice and went to talk to Mr. Mize about my project. The
first time I ever met him, he looked me up and down and said, "Have you
ever done any woodworking before?" I said, "Well, I've built shelves for the

garage and things like that, but I've never built anything that I've put a finish on or anything that made music."

And he said, "Do you have any tools?"

I said, "Well, I've got a dandy radial arm saw and some hand tools." He kinda made a face. A radial arm saw is not an instrument builder's friend. There are good applications for its use, but building a music instrument is not one of them. So he said, "And what kind of wood did you want?"

"Cherry," I answered. I had my heart set on building this banjo out of cherrywood.

Mr. Mize is real strange about his wood. He's never met a piece of wood that he didn't like. He loves his wood, and now I'm the same way. Mr. Mize was thinking, "Here's this greenhorn that doesn't know what he can do, and he wants me to sell him a nice, pretty piece of cherrywood, and he'll probably go home and hack it to pieces and not have anything."

So he said, "I'll tell you what. I'm not going to sell you any wood, but I will give you a piece. I've got some sassafras lumber that is thick enough that you can make this instrument out of it. If you mess it up, you've not wasted anything real nice, but if you succeed, you will end up with a good instrument."

He gave me that piece of sassafras, and by the time I went through all the other incantations of going back and forth to Ellis, and then finding out about skinning and tanning groundhog hides from other people, and on and on and on, there were probably close to two dozen individuals that contributed to the building of that first banjo, in one way or another. If I had just stopped there, it would've been a treasure, but that was only the beginning. So that's how I got the knowledge to begin with.

When I finished the banjo, I took it back to show Mr. Mize. I believe he was amazed at the result and told me I had done good. I found out some years later that after I left he had told his wife, Maude, "We need to help that boy. I believe he has potential." Since that day, Mr. Mize has been true to his word, and we have become good friends. He taught me to build dulcimers and has helped me in my newly found vocation in too many ways to count. By the way, I still play that sassafras banjo on a regular basis. It's a good'un!

Later on, Mr. Mize passed his dulcimer pattern and construction techniques on to me. He got them from Homer Ledford, who got them from Jethro Amburgy, who got them from J. Edward Thomas, who, I've been told, sold his dulcimers out of a mule cart in the early 1900s in and around southeastern Kentucky. Each person that's had it has left his mark on it in one way or another; so although my dulcimer is not a twin brother to one of Mr. Thomas's dulcimers, it is definitely a first cousin.

During this time I was working as an engineer, but I got laid off within about a year. My family and I decided that it was more important to us to

PLATE 102  John showing Foxfire student Maggie Whitmire
how to play his dulcimer

live someplace where we felt comfortable than to move to an unknown environment just because of a high-paying job. We had grown quite fond of the people and lifestyle of upper East Tennessee and didn't want to leave.

One day my wife told me that if there was ever a time to try and make a living at something I really enjoyed, this was it, and she'd go back to work to help out. After much discussion, that's what we did. She went back to work, and I started my instrument-building career. Her working was the only way we could afford to have any health insurance. More important, staying in Bristol allowed my son to finish high school where he had started and go on to graduate from East Tennessee State University.

> **"I spent a lot of time at the feet of old men that chewed tobacco, just watching and trying to pick up that old-time lick they used, and it just took forever."**

When I was in high school, I played alto saxophone and didn't know a banjo from a boat oar! But I've always loved all kinds of music. I got hooked on string band music when I moved to the mountains and started researching the music of the mid-1800s. I found out that a good bit of what is today called old-time music is very close to what was played during the War Between the States.

Once I started going to craft shows, I quickly realized that if I was ever going to sell any instruments, I was going to have to learn to play them. I didn't know how to play a lick on the banjo when I built my first one. I taught myself to play by listening to recordings of old-time music. I found some records at the library and did tons of research by listening to old-time string bands and talking with old musicians and just hanging around and practicing until it sounded right.

I spent a lot of time at the feet of old men that chewed tobacco, just watching and trying to pick up that old-time lick they used, and it just took forever. I bought a bunch of books and they tried to explain how it was done, but they didn't help much. I listened to the music obsessively, over and over, to get the rhythm programmed in my head, and finally one day, it all clicked. I learned through trial and error—basically a lot more error. Sometimes, when I'm teaching a banjo-building class, folks will ask if besides building a banjo in five days, my students also learn to play it. I smile sweetly and give them a line I got from Mr. Mize: "In this class we're concerned with production, not entertainment."

PLATE 103 John with one of his mountain larks

Over the years, I have made a variety of instruments besides the fretless mountain banjo and the dulcimer. My contemporary string instruments all have three strings and a diatonic, dulcimer-like fret pattern. The first I made was the birdhouse banjo, which was basically a dulcimer fretboard with a small triangular (it looked like a little birdhouse) sound box attached to the end. It had a twangy sound—therefore the name. Next I conjured up something I called a one-holer. It looked like a baby banjo and had a sweet, high-pitched sound, sort of like a mandolin. It was called a one-holer because its single sound hole was in the shape of a crescent moon like on an outhouse door.

Currently, I make a little instrument with a big sound called a mountain lark; well, everywhere except Brasstown, North Carolina. I originally designed the instrument with an eighteen-inch scale length and a two-inch-deep teardrop-shaped sound box for an entry-level building class I was going to do at the John C. Campbell Folk School, located in Brasstown. Originally, I named it the Campbellin, as a tribute to Mr. Campbell. But when I would take it to craft shows, I'd have tons of people over the course of a weekend ask what it was called, and then, "Well, why'd you name it that?" I'd have to tell each one of them the story, so after a couple of weekends, I changed the name to mountain lark (except in Brasstown), and not a soul has asked about the name since. I'll let you in on a little secret. There ain't no such a critter as a mountain lark. I borrowed the lark name from a Studebaker car I had when I was a teenager!

I began to make several of my instruments because of the research I did on the history of the banjo. The gourd banjo, mouthbow, bones, and quills were all introduced to North America by African slaves.

The original bones were rib bones from cattle and horses. You can take two eight-inch lengths of bone and hold them between your fingers, and by snapping your wrist back and forth, you get a kind of castanet sound. It's called rattlin' the bones. The bones I make are wood, and I use different kinds of wood to get different tones.

If you're a mediocre bones player, you can use one set in one hand. If you're a fair to middlin' bones player, you can play a set in each hand; and if you're a real good bones player, you can play two sets of bones and buck dance and sing and carry on all at the same time. It's a real entertaining thing. If you can play two sets at once, you can get quite a rhythm with them. I'm not in that category, but I've seen people do it, and it's great.

The quills are made of different lengths of river cane lashed together, kinda like a panpipe. The mouthbow is a piece of wood with a single string to make it resemble a hunting bow. You hold it up to your mouth and strum the string and your head becomes the sound box and the notes come out your mouth. The emptier your head, the better the sound!

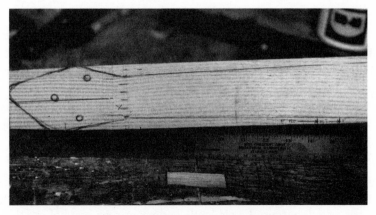

PLATE 104  A roughed-out peg head and neck

PLATE 105  A finished peg head with pegs, strings, and nut installed

The gourd banjos I make are built like the instrument would have been in the late 1700s up to around the 1840s, depending on the number of strings I use and the shape of the neck and peg head. They go mostly to collectors and living history museums like Colonial Williamsburg.

The history of the gourd banjo, or probably more technically correct, ban-jar, is that it is an instrument of African origin. It came to this hemisphere when the Africans were uprooted from their native land and brought to the Americas as slaves. They wouldn't have brought much, if anything, with them in the way of worldly possessions and were probably just lucky to have clothes on their backs when they arrived. But what they did bring with them—what they were able to bring in their heads—was their rich heritage of music, dance, and storytelling. Once they got settled in this strange land, I imagine they set about re-creating things they were familiar with so that they would feel a little bit more at home. Some of those things would have been the music instruments that they had in Africa like the gourd banjar, the mouthbow, and various percussion instruments.

We know of the word *banjar* (ban´-jer) courtesy of a man named Thomas Jefferson. Jefferson, prior to the War for Independence, traveled around a good bit. He was interested in all sorts of things: horticulture, architecture, and music. He would keep detailed journals of things he ran across during his travels. In one of these journals, there is an entry describing a group of slave musicians. They were playing music, and he writes about seeing one man playing a gourd instrument with a hide head and wooden neck. I believe he reported it had four strings. When Jefferson asked this feller what the instrument was called, because he evidently had never seen one before, the man told him it was a banjar. Jefferson wrote down in his journal *banjar,* phonetically, like he'd heard it pronounced. So we have a pronunciation and a name that goes back to the late 1700s. The funny thing about this is that when you get to talking to the older musicians in the southern mountains, they still talk about fiddle and banjar music. Many never say the word *banjo.* It's fiddle and banjar music. They have no earthly idea that they are speaking African. If the man Jefferson talked to had come from a different tribe or geographical location, Jefferson might have heard the word *banjore* or the word *banza.* There were several different African words for the same type of gourd instrument.

I base my banjars on a painting called *The Old Plantation* that was done about the year 1800. It shows a slave wedding, with a couple jumping the broomstick and two musicians off to the side. One of them is playing a gourd banjar; the other, what appears to be a gourd drum of some sort. There are two styles of peg heads that I generally use: the scroll type, for 1840 and newer five-string instruments, as shown on the Sweeney banjo in *Foxfire 3;* and the old plantation type, sort of a diamond shape, for four-string instruments, patterned after the banjar in *The Old Plantation* painting, also in *Foxfire 3.*

You put your gourds up to dry in the fall. Since they weigh several times as much when they're green because they are all full of water at the end of their growing season, they need to be dried. Some people allow them to dry in the fields. Some people put them up in barns, like in straw piles. There are lots of different techniques, and I'm not really an authority on how to do that. All I know is it takes at least till the next spring for them to be good and dry, especially if they're just laying out somewhere. I can't even grow mold in a damp crawl space, so I prefer to get my gourds from those who have that talent. That way I can be real picky.

The type of gourd I start with is called a martin gourd, which kind of has the shape of a Hershey candy kiss. Folks usually drill holes in them and hang them up for birdhouses. For cutting openings in the gourd, there are really no specific measurements. I like to end up with a six- to seven-inch opening to stretch the hide over, put a one-inch sound hole in the bottom, and leave about two-thirds of the gourd body. Each banjar is unique unto itself. I've got a kind of generic template that I use most of the time to shape the necks, but as far as the gourds go, you just work with whatever you've got. As for choosing a gourd, mostly I just look for a nice shape and then peck around the outside. Sometimes they'll have rotten spots in them, and you don't want to mess with those if you're going to take all the time to make an instrument. So if I had three solid gourds, exactly alike, sitting there, I'd probably, if I was going to pick just one, I'd probably take the one with the lowest pitch when I pecked on it 'cause I'd figure it had the thickest sides.

When cutting on the gourd I use a little keyhole saw. It has a saw blade that is kind of pointy on one end and it gets bigger as it goes toward the handle. I select the side of the gourd best suited for the large hole and set the gourd with that side facing up. I then get a block of wood or a coffee can or something I can lay a marker across the top of, and with the gourd in a fixed position, move the marker up against the gourd and slowly trace a line around it. That'll give me a perfectly even trim line. Then I'll whittle a little hole inside of the trim line and take that keyhole saw and open it up.

"You can't just go whapping on the thing, or it'll bust all to pieces! But once you get it all together, it's pretty strong."

PLATE 106 A gourd with the top cut off and
a small sound hole in the bottom

When you open up the gourd, there are all these seeds and all this dried-out crusty membrane stuff. I just use my hands to clean most of it out and a cabinet scraper to get the rest and smooth the inside surface the best I can. You can use anything that's kinda round and has got a sharp edge on it. It doesn't have to be the exact radius of the gourd, but it has to be of a size so you can get in there. You can use a piece of broken glass. The old-timers used that. They may not have had a cabinet scraper, so a broken Coke bottle is what they used. But a scraper's primary use is on wood, and I've smoothed many a banjar neck with one.

Once your gourd is cleaned out, turn it upside down on a big piece of fairly coarse sandpaper and sand the lip of the head opening until it's nice and flat and smooth. Just keep in mind that once you cut the gourd apart, it is much more fragile than when it was in one piece. I reinforce the lip 'cause when you put on the head, if you just drive the tacks into the side of the gourd, they won't hold worth a hoot. You have to have something hard behind them. I steam bend a piece of oak or a piece of walnut with little kerf cuts [notches] in it to aid the bending and shaping, contour it to fit on the inside edge of the gourd, and glue it into place. After that, you have to predrill the holes before you put in the copper tacks because you can't just go whapping on the thing, or it'll bust all to pieces! But once you get it all together, it's pretty strong.

I turn the taper on the tuning pegs on a small lathe. Where they go through the top of the neck is called the peg head. The narrow strip of wood or bone that goes perpendicular across the neck and keeps the strings spaced apart, up on the peg-head end, is called the nut. So the fingerboard section of

PLATE 107 The gourd showing the
reinforced lip and wooden end plug
for a square dowel stick

PLATE 108 View showing head secured to gourd with copper tacks, bridge, tailpiece, and dowel stick extension

the neck goes from the nut down to the pot, which is the round part; whether it's a gourd or a wooden hoop, the round part is called the pot. The head is stretched across the pot and tacked in place. The bridge sits on top of the head and spaces the strings and transfers the sound vibrations to the head. The piece that holds the strings at the tail end of the instrument is called, you guessed it, the tailpiece. The wooden part that comes out of the base of the neck and runs through the gourd is called the dowel stick. If I were to take the strings loose up at the tuning pegs, the pot would slide off the dowel stick. The only thing that holds the pot in place is the string tension.

To keep from wasting a lot of wood, I make the dowel stick from a separate one-inch square piece of wood. It's rounded at one end, like a spoke, and glued into a one-inch hole I bore in the base of the neck. The reason I leave the dowel stick square is so the gourd doesn't spin around on it. Its length is dictated by the size of the gourd. I let my dowel sticks extend about six inches out the bottom of the gourd. This gives you something to hang the tailpiece on, and you also prop the stick inside your thigh to help you control the instrument while you're playing. By the way, this instrument is designed to be played sitting down. There's a dowel stick in a modern banjo as well. You just can't see it because it's inside the hoop, and there's a resonator on the back.

The gourd banjos that I make are strung with either nylon or gut strings. To me, they sound about the same. All instruments with the hide heads are susceptible to humidity changes. If you're playing outside on a rainy day, the head absorbs the moisture but will dry out later. It's just a natural characteristic of the hides. Gut strings are kind of the same way. They'll also absorb moisture and soften, so on a humid day you have to retune a good bit, but they are historically correct. Nylon strings aren't bothered by humidity and

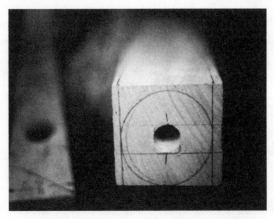

PLATE 109  The hole bored in the base of the neck for the dowel stick

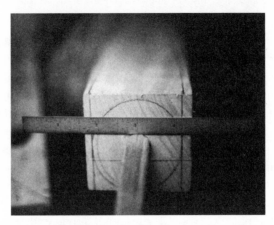

PLATE 110  The dowel stick is glued in position on the neck.

are less expensive than gut, so on the basic gourd banjar I make, I use nylon strings. They look the same unless you really get close to them.

I don't have gut string-making technology, and people always talk about cat gut strings—you've heard that term. I've never run into anybody and haven't been able to find any old-timer who ever knew anything about that. The gut strings I get come from a place up in New York. I think it's called E & O Mari. They are like a fifth-generation gut string manufacturer, and they told me they make them out of sheep intestines as opposed to the legendary cat innards. A fun thing about this was, I was building a banjar for a local museum, and they wanted gut strings on it. Well, I wasn't smart enough to order the strings when I started work on the banjar. I just waited till kind of the end, and I called my supplier and they said because of mad-cow disease, they weren't able to import any gut strings. Later I thought, "If

PLATE 111 The finished gourd banjar

they were made out of sheep, how come the mad-cow disease is bothering them?" At any rate, I didn't get the strings and had to put nylon strings on that banjar.

Goin' back to the late 1850s, the first factory-made banjos were fretless. They remained that way through the Civil War and up into the 1880s. This whole thing, the whole banjo evolution thing, is an interesting story. In the 1880s the people who made banjos wanted to expand their market. Because of the stereotypes associated with the original banjo, a lot of upper-crust folks didn't want much to do with such a "coarse and vulgar" instrument. So the manufacturers set about trying to figure out how to sell their banjos to this untapped resource. It's really funny, but it boils down to this: The reason there are frets on a banjo today is because of a marketing scheme.

A fret is a thin piece of metal that goes perpendicular across the fingerboard, and it gives you an exact position to get a note. You will see them on guitars, and you will see them on modern banjos. Their positioning is very precise so as to assure accurate noting of the instrument.

Sometime in the 1880s, the banjo manufacturers started playing classical music on their instruments to appeal to their newly targeted marketing segment. Most old-time banjo tunes are played in what is called "first position," meaning, basically, the first five noting positions on the neck. When you start playing classical music, which is obviously more complex than hoedown tunes, to get all the notes, you have to play what is known as "up the neck." But without frets, the further you move away from first position, the foggier the note positions get. Down in first position you've got little landmarks like the fifth peg and maybe a knot or piece of grain in the neck to guide you. But once you start to move up the neck, the note positions get closer together and harder to find. If you look at some of the later factory-made fretless ban-jar necks, you'll find scallops on the side of the neck so as to give you a new point of reference for playing up the neck. That was one solution, but frets were a lot easier. So manufacturers decided to put frets on them and deco-rate them with ornate inlay work, carvings, and German silverplating. And they sold like hacksaws in a hoosegow [jail].

Well, back up in the mountains, being able to play Beethoven wasn't a big selling feature, so a lot of folks made their own banjos well into the twenti-eth century, partially because of a lack of availability and partially because of economics.

According to tax records of the times, there were not a lot of slaves in the southern mountains. The terrain is just not well adapted to large farming operations. Consequently, most folks who had slaves around these parts only owned one or two and, in many cases, worked with and lived in close prox-imity to them. Because of this, I believe there was much more cultural inter-change between the Africans and the Anglos in the mountains than in the deep, plantation South. This allowed music, playing styles, and instruments like the banjo or banjar and the mouthbow to cross cultures.

That is not to say all these instruments were commonly found in all mountain homes. There simply wasn't a banjo, mouthbow, dulcimer, and fiddle in every log house in the southern mountains. If you had somebody in your community that happened to have a talent for building or playing some of these instruments, that is probably what you had in your area. Even the playing styles were very localized. It used to be you could tell where a musi-cian was from just by the way he played his fiddle or banjo.

The main difference between the gourd banjar and the mountain banjo, besides looks, is sound. There's no way you can physically get the head as tight on a gourd banjar by stretching it by hand and tacking it as you can on a mountain banjo with its wood frame and metal tone ring. Because of the tighter head, the mountain banjo will be louder and brassier sounding, although not nearly like a modern plastic-headed banjo. But it'll just have more of an edge to it if you compare it to the soft, mellow sound of a gourd banjar with a tack head and nylon or gut strings.

These instruments that we're talking about—the old-timey instruments—were never designed to be played on a stage or at a performance. Music at that time was much more intimate. The term *hoedown music* came from the time at the end of the day when you were done working and laid your hoe down. That was when you might play a little music to relax or have some fun. And that's the truth. You'd quit work for the day, have your sup-per, and the family would spend some time together instead of running off to soccer games or doing computers or whatever folks do nowadays. You know this was a time of families coming together, and they would sing ballads, play music, dance, or they might tell stories. So they were front porch instruments—front room instruments. They didn't have to be loud.

Well, time marched on, and people started playing on stages. They needed louder instruments because it was before the microphone was invented. The high-pitched fiddle carried out pretty well, but the banjo needed help. If you have an open-back wooden-hoop-style banjo, and you're standing up playing it, a good bit of the sound will be absorbed by your belly. So someone came up with this wooden hubcap sort of thing that attached to the back of the banjo and reflected the sound forward. It was called a resonator and began to show up on banjos around the turn of the twentieth century and is now a part of every bluegrass banjo you see today.

One of the most frequent questions I am asked is "How long does it take to build one of those things?" When I'm making mountain larks, I usually do them in batches of ten. They end up looking and sounding different because of all the different woods I use. The reason I do them in batches is to be more time efficient, and mostly it has to do with the drying times of the glues and finishes I use. If I did them one at a time, it would take days. In batches it takes probably six to eight hours each, depending on how the wood works and how fancy I make them. That's per instrument, so if you multiply that by ten, it takes me about sixty to eighty hours to make a batch of ten.

I can build probably two to three dulcimers in a forty-hour week if I have some of the parts roughed out ahead of time. The mountain banjos take probably thirty to forty hours each because they have a good bit more handwork in them, and the hide tanning takes extra time. I don't even like to think about the time I have in a gourd banjar. Some things you just do because you figure they're important. Speaking of important, groundhog hide tanning is something that ought to be part of everyone's education.

When I was researching the old-time music, I was fortunate enough to run across a left-handed fiddler named Uncle Charlie Osborne. When I met Charlie, he was ninety-eight years old. Born in the year 1890, he had hardly ever been out of Russell County, Virginia, in the mountains of southwestern Virginia. He was the purest example of an old-time fiddler that I have ever run across. He learned to play from his father and had not had a lot of outside influence on his music, so he played those tunes basically the way he had learned them eighty years before. He was a great old-time musician. As I got to know Charlie, I was able to play a little bit of music with him and learned a lot of different old-timey things. He'd tell stories and talk about what times were like when he was growing up.

When he died at the age of a hundred and one, he left behind a number of children who at the time were mostly in their sixties and seventies. Two of his sons in particular liked to varmint hunt. Homer and Creed Osborne would go out to shoot groundhogs on a fairly regular basis, and occasionally I'd go with them. Out in rural areas, groundhogs are a real nuisance. They dig holes that can trip cattle and horses and cause them to break legs, and they can destroy a garden in record time.

If I'd call and say I need half a dozen or so hides, they'd start saving them up for me. Once they'd shoot the groundhogs, they'd skin 'em on the spot, put the hides in an old Wal-Mart bag, and store them in a freezer until I'd come up to visit. Then I'd bring the hides home and keep them in my freezer until I had time to tan them. I usually tan three or four at a time and tack them up to cure on the shed behind our house.

Groundhogs aren't bad eatin' either if you cook them right. They've gotta be parboiled a good bit to get all the gaminess and grease out of them, then baked and layered with onions and sweet potatoes. That was what Charlie's daughter, Margaret, would fix him for Christmas dinner every year. They invited me and my wife, Sandy, and my son, Jay, over for Christmas dinner one time, and that's what we had. A groundhog is a lot cleaner animal than a chicken. When you get right down to it, a chicken is a nasty critter.

PLATE 112 John thinning down a groundhog
hide on his fleshing bench

The old-timey way to tan a groundhog hide is to first soak it in a mixture of oak ashes and water. The old term for this mixture is *ooze*, and the ratio depends on a number of variables, like how many hides you are doing at once, the air temperature, and the quality of your ash. You just have to play with it. If the next morning your hide looks like a giant hairy raisin, you maybe could have used a little less ash. The container you use can be made of anything that isn't metal, and ideally it should be roomy enough that the hide can be laid out flat. The amount of time you leave the hide in the ooze depends a lot on the weather. If it's a really hot day, you can set your container of ooze in the sun, and the hide will generally be ready in about twenty-four hours. If it's only fifty degrees, it may take three or four days. The way you tell that the hide is ready to come out of the ooze is by taking a stick and scraping back and forth on the hair. If the hair layer breaks loose from the hide and peels off, kind of like peeling sunburned skin, the hide is ready to rinse. Otherwise, it's back into the ooze a while longer. Once the hide is rinsed, it needs to be fleshed to get all the extra meat off the inside and get it down to a good thickness for a banjo head. I do this on what's called a fleshing bench.

The benches that were used in local tanneries back in the days when cattle and other large hides were manually fleshed were much larger than the one I use. I sit straddling the lower end of the bench and spread the hide across the top end. I added a little trough about halfway down the incline to keep the runoff from the hide from soaking my britches.

A good banjo head is fairly thin, so you spread the hide over the bench, meat side up, and work your knife in a circular motion, all the time pulling back on the excess flesh you're cutting away from the inside of the hide.

The top surface of the bench is rounded. Generally, it is the same contour as the outside of the tree you made it from. The curve keeps you from gouging holes in the hide. If you put a hole in it, it isn't worth a hoot as a banjo head. That's when you make it into shoestrings.

> "The Lord made trees a bit like he made people. They all have different characteristics, and if you look hard enough, you'll find something they're good for."

I'm real fond of cherrywood for making instruments. I love working cherrywood. I like the color and smell of it. I believe out of all the instruments I've made, my ears tend to like the cherry ones. Your ears could be different. I expect over the years I've used just about every kind of tree that grows in our area to make some part of an instrument. The Lord made trees a bit like he made people. They all have different characteristics, and if you look hard enough, you'll find something they're good for. Some are pretty on the outside and rotten on the inside and vice versa. But the way you find out is to work with them. Every once in a while, I use some fancy kind of wood. By fancy wood, I mean figured wood, or wood that has a lot of grain in it such as curly maple or flame maple or tiger maple. My son calls it hologram wood because the grain pattern looks three-dimensional. It's almost as if you could reach down into the wood and touch the ripples.

When I first started out, one of the hardest things for me to do was finding good wood. Since I have been in the craft for a while, now wood sometimes finds me. A couple of years ago, a friend of mine, a former student, called me and said he had a friend in North Carolina who was moving to Florida and had a quantity of American chestnut framing timbers that he couldn't take with him and wondered if I might have an interest in them. Well, does a bag of flour make a big biscuit? The American chestnut tree is, for all intents and purposes, extinct, so I was off like a shot. Because of the size of those beams, I am now able to make solid American chestnut mountain banjos because I have wood at least two inches thick from which to carve the necks.

The mountain banjo is my favorite instrument because of the idea that the old pattern was handed down to me. I build them like Mr. Wolfe built them, and he built them like Stanley Hicks, who built them like his dad, and his dad built them . . . well, you get the idea. I won't change that pattern for anything, and it doesn't matter if I never sell another one. They are just what they are.

I have my doubts about my son going into instrument-making anytime soon, unless he can figure out how to do it with a computer. Right now, I've got a young man down around Atlanta that I'm trying to help along the same way Mr. Mize and Mr. Wolfe helped me. And over the last six or seven years, I've been blessed with dozens and dozens of students at the Campbell Folk School and other places, and I'm sure some of them will carry on the tradition as well. You know it takes only one person to keep it alive.

I got started into instrument-building kind of late in life, but because of the Foxfire connection that steered me on to Mr. Wolfe and Mr. Mize to get me started, I feel I've been given a level of mountain instrument-building knowledge equivalent to a Yale law degree. This whole saga started back in 1990, and over the years, the Lord has continued to be faithful to provide both the knowledgeable people and the incredible opportunities that have brought me to where I am today. It's sure nothing I could have done or planned on my own. To think that a forty-something city boy with zero knowledge of woodworking, instrument building, and old-time music is able to be doing what I'm doing—well, it boggles my mind. God is still in the miracle business!

***Editor's note:*** As John Huron sat reviewing these pages, he got the sad news that his, and our, good friend Robert Mize had suddenly passed away. John wanted to add this: The unexpected death of Robert Mize left a lot of holes in a lot of hearts. In the years that followed our initial encounter, he became very dear to me, and I could always count on extremely candid answers to all my questions concerning my newly found vocation. I believe I shall miss him more tomorrow than I do today. As time passes, he will no doubt be remembered as the builder of nearly 4,000 mountain dulcimers. But he was much more than that. Even a brief encounter with Mr. Mize— whether at a craft show, at a dulcimer gathering, or in his dusty old shop— became a treasured memory to the many thousands of people he touched. But his most important products were not dulcimers or tall tales. He and his wife left behind four fine children, many grandchildren and relatives, and innumerable friends, each with bushels of very personal memories of Mr. Mize and Mama Maude. What better legacy could you ask for?

# TIMPSON CREEK
# MILLWORKS AND GALLERY

*"I've always said to treat your customers like your mother,
and you won't ever have any problems."*

Ever since I was nine years old, I have worked with my mom cleaning houses during the summers. One summer we were cleaning a new construction house when a man came in and began hanging a chandelier made of antlers. The handiwork and its effect were absolutely amazing! Mom told me that Dwayne Thompson was the mastermind behind that project. I was astonished; I wanted to know more about this extraordinarily talented man. A Foxfire article gave me the perfect opportunity. When I called to set up an interview, he was eager to speak with me.

The attendant at his gallery showed us how to get to his workshop. Carrying the tape recorder and camera, we had to go up a set of spiral steps. I could see myself falling over the side! When we reached the top of the stairs, Mr. Thompson was there to greet us. He invited us to sit in rocking chairs on the front porch of his shop and took us on a tour to view his handiwork. I invite you now to sit back in a rocking chair and enjoy this story of how such an unbelievably talented man began his artistry and the photos of his incredible work.

—*Kandi Lacretia Gay*

MY NAME is Dwayne Thompson, and I was born right here in Rabun County in 1953. I was raised right here on this creek [Timpson Creek]. I went to church right out the road here. There used to be a small general store right here on the creek, too, that everybody here used. I went to school at Rabun County High. I don't know what else except I just growed up right here on the creek, more or less.

My daddy was R. E. Thompson, and my mother is Bernice Thompson. My mother was a homemaker all of her life. My daddy worked on the state highway, and he was a bootlegger here in the county. He was killed in 1971; my mother is still alive, and she lives right up the road here. I've got one sister; she lives over on the creek here, too. Her lovely name is DeLois Edwards. She married a boy out of Cleveland, and he is Lamar Edwards, who is the county surveyor.

My wife and I went to high school together, and we knew each other in high school. As she was graduating college, in the summer she did the riding program over here at High Harbor Camp. Some of the little kids would stop by here since the shop was on the road here, and I'd give them little wooden blocks for the kids to paint. She was stopping by, and we just got to talkin'. We went out, and it went from there. We have been together for a lot of years now. We have one daughter, and her name is Anne Neal Thompson. She was born on September 4 in 1986.

I had fun growing up. I played a lot, but I also worked a lot—all the summers I worked, but we had fun. We did a lot of fishin' and a whole lot of huntin'. I hunted all the time, every spare minute I had. We did a little bit of campin' in the mountains. When I got a little older, around the age of thirteen and fourteen, we all had little motorcycles and stuff like that, so we'd just stay out all day in the woods on motorcycles most of the time. As we got older, we did things more for the adrenaline rush: dune buggies, riding motorcycles, hang gliding, and Jeeps, anything fun and recreational.

I remember going campin' a few times with my parents. I remember that real well. I remember the first time I ever saw Atlanta. I remember being so small I had to get in the pen and catch hogs. I'd ride 'em. I also remember

PLATE 113 Dwayne Thompson

deer huntin' with my granddaddy. I remember my granddaddy taking me to a couple of stills. I did not know where in the h—— I was. I was lost. I remember that real well. I remember my granddaddy being so much fun. My granddaddy Thompson was in the first *Foxfire* ever done [see *The Fox-fire Book*, 1972]. He was probably the most fun man I've ever been around. He enjoyed kids, and he kinda let y' get by with stuff that Mom and Dad wouldn't let y'. I really enjoyed him.

There is a lot of difference in schools today than before. I think there is a lot more pressure on the kids; I think you guys have it a lot harder. I mean a *lot* harder. My daughter has to study all the time. When I was growin' up, I used to breeze through almost everything. There just was not as much pressure. Everything now has to be on a computer. You gotta drive a car at sixteen. You gotta have a car at sixteen, and you gotta keep up with your classmates and everybody. I also think the education and sports are more involved, and I think your home life is a lot more involved now. I think you guys have it harder than I did. I know a lot of people say that the old-timers had it harder, but I don't believe that. I think y'all do. Really 'n' truly, if I could give advice to teenagers, I guess I would tell them to find a time to breathe. They've gotta find the time to just say "The h—— with everything" and just kinda relax a lit-tle bit. You don't have to be movin' all the time. You can stop!

Really, my responsibilities as a kid were not real bad. The only animals I had to take care of were cows. I milked cows for my grandmother. I did that for about two years when I was in elementary school and some in high school, that and helping with the wood heat. We had a very, very small cookstove in the kitchen, and I helped keep it goin'. I would cut the grass and whatever a boy could do. We didn't have a farm. We kept up hogs all the time. That's about it. Like I say, when I got older, my dad got me a job, and I had to work. From about the sixth grade on, I worked. I had a couple of household chores, not many. My sister and me, we did a few, but Mother did most of them.

I had many jobs when growing up. When I was in about the sixth grade, I had to go to Dillard. I went up to the Flats [in Dillard, Georgia] to pick and sack cabbage. I went up there in the late summer and picked beans, and I picked up taters. That was the worst job I ever had in my life. One summer, I sold produce in Dillard at a produce stand. That was a pretty good job. I made twenty-five bucks a week. I worked six days a week. One year I worked at a janitor program at the high school, but I lost that job 'cause I wouldn't cut my hair. They told me to either get a haircut or not work, so I said that I guessed I wouldn't work. That was about my eighth-grade year. As I got older, I worked with a carpenter on the lake. One summer I worked with my brother-in-law surveying; I enjoyed that. I enjoyed being out in the woods, so that was a good summer job.

Really, I got interested in what I do today in high school. The shop teacher, Jack Prince, and the agriculture and FFA [Future Farmers of America] teacher, Jack Martin, they were just real good to me. They let me work. It was just so easy for me. Once I got started, I never quit. I went right out of high school into trade [vocational] school. I got a job at a furniture company, designing furniture and building prototypes. I never got out of it.

When I started my business, I borrowed fifteen hundred dollars from my aunt and bought me some tools. I subcontracted and built some furniture for a couple, and this got my business started here. I never turned down any job comin' through the front door, anything dealin' with wood, whether it meant chainsawin' a log or puttin' an ax handle into an ax or buildin' somebody a wooden box. I just didn't turn anything down. By doing that, I just ended up gettin' a lot of work.

I'm kinda into the lucky point now when it comes to the pieces I make. I've got the experience and enough time under my belt. I do about 50 percent commissions, and I do about 50 percent of whatever I want to do and sell those. Even my commissions are mine. Somebody can give me what they want, but the look of it is mine. If they come to me, then everybody knows me enough so they know the look that they're gonna get. I usually draw and sketch everything I do. I usually draw it out to give them a general idea. I say, "That is pretty well what I'm gonna do, and it may change."

Most of the time, when I choose my materials, I work with stuff that is thrown away. If somebody is trimming a road, I will ask 'em if I can pick up what's on the ground. What I usually do is stockpile this wood. I have it all in a pile. If I get something in my mind, then I will go out there and look for something to use. I kinda look for it in my pile rather than going out in the woods and cuttin' a piece. Material-wise, that's how I get it. I look for curved pieces; I look for stumps. I look for everything and put it up as inventory. I collect old dull paintings and just objects. It may be somebody else's art to go with mine.

It's almost impossible to say how long I spend on one piece because I build from little to big, so I'm gonna say anywhere from a week to three months. I'm gonna start a piece soon that will take about four to five months to build. I get frustrated, and that's when you just leave it alone and go somewhere else. That's when you look for that third piece. I've run against the wall so many times. I don't really get flustered anymore. I just walk away.

I have to work on more than one piece at a time—sometimes you get kinda socked in on a piece, and you get blind to it. I just have to walk off. I have been working on this chandelier, and I am stuck. I cannot get any further than where I am at because everything I do, I don't like. I'll just quit, and then one morning, all of a sudden, it will just come together. I never

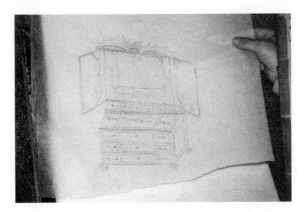

PLATE 114  A draft of a soon-to-be masterpiece

PLATE 115  A completed piece that is a
variation of the draft
(*photo courtesy of Scot Roberge Photography*)

work on just one piece, never. Plus, some stuff you do is boring, so about a day or two of that boring stuff and I push that off and work on something interesting. I kinda shift them. I work on anywhere from three to five pieces at a time. When beginning a piece, I usually get an idea in my head, and then I do a rough sketch. If it's not a real complicated piece, I'll just draw the mechanics of the piece. I don't really know how exactly it's going to look. I'll go ahead and draw and get the big pictorial of it. Then I'll look at that and say, "Well, that don't look too good," then try to make all of my changes. What then happens between the paper and the wood is I can't find the wood to match what's on the paper, so you gotta change that. Using rustic material like I do, some things just don't work. It ain't like standard cabinet stuff:

PLATE 116  An armoire created by Mr. Thompson

Sometimes I have to make the materials I need. Recently I had to make the hinges for a piece I was making because nothing worked like I wanted it to. A lot of times I'll have a SciTech [idea] of something, and if it's real complicated, I'll have a sketch. I'll go from that to a carcass and put drawers, shelves, or whatever I need. Then I'll start doing the exterior from that. I then decorate it, unless it's a piece made out of logs. Then the logs would be the structure. If you had a cabinet, then the first thing you'd do would be build a box. In this box you might have drawers or shelves. A carcass is basically a framework; that's how you start. Everything you build is a box, and from there you just decorate the box.

The difference in how I find jobs now and when I first began is mainly I don't have to listen to the customer as much as I did. It's my way or the highway. I pretty well do it like I want to do it. If it ain't gonna look good and won't be up to what I want, then I don't do the job. If they want it either cheaper or in a style that I know when I get done it won't look good or look like I made it, then I don't and won't do it. I look at my work just like climbin' a set of steps, and I just need to keep on a-climbin'. I can't stop. If I stop and back up, then I'm not learning. Every piece that I build, I back up, and I look at it. The first question I ask myself is "What is wrong with it?" If I do find anything at all wrong with it, I either change it or change it on the

PLATE 117  A finished chandelier

next piece. If there is nothing wrong with the piece, then I see what I could do to make it better. By doing that to myself, it gets tough sometimes, but I keep myself goin', climbin' those steps. I keep tryin' to make it better, and I really enjoy that.

Right now, what I'm really proud of is I'm learning how to cast and make molds. I'm also doing ironwork. I use a lot of found pieces to go in my work. I spend a lot of time out looking and going to antique shows. I find stuff that I'll never find again, and I'm always sad. Now I'm learnin' how to take what I find and reproduce it and save my original. I'm real proud of that. My business has grown over the years 'cause I keep improving on the work.

My wife, years ago, was insistent on a nice yard. She wanted to keep the place up. I was a bit reluctant for a few years; then it really did get extremely enjoyable. Keeping a good and respectable appearance has actually gotten to be something I enjoy and am really very proud of. I have flowers and trees and playhouses, stuff for the public to be interested in. The people that come in our store, we just try to be friendly to them. I've always said to treat your customers like your mother, and you won't ever have any problems. That is pretty much what we do, and, by doin' that, we have people that come in the store that we really enjoy. We always enjoy seeing them come back, whether they are buyin' something or just coming by. We have just slowly built up a clientele in such a manner that we enjoy them, and they enjoy us.

# THE UNIQUE ARTWORK
# OF TUBBY BROWN

*"When you get old and you start having aches and pains, you just get you a hobby. Everybody ought to have a hobby."*

I first became interested in interviewing Tubby Brown because I saw a few pieces of his work in the Foxfire Museum. When I discovered that the artist of the interesting work lived just an hour from me, I decided that this was going to be my next project. Mr. Brown was a very gracious interviewee. The interview was very entertaining, and I fell in love with more than one piece of his artwork that I would have loved to take home. When I returned from the interview, I began transcribing immediately. Somehow along the way, I became sidetracked. This school year, a friend of mine, Missy Watts, decided to finish the article. Since I am a senior editor in the Foxfire classroom, I had the opportunity to help Missy with our shared article on the folk art of Tubby Brown.

—*Candi Forester*

MY FULL name is Rutherford (Tubby) Brown, and I am sixty-eight years old. I was born in 1929 during the Depression, about three or four miles outside of Jefferson, Georgia. I grew up living right across the street [from this house], most of the time. I was born out here in the country. My daddy was a sharecropper; that was just an extension of slavery, y' know. They tried to get all they could out of the people and not pay them nothin'. They'd furnish all the livestock and mules and all. It was supposed to be half on tax, but the landowner usually gets more on tax. They get most of it. Colored man told me one day—he was a good friend of mine that trades with me—he told me he went out to settle up with this man he was working for, you know, sharecropping. Said he knew he cleared a couple thousand, and they was gonna have a big Christmas for the kids and all. Said he went down there, and they was settled up on the back porch, said he just sat his hat down on the floor. He sat down there with a man and his wife. The man looked at the books and says, "Here, Mama, I can't tell nothin' about these books"; he handed them over to his wife. Said his wife looked at him and said, "Oh, Daddy says he'll never get out of debt." He said he just picked up his hat and left and moved the next day. You know, that's the way they would do it.

Nobody worried about us kids. We were gone everywhere. They tried to get you in at dinnertime. If you didn't come in, they'd whip you at dinner and supper. They'd get out there and call you; you might be around, you might not. We just played mostly when I was little. When you got big enough to work, you went to work. When you got eleven, twelve years old, they had you a job waitin' on you. My daddy always had me a job. When I was about eleven or twelve, I'd plow up the place on the side of the house; I had a garden. Daddy said, "I'm gonna buy everything you make at some price." Of course everything was cheap. I worked in that garden all the time. A lady was goin' on vacation, and she wanted to get me to work her garden when she was gone. She thought I was doin' a real good job. She wanted me to work in it for two weeks, to keep it clean and everything. It was real grassy! Boy, I had to work. I worked every day for two weeks, staked the beans and everything. She had a big old garden. People had big gardens back then. They canned a lot of stuff. [When] she come back from vacation, she give me two dollars. I told my daddy, I said, "I hate that old lady." He said, "You ought to asked her what she was gonna pay you before you started."

I've got a grandson who's just started driving. You'll wreck your first car. I did mine. When I was younger than fifteen, Daddy bought me a little car, and it was a twenty-something Chevrolet. It was a little coupe. Daddy said, "If something happens to that car, don't be pushing it around with my new truck. You'll skin it up." So that's what happened. The battery went dead, and I got my sister to push it with Daddy's new truck. We bent the grill on the new truck, and he just took my car and sold it the next day. Parents didn't mess with you back then. They didn't have to whip you but one time. I appreciate being brought up sorta straight and all now. It helped me. Of course my family was always good to me. They gave me a lot.

Also, when I got fifteen, Daddy got me a job with a carpenter building a house. Me and this old man built a house one summer. We worked all summer on that house. Didn't have nothin' but a handsaw back then. You didn't have no skill saw or nothin'—handsaw and ax and a hammer. I worked all summer, twelve hours a day, two dollars a day. I thought I was makin' good money. A lot of people were working for fifty cents a day back then.

My daddy was a sharecropper. He did that for a few years and then got into the grocery business. That's how we got in it, too. He run it for a long time. I had a grocery store, me and my brother, for thirty-five years. It was called Brown's Grocery. That's logical, ain't it? We run the store for thirty-five years. Grocery stores are a lot of hard work. I worked ten or twelve hours a day, every day in a grocery store. Me and my brother owned the store, and we had one person helpin' us work sometimes. I did meat cuttin' and deliverin' and goin' to the bank and all that. My brother, he kep' the books and all. I enjoyed that. I enjoyed the people. I've wrote down a bunch of stuff that people used to tell me—old jokes and things out of the store—old corny stuff. Kids now, they wouldn't appreciate it, I guess, but we did back then. We'd sit around. Way back then, we had an old potbelly heater; we'd sit around there, and somebody was always coming up with somethin'—jokes or somethin' that had happened to them or somethin'.

**"When you get old and you start having aches and pains, you just get you a hobby. Everybody ought to have a hobby."**

I went to high school here in Jefferson. I went to Piedmont College for two years and then to the University of Georgia two years. I majored in education but never did teach. The Army got me. I went into the Army in 1950, and served two years during the Korean War. That's my daddy in that photo when he was in the First World War in France. I was in the Korean War. My brother was in the Second World War. They had a war for all of us. My daddy was the only one who got wounded. He got shot in the leg, and then he got gassed with that old mustard gas. But I never did get in combat. My brother was in Russia, and the airfields were bombed where he was at in Russia. They had an airfield over there, and they shot and bombed Germans. They'd go from England to Russia and back—went back and forth. He was in Russia. One of the few people that was in Russia, I reckon.

My whole family likes art. My son, Andy, he used to help me a little bit. He teaches school; he paints, too. He paints, and my wife, Betty, paints. She helps me and gives me encouragement. We all paint. Everybody in the family makes a little bit of money. I have three children, two boys and a girl, and they ain't as old as I am! I have five grandchildren. They range in age from twenty-two to nine years old. All of them are good kids.

I have been producing artwork about thirteen or fourteen years. I just gradually got into it. I was just foolin' around with it. I thought people might like it, so I kept doing it. It gives you somethin' to do. It relaxes you. When you get old and you start having aches and pains, you just get you a hobby. Everybody ought to have a hobby. I sat down when I first retired and sold out the store. I sat down and stayed sick all the time. You get to worrying about yourself. Since I started doing this, I have met a lot of nice people. I paint a few pictures every once in a while. I like the woodwork better. I like to work with the bandsaw. I'd be layin' in bed at night, and I'd start thinkin' about somethin' that I wanted to make. If I didn't write it down, I'd forget it

PLATE 118  Mr. and Mrs. Brown with several of his creations

before the next mornin'. That is the way I got a lot of my ideas. I started sell-
ing my stuff after I was up in Gainesville one time. I saw a video of Mr. R. A.
Miller and Howard Finster, and I saw what they were doin'. I told my wife,
"I can make some stuff like that." I was lookin' around for somethin' to do.

> "He started buyin' 'em, and that's how I got started. He was takin'
> 'em to New York and sellin' 'em—givin' me a dollar for one. He was
> makin' money on me, but that was all right. It gives me somethin'
> to do!"

I started makin' stuff, and the first thing I made was cuttin' out faces on my
bandsaw. I started sellin' 'em to a man from Atlanta. He come by, saw 'em,
and he started buyin' 'em, and that's how I got started. He was takin' 'em to
New York and sellin' 'em—givin' me a dollar for one. He was makin' money
on me, but that was all right. It gives me somethin' to do! You got to have
somethin' to do when you retire or you'll go crazy.

The style that I do is called folk art. It's art that people create on their
own. They don't have any formal art training or anything. They just come up
with their own ideas. There are a lot of people doing folk art now. I never
had any art lessons. I never did know I could do nothin'. No, I knew I could
paint a house, but that's about all! When I started in the Army, I told my

mother I had a week before I was gonna have to go. I told her that I was gonna paint her house, and I painted her house. I knew I could paint a house, but that's all. One day I just sat down and started doin' paintings. That's all you gotta do. Just sit down and get you some paint. First thing to do is just paint your arms and face and everything—you don't have to worry about it then. As I sold out my grocery store, I started full in with paintin'. I used to collect antiques, junk—you can see out there in my garage. I got it full of junk; I'm gonna get it straightened up, I told my wife. I don't know when.

I guess *Noah's Ark* and some of the Bible scenes that I have done are my favorite pieces of artwork. I made a tin boat and a wooden little house to fit in it, and I cut the animals out of tin. People like the tin stuff a lot. The pieces that mean the most to me, I usually carry them upstairs. I got a few things up there that I made. I've got some driftwood stuff I made. I like the cat, a devil, and several more things. I make some driftwood items. I just always liked the Noah's Ark from the time I was a little kid going to church and they had one back in there in the room where the kids played. They had a Noah's Ark, y' know. I've always liked the story of Noah's Ark.

### "I didn't just plan to get started in the folk art business. You don't plan stuff like that."

I just gradually got into art. That is the way everybody does, I guess. You make a little stuff and find out that you like it, and you just want to make something else. It is always exciting to make something new. You can't wait to get finished. This is more like a hobby. You just enjoy it like people do fishing or anything else.

I didn't just plan to get started in the folk art business. You don't plan stuff like that. I was up there at Main Street Gallery in Clayton, Georgia, one day, and I told her that I made some stuff. She came down here and started buyin' stuff. I sold them a lot of stuff. I've had a lot of galleries that I have sold to. Business has been slow here lately. I think the Internet probably is getting a lot of folk art stuff on there and all. I did have some ladies from Delaware come by yesterday. That was the second time I've had anybody from Delaware. They bought a *Jonah and the Whale.* I've got some *Jonah and the Whale*s out there. It's got Jonah up in there cookin' fish up in the whale. They bought one of them.

I just do it because I really enjoy it. I just want to be able to quit when I want to and work when I want to. If I want to work an hour or two a day, I work, but if I don't feel like working or if there's a ball game, I don't work. I just do it when I feel like it and can enjoy it.

PLATE 119 *Jonah and the Whale*

I sometimes go to art shows, but not many. I don't take stuff to shows any-more. I used to go over to Alabama and Kentucky over there. It's a long ways over there, and it just wears me out. You have to stand there two days and talk, and, you know, people wanna take your picture and everything, and talk wears you out more than you think. I go to some shows out in Atlanta and places like that. That's comin' up in not too long. But I like to go. You get inspirations when you go to other shows. You see other people and their work. You don't want to copy it, but it gives you ideas. You get inspirations from other people's art. I do.

"I've always been a woodworker, so I like working with wood . . . I used to make birdhouses for my mother when I was just two or three years old."

The amount of time I spend on any one project all depends. If I'm painting a picture like that right there, it usually takes me about half a day. If I'm workin' on something like that big piece over there, it might take me a couple of days. I usually make three or four of the same thing at a time so I can cover more ground that way than I can just making one at a time. See, you get your saw and set it up and everything and get ready to go. I make a bunch of stuff up, and if people see it and keep callin' for it, I keep makin' it. The aquariums and *Noah's Arks* are the most popular of my pieces. I've got several things—bird trees and such—that I make that customers like. You can't rush the art to just make money out of it. You have to take your time. I want to think it out. I usually like to make something I saw when I was a kid or somethin'.

I don't have any idea how many projects I do in a year. Let's see. I guess I do a couple hundred different things. I've got a book in there that has pictures of everything; I've took pictures of everything I've made. I used to make a lot of big stuff—chairs, benches, and things—but I've got away from that. It's too much work for me now. When you get seventy-three, you're getting old, a little bit of age on y'. When you get seventy-three, you'll find out.

PLATE 120  Devil jugs

I make all of my artwork mainly with recycled stuff. I buy a lot of wood and paint. If you paint anything that goes outside with oil, it's really expensive. I got a lot of tin. You can buy a lot of tin items anywhere they tear down old chicken houses. I use mostly acrylic paints for stuff that goes outside. I like the smaller projects better.

I've always been a woodworker, so I like working with wood. First job I ever had was bein' a carpenter, buildin' a house, and I've always liked to do woodwork. I used to make birdhouses for my mother when I was just two or three years old. My daddy had some houses he fixed up, and I'd go down there and then I'd slip out enough lumber and nails and stuff to build a birdhouse. He'd always get on to me all the time about getting the lumber. Of course I would just get the scraps and stuff—drive big ol' nails in little old boards. That's the way kids are.

I like to paint, too. I've got a lot of paintings I've made. I painted pictures of things I did when I was a kid, like catchin' toadfrogs. In the sand yard, they used to have sand. I'd go up to my uncle's. I'd make ice cream, and all of us kids would get out there and catch toadfrogs. They'd come in on that sand when it got cool, come in on that sand at night, and we'd catch 'em. They make warts on your hand, they say.

That painting is the one hundredth anniversary of when they discovered ether; I call it *Crawford W. Long Day—1941*. He discovered ether here in Jefferson. That was the day they dedicated that building over there. Craw-

PLATE 121 Crawford Long painting

ford Long was from Danielsville, and he started [a medical] practice over here in Jefferson. They had this stuff they called laughing gas back then. They discovered it was an anesthesia. He operated on a man. The man had somethin' on his back, and he cut that off over there in his office.

**"A lot of my ideas come from my childhood. We didn't have television back then, and when school was out, we were just like a wild bunch."**

That was the first time it was used, I reckon. There was a Morton from up north, a dentist, that claimed that he was the first one to use anesthesia, but they haven't argued about that for years. I reckon Crawford Long gets the credit for it. You know, they've got a museum over here and a big one in Atlanta. Ether was around, but he was the first to be able to put it on your face and not kill you with it, and it was an anesthesia. They used it for years and years. Of course, they've got several different kinds [of anesthesia] now. See that horse [in my painting] is runnin' away there—that's what happened over there. Some fellow got a team of horses started and run down through the crowd. I don't know if you can tell it real good or not. My paintin' ain't too good, about like a third-grader. Well, he just got to actin' up at the top of the hill (there's a hill up there), and he, I don't know if he meant to run them away or not, but they run away down through the crowd. A feller there, a great big ol' feller—he was about half drunk—he reached up there and grabbed them and stopped them. That's what I remember from the Crawford Long Day in 1941. I was just a kid, [but that's] one thing I remember. I painted it about three or four months ago.

I paint just things I remember; I got a lot of paintings in there. I paint anything that I can think of. A lot of my ideas come from my childhood. We didn't have television back then, and when school was out, we were just like a wild bunch.

The prices of my artwork come from just whatever the galleries will pay. They have to make money on it; they have a lot of overhead. When I come up with my prices, I just try to put a hundred dollars on everything and come down a little bit on it!

I just take my time on my projects. Some pieces you can do a lot quicker than others. It doesn't matter about that. I don't keep down my time or anything when I'm makin' somethin'. I just make it because it's fun. If I didn't enjoy doin' it, it would be rough tryin' to make it.

I had an uncle—he is dead now—who lived in McCaysville, Georgia, on the Tennessee line. He was one of the most famous carvers in the United States. My uncle, Carl Stepp, was a craftsman; he was listed as one of the real craftsmen. He has some art at the historical museum in Atlanta. Now they are showing him and people like Lanier Meaders [see *Foxfire 8*]. Famous people like that are exhibited in the museum. He done a lot of carvin'; he made gun stocks and furniture. When he carved out a horse, he carved out all the muscles. He'd do all that; he was real good. I want to make something sometime good enough to go out there, but I don't know if I ever will. I have a dollhouse I have been working on, and I've set it aside. I need to go back and finish it. The dollhouse is going to be real nice. I made all the furniture for it and all. I couldn't do it now because I can't see that good, but I started the dollhouse several years ago, and I just never did finish it. I went around the house—we have a lot of antiques—and just drew them up and made them to scale.

I have a little workshop at a little red building where I do all my sawing. I started out in the barn; then I had that little building built. I've got all kinds of saws. I bought all my saws secondhand. I couldn't afford to buy all the high-priced equipment. To make somethin', you start just like everything else; you start with raw material. You got to have the idea first and then the material, and then start with the tools. I cut those out on a bandsaw usin' the smaller blade. A lot of people like to use these jigsaws, but I never have found one of them that I can do anything with. I got the big ol' bandsaw. The only thing I don't like about it is that they throw a lot of dust.

I don't make as much stuff now as I used to. I used to have a cabinet shop that I would go get my wood from, but I've got my barn full and I just quit goin'. I got enough to do me. I do most of my work up there in the work-shop—two or three buildin's up there. If I fill one of them up, I have to move on to another one.

# HOW TO

"That is why it is so unique—

there are no two alike."

—*Ruby Cheek*

The activities featured in this section are as varied as the people who have shown us how to do them. Many Foxfire books have featured Kenny Runion. He was a multitalented, friendly, knowledgeable person who graciously shared his skills with numerous Foxfire students over the years. Every time I saw Kenny, he had to give me one of his mountain laurel rings. I still have them tucked safely away. They are keepsakes, and I hope someday my son with see the value in them. Not only did Kenny make rings and necklaces out of mountain laurel, he also created excellent mountain laurel furniture. Featured in this section is how to make a Kenny Runion mountain laurel chair. While the maestro will not have made the pieces you create, they can still be beautiful and functional.

Ruby Cheek is a kind, friendly lady who showed us how to make rose bead necklaces. Her love for roses is evident in all the varieties she grows in her garden. When a friend gave her an article about making the necklaces, Mrs. Cheek began making keepsakes for her family and friends. She has perfected her technique over the years and added touches that make her necklaces even more unique.

Harley Thomas is a gentleman Foxfire interviewed several times about subjects that were as varied as Mr. Thomas's talent. While interviewing him for fiddle-making, Foxfire discovered that he also knew how to make coffins. Naturally, we asked him to make us one. It is still displayed in the chapel at the Foxfire Center in Mountain City, Georgia. We realize that not everyone wants to make a coffin, but with soaring funeral costs, it might be a skill worth knowing. In days gone by, statistics reveal a high mortality rate for children. The coffin featured here is a child's coffin. However, the measurements can be adapted for an adult-sized coffin.

Lindsey Moore and Lillie Lovell showed us how to kill, dress, and cook a mud turtle. According to both of them, it is some of the best meat you will ever eat! They take us step by step through the process, and they shared personal stories and remembrances. I personally could never eat a turtle. But, hopefully, some of our readers will find the article informative and useful. It is certainly an alternative to the high-priced meat at the grocery store!

—*Kaye Carver Collins*

## KENNY RUNION CHAIR

The photographs and diagrams in this article are of a chair made of mountain laurel by Kenny Runion in 1935. Mr. Runion uses the natural crooks of mountain laurel to the best advantage for each section of the chair.

The owner of the chair had brought it to Clyde Runion, Kenny's nephew and also a maker of this type of chair [see *Foxfire 10,* pages 404–408], to be repaired. Clyde contacted us to show us the chair and allowed us to photograph and measure it.

***Editor's note:*** Clyde's article, in *Foxfire 10,* showed none of the measurements or diagrams of a mountain laurel chair. Since we have received numerous requests for chair diagrams, we decided to print Kenny's in this edition.

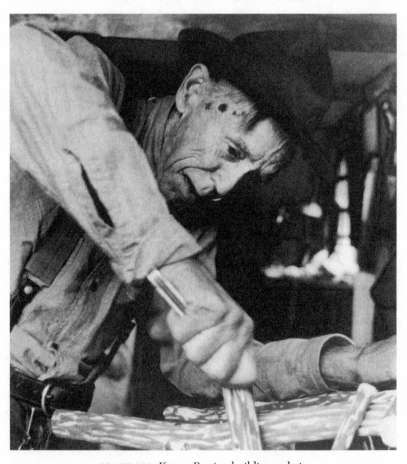

PLATE 122   Kenny Runion building a chair

PLATE 123  This view of Kenny's chair shows the rocker notches on the end
of one of the four posts and one of the seat notches that is made in each
of the posts.

## Back Post

Length from top to notch, 21½ inches

Seat notch, 1 inch

Length from bottom to notch, 10 inches

Rocker notch, 1 inch

## Arm

Arm length, 22½ inches

Seat notch, 1 inch

Length to the end of notch, 5½ inches

Notch width, 2½ inches

## Front Post

Length from top to notch, 9⅝ inches

Seat notch, 1 inch

Length from bottom to notch, 11 inches

Rocker notch, 2 inches

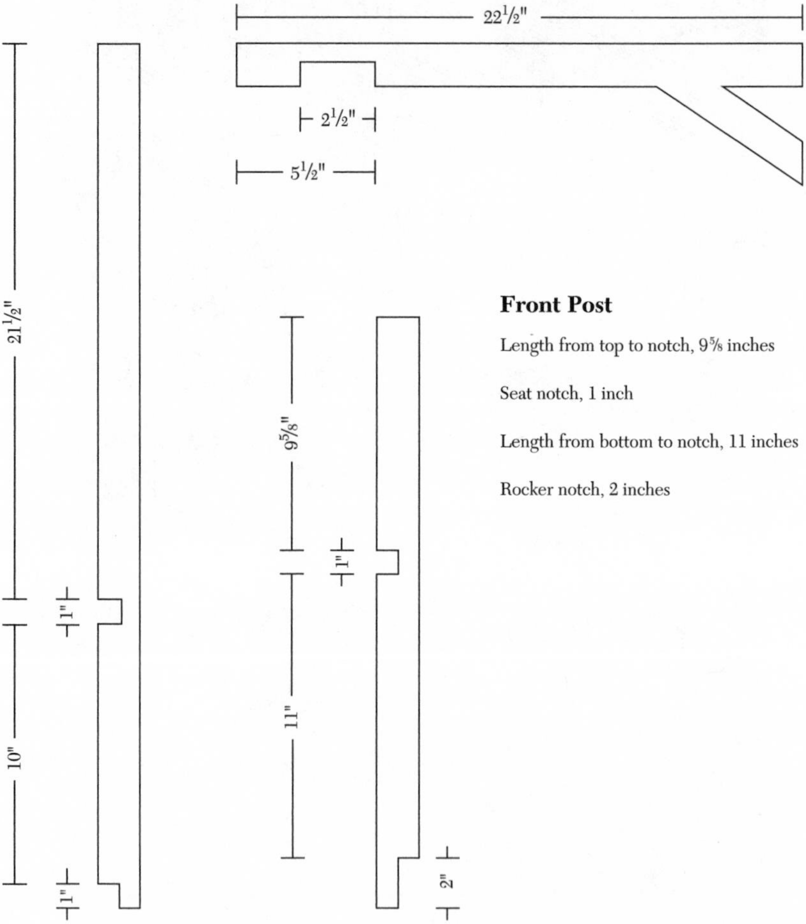

PLATE 124 Diagram of arm, back post, and front post

PLATE 125  As you can see from this photo, a notch is
made in the arm of the chair to fit over the front post.
Kenny also used a piece of wood on the side of the
chair for extra support.

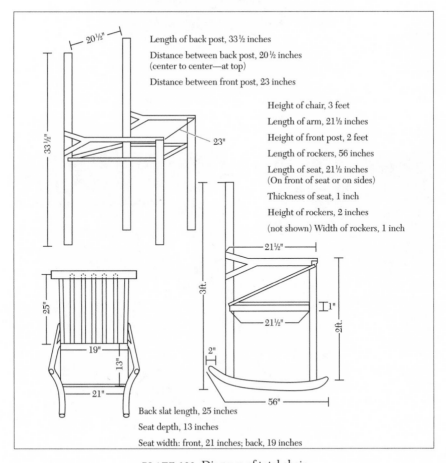

Length of back post, 33 ½ inches

Distance between back post, 20 ½ inches
(center to center—at top)

Distance between front post, 23 inches

Height of chair, 3 feet

Length of arm, 21 ½ inches

Height of front post, 2 feet

Length of rockers, 56 inches

Length of seat, 21 ½ inches
(On front of seat or on sides)

Thickness of seat, 1 inch

Height of rockers, 2 inches

(not shown) Width of rockers, 1 inch

Back slat length, 25 inches

Seat depth, 13 inches

Seat width: front, 21 inches; back, 19 inches

PLATE 126  Diagram of total chair

PLATE 127  Note how Kenny used crooked
and forked wood for the arm to give
more support to the chair.

PLATE 128  Back view of the chair. The back slats
are nailed to the back of the seat.

PLATE 129  Holes are drilled into the top for back slats to fit into.

PLATE 130  Kenny also used pieces of crooked wood as supports for each underside corner of the chair (upside-down view of the chair bottom).

# THE MAKING OF ROSE BEADS

"Roses are just like children—each one has its own characteristics, and you treat them like your child."

When Mrs. Angie Cheek, my Foxfire advisor, told me what an amazing woman her mother-in-law was, I really wanted to meet her. Her unique hobby of making rose beads interested me, and that was just the surface of a really charming lady.

As my advisor and I pulled up to the white house on Hayes Street, in Toccoa, Georgia, the yard was surrounded by trees and filled with beautiful flowers. When I knocked on the door, I met Ruby Cheek, a grandmotherly woman with gray hair and a bright smile. I soon realized she wasn't just an average woman but a woman with many talents and abilities. She was extraordinary! She was very hospitable and definitely had a knack for gardening. A beautiful rose garden was not all that she had: Her vegetable and flower gardens were magnificent as well. She showed us her gardens and shared her knowledge of them, and she spent an afternoon demonstrating the making of these wonderful beads.

After our interview we ate a delicious lunch, fresh from her garden. Telling me that she would have to treat me like family folk, she handed me the dinnerware to set the table. When we sat down to eat, we talked like family and had a wonderful time. I felt at home. In fact, I felt as if I were going for a visit with my own grandparents. Ruby Cheek and her husband, Coy, were gracious and very welcoming to a total stranger who invaded their home with a tape recorder and a camera.

—*Kari Hughes*

I HAVE been growing roses for more than thirty-two years. My roses are my favorite plants. You will never find another plant that will give you that abundance of flowers, if you treat it right.

Roses are just like children—each one has its own characteristics, and you treat them like your child. I have around seventy-eight rosebushes.

My friend May Trucano found an article on rose beads and brought it to me since she knew I grew roses. I decided I was going to make them. Most of my roses are hybrid teas, so I thought I could wear the roses around my neck that I have enjoyed working with, such as the Bob Hope, Garden Party, and Mr. Lincoln, just to mention a few. Joy Walker Stuart published the article. She noted that monks made rosary beads, and she acquired her information from them. She has tried to improve the original method the monks used. Roses are as old as the Bible; they are mentioned in both the Old and New Testaments. The Christian monks made them for worship, and they used sticks to put a hole through them. It is thought that the monks used them as rosary beads. Rose beads last over one hundred years and some make them as an heirloom. I decided I wanted to make some for my daughter, granddaughters, and daughter-in-law.

*Materials Needed*
- eight cups of fresh rose petals
- blender or food processor
- water
- a large cast-iron skillet
- six to ten rusty nails
- stove
- a wooden spoon
- a plastic container with cover
- a roll of absorbent paper towels
- a melon baller
- one package of T-pins
- one large piece of Styrofoam
- a spool of buttonhole twist thread
- a needle

PLATE 131 De-petaling the roses

Gather the spent roses that have already bloomed but are still in good shape. Pull the petals off and discard the other part of the flower.

It doesn't matter about the color of the petals. I think the more color it has, the better it is. The first step is to de-petal the flower; then pull the fresh petals out and discard the brown ones. Next, you need to puree the petals. I put them in a blender. Add about enough water to the blender just so they'll puree real fine. Keep adding your fresh rose petals until you get [enough to fill] a skillet. If you have too much water, strain a little of it off, but if you don't have enough water, the dough will crumble up. You will have to use your own judgment, but the recipe calls for eight cups of pureed petals. My cast-iron skillet holds only five cups. Add the pureed petals to the skillet. Next, put in six to eight rusty nails. Put the pureed petal mixture in a skillet on the stove. As you cook it, the rusty nails cause a chemical change. Turn the temperature of the mixture down to where it is barely simmering and stir with a wooden spoon about three or four times. Cook for two hours each day for three days straight.

You may need to add water as it cooks. Always use enough liquid to keep it simmering. You don't have to cook the mixture at the same time every day. I have done it in the morning, and the next day, I did it at night. It will start splattering a little, so I put a cover over it for protection of the stove. Don't be concerned at the odor—that is normal. After the three days of cooking, set aside the mixture, covered, for two days. You will have a handful of black

PLATE 132  The pureed petals simmering on the stove

dough. The mixture can be scooped out, put in a plastic container, and stored in the refrigerator or frozen.

The dough can be finished at a later date. You have a mass of black dough, and you need to find an absorbent paper towel to get as much moisture out of it as you can. Work out most of the moisture by patting the dough with half a paper towel. If there is too much moisture, then it will not stick together as well as the dry dough. The dough falls apart when it is too moist. Knead the dough just like you would knead bread dough. Put the dough in plastic wrap and put it back in the refrigerator. I would not leave it in the refrigerator for over a week, though.

Use a melon baller to form the beads. There are different sizes of melon ballers. Use the size you prefer. The smaller end of the melon baller is a good mold that will help to create the size as well as the form of the bead. I roll the beads by hand. The dark color will wash off your hands by using a little bleach or lemon juice. It does take a long time to work the dough. The more you roll the dough ball, the rounder the beads will get. I have found out that to use a metal measuring spoon is a great help: It smooths and levels the dough just right. It is hard to get all of the beads the same size, but they say that is why it is so unique—there are no two alike.

I find the bigger beads take longer to dry—I put them under the hair dryer. To get the pin through the center is the hardest part of making rose beads. It is best for the pin to go in the middle, but it's hard to get them perfect. Sometimes you have to pull out and start over. It's called a T-pin, which you can find at a fabric store. The T-pins are labeled Ladelon number 85T, and it's hard to get a T-pin just right. The size I use is Porter's 101Q, Size N, 1½ inch or 38 millimeters. Then I stick the T-pin in the large piece of Styrofoam for the beads to dry. Drying depends on the humidity. I have read that

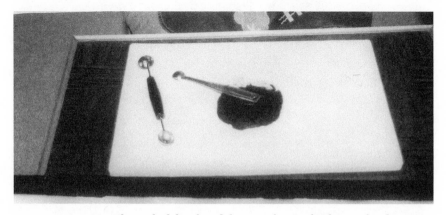

PLATE 133  The cooked dough and the utensils to make the rose beads

PLATE 134  Ruby Cheek rolls the dough by hand.

turning on a fan dries the beads quicker. If you don't dry the beads quick enough, they might mold on you.

When they are large, they will slide down on the pins that hold them in place on the Styrofoam while they dry. It's best to let the air go under and over them. You need to let them dry for about a week or more.

Be sure you let the beads dry before stringing them. The beads will shrink a third or a half of the original size. The beads are not perfectly round, and they do crack a little.

They are not hard to string. The type of thread needed is black button-hole twist thread. I have found that gold beads in between bring out the

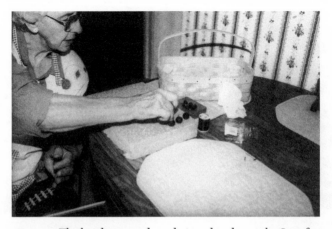

PLATE 135  The beads are made and pinned to dry on the Styrofoam.

color in them. I use the bigger gold beads for the larger rose beads and the little gold beads for the smaller rose beads. I string them, alternating a rose-bud bead and a gold or silver bead.

The hardest part is to end the necklace. I guess, to be wise, you should get a jeweler to tie a knot in the necklace. I tie it like I am tying my shoestring and get it good and tight. I then go through the rose bead to the right of the knot and then tie again. Next, I bring it back to the left, through two rose beads, and tie one more time. I clip them with nail clippers. At the ends they have a little piece of dough left on them from where the pin goes through. I keep a nail file near so I can file down the beads before stringing so they will look rounder. When you wear them on white clothing, they show up better. Some people use a regular necklace fastener on the beads, but I think the beauty for elderly women is it's easy for them to put the beads over their head if it is a solid strand. It is hard to fasten when you get older.

The first ones I made, I used rubber gloves, and they turned out crinkled. Some people like the crinkled beads. My daughter-in-law loves the crinkled ones! I have tried to trade her beads for the smoother ones, and she will not give them up.

The last step, which is optional, is to dip a T-pin in rose oil and put it in through the bead. This will make the necklace smell more like the wonderful fragrance of roses. Put the beads in a plastic bag and let them saturate for a week. Mrs. Stuart recommends keeping the rose beads in a plastic bag for preservation, if they are not being worn. After this step is complete, then you will have a remarkable set of rose beads.

## A WOODEN COFFIN

Many people of the Appalachians, as late as the early 1940s, were buried in homemade coffins when they died. Usually, the tradition was to have some of the men in the community build the coffin after a person had died, and the ladies would sew a lining for it while the men built it; so it was usually ready by evening. There were several men in the community who were regularly called on to make coffins. They kept lumber cut and cured, ready to be used when needed.

One such person in our community was Harley Thomas, a man who makes spinning wheels, repairs and builds cabinets and gun racks, and can do almost any other kind of woodwork, including making fiddles.

Some people liked to build their own coffin or have it made to order long

PLATE 136  Harley Thomas

before they needed it. It was usually kept in the hayloft of the barn. Various people in our community told of having seen one stored in one of the farmer's barns near here, or had heard about it. We inquired about its history and asked if we could see it, or even buy it if they didn't want it. The story goes that it had been made for this farmer's uncle, but since he was staying with a daughter in another state when he died, the family had him buried there. The kids remembered the coffin being up in the barn for years after that, but it had since disappeared.

We asked Mr. Thomas, since we couldn't find one already made, if he would make us a child's coffin, so that we could see how they were made and how he decided on the measurements. It took him quite a while to acquire some suitable white oak wood, and he never was able to procure brass hardware like he wanted for the handles. So he improvised, as he would have done fifty years ago, and made wooden handles.

Mr. Thomas told us that during the Depression, when the CCC [Civilian Conservation Corps] camps were located throughout this area, he had a contract with the government to build coffins. His regular job was running a sawmill and building cabinets and furniture, but he made coffins as needed.

When we lifted up the coffin he made for us, we were startled at how

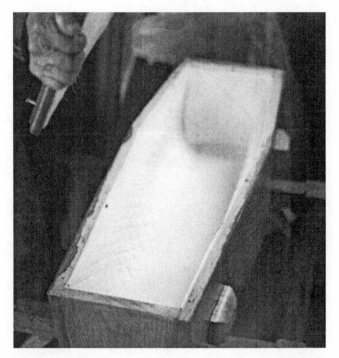

PLATE 137  The interior of the coffin, showing the satin lining

heavy it was for something so small. He stained the white oak wood with a light brown varnish and lined the inside with cotton batting, and quilted white satin was tacked on over that.

Mr. Thomas shapes the bottom of the coffin with the sides angled out somewhat to make room for the shoulders of the body. He decides on how long the coffin will be made by adding a few inches to the length of the person to be buried in it. The widest part of the coffin is one-third the way down the length of it. It then tapers back inward with the foot of the coffin being one inch narrower than the head.

The head piece of this coffin is 7⅞ inches wide, while the foot piece is 6⅞ inches wide, and both end pieces are 8½ inches high. He nails these onto the bottom of the coffin first. He cuts two white oak planks 8½ inches by 33 inches long for the sides. To bend these pieces to fit the bottom, he cuts three grooves with a handsaw from top edge to bottom edge about a quarter of an inch apart and about halfway through the boards, as shown in the diagram (see page 289).

Starting at the head and forcing the side to meet the bottom by placing the nails rather close together, he then nails on one side. By the time he reaches the foot, the board is securely attached to the end. Now he does the

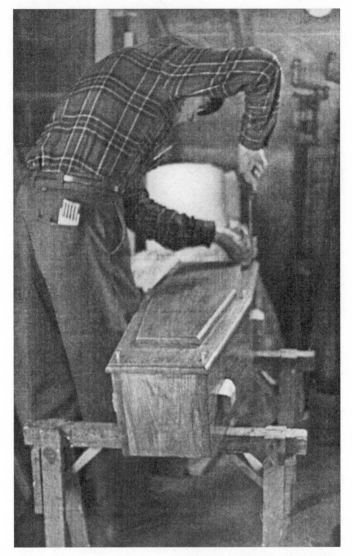

PLATE 138  Mr. Thomas screws down the top of the finished coffin.

other side the same way, and when he is finished, the entire coffin has the shape of the bottom.

He shapes a top to fit the coffin and glues on a smaller piece of wood shaped like the top as a decorative touch. The top is attached to the coffin with three screws placed on either side. He uses two wooden handles on each side of the coffin, although when he could get it, he used to use brass hardware.

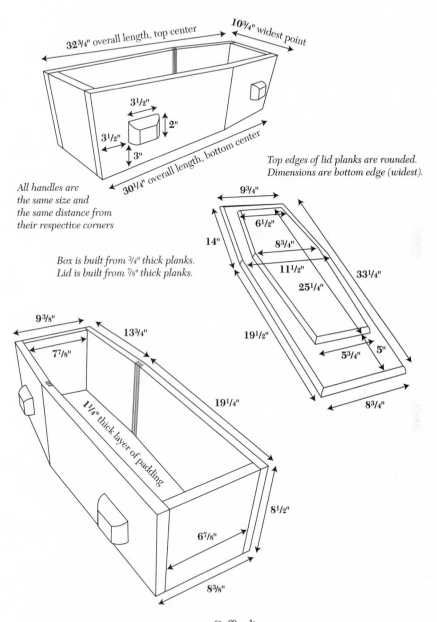

32¾" overall length, top center

10¾" widest point

3½"

2"

3½"

3"

30¼" overall length, bottom center

All handles are
the same size and
the same distance from
their respective corners

Box is built from ¾" thick planks.
Lid is built from ⅞" thick planks.

Top edges of lid planks are rounded.
Dimensions are bottom edge (widest).

9¾"

6½"

14"

8¾"

11½"

25¼"

33¼"

19½"

5¾"

5"

8¾"

9⅜"

13¾"

7⅞"

1¼" thick layer of padding

19¼"

8½"

6⅞"

8⅜"

PLATE 139  Coffin diagram

# TURTLES FROM CREEK TO CROCK

"It makes you kind of mad, though, when you go to your hooks and find half of your bait gone and your line twisted up around another bush."

—*Lindsey Moore*

We heard of a woman in Clarkesville, Georgia, who had quite a reputation in the area for cooking turtles. Her name was Mrs. Lillie Lovell. We sent a team to meet her, and she agreed to show us how to prepare and cook a turtle—if we would catch one and bring it to her.

After a number of failed attempts at the lake behind our school (the turtles simply stole the bait each time and left a bare hook behind), we were about to give up when Lake Stiles, one of our contacts and good friends, heard of our struggle and caught a live turtle for us! We kept it and fed it until the day of the interview when, with mixed emotions, it was cleaned and eaten.

Mrs. Lovell passed away before the article was completed, so students took the photographs from her interview to Lindsey Moore, a local resident who could tell them what was happening in the photos. He also shared his method of catching, cleaning, and cooking turtles.

—*Pat Marcellino and Kenny Crumley*

**Lindsey Moore:** You'll find the cleanest turtles in a fishpond. Just about all of the ponds around here have them. And you know what a bullrush or a swamp is? Well, now, if you get a turtle out of there, he's goin' to have leeches on him, which is a little worm. It don't hurt him, but it don't look good. The turtle is awful dark and nasty looking when you get him out of the swamp. But I would advise anybody that's huntin' for turtles to get them out of a pond or a river. It wouldn't be a good idea to get him out of a marsh.

You get you a chicken gizzard or fat meat for bait. You need to use what they call carpenter's twine, and you want to use a tough hook. When you buy your hook and your line, you'll have to make allowance for where the line goes through your hook, 'cause if you don't, you're going to get your twine bigger than your hook eye. Now tie your line in a fisherman's knot on the end of the twine, and it ain't going to slip. You run it back through your hook eyes, and then you pull it, give it a yank, and it ain't going to go nowhere. The turtle will be there when you get there.

Now you want to tie your line to something that gives, like a limb, 'cause when you hang a monster, he's going to yank real hard; and if you tie it to a tree, he's going to break your line. If he is around a limb that gives, he'll be there when you get there, unless he chews the line in two or somebody cuts him loose.

I'll tell you, what I generally do is set out my bait about one o'clock in the afternoon. You can't do this at night unless you ain't got nothin' to do but loaf. It's best to check them every three hours 'cause he might accident'ly break that line if he's a pretty good turtle. I've been settin' mine about one o'clock, but most any time will do.

I'll tell you, another way you can catch them is to get you some milk jugs and tie a line two and one-half to three feet long on the milk jug and bait it with chicken gizzards or fat meat and throw it out in the pond. If he hangs himself, nine times out of ten, he's going to go to the banks. You don't have to go out in a boat and get him. He'll hunt him a brush pile. He thinks he is getting away. They're funny creatures.

I'll tell you, in catchin' a turtle, it's the art of outsmarting it—just like killin' a crow. If you kill a crow, you say, "Well, I outsmarted him!" It makes you kind of mad, though, when you go to your hooks and find half of your bait gone and your line twisted up around another bush.

PLATE 140  Patrick Marcellino, Ken Crumley, and
Lindsey Moore discuss cooking turtles.

The biggest one I caught was at Toccoa Falls [Georgia]. I guess he weighed twenty pounds. Me and him couldn't agree at all. I tried to get the deputy sheriff to give me his gun to shoot it, but there was too many people around there and he wouldn't do it. I dragged him over the highway and got me a pair of pliers and a knife and just cut his head off!

You'd better believe turtles can move fast. When they snap, they snap. They don't fool around about it. You get one mad, and he's really mad. The best thing to do when you get one is shoot him right in the top of the head. If you do that, then he won't snap you! If you try to handle that rascal—for instance, if he's hung on a hook and you pull that hook out—he's liable to jerk that string out of your hand and snap you. So if you have a pistol or a rifle, just shoot that rascal right quick like so he can't snap you.

If a snappin' turtle bites you, all I know for you to do is to take something and pry its mouth loose. You don't want to pull it, or he'll bring a hunk out of you. You will just have to get a screwdriver or board or something and pry his jaw loose.

You can cut one's head off and hang him up, and in the morning that turtle will still be movin'. I've taken the heart out and laid it on the table, and its heart will still be beating. Those things are hard to kill. The old saying is they'll hold you till it thunders. [If one grabbed me,] I'd pray for rain right quick, or get somebody to do a rain dance!

I have heard that there was seven different types of meat in a turtle. According to the Bible and the old people, there's meat for every day of the week. Now which one it is, I couldn't tell you. I never did pay attention to that. I just ate it!

[How long I cook it] all depends on how big it is. If it's a young one, I'd fry it; and, if it's a large one, I'd put it in stew. The reason for that is the larger ones are tougher, and the more you boil it, the better it is to eat. If you take a turtle that weighs fifteen pounds, you'd want to boil him and put him in a stew. I don't have any special recipes. I just fix it like a regular stew. Now some people might have some special recipes, but I don't. I'd say to boil a big one at least eight hours. Don't get the water boiling hot—just slowly turning. Every once in a while, take your spoon and stir him up or shake him or whatever.

Now, I'll tell you something else that's a good idea: When you boil it, chip up an onion and sprinkle it in there. The reason for that is sometimes they don't smell too good cooking, and the onion will help.

**Lillie Lovell:** Turtles don't get too big around here now. They get up a pretty good size, though. Carlos brought one in that was about as big as the top of that stool. Now, he was a huge 'un! I had a big dishpan, and we couldn't put it down in the dishpan. He caught him out of the pond. We caught sixteen out of that pond once—and four of them were big—but none of them were as big as that huge one. But I don't know if them smaller-sized ones ain't better than the large ones are.

You can gig turtles, but we never did. I think you gig them in the back. I never did gig one, but now they've been gigged. Them shells are hard, though. [Instead of trying to go through his shell,] you'd be better off to catch him with his old head out. Then you have to be sharp. I don't think I could do that!

My husband always got 'em by the tail. He'd just catch 'em! Keep their head away from you, though, 'cause they'll bite you, and they are mean, too.

And we've caught 'em with a hook. But now we had mud turtle hooks—great big 'uns. I ain't seen one of them in a long time. You can use a regular fishhook, but you have to be awfully careful 'cause they'll get loose from that now! They'll snap it so quick you'll [lose them]. I guess they still have mud turtle hooks in fishing stores, but I ain't seen none since Daddy used them.

Now, for bait, put a piece of fish or chicken on the hook and set your hook out in a pond where it won't float up and get in trash or anything. You'll more than likely catch one!

Now Virge, my husband, always, when he was livin', I'd go with him, and he'd catch a chicken out of the chickenhouse—just a small little ol' chicken—chop it in two, and put half on each hook good. Go back the next mornin', and he had two mud turtles. Put the chicken on the hook and throw it right over in the pond and go back the next mornin'; that mud turtle will just pooch down in the mud, and there you'll get him! But you better be careful when you go to land him, now, 'cause he could get loose. Be very easy.

Now I like to cook these turtles when I clean them, unless I'm going to cut them up and freeze them like you would chicken or any other meat. When I cook them, I put them on and cook them till they're tender in salt and water. If you want to, you can put a little pod of pepper in. It won't hurt them a bit—gives that whang to them that they ought to have. Now if you boil the meat too long, it'll just come all to pieces, and I don't like it that way. I like to still have the pieces whole where you can pick them up just like a piece of chicken. It's pretty meat, and I don't want it to come off the bone if I can keep it on.

The boiling part doesn't take too long. It depends on the size of the turtle. One great big one I cooked took me nearly four hours, but they usually don't take that long. I always take my fork and test it and see if it's tender enough. When it is, I take those pieces out and fry them in a frying pan—brown them up nice.

Lots of times I've found thirty or forty eggs in them. You know the size of a partridge [grouse or pheasant] egg, don't you? Like that size. The last one

I cooked had thirty-five or forty in it. I took them out and put them in a bowl in there, and they filled a pretty good-sized bowl up! I don't care for the eggs too much, though. You can't hardly cook them. They're a kind of rubber, kind of a watery thing! They don't taste right to me. But, now, they say they make the best cakes there are, but I ain't done that now.

You'll get enough meat off an average-sized one to feed a good family. I've had them about the size of a dinner plate, and we'll have turtle for supper and two pieces left over to give to the cat! There's plenty of meat in them. I guess two pounds and a half in one with any size to it. Lots of times you can't eat a whole hind leg by yourself. There's plenty of eating in it, and it's good meat, too!

And I've always heard there's seven or eight different flavors of meat in them, and I've read that, too. But now, I don't know. They say the neck part is [like a] chicken breast. And they've got beef flavor in them—I hear that now. I don't know whether they've got hog meat. I don't think they have. But I just love them better than any kind of meat. And we've cooked them large and small.

Once we had a man that worked here, and we had a pipe—almost like a stovepipe—that carried water from the pond to the chickenhouse. Well, the water kept bein' cut off, and he'd come to the house and say, "I can't get nothin' out. The water's gone, and them chickens is starvin' to death!"

**"That head'll bite you, now, after you've got it off. Yes, sir, the reflexes keeping goin'."**

So Virge said, "They's somethin' in the pipe up there." So they went up there and worked and piddled and couldn't do nothin' with it. So Virge just went in the pond and got down in there, and it was a mud turtle about the size of a dinner plate had stopped the hole up!

We had some men come here about fourteen years ago, and they drove up out there in the yard and said would we mind them a-goin' turtle huntin' in our creek? And I was at the door. I said no. And then Virge come walkin' to the door, and I said, "Virge, this man wants to go down and see if they can catch some turtles."

Virge said, "Go 'head, but I don't believe you'll catch any there."

They went down the creek, and they come back with six! I don't know how they did it! The man said, "They're under the bank. We know where they're at." They'd reach in under there with their bare hands. This man had nothin' but his hand! I wouldn'ta put my hand down under there! There coulda been anything under there! But they come back with 'em. Said they caught six back up at the upper end of my field.

PLATE 141 Foxfire student Keith Head holding
the mud turtle by the tail

## COOKING THE TURTLE

**Mrs. Lovell:** You always want to hold that live turtle away from your body. They can bite you bad! That's how come we cut the head off, 'cause they've got strong teeth.

First, you have to cut the head off. You have to give 'em a stick and pull their head out and get 'em on a block or something. They'll grab a stick. Just pull the head out and pop 'em with the ax. That head'll bite you, now, after you've got it off. Yes, sir, the reflexes keep goin'.

**Mr. Moore:** See how cautious she's handling this turtle? They're very dangerous. You see how pointed his bill is? You have to take caution. Now if you can get him to hold on to that stick and pull his head out, you can cut his head off. But, nine times out of ten, he won't hold on. If he won't, get a long pair of pliers and pull his head out just as far as you can. When you're cutting the head off, you want to cut it just as close to the head as you can 'cause he's got a neck four to six inches long. There's a lot of good meat in that neck; you don't want to waste that.

After you cut the head off, you want to dispose of it so the kids or you don't get ahold of it. That head will bite you three hours after you cut it off. After you cut the head off, you want to hang the body or lean it up against something to drain all the blood out of the shell. If you do that, it will make it cleaner and better to eat. If you lie it on its back, all the blood will get mixed up in the meat.

There are two knives I use to clean them with. You want to keep them extra sharp. For cutting in those joints and around the top, you want to use the big knife. The little knife is the one you use to cut out from under his hull 'cause he's really stuck in that hull. I'd advise you to use this larger knife to cut the breastplate off, and cut it just as close as you possibly can. There's a lot of good lean meat in there, and if you don't cut it close, you're going to pull all this meat off.

**Mrs. Lovell:** As soon as it quits dripping [blood], I put it in boiling water to scald it. Have your water good and hot and just set 'em down in that water.

PLATE 142 Mrs. Lovell tries to get the mud turtle to snap
at the stick so its head will protrude and be easy to cut off.

When you scald 'em, now, they'll move and crook their feet up and wiggle good and just knock water and go. But the hide comes off easy after you give 'em a good scalding. You can let the hot water out after you give 'em a good scalding. You can test it and see if the skin will peel. If it will, you got it ready.

You can run hot water over them to scald 'em, too. The water there in the sink is hot enough to scald 'em. Just set 'em down in a big pan, turn the water in on 'em, and let it run a few minutes; then you can scrape that [hide]. It all comes off white and pretty. They're easy cleaned. I don't mind it a bit, but, law, lots of people wouldn't clean 'em for nothin' in the world. I guess you could keep one a day or two before you cleaned it, but I wouldn't want to. I'd rather dress 'em when they're first caught.

**Mr. Moore:** I like to wait till the following day to dress one. I don't have as many problems with 'im that way. If you clean it right after you kill it, its reflexes will still be so strong that it'll try to jerk its legs back into that shell.

**Mrs. Lovell:** After I scald it, I run cold water over it. That hot water draws 'em up, and then the cold water straightens 'em out. Next, I scrape 'em and get ready to start cuttin'.

**Mr. Moore:** When you first start cuttin' around the breastbone, you've got to turn the blade of your knife down. You have to give it a little pull to get it started. You want to keep that knife sharp as possible. Then, after you get it started, you want to turn the blade of your knife up to where you won't cut your meat. Just keep goin' all the way around the breastbone. Another rea-

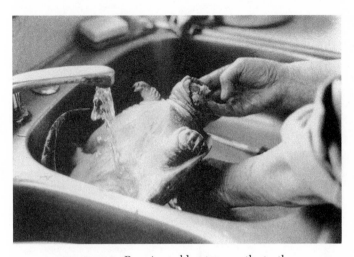

PLATE 143  Running cold water over the turtle

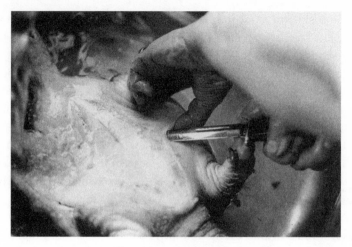

PLATE 144  Beginning to remove the breastbone

son for keepin' your knife turned up is so you won't cut the innards and ruin the meat.

Sometimes I keep that breastbone for a souvenir. My daddy always used to put it up above his door for some meaning, but I don't remember what it was. I generally just throw 'em away.

**Mr. Moore:** Now she's getting ready to go in there and take the joints [legs] out. The tail of the turtle is good meat, too. A lot of people throw that tail away 'cause it looks boogerish and mean, but it's okay. All you've got to do is clip those little ridges off and put that son of a gun in the pan. It's the best eating you have ever seen.

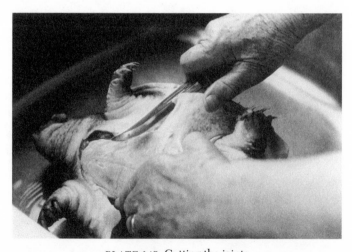

PLATE 145  Cutting the joints

In this photo, she is taking the joints out now. Those things have got joints from the claws right back up into the hull. I take it apart just like she's doin'. Start with a small knife. Then when you get all the joints cut [the joints that attach the legs to the inside of the hull], you want to go to a knife that's about ten inches long. That meat is really hung on to that hull, and you just can't pull it out. You've got to get in there and twist and pry to get it loose from the hull, and if you use a little knife, you'll break it.

**Mrs. Lovell:** There's a joint in there, and if you catch it, you can get it off easy; but if you don't catch it, you've got a hard lick. It's hateful.

After you get the breastbone off, the intestines and stuff is still in there. They should be removed before you start workin' on that turtle. If not, you might go in there and bust a gut, and it would ruin the meat. Just reach in there and pull them out. If you're around a spigot, just run that whole thing under there. It's cleaner, and your hands won't get as messy.

**Mr. Moore:** Now some of your turtles is dark-meated and some is light-meated. I believe the male is light, and the female is dark. So, if you think the turtle ain't no good 'cause his meat is dark, don't worry. That's just the nature of the turtle.

**Mrs. Lovell:** When you get done cuttin' it up, you have a tail and four legs and a neck. The only thing you want to dispose of is the innards and the head. After I get it cut up, I cut the toenails off the legs. Then I either take the skin off or not, depending. Some people don't like it cooked with the skin on, but it don't hurt it. It fries just as nice as chicken.

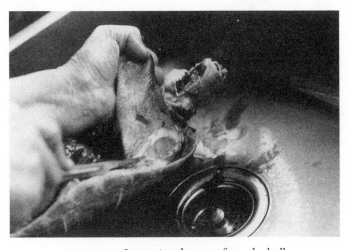

PLATE 146  Loosening the meat from the hull

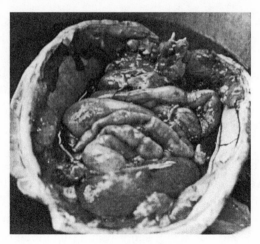

PLATE 147  Internal organs

**Mr. Moore:** She cut those claws off, but if you scald it good, you can just take your fingers and pick those claws off there—just like pickin' berries, if you want to. It's awful easy. And there she's pulling the hide off one piece, but you can leave it on. It won't hurt that turtle none whatsoever.

**Mrs. Lovell:** Next, I put all the pieces in cold salt water. Don't use too much salt—just enough to draw the meat. It makes it good. They'll move after you salt 'em. You go to puttin' salt to 'em, and they go to movin'. Any time you catch fish or any kind of wild game that comes out of the water, if you'll put salt on him and soak him for a few minutes, you'll get that muddy taste out. Let it soak for a few minutes in that salt, and it'll make the meat taste better when you get ready to eat it.

PLATE 148  Turtle meat

PLATE 149 Cutting off the toenails

Now I rinse it, put it in fresh water with more salt and a pod of red pepper. Then I put it all on the stove and boil it till it gets good and tender. I'll boil this one for about two hours.

**Mr. Moore:** Remember that the older the turtle is, the tougher it is, and the longer you have to boil it. When I get ready to fry it, I put it in Shake 'n Bake—or just plain old flour and salt—and give him a good shakin'. When you're fryin' it, I usually have the pan full of grease, enough to cover it up. You probably could make something similar to chicken and dumplings out of this—you know, make a thick-like gravy. I've never tried that. I usually

PLATE 150 Soaking the meat in salt

PLATE 151   Boiling the meat

just put the turtle in a soup with tomatoes, onions—whatever comes out of the garden.

**Mrs. Lovell:** After it's through boiling, I roll the pieces in cornmeal and black pepper and fry them in about half a cup of grease. It don't have to fry too long—just so it's browned good. And don't stir it too much or it'll make the meat come off the bone. If the grease goes to poppin', just turn the heat down a little. Now sweet potatoes is the best thing you ever ate with turtle. Now see, we've got a real pile of meat. What about that!

PLATE 152   The browned turtle meat

# WORLD WARS

"The war affected my life in many different ways. I suppose the best part of it was that it made a man out of me. I guess I learned to appreciate freedom, the United States, and everything we have here. The only thing is that it was rough, but sometimes there were good times. I hope to the Good Lord that others don't ever have to go through it."

—*Mack Suttles*

The United States has survived two world wars punctuated by the Great Depression. Today's youngest generation of Americans, however, has never seen its boys drafted to serve their country. With the September 11 attack on the World Trade Center towers in New York City in 2001, we felt the national shock of a major event reminiscent of the Pearl Harbor attack that initiated American involvement in World War II. The September 11 attacks initiated our involvement in the war against terrorism. Courageously volunteering, our men went to fight in Operation Desert Storm and Operation Iraqi Freedom, and they have died there on the desert sands. We have not, however, heard the sweet ring of victory from men who have come home from battles such as those of World Wars I and II.

"They Give Their Lives—You Lend Your Money"
U. S. Treasury Department                    Courtesy King Features

PLATE 153  An advertisement published by the U.S.
Treasury Department in *The Clayton Tribune* on
Thursday, April 15, 1943, attempting to sell
more war bonds

Society's view of war has changed since the time of the world wars and the Depression. We have not seen the adulation and national pride shown to the troops during both of the world wars. Those hurrahs are limited to national holidays and parades. We respond to reports of casualties on the front with protests rather than unwavering support. We see the news coverage, but we do not feel the human effects of the events we witness. What has happened to our regard for humanity and human rights issues?

The new generation of Americans is too young to remember the segregation of the military during World War I, the ration tickets of the Great Depression, or the Victory Gardens of World War II. We have seen our nation pull together after the events of September 11, but once we challenged those responsible, the support for our desert endeavors dwindled from a roar to a whimper. In World War II our local paper, *The Clayton Tribune*, ran a weekly column called "Rabun County Men on our Fighting Fronts." This column featured letters from the troops from this area, as well as address updates for the boys overseas and news reports about their well-being. Today, seemingly as part of a public relations effort, we make heroes of a few surviving soldiers. When Jessica Lynch returned home, folks treated her as a national hero. She is; however, eleven other brave soldiers died in the same attack she survived. They are also heroes.

During World Wars I and II, heroes emerged on foreign fields and on the homefront. The war affected every member of the community. During World War I, citizens pulled together, backed our troops, and aided them by donating everything from car tires to clothes, by buying war bonds, and by praying for them. Men went to war. During World War II, women stepped in by working factory jobs, as well as raising their children and caring for their homes. Some women, however, volunteered for foreign service as nurses.

Those who went to war, men and women, have had a part in some of the most important events in our world's history. These are their stories. Some are happy, some sad, some funny, and others simply gut-wrenching, but all are equally important to the preservation of a time when the United States had no choice but to take up arms against aggressors.

Thucydides, a Greek historian born in Athens, describes soldiers: "They are surely to be esteemed the bravest spirits who, having the clearest sense of both the pains and pleasures of life, do not on that account shrink from danger." General H. Norman Schwarzkopf defines a hero in a television interview with Barbara Walters: "It doesn't take a hero to order men into battle. It takes a hero to be one of those men who goes into battle."

The men and women featured in this section have survived danger beyond our comprehension. They have survived those trials to return to these mountains to contribute to their families, their friends, and their communities. Though they have experienced hard times, they still can say they have lived good lives. Mrs. Teenie Howell, a World War II nurse, says, "Since I was in the war, I was happier to get home and start my life. I guess the war changed my way of thinkin', too . . . I have had a very happy life."

The people I interviewed opened their homes to me, dug through countless boxes of pictures with me, and entrusted me to retell their stories accurately. Although I found many who would not or could not speak about the war, those who did had to relive the difficult events of their past so that we can know the truth, for if we do not learn from the past, we are doomed to repeat it.

As you read, you will notice the soldiers consistently speak about the good homecoming they received: They came home to crowds cheering and flags waving. As Melvin Taylor says, "We did them Vietnam boys wrong." J. H. Cannon agrees: "They [the community] were really, really appreciative—not like the Vietnam War. No, nothin' like that. We let those boys down; you know, they fought for their country. That was a bad situation. The community was really supportive of us." We must be grateful to those willing to sacrifice their very lives for our country.

My hope is that all of us, especially the youngest, can understand the sacrifices people made in order that we may live free. History books preserve forever the names of the presidents and great generals of the world wars, but they are not the true heroes. The foot soldiers, pilots, and nurses, as well as those at home who supported the war effort, are the heroes. Others who have gone before us have created a strong nation and left us a legacy of heroism and hope. This section is compiled in memory and honor of all the men and women who made the ultimate sacrifice so we can live free today.

Our country has experienced enormous changes, but one fact remains true: We have always had heroes. These soldiers are the heroes on whom our nation relied. They have fought communists, imperialists, territorial expansionists, and those who practiced inhumanity toward their fellow man. Yes, they were war heroes, but they have remained heroes, for they have lived their lives well.

*—Stephanie Jobbitt*

# WORLD WAR I AND
# THE GREAT DEPRESSION

Fought mostly in Europe, World War I began in 1914 and ended in 1918. Before it was over, the horror had spread into twenty-eight countries and onto all oceans. Because of its scope, this was a world war. Germany's military ambitions and its desire for territorial expansion incited the conflict. The superpowers—the United States, Great Britain, and Russia—were trying to halt Germany's attempt to create a European empire.

In the summer of 1914, Germany was prepared for war. Suspecting that Serbia had aided in the assassination of Archduke Franz Ferdinand and the Duchess of Hohenberg, the now crumbling Austro-Hungarian Empire attacked Serbia. On another front, seeking to break up the Entente Powers (Britain, France, and Russia) and hoping that France and Britain might refuse to support Russia, Germany attacked Russia. Germany concentrated its aggression on the eastern front until 1918, when it attempted to force Britain and France out of the war by blockading its borders. The gamble failed, and the western Allied forces ultimately defeated the Germans. This war had a detrimental effect on the entire world, but the other possible outcome, had Germany been allowed to expand and become an empire, remains unthinkable.

In October 1929, on what has come to be known as Black Friday, the stock market crashed. Both the national and the European markets suffered repercussions. In 1930, the U.S. Congress passed a high tariff law, against the advice of economists. This law caused foreign governments to set high tariffs as well; world trade dried up. The American people demanded the repayment of war debts, and the government had no money to pay the debts back. Factories closed because the need for production had diminished, but more people needed jobs because the soldiers were also out of work. The demand for industry had died; unemployment reached an all-time high all over the world. Buying necessary food and clothing items was at times difficult, if not impossible. Many families went without basic necessities. Exacerbating the situation was that the agricultural industry had overproduced, and the markets were full. Some farmers refused to harvest their crops because they could not sell them. Therefore, they had no need to hire pickers, and unemployment fell further.

The Great Depression was not, however, the first of its kind in history. Typically, a depression follows the industrial boom caused by the need for extreme production during a war. The Great Depression lasted from the stock market crash in 1929 until 1938, when the country's economy stabilized and unemployment dropped.

—*Stephanie Jobbitt*

*Reference*
King, Jere Clemes. *The First World War.* New York: Walker Publishing Company, 1972.

## MACK DICKERSON

**"Everywhere I go, where my hat is on my head, it's home to me."**

I started enlisting for radio, a wireless radio, you know. Then I got up there and stayed in North Virginia and the war broke out and they left us there. Then we stayed around there and couldn't come home, couldn't do nothin'. I had a radio, and a wireless one, too. It had three sets on there. They just took on Navy messages, you know. The admiral up there, he'd check up on all the Navy business, and a lot of it was coded stuff. You'd have to go on and check the code book and see what they said. That's what I did. We used the code book to code words out. You couldn't tell what they was, you know. I used to use Morse code. 'Bout forgot it now, but there was other codes. Morse code has dots, dashes, and straights. We used a telegraph.

Everywhere I go, where my hat is on my head, it's home to me. I just volunteered up there and went on in. I joined in 1918. The war started earlier. I never went until about a year. I believe I enlisted some time in May, and they didn't have any barracks for me. They let me come home and stay until the last of July. Then I went back, got on a ship, and went down there in the Azore Islands, and we waited. They left New York up there, refueled, and went on across the Atlantic—war 'as done ended by then, though.

I think they 'as six or eight of us there a-volunteerin' to go on a ship. Well, we jumped up—five or six of us—and went on. They sent us to Norfolk. We stayed over there together, and we went up there to Norfolk, Virginia. They had a regular old boat out there, and that took us out to the USS *Supply.* It was an old ship, three hundred and sixty feet long. We stayed on that thing, went to Guantánamo Bay, and maneuvered down there. We stayed for about, I guess, two and a half months. We stayed down there on maneuvers. It was shootin' and target practice. I did basic training at the Marine base down there.

PLATE 154 "I just volunteered up there and
went on in." —Mack Dickerson

They'd go out on a ship, and they'd give us a little vacation. We went to
the Jamaican islands—that belonged to Great Britain. Down on the Great
Britain end, they had plenty of old liquor, and the boys all got drunk.

When we got on the ship, well, I got sick a little the first night. There 'as
about eight of us sick, but you get over it in a day or two. They'll feed you
eggs every time; you'll go right out there and spew them right on the side of
the ship. They'll give you eggs every time. They're pretty good cooks,
though. They had something they'd feed you a certain day of the week. We
had quite a bit of meat. Water was scarce on there, though. They'd give you
a gallon of water, and it had to do for about a day and a half or two—made it
bad on you. Well, we had a big ol' room, and we'd sleep in hammocks on
each side—two on each side. We'd sleep down on the floor most of the time.
If you went on watch, you got up at eight o'clock, and you got off at twelve.

"There 'as three men from Clayton went in the Marines. One of
them never did come back. The others got wounded over there.
They took one of 'em to Parris Island, South Carolina."

There was one guy from Cumming, Georgia, and one from somewhere else
down in Georgia. I've done forgot his name. I never could think of it. He's a
darn sorry 'un. One night, he was supposed to come take my watch at twelve
o'clock, and some of 'em woke him up, and he never would come. Never did
come, and so we took them hammocks and started 'em swingin'. It turned up
and he fell right out on the floor and he come around there wipin' his eyes.

There 'as three men from Clayton went in the Marines. One of them
never did come back. The others got wounded over there. They took one of
'em to Parris Island, South Carolina.

Now them German prisoners were at a Marine base in Charleston. They
just dumped 'em there, and it wadn't even fenced in or cleared up or nothin'.
Then the commander said they called 'em all out one mornin'. The Army
wanted some man that drove a mule team who knowed how to harness 'em
and what to get and everything. One boy, a German prisoner of war, just
stepped out, and he stayed down there during the entire war. The city folks,
they didn't know nothin' 'bout farmin'. They had them Germans a-drivin'
mules and plowin'. It's said that one of the captains, or a lieutenant or something, came out there and his truck got stuck; they just pushed and pulled
and never could get him out. Finally, they called the German prisoners, who
put that big chain around the front of it. They went to pushin' and pullin', and
they pulled the dadgone truck apart—wheels and all out from under it.

I got paid twenty-eight dollars a month. Insurance was eight dollars. I got
about fifteen dollars out of it—had to buy my own clothes. I didn't spend my
money when we stopped. No, I kindly took care of mine so when I got out,
you know, I'd have some money.

We never did go overseas. The biggest fleet'd pick 'em up about three
hundred miles off the coast of France, and the American ships'd come back
to the States and get another convoy. You know, they took 'em in convoys.
We were just a regular Navy patrol, had a little old thirty-inch gun on the
thing—couldn't hit much with it. Had a bunch of those Navy guns on there,
you know. It'd take three enlisted men to fire the thing when it got to goin'.
There were, I guess, a hundred of them guns.

"All kinds o' ships. We had the . . . *Georgia*—it 'as one of the most
proud floating ships."

Our ship, it was a communications ship. Them admirals had to know what
was a-goin' on, sending messages back'ards and for'ards. Well, there wadn't
no planes then but a few in the Army over there. And the Americans . . .
United States didn't have no planes at all. They was a-buildin' over there.
Those aviators over there, they used British planes.

Durin' the last of the war, the fleet was on maneuvers down there—practice shootin', you know. All kinds o' ships. We had the *New York* and then had part of that old Spanish fleet, and the *Georgia*—it 'as one of the most proud floating ships—and the *Mississippi* down there. We had the *Georgia,* the *Vermont,* the *South Carolina,* the *Tennessee,* and the *North Carolina.* They was old ships. Kept 'em over from the Spanish-American War. You know how old they were, but they was good ships.

## HARLEY PENLAND

"At first I wasn't expecting to get back, so I sent nine hundred dollars back to my sister. When I seen we was goin' to get away, I went to spendin' . . . It didn't worry me then. Don't worry me much more now than it did then."

My father and his mother came from Danielsville, Georgia. His father was a slave, and my daddy was born into slavery and freed a little while after he was born. My mother was Georgia Scruggs. She was from here. We lived in a little two-room mud house in Clayton.

We went across the water in 1914 to fight in World War I. I heard that they treated all the men, white and colored, the same. I just didn't believe it, see. I was raised here in Rabun County. I was single when I was in the Army, stayed in there three years. I was drafted—never volunteered to go, no, sirree! See, when they loaded us up, they run a train; it ran in here. Then me and my brother, we went on it to Cornelia [Georgia], and they gathered up a bunch there, too. So we had a trainload when we got to Atlanta.

I went overseas on a ship. I didn't believe we was goin' to find no land: I didn't believe there was no land when we stayed on the water seventeen days and nights. We had to go around by where the Germans had that ocean planted in mines. We was tryin' to dodge 'em, and we went clear around out of the way. That was what took us so long. The ship was named *President Grant,* and it got blowed up before I got back to the States.

I was in British-occupied France. Then they moved us down to Saint-Nazaire. That was close to the foreign line, and boy, they had soldiers there! Every week or two, they moved 'em in—was killing 'em so fast. They'd load 'em up and carry the train up to the front, and that was the last we seen of 'em. That'd be the last of them 'cause they loaded a lot of dead folks.

You could use those French. They would come out to the camp, get the laundry, an' wash it. It wouldn't cost you over fifty cents. I never did have to pay over a dollar that I know—fifty cents sometimes, but the one we used was only twenty cents. I'd go down to the curb market and get a pack of them Brazil nuts. You'd get them, and they wouldn't cost over about two francs. I'd bring 'em back to the boys. I'd bring 'em back, peddle 'em out, and get away. I was spendin' some, but I wasn't gettin' much back. It didn't worry me, not then.

"Some of the boys stayed over there [after the war was over]. I had my bag packed ready to get on the first plane that was comin' home."

Nothin' we could do about some boys, and there was so many of them just went crazy. They had a pen to put 'em in, boys I knew. One of 'em was from right here below Gainesville [Georgia].

PLATE 155 "I had my bag packed ready to get on the first plane that was comin' home." —Harley Penland

When we were there, there was a place to go out and swim. The water was shallow, but there's plenty of water out there. I'd go out there and bathe in that salt water. That salt water sure is good for you to bathe in—helps your legs, or is supposed to. We had to wear boots there in France all the time through the winter—old rubber boots, hip boots. They'd come on up to your hip, and you'd hang 'em in your belt. Where I was workin', I kept mine rolled down 'cause I wasn't outside much. I was at the shipyard all the time, unloading heavy stuff. I stayed there until I first went to the hospital in British France—stayed there till I got better. Then we went down to Saint-Nazaire. They was burnin' every hour of the day at that hospital. They had an Army regular takin' 'em to the hospital, then another takin' 'em to the graveyard.

France is a old country. They had them rocks on the roads shaped down, cut out, and they curved. That was the streets there. Boy, them streets was rough—rough ridin' where the rock had wore out. The rock would be 'bout worn out and have a six-inch head on it in places.

At first I wasn't expecting to get back, so I sent nine hundred dollars back to my sister. When I seen we was goin' to get away, I went to spendin' some, but I wasn't expectin' to get back. It didn't worry me then. Don't worry me much more now than it did then. Nothin' you could do about it, but there was so many of them that must've went crazy.

Some of the boys stayed over there [after the war was over]. I had my bag packed ready to get on the first plane that was comin' home. I really came back on a ship. I've never flown in a plane and don't aim to now.

## EDITH CANNON

**"We didn't have any money, and Mama would send us a quarter now and then . . . for Rose and me to ride the train up to Tiger, and then Dad would be down there with the wagon."**

The Depression was the year I graduated from the seventh grade. Then we went down to Tallulah Falls School. All during the time I was at school at Tallulah Falls, it was during the Depression. We had fairly enough to eat, but it wasn't nothing extra—not like they are now. We didn't have good food down there like they do now. We didn't get to come home from down there but about twice or three times a year—Thanksgiving and Christmas, maybe Easter. We didn't have any money, and Mama would send us a quarter now and then in an envelope in a letter to us. It said it was for Rose and me to ride the train up to Tiger, and then Dad would be down there with the wagon. He'd bring some old coats, or he'd heat a rock sometimes for us to put our feet on. He'd bring us up the four miles home from the train, and then, on Sunday evening or whenever we had to go back, he'd take us back to Tiger. There we'd catch the train and go back to Tallulah Falls and walk from the train station up to the school. We didn't have much luggage to carry—only our clothes. We had plenty to wear but nothing extra—not like the girls do now.

Oh, well, now World War II . . . I remember World War II very much. I was married when World War II went on. We lived in this old house about a mile out from Tiger and we didn't have a car then, so Robert, my husband, and I walked from Tiger, one mile east of Clayton. We walked out there, and then a mile from Clayton out to Mr. and Mrs. Cannon's. Mr. Cannon hollered at us 'fore we got to the house. He yelled, "Listen, kids," at us 'fore we was at the house and says, "we are in war."

We listened to an old battery radio. They didn't have electricity either then, and so we listened to it on the news on the radio. We heard we was in. Robert didn't have to go to the war. He was turned down 'cause of his age, but most of my family had to go to the war. My brothers-in-law had to go,

PLATE 156 "Women didn't go to the war.
I mean, they didn't go to the service
like they do now." —Edith Cannon

but my brother didn't have to go. No, J.C. and R.E. didn't have to actually go to the war. I don't think they had to go overseas, but they went to the Army. You know, they was drafted, I guess.

I can't remember back. It's been so long, but I know we had a hard time during the Depression. They rationed our food. We had ration books to get sugar. I don't know whether it was flour, too, or not, but I know gasoline was rationed. I guess all of our food was. We had little stamps in little books. All of us did. I've got some of them somewhere. I'm a pack rat; I keep everything, but I thought maybe the children someday would like to have their ration books 'cause their names is on it, you know. We'd tear our little coupons out and give them wherever you bought gas. You just could only buy so much, only so much sugar during the war. It was a tough time during the war. We lost a lot of our men during that time, and women, too, I guess. But the women didn't go to the war. I mean, they didn't go to the service like they do now.

# WORLD WAR II

World War II began in 1937. It was a two-front war. The Germans were attempting to control all of Europe, and the Japanese wanted Asia. The U.S. involvement was the link that made it a world war. No one in any part of the United States could avoid being affected by the war.

World War II began as two separate wars, both fought for very different reasons in very different places. The war in Asia began because of Japan's attempting to fill a power vacuum left by China. The war in Europe was basically a resumption of World War I caused by military Germany's power and quest for territorial expansion.

Japan emerged as an industrial producer in the 1860s because of new Western influences. In 1895, Japan defeated China with a modern army and navy. In the late 1920s, Japan experienced a population explosion: 30 million people in 1870, to 55 million people in 1920, to 80 million people in 1937. This rapid population growth caused Japanese society to become very concentrated in large cities. Industry and exportation became the economic mainstays. This new economy went hand in hand with the development of democracy. When the Depression of the 1930s hit the entire world, the unrest caused the recovery of the political power of the national army and navy. By 1933, Japan's empire covered Formosa, Korea, Manchuria, and the Marshall, Caroline, and Mariana Islands. In 1935, Japan refuted the Washington Naval Treaty, which was negotiated in 1922, by building a naval fleet that would equal the British and American fleets.

The Allied armies defeated Germany in World War I and were subject to the Treaty of Versailles, by which Germany's military and economic advances were controlled. This treaty was designed to keep Germany from being able to renew its cause. The leaders signed the treaty, but they signed it under protest on June 28, 1919. In 1932, after an economic recession causing unemployment and inflation, the National Socialist Party, or the Nazi Party, led by Adolf Hitler, won 37 percent of the popular vote to become the largest party in parliament. In 1933, the German people voted Hitler chancellor. Once in power, he discredited the democracy set up by the Allied powers. He rearmed and remilitarized in 1936, with the intention of territorial expansion and the creation of an empire. In 1938, he took much of Czechoslovakia; then, thinking that the British and the French would stand aside, he invaded Poland in 1939. By the time the democracies were driven to declare war in December of 1939, Germany had overrun practically all of continental Europe.

The fighting, which initially began as a regional conflict, actually began in 1937, when Japan invaded China. The wider war in Asia stemmed from Japanese military expansion. Japan wanted to preempt the American response by attacking first. On December 7, 1941, the Japanese attacked Pearl Harbor, Hawaii. Their strategy was a gamble, which they lost because their initial success only made America resolve to destroy Japan completely.

Japan and Germany had similar agendas and ideologies: national pride, militarism, hate for "inferior races," and a counter to the effects of an economic recession. The United States of America and the Soviet Union intervened on both fronts and instigated the world war.

Hitler's conflict with the United States would win him support from Japan. The German chancellor wanted Japan to keep the British forces occupied while he fought the Americans in the Pacific. The Allied forces—the Soviets, the British, and the Americans—converged simultaneously on Berlin, overpowered it, and ended the war in Europe.

On May 8, 1945, German forces surrendered unconditionally to the Allied forces. The conclusion of the war centered entirely on the Americans' development of the atomic bomb. On August 6, 1945, American planes dropped one bomb on Hiroshima, Japan; and then, on August 9, 1945, another bomb on Nagasaki, Japan. These bombings ended the war and left Japan powerless. On September 2, 1945, the Japanese government presented a formal surrender document to the Allied forces, a document that ended World War II.

Human sacrifice, which can never be explained and for which there will never be any consolation, wrecked the lives and hopes of many people left at home. Decorations of valor from the battlefield did little to comfort distressed and helpless mothers and widows and fatherless children who are inevitably the real victims of any war. Many men and women went to battle, never to return, yet others fought and lived to tell the truths of what happened during World War II.

*—Stephanie Jobbitt*

---

*Reference*

Ross, Stewart. *Causes and Consequences of World War II.* Austin: Steck-Vaughn Company, 1996.

## LEWIS FREE

"I had to work seven days a week. We had to fly two or three times a week. I was in charge of eight men, and we'd go to work at seven and get off at seven. Everybody says, 'Go in the Air Force. They don't do anything.' Huh! We worked ever' day, all day!"

We was married on June 7, 1941. We lived in Rabun County before the war. My first child was born the next July. We had my baby girl then. (We had the boy after I got back.) About three months later, I was called. I was drafted. I got my letter to sign up at Liberty [Baptist Church]. I didn't know when I was supposed to go, so I went and signed up late. They said I better go in a hurry. It was in September of '42. I went over on a plane, but when I came back, it was halfway on a ship and halfway on a plane.

I started off going to Mississippi. I went to school there for nine months. In Mississippi I went and took most all of the startin', basic courses at night. We went every night and every day. Then I left there for Florida. We stayed

PLATE 157 The picture of Lewis in his airman's
uniform that he sent home to his wife

in a hotel there. It was their biggest hotel at that time. The hotel was nice, and we had a room on the tenth story of a ten-story building. This was nice except we didn't have no elevators. When the war started they had to take all the elevators out to use their parts, so we had to walk up those ten flights of stairs. It was great exercise. We got good exercise. We went up there about four or five times a day. One day there was some fellers that was bringin' a airplane in. It was comin' in too low, and it hit the ocean. It was standing up with the fin out of the water, and when I left that town it was still stickin' up. Those two boys was gone; it killed them.

> "The bus driver . . . I told him, 'I got a way to go, and that ol' lady won't give me a ticket for gas.' He said, 'Don't worry 'bout it. Here's eight.' Then he told me if I used them eight up, then he'd give me twelve, so I was right excited. It's good to have friends like that."

My wife's baby sister died when I was down in Mississippi. I finally got back up here after she was buried. I come up to see what was goin' on. When I come back, this lady was up there in the old bank. She was over the gas 'cause, you know, it was rationed. I wanted some gas, so I asked her. She said, "I can't give you no gas ticket." She put the limit on who got what when. I said, "I just got back home, and I need gas." She said she couldn't sell me no gas. They can't sell gas to everyone who comes in wantin' some. I said, "Well, all right." So I walked down to the center of town. There sat a big bus. The bus driver was an ol' feller I knew that lived on Flat Creek, so I told him, "I got a way to go, and that ol' lady won't give me a ticket for gas." He said, "Don't worry 'bout it. Here's eight." Then he told me if I used them eight up, then he'd give me twelve, so I was right excited. It's good to have friends like that. I reckon he just took them off of the school bus gas. I never did know how he got out of it.

I went to Mississippi, Florida, then to Kansas City, Kansas, where I did my Air Force trainin'. In Kansas City, we went to school for three months to read all the flight manuals and to learn the instruments. They said if we didn't make above an eighty on the test, then we can't go. I made an eighty-five, so I went. I was always smart.

Now this one boy from our base, he got to go home, so he hitchhiked back. You could hitchhike anywhere in the Air Force. He got down there to his girl, and she was married to somebody else. He come back, and he was the top notch of the runway. He could do anything with a plane. He was just about to be promoted, and one night he shot hisself 'cause he thought he was goin' to marry that girl, and when she found someone else, he just killed himself. A lot of the guys got "Dear John" letters. Another wrote a letter home, and his girl sent a picture back. He could tell she was expecting, so he went to the financial and got them not to pay her anymore. You know, his girlfriend was gettin' his pay, and he stopped that. It happened all the time.

> "To pass, you had to tear the piston of your gun apart. The Air Force had us doin' that, and we stayed up there until we got to where we could put that rifle and piston together in the dark."

I went on to school, but they let a lot of 'em go 'cause they couldn't pass. We went to Albuquerque, New Mexico, for the gas trainin'. They stopped us, and trained us to go through these camps that was about the size of a room. You had to wear a mask and put open your shirt. They made sure you was all right before you passed 'cause they put us through the poison. We had to go through the poison to leave. If you messed up, you had to do it again. I went through, but some boys didn't make it. We had to go to school about three nights a week. To pass, you had to tear the piston of your gun apart. The Air Force had us doin' that, and we stayed up there until we got to where we could put that rifle and piston together in the dark.

Then we went to Fort Mack [McPherson in Atlanta, Georgia]. That's where they sent us to get our suits and uniforms. So we got on our fatigues when we got out there, and they called us to attention. The commander, he was sayin', "I been 'round here two or three days, and I been waitin' for that dirt to be moved. I don't know what to do with it." I said, "I'll tell you what to do with it." He said, "What?" I said, "Dig a hole to put it in." Man, he got mad. That was the way I talked back then. Then we rode a train to New York.

Then we went to Florida, somewhere south of Clearwater, for more trainin'. That's where we crossed the water from. We got on a plane and went to Pakistan. We were already at war. We got on the plane and loaded it down with equipment. Then when we got all the way to the base in Pakistan, they transported us to different places. Everybody that went to school together, they separated. They scattered us out good. I guess they didn't want us talkin'.

I was scared to death. There was so much lightnin' when we came into Pakistan. It was lightnin' so much it seemed like daytime. It looked like daylight. We couldn't see nothin' but the lightnin', and when we went to land, our plane was wobblin' quite a bit. I got kinda scared then. I don't know why that pilot flew right into that storm instead of goin' 'round it. I guess he had his reasons. I got kinda scared then. We was straight in the middle of the storm when we landed.

"We were in the tunnel, and we were standin' in about three feet
of water. There was a little boy out there . . . That lieutenant went
for him . . . They didn't drop bombs or anything. They just shot
them from the plane . . . He went for that little boy, and when he got
to him, they shot him."

The first job I had was runnin' a fuel pump. I used to get the gas for their
planes. We was underground, so the Japanese didn't know where we was
at. That was my job. We went all over the base fillin' planes with fuel. All
we had to do was to drive around. I drove an oil truck first; then I drove a
tanker. I drove a tractor-trailer. My route was seven at night to seven in the
mornin'. I got to put the gas in all the planes that came in. They come in
every three minutes and left every five minutes. The boy that drove my oil
truck after me, I told him, I said, "When you go down this runway"—there
was a road beside the runway—I says, "You go down there; you be careful
when you go 'round that curve 'cause that thing'll turn over." He said, "I'll
think of it when I get there, I guess." So he took off, and he got down
there and turned it over. Another week, somebody busted the top of a
fifty-five gallon barrel of gas; then they set it on fire. Somebody did it. I
don't know who did it. It was just fire, fire, fire. It just about caught everything else on fire. We were then out of fuel, but a freight train brought us
some more.

On down deeper in China, the Japanese started comin' in. They would
come with twelve planes every day. When they come, there was twelve
bombers; each time it was twelve. We had a ditch dug that was about four
feet wide and about eight feet deep. I did march to it, and I was a sergeant.
We were in the tunnel, and we were standin' in about three feet of water.
There was a little boy out there; he was about yea-high [waist-high]. That
lieutenant went for him, and both of 'em got killed. They didn't drop bombs
or anything. They just shot them from the plane. He should have stayed in
the tunnel, but he went for that little boy. Both of 'em got killed, so that was
a bad day. He went for that boy, and when he got to him, they shot him.

Every day, twelve planes would come over and drop bombs. They were
straight and had five guns in the front of the plane. They would shoot at anything. You didn't disobey an order and be out at the wrong time. We dug the
ditch, or someone dug it, so we could hide when the planes came by. There
was certain hours where you couldn't go outside at all.

This pilot and copilot was about to go up for a trainin' mission, and I
wanted to go. I went to the office, and told 'em I wanted a job on a plane. So
they told me to be a flight engineer and go up with those boys—meanin' the
plane about to go up. Well, I went up, but they was testin' a plane. They'd

wobble it; they'd fly it on its side, fly it straight up and straight down. It would get hot, and they'd turn the engines off to see if it would still run. When I came down, I said, "I'll never do this testin' again," but they let me as a job. I missed flyin' when I got home.

We was drivin' fuel and food across the Himalayas. You've heard of Mount Everest—we flew around it. We couldn't fly our big ol' supply planes over Mount Everest, but those little fighters could. They would go over it and look at it. It's the biggest mountain in the world. We flew around it 'cause we couldn't go that high. I flew from Pakistan to China about twice a week. We just flew supplies to China. We flew those big cargo planes. China was on our side, too.

I kept goin' and workin' hard, and I got to fly. I was a flight engineer on a plane. Our outfit was called the Flyin' Tigers. There was a pilot and a copilot, and they got somebody to direct them where to go and help with any mechanical problems. This one pilot flew with me for two years. I was back there where the load was. The load was in the back, and I was checkin' it, when this copilot came back there. He said, "Sergeant, put on your parachute." I had it layin' there, and I said, "What for?" He was sayin' that one of the engines was runnin' hot, and he didn't know what to do 'cept bail out of this thing. I said, "We're not gettin' out of this thing. We gettin' it where it's goin'." He went back to the cockpit and said, "Well, if you don't want to bail out, then you better figure somethin' out." I says, "Your water is too low; if you put that water up 'bout three notches, then you'll cool down." I left to check the rest of the load. In about forty minutes he came back, and he said we was right—"it's runnin' cool now." That's what a flight engineer was for. See, if it weren't for the flight engineer, they'da had to bail out, and we'da lost a million-dollar plane and some fine people, too. That's 'bout the closest thing I had come to crashin'. We helped the Merrill's Marauders, that flyin' outfit. We helped 'em to get loaded before they went on bombin' raids.

We flew at 27,000 feet to one of the missions, and when we went to land, the planes were so close together that we had to wait. They had thirty-something planes that are wantin' to settle at the same time, so they just stacked us up. We would make a pass and call them on the radio. Then they would tell you where to fly. We would circle at that elevation until the radio said, "Drop one thousand feet," and we would go around and drop another thousand feet. The planes in front and behind of us did the same thing. Eventually, we were on the bottom, and we got to land. We were way up there at like 28,000 or 29,000 feet. They put a lot of planes in the air. We would be way up in the sky, and they'd be tryin' to get a place to land. It took almost as long to land as it did to get to China.

"He bailed out then. It took him three months to get home or back to the base. He walked and walked. He was covered up with leeches. There would just be scars and sores up his arms and legs from where them leeches had sucked on him."

The mountains over there are a lot different than they are here. They ain't got trees or bushes. It's rocks; boy, they'd be high! High rocks . . . so high that we had to fly over them. That's the reason I didn't want to bail out. Those things could kill y'. I didn't want to hit a rock. A friend of mine, he went over there. He bailed out or was gonna bail out, but they shot the plane down. He bailed out then. It took him three months to get home or back to the base. He walked and walked. He was covered up with leeches. There would just be scars and sores up his arms and legs from where them leeches had sucked on him. What they do is suck your blood out. He had to walk back to the base, and he had to be careful 'cause those Chinese would kill you. The government supported us, but not some of the people. When you flew, you had to wear a leather jacket with an American flag on the back. You'd fly with it on your back, so if you crashed, they would see it and not shoot you.

When we went to this little runway in a field, we landed and picked up eighteen barrels of gas, which is about a ton. We had to circle around a time or two to see anything. There was a truck and a little ol' buildin' there and a trail between two jeeps for a runway. We landed, and the pilot and copilot went to eat lunch. They left me to watch the plane and the supplies. When they came back, we took off. The pilot went wide open, but there was big ruts, almost knee-deep, from our landin' before. With that mountain comin' at you, it was worryin' me. It looked just like Black Rock Mountain in Mountain City, Georgia. We ran out of runway real quick like, and I asked him what he was goin' to do. He just turned that thing up on its side like that. Boy, it scared me 'cause I know that if you turn a plane too steep, it'll slide off. I 'as afraid we was gonna slide off. We didn't. He was a pretty good pilot. It was called humpin' when you flew so low that the belly of the plane hit the ground, and that was what we did most of the time. We flew low to the trees.

There was one guy that was a comin' back from a mission, and he was bein' followed by a Japanese fighter plane. He was followin' but not shootin' at 'em. He didn't shoot 'cause he wanted to know where he was goin' to land. That Jap was just watchin' the plane; he was just followin'. They was runnin' toward a mountain that was real big. They was C-46 gas planes. Then they was goin' toward the mountain, and our boy pulled the plane at the last minute. The Japanese plane wasn't watchin'. He went right into the mountain and blew up. He was watchin' the other plane, not the ground or the gauges.

There was some Japanese, girls and men, who would back into the propellers on the plane. You know they have to sit on the ground to warm up. Well, they would be tryin' to clean the devil off them, so they backed into the propellers and got chopped up. They was gettin' the devil out of 'em. They didn't do their dead like we do. If our guys got killed, they got buried. Them others, they would just lay the body out on the ground and get a dump truck to dump dirt on top of 'em. They made like a little mound on 'em. They did a lot of things different over there.

We was down in China, and it was dark. We couldn't see. We was flyin' with instruments. That's what they were for when you couldn't see or nothin'. So we started to cross the mountains, and all of the sudden, we had no instruments. I said, "We'll have to call somebody." All the planes, they all had radios then, so they called 'em and got ahold of the pilot. He told 'em where we was and what degree and everythin'. They called us back tellin' us which way to go. So we come back in; I was so glad to see that runway! That was the scariest thing that you can imagine—being up there with only three people, doin' a hundred and thirty miles an hour, and lose power and direction. Maybe that's what's wrong with me now—all those quick turns, landin', and all.

**"I slept in the same bed for three years and didn't change sheets. We had it rough. We should have had more supplies."**

I was at one base, and then they sent me to another base. When I got there, there was a tent for me. There was one boy who stayed in the tent with me. He got on a plane, got caught up, and had to bail out. They was droppin' the food on the front lines. They was supposed to drop it down over the lines for the men, but 'cause of the Japanese guns, they could never get close enough. On the way back, they ran out of fuel. They had to bail out; he lived through the crash. He was alone for months. He walked back to the camp. Somehow he made it back. He avoided the Chinese, and he got to the camp, finally.

I slept in the same bed for three years and didn't change sheets. We had it rough. We should have had more supplies. We had a whole lot of water, but no ice. We had loaf bread. They were pretty-good-sized loaves; it wadn't wrapped. I seen this truck filled with bread about knee-deep, with these young boys ridin' up on top of the bread. They was workin' on it, but we still ate it. When you went to eat, you had to look out for bugs, worms, and everything. It was terrible. I think that's why I lost so much weight [laughter]. I was hardly anything. The government didn't send us anything. They left that up to the captains and first lieutenants. We didn't have no ice or no coffee. We had a lot of hot tea because we grew it. We were in tea country.

When I went in, I weighed 157 pounds. I weighed 110 when I left China. I told my commander that I weighed 157 when I checked in, and I weighed 110 as I checked out. He said, "Mmm-huh." I didn't say nothin', though, but I ain't never gained it back. I had black, wavy hair when I left, and when I came back, I had gray hair.

**"I got mail, but back then, everything was censored. When I wrote a letter to my wife, I had to go get a captain to read it and sign it before I could mail it."**

We was the Allied forces, but I don't think I ever met anyone but American soldiers. I was in China, but I never met a Chinese soldier. I saw the emperor of China and his wife. They stayed at our base one night. I saw 'em. 'Course, I didn't get to meet 'em. Generalissimo Chiang Kai-shek and his wife stayed the night. Generalissimo Chiang Kai-shek—that's a long name, but I guess he's carried it all his life. I guess they had nicer quarters. They probably wadn't outside in no tent like we was. I got a letter of appreciation from the Chinese Air Force. It is written in Chinese and English, too.

I got mail, but back then, everything was censored. When I wrote a letter to my wife, I had to go get a captain to read it and sign it before I could mail it. If it mentioned anything related to the war, they wouldn't let me send it. If you went to a restaurant in town and you was talkin' about the planes, the trips, or anything, then they would arrest you and put you in jail.

I had to work seven days a week. We had to fly two or three times a week. I was in charge of eight men, and we'd go to work at seven and get off at seven. Everybody says, "Go in the Air Force; they don't do anything." Huh! We worked ever' day, all day!

We stayed over there 'bout three years. That's a long time to be gone. I stayed in the same tent with a dirt floor for three years. We had no runnin' water, no ice, and no toilet. We had thousands of boys like that; they were always in and out. Once a new shipment of boys came in, and a young man come lookin'. He asked, "What you reckon we be doin'?" I said, "Well, they probably be takin' you to the front line of China." He got a little wrong about that, and he just shot himself. He shot himself in the forehead with his .36 gun. The top half of his head was gone. The captain came down there to see what was wrong, and when he found out, he said he wanted every piece of him. Them boys was up all night.

We went through the Red Sea, the Strait of Gibraltar, and the Suez Canal. I went through the Suez Canal on a ship. Goin' down the canal, we had 'bout three feet on both sides. It was a tight fit. I looked all the way through the trip for a house or fishin' boat or anything hidden like back on the bank or somethin'—wadn't nothin' but grass 'bout two inches high. No tree in sight; wadn't a person in sight; wadn't an animal in sight, nothin'. The whole trip, we didn't see nothin', and I was lookin' hard. I always was curious 'bout why that was. We saw the Red Sea. The Red Sea is the one that God divided so that Moses could go through to lead his children out of Israel. He parted the Red Sea, so there was a dry path all the way through.

I think they had it the hardest on them islands. They was sellin' their cigarette ration to get food. They was doin' all they could. They sold everything to the Indians—India Indians.

Gettin' out of that place was a lot harder than gettin' in. We had to get all the planes out before we could leave, 'cause if we left, they wouldn't have no gas or people to run 'em. We just had propellers on our planes back then; we didn't have that jet stuff. We flew from the place we were stationed in China to Pakistan. We flew on C-46s. We then got on a boat to come the rest of the way home.

The sea was pretty rough when we crossed to come home. Some of them boys was real bad sick from crossin'. We laughed at 'em. When we come back, we landed in New York. When we came back to a fort in New York, they sent us on a train to Fort Gordon in Augusta, Georgia, where we had to sleep on the ground 'cause they didn't have no place for us to go. When we

PLATE 158 Lewis pauses to smile as he explains the medals on his uniform.

landed, there was one man come to greet the three thousand. He was the man who was tellin' us who was goin' where and when, but wadn't nobody to greet us in New York. Nobody knew we was back. Durin' World War II everything was a secret. We didn't know anything. My wife didn't know when I was comin' home, when I was shippin' out, or anything. Everything was a secret; there's no secrets now. We got on a train when we was in New York at a fort of some kind—Army, I think. When I went into the kitchen of the fort, it was full of Germans. They was doin' the cookin'. They was prisoners who had been brought to the States; they had on white uniforms and big hats. The kitchen was full of Germans. From there, we got on a train to come back to Georgia.

After that, we was leavin' New York on a train. As soon as we was on the train, them boys started drinkin'. I didn't drink. The train stopped at some station. That's when they got the MPs and put them on the train. Then if them boys got to drinkin', they had to get off the train. They'd have ten or fifteen at a time just standin' out there. They just had to walk home.

Rabun was a lot different when I got home. Ever'body still had rations for everything. We couldn't get no gas—still had to have a coupon. The people at home had it hard, too. They couldn't get lots of things. My wife had no butter, and that ol' margarine was so white. The margarine was sent with a little ol' packet of orange food colorin' so you could make it yellow if you wanted to. I guess you would have to mix it with your hands in a bowl and then press it back out into a block. We couldn't get no meat either. We still couldn't get no coffee. It was hard to get anything.

> **"I was glad to be back once I got home. I didn't miss any of the other countries, but I do miss the planes and my job."**

Our son went in the Air Force, too. My daughter married a man who was in the Army. They traveled alone. He went to Vietnam twice: once 'cause he had to and then 'cause he volunteered. He retired a major. The service is different now. I am eighty-five, and it was different when I was in. The war that I was in was not like the wars are now. World War II was a world war, and it was more man-to-man fighting, and more people died.

I felt free at home. We built this house here right after the war. Me and my wife could be together again and do what we wanted to do. I had to get acquainted with my daughter. She was a three-year-old when I came back. She was three months old when I left. She didn't like "that man" none, even though she carried my picture, but she sure loves me now, though. I was glad to be back once I got home. I didn't miss any of the other countries, but I do miss the planes and my job.

## MACK SUTTLES

"Boot camp was rough. Most of us were just young boys. They really put us through the mill, too . . . We learned everything we could about warfare. It was tough, but we made it through."

When I joined the Army, I guess my family was upset in a way when I left, but that was one thing I had to do, and so I went and did it. I wasn't married at that time. Boot camp was rough. Most of us were just young boys. They really put us through the mill, too. We learned to march, drill, hand-to-hand combat, how to handle the weapons, how to handle grenades, how to throw a grenade. We learned everything we could about warfare. It was tough, but we made it through. I took my regular basic training, and then I took six weeks of hand-to-hand combat training, which was Ranger training. I started in the Rangers with 169 guys; all you had to do was drop out just one time, and you were automatically out of the outfit. In six weeks when we fin-

PLATE 159 "I joined the Army . . . That was one thing I had to do, and so I went and did it." —Mack Suttles

ished our basic training, there were 69 of us left. Then I also had two weeks of survival course. I took my physical at Fort Jackson in South Carolina. We had malaria, typhoid, and yellow fever shots. We also had plague shots, and just about any kind of shot you could name, we had it. I went from there to Fort Bragg, North Carolina, for my induction. From there I went to Camp Croft, South Carolina, in Spartanburg, where I took my basic training. From there I went to Fort Ord, California, for two weeks and was sent from there back to Camp Picket in Virginia, where I joined the 65th and the 218th, and that is when I left to go to France.

My older brother spent four years in the Reserves for the Navy. Then I had one brother that was in the Air Force during the Korean War. He was in the Air Force during the Vietnam War when he retired. I also had another brother that was in service during the Vietnam War. He spent his time in Germany.

We really did not have a special time to get up during the war. Whenever they kicked you out of a hole, somewhere or another, either you were on the move, in a skirmish, or else you were in a foxhole on guard. When a commanding officer came in there and said to get up, that's when we got up, but our regular time was usually at about five o'clock in the morning if we were in basic training.

**"The only hot water you had, you heated in your helmet . . . If you didn't do that, why, you had cold water."**

It was very cold most of the time. Whenever you got a break, you were sent back to where you could take a bath and get clean clothes. Other than that, you washed in a steel pot. The only hot water you had, you heated in your helmet. If you were out there, you could take your old helmet and put water in, and if you were where you could build a little fire or something under it, why, you could heat it that way. If you didn't do that, why, you had cold water.

They would have chow lines. In the Army, we called our food chow. If you were up on the front lines, they would usually eat K rations or C rations. In each C ration there were four cigarettes. There was a can of some kind of meat or lima beans, a raisin bar, and also two "heart attack" crackers, which were crackers that tasted so bad that they would give you a heart attack.

In a fight, well, we slept in a foxhole, in what we called a slit trench. You carried an old blanket with you. The foxhole was dug deep, and a slit trench was about two foot in length, most of the time, where you could stretch out in it.

You did not build fires during combat. You would get your head blown off. You could hear gunfire almost all the time. Sometimes the Germans would catch you in chow lines. Or they would catch you by creeping up, and they would throw an 88 barrage on you.

For entertainment, why, we would go to the USO or to a dance some-where or another if we had liberty to go. I made a lot of new friends while I was over there. The majority of the time, the morale of the GIs was good. Sometimes it would get pretty low, but as long as guys depended on the next guy, why most of the time the morale was pretty good.

We had a lot of heavy artillery. We had 105s, AK guns, tanks, and 157s. The Germans had 88s and what we call screaming meemies, which was their big guns. They also had AK guns, machine guns, and what we called the burp gun, which was more or less a little machine gun that they carried. Of course they also had their rifles and tanks.

We had good weapons. I don't know, but I believe they were. And it was the planning, I think, more than anything, that beat them. As far as I am concerned, they beat their own self by squabbling back and forth among their commands.

PLATE 160   Mack Suttles shows off one of the
weapons used during the war.

Once we were going into Germany, but the Germans had blown up the bridge that crossed a big river. We had to set up pontoon bridges across the river to go across. The bridge was a main link from one place to another across there, and they blowed the bridge behind them when they crossed. We had an order to get tanks, men, and everything else across the river. With it being ice cold, we had to build the pontoon bridges so that we could go across.

"There were no stores over there. I mean, everything had been blown up. The city didn't look like a city after a battle. There was not a whole lot left. It was just jagged edges."

The only Christmas we celebrated was in '45. We did not have much to do. We had church service. We had Christmas dinner, which was served to us, but other than that, that was about all. We did not have any plays or anything like that. The people that lived in Europe celebrated their Christmas, I guess, about the same as we celebrate ours. I don't remember seeing any Christmas trees at all, but when we were over there, there was nothing goin' on, and there was nothing to be had, as far as that goes. There were no stores over there. I mean, everything had been blown up. The city didn't look like a city after a battle. There was not a whole lot left. It was just jagged edges. A lot of them had been bombed and shelled out. It was a mess. The only thing we had was the PX. That's where we got our necessities.

"You didn't talk about the war because your mail was censored then, and if there was anything in there about what they didn't want you to know, they blacked it out."

We wrote home every week, most of us did. Most of the guys, the ones that were married, wrote home to their wives; and the ones that were not wrote home to their families, their mothers, fathers, and their girlfriends, stuff like that. There was not too much data to speak of. Other than that, about the only thing you could tell them was if you were well and okay.

I was assigned detail at Dachau prison camp. As a matter of fact, I was there when it was took over. Then I went back to Dachau prison camp, and I was stationed there for a while. We had 19,000 SS troopers there.

We didn't know what was happening in other places. We were just concerned about our own thing, and whatever we had to do, we did it. But, as far as other commands and things, we didn't know too much about that.

I was at Le Havre, France, at the shipyard, waiting for the boat to take us to Japan over there for the invasion on Tokyo when we heard the bomb was dropped. There was a lot of celebrating goin' on. I was overseas three years, two weeks, and three days.

Most of the time, we would get paid every thirty days if we were where we could get the money. Fifty dollars a month was how much we got—that was, until we got a little bit of a rank. I was getting one hundred sixty-nine dollars a month after I got ranked a little bit higher, but when I went into service and all, for a long time it was fifty dollars a month. That was about enough to pay for laundry and have one good weekend.

I was in Berlin, Munich, Salzburg, and Frankfurt. They have got a lot of mountains in different places, but Germany has also got a lot of good farm country. They don't have single-unit houses and things over there. Everything is built together just like in these big apartment complexes. I was in the service company and drove trucks over there after the war. I hit about all of them. I stayed till '47 before I came home from overseas. When I came out, I was a T-5. I made it to a staff sergeant, and I got knocked back down. I spent a lot of time in what we call a service company over there, driving trucks. I didn't bring anything back because they wouldn't allow it.

PLATE 161 Mack Suttles standing in front of some German wreckage

"After it was over, I met a lot of nice people that were over there that weren't too bitter. Some were bitter, but generally, most of them at that time were pretty nice people. They had no freedom whatsoever."

We went through seven of what we call shakedowns before we got out. They went through and searched everything you had. Anything that you picked up as a souvenir that you didn't have a signed paper for or anything that you got in combat, you couldn't bring it home.

The war affected my life in many different ways. I suppose the best part of it was that it made a man out of me. I guess I learned to appreciate freedom, the United States, and everything we have here. The only thing is that it was rough, but sometimes there were good times. I hope to the Good Lord that others don't ever have to go through it.

After it was over, I met a lot of nice people that were over there that weren't too bitter. Some were bitter, but generally, most of them at that time were pretty nice people. They had no freedom whatsoever. They did what they were told. They couldn't say what they wanted to, and here in the United States you can say what you want to. You have got your freedom and everything, which people should be proud of.

## J. H. CANNON

"They killed the medics, so we learned real fast not to wear the helmet with the cross. They shot 'em 'cause then anybody that got wounded would get no cure, and they'd die."

I was born here in Rabun County, Georgia, on March 2, 1914. In other words, I'll be ninety years old this March comin' up. This store [Cannon's Furniture Store, Clayton, Georgia] used to be a hotel. My mother had a motel here, and my father ran the department store down there. But then it wasn't a department store. It had all kinds of stuff. It was hardware, furniture, clothin', and canned fish. Most everything they had was canned, you see, because they had no refrigeration back then. All the meat had to be sold that day because they had no refrigeration.

I was drafted into the Navy. It was scary. I was, I guess, twenty-six or -seven when I left. I was married when I left, and my wife had my child a few months after I left the States. At that point, I had a brother who was younger than me who was drafted. Then my [older] brother had a son, my

nephew, who was drafted. My brother, he was in the Air Force. He was stationed in China, workin' for pilots. He was lucky. He was not a pilot. He was
a worker. He was in charge of the kitchen for the pilots, which in wartime is
a good job, but he was in the Air Force. They flew what they called the
hump between China and Japan. He was stationed on the other front of the
war, away from me.

Training was in Cambridge, Maryland. We had basic training like they do
now, but 'cause I was a medic, we worked in the hospitals. We worked up
there waitin' on patients and givin' 'em shots. We cleaned up stuff, too. You
know, if someone had a bowel movement, it had to be cleaned up. We just
kept it clean, and we took their temperature, of course. They taught us how
to change bandages and all, you know. I never studied medicine, but I was a
medic. The ambulances before World War II—well, the funeral directors
had the ambulances. The hospitals didn't have the ambulances. After World
War II, the hospitals run the ambulances like they do today. Back then, I
drove an ambulance, and I learned the basics of handlin' a sick person.
That's what we did in the Navy trainin' program at the hospitals.

When you was drafted, the Navy would question you before they gave
you a job to see what you was good at. Some of these boys were not as lucky
as I was: They were drafted, and they went to Japan. It was worse 'cause the

PLATE 162 J. H. Cannon in his Navy uniform

medics there had to tend the wounded on the battlefield, not from a boat. They explained that they wore the cross on their helmet, and they weren't supposed to shoot you if you had one, accordin' to the Geneva Convention. It said that you wadn't supposed to shoot a medic, but that ain't what happened. What happened was that's the first thing they killed. They killed the medics, so we learned real fast not to wear the helmet with the cross. They shot 'em 'cause then anybody that got wounded would get no cure, and they'd die. Now, that was what happened in the South Pacific, you know, Japan and all, but if I was there, I don't think I'da worn that helmet either.

I was assigned to deal with enlisted men because I was an enlisted man. Well, basically, all we did was take care of the wounded. When they were curable, we cured 'em. We'd help the doctors give shots. We had shots of morphine in our pockets to comfort 'em. You could give 'em a shot if they're in pain, but when you did, you had to tag 'em, in case somebody else came by and give 'em two shots. Well, you know, that could kill somebody.

I was on the LST-150, a military transport ship. An LST was a landing ship tank. It was about 175 feet long. This buildin' [Cannon's Furniture Store] here is only 130 feet long, so you can tell about the difference. I think it was wider than this—a little wider. It was 175 feet long, and that's 45 feet longer than this buildin' here. We had different levels, you know, so it wasn't small. We had a basement, you might say. That's how they would get trucks, jeeps, and tanks to come up in the boat. They'd had these gates like doors, and when you let 'em down, they was a place to drive the truck out to. You ever seen an LST?

We worked in the Normandy invasion. The first time we landed on the shore, it was not secure. We couldn't beach. We had all the men, soldiers, in the bottom of that thing, and we had tanks and guns in what they call a duck. Now a duck was a boat that they could move men in. It was a boat that had propellers on it, and it had wheels on it. As they were taking the beach, they would let the big thing in the front that is like a huge door down. Well, they let that down, and the men and equipment come out. They'd drive these things in the water. They had wheels on them to drive 'em on land, but they had propellers to get you to shore where the wheels could take over. Now the first wave of ships—I was in the first wave—was sent when the shore was not secure, and most of the people that got in there was killed. I figure, I'm guessin', they lost half of the LSTs that went in. Now the LSTs were loaded with men. I don't know how many men, maybe like 150 men that was operatin' the ship, but then there was no tellin' how many soldiers—all in this big tank 'bout like a buildin'. It had guns in it and tanks, just the smaller tanks, though. It didn't have the great big tanks. They would come later. They had the old guns in there, some large guns, and of course, they all went down with the LSTs. We couldn't beach when I was in there the first time. When they tried to get off them ships, I 'as sure that most of 'em didn't make it.

Anyway, when we went back the second time, we made about three trips. They brought the wounded men to us in small boats. When we got 'em out, we treated 'em and then took 'em out to England. When we got to England, we would unload 'em. Then the next trip we come in, we could beach. That was when we had the most wounded comin' in. They was bad—the people we took in this last trip, we could get off at the beach. They could get off without swimmin' or ridin' in a boat, so a lot of 'em was worse. They tried to get off. They tried to get out, but they didn't have anywhere to go, you see. Now this was the first wave. They were the first ships comin' in. The first wave of ships should have never come in until we got the beach secured. They were tryin' to do that with the planes. They was usin' bombers and all. They did also have a lot of paratroopers that they dropped, but they shot a lot of 'em before they could get down. Then they dropped some of 'em too low, and they hit the water. They drowned 'cause they were loaded down with heavy guns and stuff. It was a bad day.

Now that was in the Normandy invasion. Now after they did the Normandy invasion, we changed ship; I got on another ship. It was LST-143, I believe, but I could be wrong. Then we'd made a southern France invasion. We couldn't see nothin' happenin'. We would hear shots and guns goin' off all the time at Normandy, but these others, we didn't see nothin'. The only way we figure they got to us was, they pulled 'em out from southern France toward the north where the beachheads were. I mean, that's what we figured, but we didn't see any more action at all. I'm glad because we were loaded down with all the men and equipment on one boat.

"The people at home were great . . . They were really, really appreciative—not like the Vietnam War. No, nothin' like that. We let those boys down, you know; they fought for their country. That was a bad situation."

I was stationed on a ship until the invasions were over. I was stationed in Oran, Africa. Then this doctor I was with . . . this was a Jewish doctor who was the port surgeon—he took care of the merchant ships comin' into the harbor. They'd come in with a mission from the base. They'd also come in with some type of supplies, or sometimes they had some sick. So sometimes we were takin' care of soldiers, and sometimes we were movin' supplies. They'd come up, and we'd come out with the doctor. We'd check the sick, and if they were real bad, we'd bring 'em to the hospital. If they weren't real bad, we'd give 'em some medication, and they'd go on.

I got out of there as soon as I could after the war ended. When the war was over, I came back here and ran the furniture store. Rabun was a lot different from before the war. People, people, people—we had never had so many people. After the war all the natives came back, and they brought some more people back with 'em. Then they put up some new industries for the soldiers to work, so even more people came. They put up factories. That helped us 'cause of the population needin' jobs, and we had no industry here until after the war was over. That's when we got the shirt factory and things.

**"It's not possible, or it wouldn't be possible, to fight that kind of war with that few loss of life in a war without the Good Lord. That's what I think."**

The people at home were great. Oh, yes, they loved us. There was a big parade when we came home. I was the first commander of the American Legion, and we had a big parade. All the mothers, they came out to see. They were really, really appreciative—not like the Vietnam War. No, nothin' like that. We let those boys down, you know; they fought for their country. That was a bad situation. The community was really supportive of us. When anybody went to the war and they came back, we was happy. Even our president now, that's a miraculous thing that he can have a war without losin' any more men than he did, but I think the Good Lord was helpin' him with that.

PLATE 163 J. H. in Cannon's Furniture Store,
which is now operated by his son, Sonny

It's not possible, or it wouldn't be possible, to fight that kind of war with that few loss of life in a war without the Good Lord. That's what I think.

The service has changed. Yes, it's changed. They have a lot of different things now. There's a lot of new things since I was in. See, I been out now for fifty-five years. We came home on a ship, even though they kept sayin' we was goin' to fly home. We came on a ship. Then we took the bus back here. I came home, stayed for a few days; then they sent me to Miami, Florida. I had to go there 'cause the war with the Japanese wadn't over yet. I was down in Miami, Florida. I ran a sick bay there where anybody who was sick could come get to a doctor or medicine. We didn't get out of the service until the war was over. I don't think it was too long after we got back to the States. It might have been six months or twelve months. I don't remember. Then they let us come home. They let everybody come home then. We didn't have to serve for a specific time. We got our discharge when the war was over, and that was it.

I think that this president [George W. Bush] that we got was anointed by the Lord years ago, to be our president at this time. He is a man of the Lord; he believes in the Lord, and that's the way it should be. I think that president during the war was probably a man of the Lord, too. I'm glad that we got the president we got and the government we got. I'm glad the people are backin' him up like they should, like they did in World War I and World War II.

## TEENIE HOWELL

"I can't say that I enjoyed the war, but I'm glad I went. I did my part. It was quite an experience 'cause I was young then, you know—twenty-one years old."

At the end of what they call the Depression, I was raised in Roswell, Georgia. It's north of Atlanta near Alpharetta; that's where I was raised. Livin' in a small town, I think I was better off durin' the Depression than girls who lived in the city 'cause most of my friends were in the same standard of livin' as I was, you know. Our mothers made our clothes. We never did go without food or anything, but there was a lot of families that did. They had the CCC [Civilian Conservation Corps] Camps that built roads up here. The money those boys made, they sent home to their families to buy food and everythin'.

When I finished nursin' school, I went into the service, and that was durin' World War II. They needed nurses so bad, and so I went in at Atlanta to Lawson General Hospital. I worked there for a little while, and then they

PLATE 164 Teenie Howell, one of the
many patriotic women who chose
to join the war effort as a nurse

sent me overseas to the station hospital in Italy. I was in Oran, Africa, and
then I went on to Italy. Then we moved our hospital as the troops moved. I
was over there two and a half years. I can't say that I enjoyed the war, but
I'm glad I went. I did my part. It was quite an experience 'cause I was young
then, you know—twenty-one years old.

I had to wait until I was twenty-one until I could get my license and go in
the Army. I went home and stayed with my family for a few weeks until I got
to twenty-one. While I was there, I helped a doctor take out some tonsils.
That was the first money I ever made, and he gave me twenty dollars. He
was a doctor who came up there just to take out tonsils in Roswell. I remember that. I thought that was just great that he paid me twenty dollars.

I was in the Army. We had different uniforms. We wore the olive green in
the wintertime but beige in the summertime. That's one thing: I never did
take a lot of pictures or anything; I should have.

When I got my state license, I went into the service. Two of my friends went
in, too—at the same time. We stayed together until the war was over in Italy;
then they split up our hospital. I came back to a general hospital in Naples,
Italy; then I came home. We stayed together as long as the unit stayed
together.

At that time, nursin' was not connected with the college. I went to Georgia Baptist Hospital in Atlanta. That's where I got my trainin', but when I came home out of the service, I went to Georgia State College. I took some courses there that would help me with the Visiting Nurses Association; I did not get a college degree. I am an RN, but now, you know, you have to get a college degree. All the nursin' schools like I went to, they closed all that. They called 'em diploma schools. My nursin' school is with Mercer University now. It was with Georgia State College, but then they moved to Mercer University.

**"I had one that was in the English Air Force . . . He would write me a love note every night and put it in under my report on my desk. That was before I ever got married . . . So, like I say, I've had mine!"**

In the meantime, though, I got married while I was at Lawson General in Atlanta. I had been goin' with my husband for two years. He was in the service. He was drafted, and he was down at Fort Benning for a long time. Fort Benning is where they do all the Ranger trainin'. He was in the Army, and he was in the Signal Corps. He did codin' and decodin' of secret messages. He had a very interesting job, and so, then, when I was sent overseas, he volunteered to go. They sent him to the Aleutian Islands, across the—I can't say across the country—but I was in Europe, and he was in the Aleutian Islands. He left after I did and got home before I did, so we didn't see each other for two an' a half years.

When I first went in, I didn't even know one officer from the next in rank, and I went to Lawson General where they put me on a officers' ward. I was young, you know. I walked down through there; they whistled at me and everythin' else. They were officers; they could get by with it. Now, enlisted men couldn't do that. They aggravated me all the time. I thought that I should treat them just like I did in civilian life: The patient comes first. They gave me a hard time. One time I was workin' night duty, and one of 'em got my shoes and put 'em in the men's latrine. I couldn't get my shoes back. They had me fixin' 'em egg sandwiches at night. I thought I was supposed to do that if that's what they wanted. Then the day shift come on and said, "What happened to our eggs? We didn't have any eggs for breakfast." I told 'em I gave 'em to the patients last night. I wadn't supposed to do that, but I had to learn the hard way when I first went in there. I remember we had urinals for the men. This one guy, he thought he was so smart. He kept sayin', "I need a duck." I didn't have a clue what he was talkin' about, and he knew I didn't. He just kept on and on, and finally someone told me what a duck was. It was a urinal, and he thought that was so smart. They gave me a hard time. Then I had one that was in the English Air Force; he was in Lawson

General. I don't know how he got there, but, anyway, he would write me a love note every night and put it in under my report on my desk. That was before I ever got married. He was a cute boy.

I went from Atlanta up to New York. We went to Camp Shanks in New York; it was a port of embarkation—a port where ships embark for foreign countries from. It was in an era where it was very secretive where the ports of embarkation were. When we got there, they told us to be ready, that they would call us out at most any time of the day or night to board the ship. So they called us at about two or three in the mornin'. We put on our dungarees, our high-top boots, and everythin'. Then we got on a ferry and went across from Camp Shanks to this port in New Jersey. When we got off the ferry, they were playin' "You Must Have Been a Beautiful Baby, but Baby, Look at You Now." We were just loaded down with backpacks on our backs. We all had a bag that was filled with pup tents and a cot. Everybody had a pup tent. All this stuff for really campin' out was in that bag. When we got off the ferry and got up to the ship, there was all these bags out there, and they said, "You know, you have to carry that in." The nurses were tryin' to lug theirs in. I had a pack in my hand, a bag on my back, and that bag with all the campin' stuff in it. We were trudgin' across that ramp, you know, goin' onto the ship, but some soldiers came down and carried our bags in for us. They were sweet, so I'll never forget that. We had a certain place in the ship that we could go out and go up on deck at certain times, you know. I was very thin then. I didn't eat much, and I was lookin' forward to the food and everythin'. I wadn't really seasick, but I just couldn't eat anything anyway. I made it fine, though. As far as you could see on this ship goin' over, there were these destroyers that were follerin' us, you know, protectin' us. It was a convoy of ships goin' over. I remember we went by all these historical places.

> "They had small quarters for the nurses . . . We had six in a stateroom. It was so crowded that we had to get up in turns."

We went over on a troop ship, and it was loaded down with troops and equipment. They had small quarters for the nurses; it was so crowded for us and everyone else, too. We had six in a stateroom. It was so crowded that we had to get up in turns. We had to take a sponge bath 'cause we only had water at certain times. So I'd get up and take a sponge bath, get back in my bunk, and then another one would get up to bathe. That's the way we worked it until we got overseas.

We got into Oran, Africa, and that's where they put us off. Only the nurses got off there. We had to get out. We stayed in these tents, but we were right on the beach where they had landed at one time. We could go down there and swim while we were waitin' to go to Italy. Some of our nurses were on "detached" service, but I didn't have to go. So we would lounge on the beach, swim, and everything all durin' the day.

Then we went on a British ship from Oran to Naples, Italy. Well, it wasn't very pleasant on that ship. The food was terrible on that English ship. It was just terrible. We got into Naples, and they didn't really have a place for us to go. They put us in one of those bombed-out buildings, and so we didn't get our stuff until . . . well, we were there two nights without any supplies really. We didn't get our packs or anything. We were just there stranded. I remember these two officers came down in a jeep. They were quartermasters, and they said, "Can we help y'all? Would you like to have some blankets?" We said yes, 'cause we were layin' on the floor. So they told us to come on up, and, oh, 'bout four of us crawled up on this jeep. We went up to this quartermaster's place, and it was all in blackouts, you know. They told us, said, "You know the Germans come over and bombed the port down here." They told us, "Always have your helmet 'cause they come over to bomb every night." While we were in there gettin' our blankets, they fixed us some hot C rations—good food. We had finished eating and had gotten our blankets. We were 'bout ready to go, and we had a air raid. The Germans were flyin' over, bombin' everything at the port, so these two officers told us, "If anything happens, y'all stick together and get in these foxholes." So we separated, and I had the hand of one of the nurses. She was scared to death; she said, "I can't get in there." I said, "Jenny, you can, too." So I was pullin' her. We crawled in. I got on a black fellow, and he was shakin' so bad. I didn't care 'cause I was shakin', too. When it was over, we just sat out and just kinda laughed 'bout the whole thing. Then what was so ironic about the whole thing was what we thought was the Germans—well, it was the Germans that were bombin' the port, but our antiaircraft guns were up on the mountain shootin' at the Germans. I thought it was the Germans shootin' at us. That was my experience of bombin's.

### "It had Mussolini's name carved up there on the entrance, and it had been chiseled off 'cause, you know, he went with the Germans."

They finally did get us a place to put up our cots and everything. We didn't set up our hospital. We went out of Naples up on the mountain and took over an Italian hospital. We took over that ol' Italian hospital. They had moved their patients out when we took it over. I don't know what they did with their patients. It had Mussolini's name carved up there on the entrance, and it had been chiseled off 'cause, you know, he went with the Germans. From there we just kept goin' on up, went all up, you know. We went all through Italy and went to Rome and all these places. While we were over there—'fore we ever got our hospital set up—there was four or five of us went down to the port to see if we could go down to the Isle of Capri. So we got on this boat and went over to the Isle of Capri. We got over there, and when we got ready to go back, they wouldn't take us back. We asked why not, and they said, "Oh, you can't go into Naples. They bombin' every night, and we can't do it." Well, we were stranded. Thank goodness we had not set up our hospital then, but everybody in our outfit was worried 'bout us, you know, 'cause they thought we'd been hit—been bombed. We finally did get back the next day. We had to go on a old boat back to Naples. So that kinda taught us a lesson to not get away and depend on the Italians to take us back.

So that was some of the best parts of bein' over there, but it was hard. Workin', you know, you were tired all the time. We worked twelve hours, and if you could, you got maybe an hour off durin' the day. There was twelve hours on at night if you worked night duty. We stayed busy.

> "I remember the first time they did that. I had my helmet off 'cause we used to take a bath out of it . . . So I was takin' a sponge bath out of my helmet, and they flew over. I was pourin' water out and puttin' my helmet on. There was water everywhere."

It was a big hospital; it was our first hospital in Naples. They dropped a bomb right at the gate. See, we had red crosses all over. They weren't supposed to bomb the red cross, but they did drop one outside the gate one night. If we had an air raid, we had to get out in the hall and get our patients out there, too, if we could, you know, against a wall. The worst part of it was, in the daytime, the Germans strafed, and that was where they would fly real low to the ground and shoot at the soldiers—not bomb. That was when they would fly over our hospital, and you could see the pilots sittin' in there. They would shoot these guns up. They were shootin' at the supplies goin' to the front. Some of it was ammunition, but most of it was just general supplies for the troops. They would go right up the road, strafin'. They were shootin' out of these planes, very low. They never did hit the hospital, but they did fly over the hospital. That was very frightenin'. I remember the first time they did that I had my helmet off 'cause we used to take a bath out of it, you know, if we didn't have a shower or anything. So I was takin' a sponge bath out of my helmet, and they flew over. I was pourin' water out and puttin' my helmet on. There was water everywhere. Some of it is funny, and then some of it was very sad, so sad.

I saw a lot of boys go down. 'Course, I saw all kinds of casualties and everything, you know, bein' in the service. I gained a lot of experience from all that. I'm glad I went, now. The thing 'bout it was, in our hospital, we would get 'em after they's off the front line. They had what they called the field hospital, which the nurses were not in it. Then they had the evacuation hospital, and nurses were in that. Then they came on back to the station hospital where I was. Then they went back to the general hospital, and they shipped 'em home from there. Along the way, they did some surgery and everythin'. They tried to get 'em to the general hospital and back to the States as much as possible. They flew some back, and some came back on ships. See, they've changed all that now.

We had doctors for every service over there. We had chaplains. We had a Protestant chaplain and a Catholic chaplain. I worked on a medical floor, and we had one medical doctor that was on my floor. Then there were also ward men that helped—privates or whatever. We had three surgeons in my hospital, three or four medical doctors; we had a psychiatrist, an orthopedist, and well, we had everythin'. The doctors were all guys. We didn't have any women that were doctors. They have 'em now, but they didn't back then.

I stayed with the same nurses and doctors the whole time I was over there. Our hospital stayed together until the war was over in Italy. Then they broke up our outfit and sent us on detached service somewhere else. Well, you have points, and I had enough points that they didn't send me out of Italy. They sent me to this general hospital, and I was waitin' to come home. I stayed there three months, and I had to be replaced by the young nurses comin' from the States before we could come home. One of my best friends that lives in Dahlonega, Georgia, now, she and I were in nursin' school together. We went overseas together, and they sent her to France. After the invasion of Normandy, they sent her over there, but I didn't have to go because I had enough points. I just had to wait to come home.

At one time, they emptied out our hospital and moved a German hospital in. There wadn't any nurses in it. There was doctors and patients that moved in there. We stayed. I don't know how long they were there, but we had captured this hospital. They moved 'em out and moved 'em in our hospital. I don't remember how long they stayed, but they were all Germans, you know. Then, every once in a while, we would get a patient that was French. One in particular that I remember was this Frenchman who, I guess, had gotten his back hurt. They had put a cast over him with his clothes on—even an overcoat—and they had this body cast on him when he came into the hospital. It was the funniest-lookin' thing you've ever seen . . . We also had some Indian troops over there where I was in Italy. I saw some of 'em once in a while, but not a lot of 'em.

Nurses didn't advance like Wacs and Waves and all them 'cause that was a new agency. Our chief nurse was just a captain, and I made first lieutenant.

That was right under a captain. Then all the other girls were second lieutenants 'cause we were nurses and women; they enlisted us as officers. They
saluted us and everything. It was a good job when we went in as young girls
just out of school. They needed nurses so bad. We could have gotten other
jobs, but they paid more, you know. 'Course, I can't remember how much I
got paid, but pay was very low compared to what it is now, you know. I think
it was one hundred and sixty dollars a month, but I was offered a job at the
hospital where I trained. At the hospital, livin' there and everythin', they
wouldn't pay but six hundred dollars a month. Nurses' salaries were low
back then. 'Course, now they're way up, and you can always get a job.

We had plenty of supplies for the hospital, and then we got rations for
ourselves, you know. I couldn't spend any money. I sent all my money home
except forty dollars a month, and that was just to buy toilet articles and
everythin'. I could not spend my money. I gave ten dollars for a tortoiseshell
comb once, though, you know. There was just nowhere to spend it.

**"This doctor said, when I was just through with surgery, 'I tell all
these boys not to marry a girl until she has her appendix out and
buys herself a fur coat.' "**

I had to have an appendectomy—where they take your appendix out—
when I was over there, and so they sent me to Sorrento to recuperate. This
doctor said, when I was just through with surgery, "I tell all these boys not to
marry a girl until she has her appendix out and buys herself a fur coat." Most
girls have to have their appendix out. I stayed there a week, and then I had
some leave time. That's when I went to Milan, Italy, and over into Switzerland. I had a lot of leave time since I had been in the service. After I went
into this general hospital, they let me take some of it.

I did go to Switzerland while I was over there. I flew from Naples up to
Milan, Italy, and rode the train over to Switzerland, which I enjoyed, but
outside of that, I didn't get out of the country the whole war. If you know
anything 'bout the history of Italy, you know Mount Vesuvius erupted while
I was over there. I went to the Isle of Capri, Sorrento, the Amalfi Drive, and
all these historical drives. I went to Pompeii, which is a city that was covered
in lava at one time. Then I went up to Rome, and, you know, went to the Vat-
ican. Had to go to the Colosseum. I did not get to Venice, Italy. I did see the
Leanin' Tower of Pisa. We flew over that. I saw all this stuff in Italy. I have
no desire to go back. It's so dirty in Naples especially. It's just dirty, filthy.
Switzerland is a clean country. It's so clean and mountainous. It has a lot of
snow, lakes, and stuff. It was really pretty, but Naples was the worst place. I
don't think it helped that I had to work twelve hours a day when I was there.

Roosevelt was the president durin' that time. I remember when he died. We had a bulletin board outside, and as you come outside to the mess hall—that was where we ate—we had this big ol' board. It would follow all the troop movements—advances and all. That mornin' we came out, and there was a big picture of Roosevelt. He had died durin' the night. That was one thing I'll never forget: walkin' out that mornin' and seein' that he had died.

When I wrote my husband, it would come to the States first and then go to the Aleutian Islands. He wrote me every day. I wrote him every day, but by the time we got answers, it was long. He would ask me something, and by the time he got my answer, he'd done forgot what his queston was. We didn't have all this telephonin' and all that stuff like they have now. They're on TV talkin' and all; we didn't have that back then, o' course. We didn't even have TV back then. We had to censor the patients' mail. We had to do a lot of that. Especially if you were workin' the night duty, you had to censor the mail. They were so afraid that they were goin' to give away somethin', and now, you know, they tell everythin' on TV. Back then, everythin' was a secret.

### "They told 'em that when they got there, there would be a woman behind every tree, but when they got there, there wadn't any trees."

My husband and I were never together till after the war. My husband was sent to Fort Benning after he was drafted. Back in World War II, they were draftin' 'em like everything. He was twenty-three when they drafted him. They sent him to Fort Benning; he was down there with all these old soldiers and regular Army men, you know. He was tryin' to get out of that. So I think his IQ and everything helped him to go into this Signal Corps, where he was codin' and decodin' messages. At one time he said he was goin' to OCS—officer trainin' school—but he decided that he liked this so well that he stayed with it instead of schoolin'. Before I went overseas, he went to Camp McCall, North Carolina. See, his commanding officer and him were the only two that could code and decode these secret messages.

We had the FBI and everything checkin' on us back then because he was in that type of secret thing. They checked where he lived, where he went to church, all his friends, mine, and everythin'. Then when he went to the Aleutian Islands, their whole outfit was the Signal Corps. They were close to Japan. They were on the other front. They were on Adak, the island; it's not too far from Japan. They were connected with the Air Force. They went out of Seattle, Washington. They told 'em that when they got there, there would

PLATE 165 John and Teenie Howell before
they left to serve overseas in
World War II

be a woman behind every tree, but when they got there, there wadn't any
trees. It was snowin' all the time. They had ropes to put from the mess hall
to the office and everythin'. They had to hold on to this rope to get there
'cause there was so much snow. He tried to learn how to snow-ski when he
was there. He had some pictures of that; it was awful. I think he really
enjoyed his job 'cause it was so interestin'.

I was over there in Italy for two and a half years. I stayed there until the
war was over in Italy. Then there was the invasion of Normandy and France.
It ended before I came home. I'm pretty sure that they finished the war with
Japan before I came home. The nurses that I knew that went to France, you
know, I lost track of 'em, but I think I got home before they did. I think the
war was over not too long after I got home.

"I was lookin' forward to comin' in 'cause I had heard everybody say that you get a steak dinner when you come back to the States. Well, we got turkey."

When we got off of the boat in Camp Kilmer, New Jersey—they were tryin' to get us home for Christmas—they had put the nurses up in the quarters for the pilots. We were in on an aircraft carrier. You know, that's where they bring the planes in and all. I was seasick the whole way home. We ran into a storm, and it was just awful. Well, we were supposed to be home in ten days. They were tryin' to get us home for Christmas, but we didn't make it. We got to Camp Kimbleton, New Jersey, and got off the ship. Then they took us by bus up to the quarters to where we were goin' to stay. I was lookin' forward to comin' in 'cause I had heard everybody say that you get a steak dinner when you come back to the States. Well, we got turkey, I think, 'cause it was Christmas. We got turkey, dressin', and stuff, but I was lookin' forward to a steak. I was back, and I was callin' home to tell 'em that we had just gotten back to the States. I had to stay up there awhile to get out and be processed, and then I went to Fort Bragg, North Carolina. From there, I came home by train. My husband was glad to see me. He got home before I did. That seems like a dream, a lot of it. It's been so long.

When I came home, I didn't realize that things were rationed. See, while we were over there, you couldn't get sugar, margarine, and, oh, a lot of things here. You had to have coupons to get 'em. When we came home, that was still in effect. What happened was they took all these manufac- turin' companies, and instead of makin' clothes for civilians and everything, they made Army clothes. They took over doin' that. They did not build any cars. They were just buildin' vehicles for the Army. So when we come home, you couldn't buy a car. My husband had a car, and we left it. So all the boys who came home on leave drove that car when they were on leave while we were gone. When we got home, we had a car, and nobody else had one. You couldn't find a place to live 'cause there wadn't many houses bein' built. We had a friend that lived across the street from my husband's family, and this lady had a duplex. One side of it had become vacant, and she saved it for us. We had a duplex, but we had no furniture. We had to take makeshifts and what people would give us. You couldn't buy anything. We got a gas refrigerator from a man on the street who was with the gas com- pany. He let us have the gas refrigerator, and he finally got us a gas stove. You just couldn't find any furniture or anything. We finally bought a bed- room suit, and it was awful. The drawers were like pasteboard, but it was all we could find. We found a breakfast room suit, brought it home, and had to paint it. See, all the furniture companies went into the war effort. Everything went into the war effort 'cause the U.S. was not prepared for it. So everybody pitched in in World War II. Women who had never worked before worked in the factories where they built the planes and vehicles. I had two friends that worked over at Lockheed in Atlanta, so everybody pitched in. If they hadn't, we'da never won the war 'cause we were ill prepared for it.

You couldn't buy clothes. I could buy some clothes, but my husband couldn't buy any clothes. It had changed a lot. I remember my mother-in-law . . . She had a man that came by from a bakery, and he'd bring bread, pies, and all this stuff, you know. So when he came by, I went out to buy some, but he wouldn't sell it to me. He said, "You're not a regular customer of mine." That was very disappointing. Then, if you went to the grocery store, you had to be there at a certain time if you wanted to get some meat. You had to stand in line. That bothered me. It didn't take too long to get adjusted. Then durin' all this, I had three pregnancies and three miscarriages. I don't have any children.

Later, we bought a home, and bein' in the service, we had saved money. So we were able to buy a house, but we weren't able to buy any furniture. We got a new automobile, practically new. It was from a man who was a state patrolman. He had bought this car and he couldn't pay for it. Somebody told my husband about it. It still had the paper on the steerin' wheel. I was so proud of that car. I was standin' on that porch waitin' for my husband to bring it home. It had a mother-in-law seat in the back, if you remember them—a little ol' seat in the back—but it was very comfortable in the front. We were so happy with the car, you can't believe. You couldn't buy a car. We had the old car, and we went to the beach one summer in that car. We had to have it worked on down there and back. While we were in Daytona Beach, my husband could have sold it. He said, "I can't sell you this car. We don't have any way to get home." They said they'd take us to the bus station. We said, "No way. We're not gettin' rid of this car." So we kept it until we got a nicer car.

So then, after I came home, they still were beggin' for nurses so bad, and my husband didn't want me to go to work. We bought our first home then, and he did not want me to go to work. Well, they kept buggin' me 'cause they were startin' a new agency called the Visiting Nurses Association. That was the beginnin' of home nursin'. I was the first staff nurse. I had finally talked my husband into lettin' me go. He said, "Well, we'll try it for a while." So I went. I worked for the Visitin' Nurses Association for twenty-six years. I guess I tried it for a while. I stayed there for twenty-six years, so that's about all of my career.

"The nurses were the only females in the service at all—in the
Navy and in the Army and even in the Air Force. The Marines didn't
have any nurses."

When I think about all this now, how much publicity and everything they've
gotten from this new conflict and even in Vietnam . . . Vietnam was terrible.
Those boys fought for us, too. World War II veterans didn't get much publicity when they came home. Now I belong to the monument in Washington, D.C. It is for women who were in the service. I don't know how I got an
application to join, but I did join it. I haven't been able to go to Washington
to see the buildin', but it's for all women who were in the service. That was
the Wacs and the Waves. See, they all came after we went in the service.
The nurses were the only females in the service at all—in the Navy and in
the Army and even in the Air Force. The Marines didn't have any nurses.
Then the Wacs and the Waves came into bein' later. Then, back in the
States, while I was gone, they recruited and were trainin' some nurses for
RNs. That was while I was gone.

Everythin' has changed now. They kept such a secret about everythin';
now they show the troops here and there on TV. It's just been so open. I
don't know whether that's good or not. They know what's goin' on over
there. We're still losin' boys over there now. I tell you, if my boys was over
there, I'd be worried.

I went in the service in 1942, and by the time I got home, it was about
1945, or somethin' like that. I am eighty-two years old. Now, at my age, I just
kinda live in the past. That's just about all on my history. That's the story of
my life.

"I told one of the nurses when I was workin' one day, 'If I never
have any fun anymore, I've had mine.' I've had some sacrifices while
I was in the service, but I think that was good for me. I grew up a
lot."

Since I was in the war, I was happier to get home and start my life. I guess
the war changed my way of thinkin', too. I guess I thought we could just
come home and buy everythin', and we couldn't. I have had a very happy
life. I really have. I had a good husband, and even though I don't have any
children, I've had a happy life. I told one of the nurses when I was
workin' one day, "If I never have any fun anymore, I've had mine." I've
had some sacrifices while I was in the service, but I think that was good
for me. I grew up a lot, 'cause when I went in, I was young—twenty-one
years old.

# MELVIN TAYLOR

> "I went down there and looked in one of them big cruisers; boy, I could see myself on that thing. It was the first ship I'd ever seen—first time I'd ever seen no ship."

I've lived in Rabun County all my life, born and raised here. While I was still in high school, I was in high school when I turned eighteen on the twenty-sixth of October. After being drafted, I left for the service on the sixteenth day of December. I was gone for two years, two weeks, and eighteen days; I came back when I was twenty years old.

I was in the Navy. I was a corpsman—that's the same thing as a medic in the Army. In the Marines, they ain't got no medical force, so the Navy takes care of that. So I was in the Navy, and I went to hospital corps school and stuff. I didn't want to be stuck in a hospital or nothin'. I thought I'd never be in no war or see action or nothin'. So, you know, I was up there in the hospital corps school in Great Lakes, Illinois, and an older fellow that was there, I told him I wanted to get out of the hospital corps. He said, "If you want to see action, you're in the right outfit." I'd never heard of the Fleet Marines or nothin'. I finished school there and went on to school in San Diego and worked in a hospital. Then I had to stay there three weeks. I went down there and looked in one of them big cruisers; boy, I could see myself on that thing. It was the first ship I'd ever seen—first time I'd ever seen no ship.

PLATE 166 Melvin's unit at Great Lakes, Illinois, in 1944.
He is in the second row down, second from the left.

Anyway, I had my three weeks in . . . I began to hear a good bit about the Fleet Marines then, so I went down there and volunteered for sea duty. I went down there at lunchtime that day and looked at the bulletin board. It said to be down at ten in the mornin' of the physical to go to Camp Pendleton, California, Marine Base, but I forgot to go. I was under this lieutenant JG [junior grade] lady. She was real old, and boy, she was a mean 'un! She had us all workin' over there, and I forgot to go take my physical. They said Commander So-and-So wanted to see me. I wanted to know what some commander wanted with me. When I got there, this nurse reamed me out and said he wanted me to go get my physical. So I went over and took my physical, and I done a little bit better than they told me to. I was in a hurry when I was leavin' and ran right slap into that nurse, and boy, she got ahold of me again. But anyway, I went on to Camp Pendleton. I went through field medical school there and combat trainin', and then we went overseas on the troop transport named the *General Harry Taylor.*

"I saw 'em bring the *Benjamin Franklin,* the carrier, through. It had been torn all to pieces. It was burnt out; you could see slap through it through a black hole."

PLATE 167   Melvin Taylor in his seaman's uniform in 1944

PLATE 168  Melvin proudly holds the wool corpsman's
uniform that he wore in World War II.

We went to the South Pacific with the First Marine division. I went over
there in September of '44. We was trainin' over there. The division was on
furlough, and I was on operation. We were the replacement division. We
would replace the ones that got hurt or killed or the ones that went home.
We started trainin' and stuff. On the first day of trainin' we went to Guadal-
canal. We went there trainin', and we loaded the ship in the last of February.
We loaded up. We took our mattresses and everything. We needed somethin' to sleep on in that transport. We stayed on the transport for thirty-six or
-seven days. We didn't know where we was goin'. We practiced beach
landin's goin' up and down the sealing ladders. So we finally go to Ulithi,
which is one of the Caroline Islands. It was a stagin' area. While I was there,
I saw 'em bring the *Benjamin Franklin,* the carrier, through. It had been
torn all to pieces. It was burnt out; you could see slap through it through a
black hole. The superstructure was turned up sideways. It had a small number of sailors on it. Our ship would go out to sea every night, and we would
be sittin' in the same spot when daylight come. We still didn't know nothin'
'bout where we was goin', so one evenin', 'bout four o'clock, there was ships.

Everywhere you could look, there wadn't nothin' but ships. We saw the
LSTs, and they're slow, really slow boats; they carry tanks and equipment
and all kinds of stuff—you know, heavy stuff. They began to move out, so we
figured then it wadn't goin' to be long till we got under way.

> "I was walkin' down the street in Tientsin [Tianjin], China . . . I
> said, 'I believe that's Claude English from Tiger, Georgia,' and I
> hollered, 'Claude!' down the street, and he turned. It *was* Claude
> English from Tiger walkin' down the street in Tientsin, China."

We had never heard of the island called Okinawa; we were thinkin' of everythin' in the world else. They was just briefing us on it. They was about a hundred thousand Japanese soldiers lookin' down our throats. We got there, and
there was ships everywhere you could see. There was two Japanese kamikaze
planes, those suiciders, come across, and I never seen such fireworks. That
whole fleet was shootin' at 'em. They was one of 'em that crashed in shallow
water. The side of it was covered—painted in Japanese flags; that was the first
thing I saw was all those Jap flags. The flags were how many they'd shot
down. They must have had a real good gunman 'cause there sure was a lot of
flags on it. We went on and followed a Higgins boat to the beach. They didn't
defend the beaches. There wasn't much on the beaches, so we went across
and cut the island in half, and they was a airfield on one end. There was three
Army divisions and two Marine divisions operatin'. There was all kinds of
people, but anyway, we went south and relieved the south Army division. We
went on through to the end of the island. When we got there, the Japanese
had done jumped from what they called Suicide Point. I never got to see anyone jump off. We had two wounded Marines down there, though. We had to
use ladders to get the wounded out. I wasn't up on top. One of the guys said
the bodies was just stacked up on top of one another. They killed themselves
with them hari-kari knives. We did everything we needed to and had the area
secure. We stayed around and went down on the south end, but there wadn't
any fightin' on the south end. All the fightin' was in the caves there. Some of
those caves was seven stories deep. There were tunnels that ran together and
in certain ways. That's what took 'em so long and why it was so hard to secure
the island. You couldn't get 'em out of that place. Finally, after eighty-three
days and nights of hard fightin', the island was secure. The president of the
United States presented the Presidential Unit Citation to the forces. We
went to the north end to train 'cause we knew there wadn't nowhere else to
go but Japan and the Japanese homeland.

So after the surrender of Japan, we and all of the First Marine Division
were ordered to North China as occupation troops. I stayed on China Duty

from October 1945 to February 1946. It was during this time that I was walkin' down the street in Tientsin [Tianjin], China, and I saw a soldier comin': Now the streets are real narrow goin' one way. So I saw this soldier goin' down a side street, and I looked up close. I said, "I believe that's Claude English from Tiger, Georgia," and I hollered, "Claude!" down the street, and he turned. It *was* Claude English from Tiger walkin' down the street in Tientsin, China. Every time I've seen him since then, I ask him if he's been to Tientsin lately. I was halfway 'round the world and saw a boy from here. I saw another guy—Glenn Phillips—from Rabun County, in Chicago, Illinois. That was the only two I ever saw from Rabun County, best I remember.

While on a barge waitin' to be pulled up the Pei Ho River in China, we ran out of provisions. So I went over to an Army mess hall and asked for some groceries. The sergeant told me that he had to have a requisition from an officer. I looked down that beach and I saw two officers walkin'. I ran and caught up with them. I saluted and said, "Sir." Then my feet sank into that sand about a foot when I saw the star on his uniform. He was Brigade General Jones, executive officer of the First Marine Division, with a Navy captain. I finally just went ahead and asked him for the requisition. General Jones said, "Tell them that General Jones said to feed you." The mess hall sergeant had seen all this goin' on, and boy, did he dish out food for me and my buddies then!

I picked up some relics from places while I was over there. I picked some things from dead Japanese soldiers, but I had to be careful because the

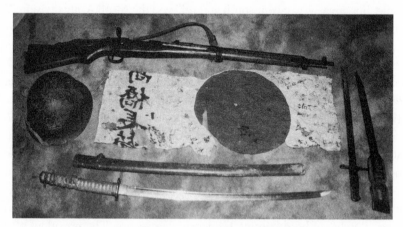

PLATE 168A A Japanese commander's sword with its leather sheath (bottom), a Japanese infantry rifle (top), an attachable bayonet with sheath (right), and a foot soldier's helmet (left), as well as a tattered Japanese flag. Almost every Japanese soldier went into battle carrying a flag such as this with messages of love and luck written on it.

Japanese would booby-trap those things so you couldn't get them. I didn't go lookin' like some people did, though. I got those flags off of some guys on the beach. I also brought back a Japanese helmet, a rifle with a bayonet, a commander's sword, and a soldier's wallet with some money. The officers didn't care what we brought back. They just didn't want us gettin' hurt 'cause of it.

I used to make necklaces on the beach made out of shells. I'd find those shells on the beach. I had to leave them out in the sun to dry out 'cause they're alive when you find 'em. I would put 'em together with dental wire and then hold 'em on that with wax. I made one this one time that was real pretty. It was about Christmastime, and this boy I was with, he wanted somethin' to send home to his girl. He had some money, but there was nowhere to buy anything, so I told him I'd sell him a necklace. I knowed he had money 'cause he sold his beer rations for a dollar. I said, "There ain't nobody in Georgia got nothin' like this from the Solomon Islands." I said his girlfriend would love it, and I needed to make some money. He paid me twenty dollars for that necklace. I sent the money home to Mama. She used it to buy the kids' Christmas. That Christmas they had more than they had in a long time. My sister still remembers the doll she got.

I did some fishin' off the deck and stuff, but for the most part, we had trainin' for battle to do. We didn't get much free time. I was 'bout ready to get off that boat.

One time we was over there, and me and a guy went to the mess hall to eat. We hadn't never seen no shrimp. The other boy looked at it and said, "What's that?" I said, "That looks like a crawfish to me." So we thought they looked like big crawfish. He asked me how we e't 'em. We didn't eat none at first. We decided to wait and watch to see what everybody else did. We watched them, and they started peelin' and eatin'. We eventually joined in, but that was the first time I'd ever seen any shrimp.

We had some big ol' lizards over there. I saw one comin' over a coconut tree. It was 'bout five feet long. It looked like a 'gater. When he stuck his head 'round that tree, first thing I thought of was, why was a 'gater climbin' a tree. It scared me. They had those flyin' fish. I know people don't believe they can fly, but they got up to the deck of the ship. They was flyin' over the deck. It wadn't no little boat either! Those fish was flyin'!

**"Well, I was a little bit nervous 'bout fightin' for a while, but the war made you grow up faster."**

We were greeted well—oh, Lord, yeah. When we come in, they had big bands. Well, they had big boats comin' in every day, aircraft carriers and all.

The kamikaze suicide planes was always goin' after them ships in Okinawa. You couldn't even see the ships. All you could see was the planes. You'd see the planes on fire, and they'd get so close that you could see the Japanese pilots sittin' up in there. The motor on that suicide plane was just a-spittin' and sputterin', and right behind him was Marines shootin' at him. They shot him down. I saw another one hit a ship. It was a cruiser. Every third or fourth bullet out of the gun is red, and it was just light enough so they could see where they was shootin'. You could see the tracers then; two kamikaze planes went after that cruiser. The first 'un, they shot him down, and he went off in the water and blowed up. The second one I seen, they shot him three times, and he went down in that cruiser. They'd go for anything. I've seen 'em go after motorboats, anything they could hit.

I remember that about three days before the end of the Okinawa campaign, several Marines were shot by Japanese snipers in a canebrake. After giving them first aid, we corpsmen carried them down to the Medical Recovery Station. While there, I saw the stretcher bearing the body of General Buckner, the commander of all ground forces on the island, who had been killed by Japanese shells. To honor him, the area was named Buckner Bay.

I was the oldest one in my family. My baby sister was only six weeks old when I left. She was walkin' and talkin' when I came home. Two years is a long time. I brought some things home with me from my time in China for my family, especially my mother.

One mornin', we was out for reveille and some guy had a little ol' battery radio and it come on and said the war was over. You never heard such hollerin'. So I didn't have enough points to get out: You had to have a certain number of points that went by how many battles you was in and how long you'd been in. We then went to North China. I stayed over there for 'bout four or five months. We went over there in October, and I stayed till February. It took me nearly a month to get home: seventeen days in a troop transport, the *Effingham,* and then four days, once I was in the States, on a train. Well, I was a little bit nervous 'bout fightin' for a while, but the war made you grow up faster. I was only twenty years old, and I was a hospital apprentice first class. I had seven brothers and sisters, and I had been gone a little over two years. When I got home, I had forgot what they all looked like—my mother and daddy included. Well, I got out, and I was a senior in high school. When I was discharged and came home, I wanted to finish my schoolin'. I met my wife when I came home from the war. I went back to school to finish my senior year, and my wife was a junior there. I went back and finished high school, and then I went to Piedmont College.

# CHEROKEE
# STORIES

"We had just a box of candy,

and that's all we'd get for

Christmas. We were satisfied.

Didn't have nothin' to ride,

no wagons or nothin'."

—*Amanda Swimmer*

Searching for what remains of Cherokee heritage is at times as difficult as finding ginseng: Both are all but gone from their former range. The glory of the Cherokees was unrivaled until settlers and the United States government tried their best to exterminate it. Now the Cherokees are reduced to two communities: the larger one in Oklahoma and a smaller one in North Carolina. The towns and rivers with bastardized Cherokee names, the rare pottery shards and arrowheads, the history books, and the dry government documents seem to be the only reminders that can tell us who the Cherokees were. With a little exploring, and what I am sure is providence, I found a few people who let me know who the Cherokees are.

When Tom Hill was a young boy and his dad was in the Navy, he spent the summers with his grandmother in Cherokee, and as he told me, "That heritage has always been a part of who I am. I didn't have to go out and find it." Now Tom works hard to share it through his lessons and stories in order to keep it alive for Cherokee's next generation.

In the beginning of my interview with Amanda Swimmer, she told me, "Don't ask me about my medicine. Now, I'm not givin' it away . . . If y' do, it ain't gonna be worth nothin'. I'll just tell you first before you ask me anything." Amanda then told me about the log home of her childhood and her long walks to school. She gave all her children both Cherokee and English names so the elders could "call them who they are," a tradition that has since faded. Amanda let me know immediately, however, that some precious elements of her life were sacred, traditions passed down for many generations. She wasn't going to share them with just anyone.

Goingback Chiltoskey, G.B. as he would later be called, learned how to carve wood from his older brother, and his skills as a model-maker led him to travel all over the United States; nevertheless, he didn't forget his Cherokee origins. In his day, Goingback was a champion with his ancient blowgun that was over a hundred years old. His wife, Mary, though a native of Alabama, worked passionately to preserve Cherokee culture. She helped change a state law forbidding marriages between races, and she saved the elementary school's Cherokee artifacts from imminent destruction. Mary also helped compile the script and plan the production for *Unto These Hills,* a drama about the history of the Eastern Band, a production that thousands of visitors see every summer.

I found in these interviews an overwhelming desire to preserve what is left. I felt joy in recording them and anxiety in writing them down, for I wanted to be certain every phrase was just as I had heard it. The stories of the Cherokee are almost forgotten, but people like Goingback and Mary Chiltoskey, Amanda Swimmer, and Tom Hill have told theirs freely so that anyone who wants can listen.

—*Russell Bauman*

# THE TRAIL OF TEARS

*"I wish I could forget it all, but the picture of six hundred and forty-five wagons lumbering over the frozen ground with their cargo of suffering humanity still lingers in my memory."*
—John G. Burnett, qtd. in
*The Removal of the Cherokee* 55

When I was a boy, I fantasized about the world of the Indians. I guess for short moments of time, I became a young brave in the world of my imagination, but soon, of course, I would have to go inside to get some Cheerios with apple juice to spill on the couch while I watched *Sesame Street*. I began to wonder even then how the Native Americans changed from their lifestyle prior to white civilization to the one they have now. How did America cause an entire society to change so abruptly?

I have heard the story of the Trail of Tears a few times in American history books, in the chance PBS documentary, and once or twice in museums. How our government uprooted an entire people is perhaps our nation's saddest story, a story cloaked in confusion. The first realm of confusion lies in separating historical fact from myth and today's modern evaluations. I think of conniving congressmen and treaty-breaking expansionists pushing the Cherokees out of their homes and council halls. The second cause for confusion is in understanding the psychology of our nation at the time. Placing a modern mindset into that of our forefathers is an impossible task, and at the outset we realize that the task is shadowy speculation.

The events that culminated in the Trail of Tears concern the struggle between two cultures. The United States had too much strength and too little foresight and was embryonic and volatile; the Cherokee Nation, governmentally disorganized, was quickly leaping ahead, trying to modernize and catch up to the new America.

Halfway through the eighteenth century, the Cherokees began to transform from their traditional lifestyle of small agricultural villages into a modern nation with an alphabet, a printing press, political parties, and economic strata, at the top of which were even Southern planters with slaves. This change came rapidly because the Cherokee leaders at the time realized the

future peril of their people. Modernization was the only means of compet-
ing with the encroaching whites. The Cherokees hoped that through adopting Christianity, white education, and an organized government, they could
succeed as a separate nation.

Simultaneously, settlers realized the value of the Cherokee land. The
southwest corner of Virginia, most of North Carolina and Tennessee, and
the northern parts of Alabama and Georgia were inside the domain of the
Cherokees. Settlers from the surrounding areas slowly began squatting their
way into Indian territory, where the land was fertile and the game was plen-
tiful. Settlement took the path of least resistance. Western North Carolina
was far too rugged for successful farming. Though this area is one of the
most visited today for the wildlife and natural splendor, it offered steep hills
and rocky soil to the homesteader. The area is still remote, and the Cherokees still live there in places such as Robbinsville, Murphy, and the Qualla
Boundary. Tennessee, which at this time was the wild frontier of Davy
Crockett, lay on the other side of the Smokies, and consequently, only min-
imal settlement existed there. Sadly, the whites had already settled north-
western South Carolina and had displaced the Cherokees and Catawbas
long before. The lands in today's northern Georgia are hilly and fertile,
sought after by those wanting a second home in the mountains. Nothing has
changed. The same hills were coveted by the Georgia settlers of the early
nineteenth century. During the first quarter of the nineteenth century, settlers moved into Cherokee territory and began pushing the Indians out of
their homes an acre at a time.

Though many Cherokees tried to hold their ground, since their nation was
neither modern nor centralized, they were unable to provide an even political front against their opposition: the white pioneers and the congressmen
who wanted Indian territory. Cherokee delegates went to Washington many
times, but these delegates often represented only small factions because a
consensus from the entire nation was impossible to obtain. Historian James
Mooney notes how the tribe was changing: "By the first decade of the nineteenth century, many Cherokees around the Hiawassee and Little Tennessee
Rivers were taking up a more sedentary, agricultural lifestyle, but many others to the south resisted the lifestyle change and still hunted game. The U.S.
government took advantage of this situation by offering citizenship to the
northern Cherokees, while they offered lands west of the Mississippi, along
the White River in Arkansas, to the hunters if they would give up their eastern lands. Later, Jefferson ratified this course of action as the Treaty of 1817"
(102–3). Some of the Cherokees foresaw the grim picture of their people's
suffering and decided to move west, even though the Treaty of 1817 did not
demand them to do so. This group acquired the name "The Old Settlers."

Modernization for the Cherokees culminated when they drafted their constitution. In the Constitution of the Cherokee Nation, completed on July 26, 1827, the Indian nation decided never to cede another foot of land to white settlement (Wilkins 203). Washington, D.C., and other places in the United States and even Europe hailed the new Cherokee constitution, but the document infuriated those who most needed to be placated. Georgia disregarded the constitution and passed legislation for the Indian Code (Wilkins 204).

The Indian Code (1827) enabled settlers to move onto Cherokee territory and lay claim to it as theirs (Wilkins 204). In 1832, surveyors further worsened the Cherokees' situation by dividing the land into sixty-acre lots for the state of Georgia to give away in a raffle system (Wilkins 249). People moved onto the Cherokee farms and called these lands their own. The whites burned Indian houses and outbuildings, and a few people died in the struggles that ensued. Since the Cherokee Nation was not part of the United States and was thereby treated as a separate entity, the Indians, whose property the whites had destroyed, could not testify in a Georgia court against a white. Those claiming anything in court needed a white witness. In almost every case, the only white witness was the wrongdoer (Wilkins 210).

To worsen and complicate matters further, a prospector found gold somewhere near present-day Dahlonega, Georgia, and started a gold rush. Known as "the yellow straw that broke the Cherokees' back," the finding of gold brought even more settlers to North Georgia, and the Indians simply could not compete with the sheer numbers of the invasion.

During this time the U.S. government, in the Treaty of 1817 and others, pushed the Cherokees to relocate to a place where the whites would never again bother them. The very thought of removal was absurd and insulting to the Indians, just as it stupefies the contemporary historian to think of the injustice, especially since the Cherokee people were inches away from adopting every aspect of white society: legally, socially, and politically. The Cherokees proved they were capable of adapting to a European lifestyle more quickly than most other indigenous peoples. All they needed was proper jurisdiction and protection. John Ridge went with a Cherokee delegation to Washington in 1831 to ask President Jackson's aid in repealing Georgia's Indian Code. There President Andrew Jackson voiced his lack of concern for the Cherokee situation: "You can live on your lands in Georgia if you choose, but I cannot interfere with the laws of that state to protect you" (qtd. in Wilkins 223).

Jackson grew up in the frontier state of Tennessee. There he frequently encountered Cherokees and came to see them as a mere impediment to his nation's progress. In the words of John Ehle, "He shared the white Tennessean's common opinion of Indians. As he saw it, they were the festering sore that afflicted the settlers and limited the colonization of this great land, the progress of this newest and best nation on Earth" (107). In the spring of 1814, Jackson quelled the Creeks in the battle of Horseshoe Bend, but he could not accomplish his victory alone. Nearly five hundred mounted Cherokees helped Old Hickory defeat the Creeks. Jackson grew in favor. During the War of 1812, Jackson and his Tennessee Volunteers defeated the British columns in the Battle of New Orleans (1815). After these two victories the frontiersman was a national hero, and with his fame came the ideas of Manifest Destiny. America was not to be a nation of the Atlantic seaboard only: She was to stretch from "sea to shining sea" (Ehle 122–23).

Major Ridge, the father of John and a compatriot of Jackson against the Creeks in the battle of Horseshoe Bend, was one of the more successful Cherokee businessmen, planters, and statesmen. He and his son fought fiercely against removal, but the two men were pragmatists as well. In 1832, they doubted that fellow Cherokees could remain in the East (Wilkins 233). White encroachment was a never-ending cycle of disappointment and harassment. Since so many Cherokees suffered injustices during the enactment of the Indian Code, the Ridges foresaw the same scenario replayed with their territories in Tennessee, North Alabama, and the rest of North Carolina. The Ridges and a growing number of constituents painfully decided the best action for the people was to move west. At first these men seemed to be traitors, but Major Ridge and his family were highly educated and understood the mindset of the whites and the impossibility of reaching a fair negotiation. The Ridges could not escape the age-old perception that all Indians were drunken heathens, even though the Ridges were literate, prosperous planters. Equality and civil rights, particularly for nonwhites, were merely ideals and did not fully become part of the dominant paradigm until the 1960s, a hundred and twenty some-odd years later. Even now America struggles to mend the endless damage of prejudices and racism.

Most of the Cherokee Nation sided with John Ross. Only one-eighth Cherokee and chief of the nation, Ross had his own platform: to remain in their ancestral homes and resist removal. The Cherokee people loved and respected Ross, who, beginning in 1828, served the Cherokee people as chief for almost forty years (Wardell 9). In light of Jacksonian democracy and Manifest Destiny, Ross's anti-removal stance was certainly the most idealistic of the times and by far the most popular. Moving the Cherokee Nation to Oklahoma was an unthinkable and absurd option. Some critics claim that Chief Ross harmed his people by persuading them to stay put, but fighting for a cause against such unbeatable odds is a characteristic of America. Who ever thought a few ill-equipped colonials could win against the British? Ross knew the risk was great, but he stood by his people. Sadly, in years to come he would lose his own wife during the removal.

Unsurprisingly, most of America, and enough of Washington at the time, supported Indian removal. Society in the early nineteenth century saw Native Americans as a people unable to assimilate into white culture. Most people thought the Indians corrupt, unable to deal with whites in business or at social gatherings. Although in remote regions of Tennessee and North Carolina, the native Cherokees and newcomer pioneers had already begun the process of assimilation through intermarriage, the greater view was that whites were racially superior. Because this superiority would undermine the Native American culture, some whites felt that moving to Oklahoma was in the Cherokees' best interest. Most Americans at that time strongly resisted the now popular, even clichéd idea of America as a multicultural melting pot. The only answer for the dilemma was relocation.

In late December 1835, Cherokee advocates for the move to Oklahoma met at New Echota, which was located in the present city of Calhoun, Georgia. Some participants in this meeting were Andrew Ross; Elias Boudinot; Major Ridge with his son John; and the strongest fighter for removal, a federal negotiator for the removal treaty, John Schermerhorn (whom the Cherokees called "The Devil's Horn"). Also joining the statesmen were between three and four hundred concerned citizens of the Cherokee Nation, a minuscule fraction (Wilkins 285–87). The decision to move was the only safe way to ensure a future for their people, so, sadly and with purpose, they drafted the treaty. The twenty signers of the Treaty of New Echota sent a small party to Washington. There a fierce debate ensued, with the Senate almost equally split. Democrats supported Jackson, but the opposing Whigs despised the idea of ratification (Mooney 128). Among notable leaders who opposed the Cherokees' relocation were Henry Clay, Daniel Webster, Edward Everett, and David Crockett. The issue was one between states' rights on one hand and federal jurisdiction and the Constitution on the other (Mooney 129). President Jackson pushed the treaty with dogged perseverance until the Senate ratified it on May 23, 1836, with a one-vote margin (Wilkins 292). A one-vote margin passed a treaty to which only a handful of Cherokees had agreed! Therefore, the Trail of Tears was only a hairbreadth away from passing into oblivion. From the moment of ratification, the Cherokees had two years to relocate.

During the two years between the signing of the Treaty of New Echota and the actual beginning of the Trail of Tears, the United States issued many warnings and notices about removal. The notices urged the condemned to move west by their own means, but Chief Ross, trying to undo the work of Jackson, made more trips to Washington, and when he came home, he encouraged his people to stay in the East. Only a few members of the condemned nation gave the government warnings any notice and moved west.

Most of those leaving were of the Ridge faction, later named the Treaty Party.

In May, General Winfield Scott, commanding a thousand troops, moved onto Cherokee lands with orders to round up all the Indians to begin the forced journey. Scott and his men built stockades and herded the Cherokees into them family by family. The Army intended the stockades as temporary holding areas while troops went out to gather all those who did not come in willingly. Scott's charges took longer than expected to gather the Cherokees. Kicking people off of their ancestral farmlands was difficult business to begin with, but the territory in which the Cherokees lived was so vast that it took more time than Scott anticipated. The troops took Indians at gunpoint from their fields, beds, or dinner tables and marched them, stunned and surprised, to the collection centers. "In many cases, in turning for one last look as they crossed the ridge, they saw their homes in flames, fired by the lawless rabble that followed on the heels of the soldiers to loot and pillage. So keen were these outlaws on the scent that in some instances they were driving off the cattle and other stock of the Indians almost before the soldiers had fairly started their owners in the other direction" (Mooney 130).

Scott built four collection centers. Three were in Tennessee: at Calhoun, Cleveland, and Ross's Landing (now Chattanooga); and one was at Gunter's Landing, Alabama (Wilkins 320). Each encampment took up approximately forty square miles, and to these places the soldiers herded the Cherokees like livestock. Many of the prisoners came to these places on horseback, but once they arrived, the soldiers forcefully rounded up the horses and held an auction right outside the stockade walls (Wilkins 321).

The weather was miserable during the summer of 1838. The heat seemed never to cease, and rains did not cool the earth until September. Normally, summer is a time for preparing for winter and eating a wholesome diet of fresh fruit and vegetables, but, in the detention camps, the farmers and hunters with all of their families ate salt pork and wormy cornmeal day in and day out. Imagine the conditions: the flies, the vermin, and the waste that must have littered the landscape of the detention camps. There the Cherokees lived in such tight quarters that diseases such as measles, whooping cough, pleurisy, and bilious fever spread (Ehle 344). Many died in these camps before beginning the trek west.

The safest, quickest, and most preferred route was water travel, but little rain came that summer. The Tennessee and Mississippi rivers were fine for travel, but the boatloads of emigrants had to go upstream on the Arkansas River, too low for safe passage (Wilkins 322). Little or no water was in the streams or rivers, the weather was stifling, and many prisoners were incapacitated from disease. Chief Ross saw the danger his people were in and knew conditions would only worsen if the nation began its journey in the summer. He negotiated with Winfield Scott and postponed the start date to October 20 (Mooney 132).

During the roundup, a small resistance movement in the mountains of North Carolina gained strength and further complicated Scott's plan. According to James Mooney, the refugees hid in an encampment at the head of the Oconaluftee River; there they subsisted on roots and wild plants, along with the scarce game they could kill (157). The far-reaching good deeds of William H. Thomas, a trader who befriended the Cherokees, enabled them to remain in the mountains forever. Mr. Thomas utilized a clause in the Treaty of New Echota: Cherokees wishing to become citizens of the United States could do so. The refugee Indians became citizens of North Carolina. The land of the Qualla Reservation remained in Thomas's name until North Carolina, in 1866, recognized that Cherokees could be landowners. (Mooney 157–59). These hardy people who fled from federal troops into the most rugged area of the United States east of the Mississippi became known as the Eastern Band.

Scott planned to send thirteen groups of a thousand each across land to Oklahoma with a three-day gap between each group, but because of the delay during the summer months, the first groups did not depart until late August, and the last departed October 23 (Ehle 342, 361). By this time, the Cherokees had been in the holding areas for months, most were sick and malnourished, and many had already died. The slow march westward naturally made conditions much worse. In the beginning, the Indians gathered edible plants along the way, and the men hunted game to supplement their meager rations. Later, after only a group or two had gone, the game became scarce, and they exhausted the wild food supplies. The drought ceased on September 23 with refreshing rain, but later, as the weather cooled and the rain continued to fall, health and morale slipped further. Soon the trail was a veritable quagmire (Ehle 352–54).

The overland route began where the Hiawassee River meets the Tennessee at Bythe's Ferry. From there they went to McMinnville, then Nashville, then Springfield in southern Missouri, and onward to the territory that became Oklahoma (Ehle 352). The bulk of traveling took place in late fall and winter. Keep in mind, the travelers had no time in the summer to make necessary preparations because they were in the holding areas! Many of the travelers walked through mud, over rocks, and in ice and snow without shoes, adequate clothing, or shelter needed to survive during the quickly approaching winter months.

The Army provided 645 wagons, roughly one for every twenty people. At first the wagons carried families' supplies, but later they carried the sick and dying (Ehle 352). The wagons provided inadequate room for the weary and the ill, and on the trail, more people became sick every day. Walking day after day was torture for the elderly, and the trip weakened the babies, too. The main enemy was disease: Dysentery, diarrhea, and head and chest colds were common, and almost everyone had intestinal cramps and other pains (Ehle 353). The dead had to be buried and mourned over, and shamans chanted every night of the journey. Cherokee custom calls for three nights of the shaman's sitting by the grave to keep the witches away, a custom that of course proved impossible to observe because of the forced marching (Ehle 357). Sometimes the travelers covered as little as five miles a day, and often as many as twenty Indians died in a day from starvation, exposure, and homesickness (Mooney 132).

A native of Maine, who remains anonymous, recounts what little he witnessed on January 26, 1839, of the Cherokees' journey: "On Tuesday evening we fell in with a detachment of the poor Cherokee Indians . . . about eleven hundred Indians—sixty wagons—six hundred horses, and perhaps forty pairs of oxen. We found them in the forest camped for the night by the roadside . . . under a severe fall of rain accompanied by heavy wind. With their canvas for a shield from the inclemency of the weather, and the cold wet ground for a resting place, after the fatigue of the day, they spent the night . . . many of the aged Indians were suffering extremely from the fatigue of the journey, and the ill health consequent upon it. Several were then quite ill, and one aged man we were informed was in the last struggles of death" (qtd. in *The Removal of the Cherokee* 44).

Chief John Ross and his wife, Quatie, took a safer route by boat, except for one short overland passage. Except for Quatie, who was nursing a cold, Ross's family was in good health. On one of the cold nights during their overland passage, in an act of kindness, Quatie gave her cloak to a freezing child. In the morning, very ill from pneumonia, she died a death similar to many of her people and was buried without a coffin in a shallow grave beside the trail. (Ehle 362)

The journey finally ended after six months of travel during the hardest part of the year. Accurate statistics on the number of deaths resulting from the removal prove to be completely elusive. No one made an accurate count before or during the march, and the numbers change according to the sources. Somewhere between three hundred and two thousand perished in the temporary holding camps, and the estimate for the trail is much the same: between five hundred and two thousand (Ehle 390).

Historian James Mooney interviewed one of the Georgia soldiers who witnessed the removal, a soldier who subsequently became a colonel in the Confederate service: "I fought through the Civil War. It has been my experience to see men shot to pieces and slaughtered by thousands. But the Cherokee removal was the cruelest work I ever saw" (130). Through rotten politics and the consequences of Manifest Destiny, the Cherokees themselves nearly vanished, and a culture that once nearly dominated the entire southeastern United States was gone forever.

—*Russell Bauman*

*References*

Ehle, John. *Trail of Tears: The Rise and Fall of the Cherokee Nation.* New York: Random House, 1989.

Mooney, James. *History, Myths, and Sacred Formulas of the Cherokees.* Ed. George Ellison. Asheville: Bright Mountain Books, 1992.

*The Removal of the Cherokee.* N.p.: n.p., n.d.

Wardell, Morris L. *A Political History of the Cherokee Nation 1838–1907.* Norman: University of Oklahoma Press, 1938.

Wilkins, Thurman. *Cherokee Tragedy: The Ridge Family and the Decimation of a People.* Norman: University of Oklahoma Press, 1986.

# PLACE-NAME ORIGINS

T he reality that strikes me the hardest in compiling this information on the Cherokee people is their nation once covered every familiar place around my home. Each time I go to work, to the grocery, to the river, or to college in Sewanee, Tennessee, I drive on land that, not too long ago, was part of the once vast Cherokee Nation.

All we find today are reminders: a few arrowheads in someone's dresser or a friend whose great-grandmother was a Cherokee. Most obvious, however, are the names of places so familiar to us. Just near my house is the Chattooga River, a community named Satolah, Stekoah Creek, Estatoah Falls, and the Tallulah Gorge. Driving to college, I pass the Ocoee River, Red Clay State Park (once the meeting place of the Cherokee Nation), and the city of Chattanooga, just north of Chicamauga battlefield. Finally, when I am just outside Sewanee, I pass a sign that reads ENJOY GENTLE THRILLS ON THE SEQUATCHEE.

America cannot erase her ancestry because these reminders surround us. Sites from Northeast Georgia to Tennessee bear Cherokee names. In many cases the true meanings of these names are forever lost, and only myths and legends serve to explain them. I have translated some place-names, but I have also included some of the myths handed down and changed from one person to the next.

—*Russell Bauman*

## TALLULAH

Northeast Georgia owes much of its tourist appeal to the Tallulah River, which created Lakes Burton, Rabun, and Seed and, over the span of millions of years, carved out a great fissure in the earth. Though the river is only a shadow of its former glory, the chasm known as Tallulah Gorge remains a natural marvel. The Cherokees viewed the river as a place of powerful magic. This river in Rabun County takes its name from the Cherokee word *Talalu'*, which was the name of an ancient settlement some distance above the falls. The name cannot be translated.

Many stories now circulated about how this river got its name enjoy great popularity, but none of them has any basis at all in historical fact. One such story concerns some children supposedly carried over the falls. Another claims that the area got its name from the cry of a frog: *dulusi* (Mooney 417). Still a third legend tells of two hapless hunters and their encounter with unfriendly little people.

The two Indian hunters went near the roaring falls in search of game. The hunters were both quite well known, and so when they never returned, the nation became worried. Finally a group of medicine men made a pilgrimage in search of the hunters. They were gone for an entire full moon. When they returned, they were full of tales about a dreadful fissure in the earth with a stream roaring through it. The inhabitants were a race of little men and women who dwelt in the crevices of the rocks and grottoes under the water-falls. The medicine men tried to arrange a council with these little people, but their shrieks made it clear that they were unfriendly. The medicine men assumed that the hunters had been lured to their deaths by the tiny tribe in the dreadful gorge called Talulu'. From then on, the legend recounts that Cherokees avoided the gorge and the falls almost completely (Charles Lanman, qtd. in Mooney 417–18).

## NANTAHALA

The Nantahala River begins as several streams that converge on the slopes of Standing Indian Mountain in North Carolina. Campgrounds line the headwaters, and white-water enthusiasts enjoy the lower sections. The word survives because it was the name of a Cherokee settlement, *Nun daye li,* near the mouth of Briertown Creek. The Cherokee word means "middle sun" or "midday sun." In places along the stream, the high cliffs shut out the direct light of the sun until nearly noon, thus the name.

The legend goes that the cliffs were so steep that when the hunter Tsasta wi killed a deer, he would stand at the edge of the bluffs overlooking the town and throw the liver down upon the roof of his house. His wife could have it cooked and waiting for him by the time he got down the mountain.

In Rabun County the translation of the Cherokee word is commonly thought to be "land beyond tomorrow." Some believe that the word also means "mountains of the moon" in reference to the Moon and Star Maiden. She cared for white flowers and supposedly lived in the mountainous area still named Nantahala (Mooney 408).

## STANDING INDIAN

I spent a lot of time around Standing Indian Campground, named after Standing Indian Mountain between Franklin and Hayesville, North Carolina. The original Cherokee name was *Yun wi tsulenunyi,* meaning "where the man stood" or "where the man stands." The name originally came from a strange rock jutting out from the bald summit. The rock has since broken off. As the old memory faded, a tradition grew of a mysterious being that once stood on the mountaintop (Mooney 409).

As is so often the case, storytellers have recounted inaccurate variations until the original derivation of the name has become completely obscured. One of these stories goes as follows:

In the days when the Indians lived in these mountains, their practice was to place a watch atop the mountains to command the best view of the surrounding territory. When he spied anything unusual, he would light an already prepared bonfire to alert the villagers below. The post was a highly responsible one, for the whole tribe depended on the sharpness of the scout. The scout would rather die than desert his post without being relieved.

On one especially cold night, someone stood watch as usual. Rather than light a fire to keep himself warm (and perhaps frighten the village in the process), he stood quietly alone in the subzero darkness without heat. The next morning, the brave sent to relieve him found him frozen to death, still standing against the tree that was his lookout spot. For the dedication he showed toward his tribe, the mountain was named in his honor.

## STEKOAH
Two places bear this name: One is a spot on the Tuckasegee River in Swain County where the famous Cherokee agent, Colonel W. H. Thomas, lived; and the other is Stekoah Creek in Rabun County, Georgia. The correct Cherokee form of the name is close to *Stika yi*. Some think the name means "little grease" or "oil," but as was the case with Nantahala, the true meaning is lost (Mooney 409).

## TRACK ROCK GAP
In Union County, on a ridge separating Brasstown Creek from the waters of the Nottely River, petroglyphs cover the micaceous soapstone rocks on either side of the trail. The Indians named the spot *Datsu nalasgun yi*, "where there are tracks"; or *Degayelun ha*, "printed place" or "branded place," in reference to marks appearing to be animal tracks. The most accepted explanation is that early hunters resting in the gap made the marks. However, an Indian legend tells that when the earth was very new and the ground and the rocks were still very soft, hundreds of racing animals marked this place with their footprints (Mooney 418–19).

## COWEE
Cowee was originally known as *Kawi yi,* a former Cherokee settlement ten miles below Franklin, North Carolina, at the mouth of present Cowee

Creek. The name may be a contraction of *Ani Kawi yi,* "place of the Deer Clan," and was one of the oldest and largest of the Cherokee towns (Mooney 508). From the green pastures and farms bordering the Little Tennessee River, passersby can easily see why this was a settlement. The famous explorer William Bartram, in his travels through Cherokee country, showered his praises on the beautiful valley: "This settlement is esteemed the capital town: It is situated on the bases of the hills on both sides of the river, near to its bank, and here terminates the great vale of Cowe, exhibiting one of the most charming mountainous landscapes perhaps anywhere to be seen" (qtd. in Rights 175).

## WARWOMAN DELL

This spot is in the heart of what was the lower Cherokee country, now Rabun County. Although gender roles were somewhat malleable, most women planted crops and gathered wood. However, some women took on a more masculine identity. In such cases this woman was considered a warwoman. The warwoman herself was one of the most influential members of a Cherokee clan. Other names for her were pretty woman or benevolent woman. Her position was usually inherited, but if it could not be passed from a mother to her daughter, elders trained someone specially for the job.

"Nancy Ward, an eighteenth-century Cherokee woman, fought like a man in battle, and the men gave her the title of 'war woman' or 'beloved woman.' She spoke in Cherokee councils and in 1781 even conducted negotiations with an invading American army" (Hudson 269).

The warwoman also used a quartz crystal for divination. In Warwoman Dell, three streams come together. Local legend claims the Cherokees thought this spot sacred, for it was here that one of their warwomen did her divining through the use of several huge quartz crystals found in the area. The three streams, to the Cherokees, symbolized the three divisions of their nation: upper, middle, and lower.

## HIAWASSEE

Hiawassee is the name of both a river in North Carolina and a small mountain town bordering Lake Chatuge in Towns County, Georgia. The Cherokee derivation of this name is *Ayuhwasi,* which means "a savanna." A questionable legend notes that Hiawassee, "the pretty fawn," was the beautiful daughter of a Catawba chief. She won the heart of a Cherokee warrior named Notley, "the daring horseman," who in time became the head chief of the Cherokee. Their union purportedly made peace between the two tribes. Mooney notes, "The story sounds very pretty, but is a pure invention" (416).

*References*

Hudson, Charles. *The Southeastern Indians.* N.p.: University of Tennessee Press, 1976.

Mooney, James. *History, Myths, and Sacred Formulas of the Cherokees.* Ed. George Ellison. Asheville, N.C.: Bright Mountain Books, 1992.

Rights, Douglas L. *The American Indian in North Carolina.* Winston-Salem, N.C.: Duke University Press, 1947.

# FALLING FLOWERS:
# AN INTERVIEW WITH THE CHILTOSKEYS

Foxfire has known the Chiltoskeys since the sixties. Mary Chiltoskey appears in our special December 1967 *Foxfire Magazine* issue, "The Cherokee Indian," and in the Fall 1971 issue: Reverend Rufus Morgan (*Foxfire 4*, pages 394–441) mentions the Chiltoskeys in his interview, and Goingback appears in *The Foxfire Magazine* in Summer '81 and Fall '83. The 1981 publication features his unique wood carvings, a craft he learned when he was ten years old from his older brother, Watty.

I discovered the Chiltoskeys through the pages of old issues of *The Foxfire Magazine*. Although both Goingback, better known as G.B., and Mary died in 2001, after reading the articles and old transcripts, and looking at the photographs of Goingback with his carvings, I feel as if I know both him and his wife. This feeling is primarily due to talking with folks who knew them. Bob Daniel, a contact featured earlier in the personality section, and someone I interviewed in high school and have been visiting ever since, came to Foxfire one afternoon to help Mrs. Cheek clear up some questions concerning his article. He began talking to us, and suddenly I realized that he and G.B. were very similar. They are both master craftsmen, and Bob spent many years in Franklin, North Carolina, just down the road from Cherokee. So I asked him, "Bob, you didn't happen to know a man by the name of Goingback Chiltoskey, did you?"

He beamed. "Yeah! G.B. Chiltoskey!" I was very excited to have discovered such a significant connection between two contacts, yet I was unsurprised. Mr. Daniel is the kind of guy who has a friend in every town he visits and has made five more by the time he leaves. Bob elaborated: "We spent lots of time in Cherokee and used to go to the Village of Yesteryear in Raleigh. I met him through Bill Crowe, his nephew. He and Bill used to do blowguns. G.B. had the finest blowgun up there at the fair—'bout as long as from here to the wall [eight to ten feet], and the envy of all the people who shot blowguns. He could make a dart out of white locust and fletch it with Jerusalem thistle. They gather it at the right time of year . . . That's an art, watchin' them fletch it. They hold that fletching thistle and roll that dart. I was invited to go to a blowgun contest. Bill Crowe asked G.B., 'What you gonna do with that blowgun when you die?' 'Saw it in two and put it in my casket,' G.B. said."

In working on this article, I am also grateful to Mary Regina Ulmer Galloway, Mary Chiltoskey's niece, who graciously gave me permission to use some of her aunt Mary's stories featured in Mrs. Galloway's work, *Aunt Mary, Tell Me a Story: A Collection of Cherokee Legends and Tales as Told by Mary Ulmer Chiltoskey.* She and her husband, Johnny, also took me to lunch at the Dillard House, which, needless to say, was better than the peanut butter and jelly sandwich I packed for myself.

The Chiltoskeys' story is fresh and new, and what amazes me is Foxfire's last interview with Goingback and Mary was conducted when I was scarcely two years old. Their story is an important one in the history of the Cherokees, of Appalachia, and, indeed, of our nation. I'm glad to have read it.

*—Russell Bauman*

**Editor's note:** In most of this article either Mary or G.B. speaks. However, Gene Jackson, a family friend and one of Mary's very first students in Cherokee, adds important information.

**Mary Chiltoskey:** I didn't know a person in Cherokee when I came here in 1942. I was born and reared in Alabama and came here because I needed to work year-round [as opposed to seasonal teaching jobs]. I had been teaching

PLATE 169  Goingback and Mary sit with Foxfire
student Ohsoon Shropshire at one of Foxfire's annual picnics.

and going to school since I was sixteen years old. The Monday after I graduated from high school, in 1923, I started going to college; then I started teaching that fall. I had paid all of my own schooling and my parents were getting old and I needed to begin helping them a little bit. I certainly had no backlog [of savings] from teaching part of the year, so when I found out there was work year-round in Cherokee, I came here to teach.

Back then, in World War II, teachers had to do all the sugar rationing as well as the teaching. That was the first extra job handed to me, the rationing, because I had just had that job to look after when I was in Cuba, Alabama, as an elementary school principal. When I came here, I was also a Red Cross volunteer, Girl Scout leader, and all such as that, as well as my regular forty-four hours a week teaching. We went a half a day on Saturday then.

### "We were married in Knoxville, Tennessee, because it was illegal to have mixed marriages . . . in North Carolina."

There were sixty-two people in a class. We had two classes at a time because it was war times. There was a great lack of teachers. I had come here just on a temporary appointment. The person's place I took was in the armed forces, and if he had wanted his job when he came back, it was his. That spring, on Memorial Day, I took an additional Civil Service exam that just happened to be available. When I had been here thirteen months, I got a job that would not be up for grabs. I replaced a person who had died. Having taken the exam made me one jump ahead on that job coming up, though I did not know that at the time. The principal at the Cherokee Indian School had recommended that I go ahead and take the exam. He had good foresight and looked after the interests of his teachers. Shortly before I came to Cherokee, he had recommended to G.B. that he terminate his teaching job and be available for a good civilian war job. That was Sam Gilliam. He was a great man. He was a man who was able to look ahead but keep his mouth shut and let you make your own decisions. He still lives over in Asheville. He is eighty-six years old now [at the time of the interview in 1983].

I taught twenty-five years and two days at the Cherokee Indian School, and I've been doing a lot of teaching since then. I taught a three-hour class right here at the dining table this morning. [*Editor's note:* I learned two very important things from Regina Galloway, Mary's niece. First of all, Mary saved many of the Cherokee School's artifacts and stories from being lost forever. In the early sixties, a new principal at the Cherokee Indian School thought it best for them to let go of their native heritage and instead learn about more "contemporary" subjects. He wanted the teachers to collect all the Cherokee relics and burn them. Mary and some other teachers saved the artifacts by hiding them under their beds at the teachers' boarding-house. Mary also helped compile the script for *Unto These Hills,* a drama about the history of the Eastern Band.] Goingback and I courted ten years and sixteen days, and were married in 1956.

**G.B. Chiltoskey:** We were married in Knoxville, Tennessee, because it was illegal to have mixed marriages—such as marriages between a black person and a white person or a white person and an Indian person—in North Carolina. Later on, Mary played an instrumental role in getting that law changed.

> "I was born within a mile of here. My given name was James, but later, when I was two or three years old, my name was changed because I was a sickly child. The Cherokee doctors argued back and forth about what would be best for me. They changed my name to Goingback."

**Mary Chiltoskey:** That summer of 1956, I went up to Fort Belvoir with G.B. and attended school. I could have had almost any job I wanted there. In the city of Washington, D.C., in 1956, they were giving them away by the bushels. But there was a reason for my being here in Cherokee, and it involved Goingback. So I came back home. I lived down on the campus until 1962, and then I moved over here to the house we used as a workshop. We started this house when he retired in 1966. We moved into it—would you believe—in 1976? Good Friday, 1976.

**G.B. Chiltoskey:** I was born within a mile of here. My given name was James, but later, when I was two or three years old, my name was changed because I was a sickly child. The Cherokee doctors argued back and forth about what would be best for me. They changed my name to Goingback. I don't know why. That was just one of the beliefs the medicine men used. I now go by the name Goingback Chiltoskey. The first part of the name was translated into English from the Cherokee, and the last name was not translated. *Chiltoskey* means "falling flower." It was spelled out in English the way the Cherokee pronunciation sounded.

The Cherokee Indian language was the only language my parents talked. My father was born in 1850 and died in 1930. He farmed, worked around for people, and my mother kept house. Everything she said to me was in the Cherokee language. They didn't speak the English. My father had only gone to school for two weeks. What can you learn in two weeks? I didn't learn to speak English till I went down to the boarding school in Cherokee when I

PLATE 170  A young G.B. with his parents,
Will and Charlotte, and his
older brother, Watty

was ten years old. The school was located where the elementary school is now. It was run by my "rich uncle" [the U.S. government].

I don't know how I felt about going to that school then. I knew I had to go to school to learn English so I could get along. Of course I didn't think about that when I was in kindergarten and in the lower grades. I just knew I had to learn the English language, which is the foreign language. It is not an "American" language.

"If the young ladies wore long hair when they were admitted, it was automatically cut off because of the lice they assumed we had."

Gene Jackson: That boarding school was run by the U.S. government for the Indian children. The school was maintained in a military fashion. There were some rules and regulations that I always like to bring up because, if I don't, you won't know that it really happened. If the young ladies wore long hair when they were admitted, it was automatically cut off because of lice they assumed we had. We were lined up and bathed like animals, not in private.

No one was allowed to speak the native tongue because the white teachers could not understand what was being said. Your punishment was to have

PLATE 171 Cherokee Indian High School's basketball team, 1925. G.B. is in the back row, second from the right.

your mouth washed out with lye soap. Or you were locked in one of the hall closets where there was no light or ventilation, and you never knew what the time limit would be. That was changed, of course, as the years went on. In 1975, the Indian language was reinstated in the school curriculum. It is now started on the kindergarten level.

**Mary Chiltoskey:** In the 1870s there was a law passed by Congress aimed at making it easier for the Indian children, but maybe not always understood by those who had to administer that law. In this business of learning the English language, you learn a language only when you have to learn it. So the law was made that no native language should be spoken in the [U.S. government–run Native American] boarding schools, therefore making it easier for the children to learn to speak English. Of course, when people start administering a thing like that and you have a little four-year-old child and you don't let that child speak his own language to people around him, it could be cruel. If some child was left in that little dark closet overnight, that could be cruel. Those things may not have happened very often, but they happened. Well-meaning policies are not always carried out as they were originally intended. People worked to make changes, but it wasn't until 1975, after some laws had been changed in Washington, that this policy was changed. Many times, I'm sure, between 1870 and 1975, there were well-meaning people who said, "Something ought to be done about this." And they didn't take one step to do it. Every day, we run across situations like that.

**G.B. Chiltoskey:** I learned to speak the language so I could get along with the other races of people. Otherwise, I wouldn't be where I am. I stayed [at the Cherokee boarding school] through the ninth grade. That's as high as they went. I got through school down here in 1927. It took me ten years to do that. There was no transportation to go on [to a senior high school in our area], and by the time I graduated from Cherokee, there was kind of a prejudice against the Indians to go to the public schools around here. I had to go somewhere else, some distance from this area, and live with white people [to complete my education]. There's where I made use of English. There was no one that spoke my language. I got along very nicely, and I tried to be polite and cooperative. They treated me as well as I wanted to be treated and didn't have any prejudice against me in any way I knew of. But you could get it [find prejudices] right away if you wanted it. I wanted to get along with the people I was with, and I still have friends all over the country. Somebody knows me wherever I go, and I know them. We were in London one time, sitting in a restaurant eating breakfast, and this young man grabbed me by the coat and said, "Hello, Mr. Chiltoskey!" And a few weeks ago we were in Yellowstone National Park and ran across three people there that knew us.

From Cherokee, I went on to Greenville, South Carolina, to a public high school there. I finished there in two years. I didn't have any money of any kind to back me up, so I had to dig for myself. If I hadn't been able to make things, I wouldn't have been able to support myself there. I made things like a mantelpiece for the house where I boarded, and the teachers gave me permission to use the high school shop. That way I made my money to pay for my board and room to go to school. A short time ago, there was somebody visiting here from Greenville. She said the family that I had boarded with was still showing with pride the cedar chest I made for the mother.

When I went to Parker District High School, I got into mechanical drawing. I knew nothing about it. The first things I remember I had to draw were a nut and bolt with all the threads. And right there I caught on to how the thing was laid out. After I got through the drawing, the machinist could make the bolt and nut by my drawing. Then we had to learn to make blueprints out of those drawings, and that's where I learned how to read the blueprints.

I liked to carve wood when I was a kid. It just grew up with me, so I had to make a little business as I went along. My work as a model-maker just fell right in line with what I could do.

PLATE 172 *Woman Carrying a Bundle,*
one of G.B.'s more famous carvings,
was exhibited at the Smithsonian.

I had an older brother, Watty, ten years older than I, who was a wood-carver, and he shared his skill with me when I was a young boy still at home. I was always interested in woodworking. I worked carpentry down here at the Cherokee School when I was a boy, from about 1924 to 1927, and I helped make hundreds of caskets for people who died in the Boundary. [The Boundary refers to the Qualla Indian Boundary, the 50,000-acre tract owned by the Eastern Band in North Carolina.]

After I finished at Greenville, I became a dropout. I joined with a show-man going through. I rambled around for a while. That was the only chance I saw that I would have to go see the city of Washington, D.C. I'd heard so much about it, so I went with the showman and got into Washington for two weeks. It was a one-man show—reptile exhibition. I handled snakes around the neck. I made enough money to get back to Cherokee, but first I stayed with a friend of mine in Baltimore, Maryland, for a few weeks.

I had to come back here to Cherokee to be eligible for transportation to the Haskell Institute in Lawrence, Kansas. I didn't get back in time and was late with my registration, so I had to wait a little longer to earn money to pay my own way. When I went there in 1929, the Haskell Institute was a private school for Indians. It was a tribal school, and there were eighty-seven tribes represented then. It was kindergarten on through high school with com-mercial trades and a junior college. It has moved on up now.

PLATE 173  G.B. proudly carries his *St. Francis
of Assisi,* also displayed at the Smithsonian.

Then, later on, I got a job at a summer camp near Allentown, Pennsylvania, as a counselor with the Boy Scouts. I was kind of happy at the time, and that summer I made the most money I'd ever made in one season. I got all my transportation, board, room, laundry—you can't ask for any more than that— and a salary on top of that. At the end of the school year, I came back and gave my mother fifty dollars. Then I stayed away from home for three years. That's the longest time I ever stayed away from home. When I came back, my mother still had some of that money left. I told her to use that money to buy snuff. (She used snuff, you know.) I sent my money home all along, and I had six hundred dollars in the bank that I could do something with in a few years.

I went to Santa Fe, New Mexico, and studied Indian arts and crafts after I finished at Haskell. I learned silversmithing while I was there. I worked there, too, off and on, and then I was finally offered a job as an assistant shop teacher. I was offered two jobs like that: one out there and one back home in Cherokee. So I came back home in 1935, and I started the first wood- carving classes here at the Cherokee School. That teaching job was my first job working regularly for the U.S. government. While teaching there from 1935 to 1942, I attended summer sessions at Oklahoma A&M, taking indus- trial arts; Purdue University, taking courses and teaching handicrafts; and the Art Institute of Chicago. Later, while working at Fort Belvoir, I attended Corcoran School of Art, in Washington, D.C.

PLATE 174  Goingback and his sister,
Sally (center), and Gertrude Flanigan,
family friend and home
economics teacher

### "I made models, anything you can think of that had to do with war or the military."

I stayed with that job until they terminated me because World War II came along. They said they couldn't defer me from the armed forces—terminated me on account of that and told me to go out and get another job, and that'd keep me out of the military.

**Mary Chiltoskey:** The young men were getting drafted very fast. Civilian men with special abilities were needed in special places, so some employers were turning men loose if possible. If they wanted to go and find one of these special jobs, they could do it. As long as you are tied down to a job, you're not going to look for those opportunities in the service. Now G.B. was one of those folks that were caught up in that kind of thing. He turned his to a good thing. Some folks let that be the end of their special work and joined the Army.

He hadn't asked to stay out of the military, but the man who was the principal at the reservation school here was a farsighted man and knew what possibilities awaited him, so he terminated Goingback from his job. This made it possible for him to find one of those government war jobs that needed his specific training. If he had been in the armed forces, even if he were doing his woodworking, by the time he had got started on a project, say on the model of the underground installation in Greenland, his unit might have been moved to China, and all his work would have been to do over again by someone else. That is the way the Army has to operate. As a civilian worker, he could be put there on that job. He didn't have to move, you see. The reservation principal understood the workings of the Army, and those things work out right when someone knows what's behind them.

**G.B. Chiltoskey:** So, instead, I got under the wings of the military as a model-maker. That was 1942, and I went to work in Fort Belvoir, Virginia [near Washington, D.C.]. I made models—anything you can think of that had to do with war or the military. Like splitting an atom—I made models of atoms. I didn't understand what they were for. I just made models from blueprints. Then if anything had to be changed, they would change it right from that model and the blueprint. If you make a mistake, [to fix] it is expensive on the real thing, but the model shows it up. The blueprint can be changed, and a lot of money is saved.

> **"It was top secret work . . . We weren't supposed to say anything about what we did or who we worked for."**

It was top secret work, especially making terrain model maps for invasions. We weren't supposed to say anything about what we did or who we worked for, so when we went to town and got drunk, or got with the opposite sex, we didn't talk about our orders. We didn't know who we might be talking to.

**Gene Jackson:** It's the American Indian who knows how to keep his mouth shut. Another thing I like to remind people of when I have the chance to talk like this is that during the Second World War, they used our native Cherokee language as a code system. Consequently, the Japanese or the Germans never ever decoded it.

**G.B. Chiltoskey:** They did that in World War I, too. Wherever you had Indians from the same tribe in two different companies who could communicate in their native language, that could be used as a secret code.

So I went to work in Fort Belvoir as a civilian in the U.S. Army Engineer Research and Development Laboratory, and I worked there till the end of the war. Then I had itchy feet, you know, reading about Hollywood so much. I wanted to know what it was about, and I thought I'd try that. Five of us guys formed a partnership and started a model-making business in Hollywood, California. I stayed in it about a year and then dropped out to lose everything I had in it. We called ourselves Imagineering. We made architectural models and movie sets.

PLATE 175  G.B. demonstrates his expertise with his blowgun,
an heirloom over a hundred years old.

That was about 1947, and I went back to Cherokee to start teaching GIs
in woodworking shop. After about six years, that terminated, and I was out
of a job for about five months. I was looking for a certain kind of job. My former boss at Fort Belvoir asked me if I wanted to come back on the job. He
said, "I can give you a job in the machine shop." I'd had a job like that
before, and it's very heavy work. I didn't want just any kind of job. I told him
I would wait till a model-making job opened up. Finally there was a job I
was interested in. There had been five men there for that job; the boss there
knew me, and I got first priority. I wanted to stay there for five years to further my retirement. Instead, I stayed twelve years, so my retirement went
very well after that.

Mary and I got married in 1956; she stayed in Cherokee to work, and I
went on back up there to Fort Belvoir. I retired from Fort Belvoir in 1966. I
had worked for my "rich uncle," the U.S. Army Engineer Research and
Development Laboratory, in Washington, D.C., for seventeen years.

We moved back to our home here in Cherokee and began building our
new house. The only work I do now is things that are commissioned. [G.B.
has crafted many pieces for churches, schools, and other organizations.] The

commissioned pieces already have a home before we ever put a lick of work to them. One job I had was making a model of a streetlight. General Electric of Hendersonville, North Carolina, sent me the blueprint, and I made the model. I've never seen it anywhere. I don't know if they used it or not. The model may have proved it didn't work. I made it of wood and metal. It wasn't an actual working model. The jobs at Fort Belvoir are now contracted out. I could still get contracts from them if I wanted to, but I don't want to be tied down to a deadline. It's too much.

# AUNT MARY'S STORIES

*"And every time she came to visit us, it was always*
*'Aunt Mary, tell me a story; Aunt Mary, tell me a story.'"*

While I was organizing all of our information on the Chiltoskeys, Kaye Collins brought me a copy of a book entitled *Aunt Mary, Tell Me a Story*. I thought a few Cherokee legends as told by Mary Chiltoskey would be a nice addition to the material I already had. I made an apprehensive call to Mary's niece, Regina Galloway, who holds the copyright to the book. She soon replied to my phone call to tell me that she and her husband, Johnny, would in person give me the permission I sought, and they very graciously invited me to lunch.

The two filled my afternoon with funny anecdotes about Goingback, better known as G.B., and his wife, Mary. Mrs. Galloway also educated me on some of the trials that the Eastern Band faced over the years and told me of her own childhood. She, having grown up in West Alabama during the civil rights movement, came to view the world quite differently than her peers, largely because Goingback was her uncle.

The Galloways helped me to gain a more personal and insightful perspective on Goingback and Mary Chiltoskey. I regret that I did not have an opportunity to interview them myself, but talking with Mrs. and Mr. Galloway provided the connection to the Chiltoskeys I sought.

—*Russell Bauman*

## THE LEGEND OF THE CHEROKEE ROSE

When, at the age of four, Aunt Mary heard her first Cherokee legend, she had no idea she would spend over half her life with the Cherokee people on the reservation in North Carolina. She was riding down a farm road in West Alabama near Demopolis when she noticed the large growths of the Cherokee rose growing so thickly and stubbornly that it gave the local farmers problems. The prolific plant was literally taking up too much of the grazing land from the cattle.

Years ago, Mr. Larkin Eddins, a storyteller from Alabama, told Mary this legend. First, she was told never to play near the pretty, thorny rosebushes out in the billy goat field, which was the field before they turned to go into Demopolis: "Don't get too close by," he said. "There will be stickers." Then he told the legend.

More than a hundred years ago, the Cherokee people were driven from their home when the white men discovered gold in the mountains of North Carolina and Georgia. Their journey is remembered as the Trail of Tears. Some of the people came across Marengo County in West Alabama. It seems that after they had left their home, they came this far south so as not to have to climb more mountains.

It was late summer and very hot, and most of the time the people had to walk. Tempers were short, and many times the soldiers were more like animal drivers than guides for the people. The men were so frustrated with the treatment of their women and children, and the soldiers were so harsh and frustrated that bad things often happened. When two men get angry, they fight, and once in a while, men were killed on the trip. Many people died of much hardship. Much of the time, the trip was hard and sad, and the women wept at losing their homes and their dignity.

The old men knew that they must do something to help the women keep their strength in weeping. They knew the women would have to be very strong if they were to help the children survive.

So, one night after they had made camp along the Trail of Tears, the old men sitting around the dying campfire called to the Great One in Galunlati (heaven) to help their people in trouble. They told Him that the people were suffering, and this made the women spend much time weeping. They said they feared that the little ones would not survive to rebuild the Cherokee Nation.

The Great One said, "Yes, I have seen the sorrows of the women, and I can help them to keep their strength to help the children. Tell the women in the morning to look back where their tears have fallen to the ground. I will cause a plant to grow quickly. They will see a little green plant at first with a stem growing up. It will grow up and up and fall back down to touch the ground where another stem will begin to grow. I'll make the plant grow so fast at first that by afternoon they'll see a white rose, a beautiful blossom with five petals. In the center of the rose, I will put a pile of gold to remind them of the gold, which the white man wanted when his greed drove the Cherokees from their ancestral home."

The Great One said that the green leaves will have seven leaflets, one for each of the seven clans of the Cherokee. The plant will begin to spread out all over, a very strong plant that will grow in large, strong clumps, and it will take back some of the land they have lost. It will have stickers on every stem to protect it from anything that tries to move it away. The next morning the old men told the women to look back for a sign from the Great One. The women saw the plant beginning as a tiny shoot and growing up and over until it spread out over the land. They watched as a blossom formed, so beautiful they forgot to weep, and they felt beautiful and strong.

By the afternoon they saw many white blossoms as far as they could see. The women began to think about their strength given them to raise their children as the new Cherokee Nation. They knew the plant marked the path of the brutal Trail of Tears. The Cherokee women saw that the Cherokee rose was strong enough to take back much of the land of their people.

## THE FIRST WOOD-CARVER

Any number of animals had carved wood to use for tools and furniture and such, but do you know which animal first carved wood for fun or to make something beautiful?

Long ago, when the animals used to have their gatherings on what we now call the Festival Ground, Rabbit did a lot of bragging about how fast he could run. Now most of the animals were used to Rabbit's bragging, and they knew they could beat him if they tried, but Rabbit just kept saying he could outrun Deer.

He kept saying, "I don't have all the problems Deer has running through the woods."

Now we know deer do have a little problem on the rocks and in the thick bushes, but Deer was not saying anything.

He let Rabbit make more and more noise until finally Bear said, "Rabbit, tomorrow morning we'll just have a race to see who can really run the fastest. We'll start at the sycamore tree, run up into Big Cove, go around the big sycamore tree way up there and back to the tree here in the gathering grounds."

"All right," everyone said. "We'll all be here."

Up in Big Cove there had fallen a hard rain. As Beaver and his boys went home from the gathering, they noticed a big poplar tree had fallen in the river, and it was headed toward their home down the stream. They all jumped into the river, got the tree turned around, and got it up on the bank. First, they had to cut off the roots. They could use parts of the tree to strengthen their dam instead of letting it hit their home and break it.

When they got the roots chewed off, they saw a full bunch of roots, and

Daddy Beaver got an idea—the industrious beavers always like to find a good use for anything they have—so the daddy said, "I think I'll make a nice wooden decoration from that root." The family worked into the night, chewing and chewing and trying on the decoration, which was fixed up like a headpiece for the winner of the race.

Early the next morning, they put the decoration into the stream, and they had a good time floating their creation toward the Festival Ground.

When they got to the gathering place, Deer was already there, ready for the race. But where was Rabbit?

Raccoon said, "You know, I noticed something strange on the trail up the mountain. Just off the trail there were plants newly pulled up in the thicket."

Mr. Owl said, "I'd better check to see what's going on up there. It will just take a little while. You wait for Rabbit."

About that time, Rabbit showed up all excited; animals noticed that he was newly muddy. Now the beavers had worked all night and had gotten muddy, but they had a nice bath coming down the river. Maybe Rabbit thought the other animals would not notice the fresh mud on his coat and paws. Rabbit also didn't know that the other animals watched closely anyone who bragged a lot. Rabbit noticed the decoration that the beavers had brought, and he said, "Hey, what is that?" Of course he had to try it on, and he said, "It is no use to have a race because we all know I'm going to win it." Well, Rabbit looked a little silly in the headpiece, but he didn't know it.

About that time Mr. Owl, who had gone to check the trail, reported that there were fresh tracks where someone had cleared a path for a shortcut through the thicket. All the animals thought they knew whose tracks those could be.

"Rabbit," Mr. Owl said, "how did those rhododendrons get pulled up throughout the thicket?"

"I don't know a thing about it," insisted Rabbit.

"Where did you get that mud?" said Beaver.

"Yeah," said Bear. "What kind of a trick are you trying to pull?"

That took Rabbit by surprise, and he hung his guilty head and said, "I did it. I cleared a shortcut. I wanted to win the race."

"Of course you wanted to win," said Mr. Owl. "Everyone wants to win, but we win fair and square. Now we will not have a race because you have lost by default, and you will have to be punished for cheating."

"I've been punished by not getting the prize," said Rabbit.

"That's not all," said Mr. Owl. "From now on you'll have to root around in the ground for most of your food because you did not take the high ground and play fair." And that's why Deer has beautiful, proud antlers carved by the beavers, and Rabbit looks down for his food.

# AMANDA SWIMMER
# FROM BIG COVE

*"I was born right down there where that house is there. We had a log house made out of poplar logs."*

Amanda Swimmer was born a stone's throw away from where she now lives; her property borders the Great Smoky Mountain National Park, but it is past all the crowds and campgrounds that normally come hand in hand with the Smoky Mountains and Cherokee. Nobody really goes up there to bother her, she told me.

I first heard of Amanda Swimmer when I talked with Tom Hill, who is also featured in this segment. His coworker Melvina Swimmer is Amanda's granddaughter; Melvina (Mrs. Swimmer calls her Vina) proved to be a very helpful liaison between Amanda and me. Melvina gave me directions and phone numbers, and she even looked over the rough manuscript of this article. Finding Amanda took a few attempts, and during them, I learned two important facts about her: She is very busy, and everyone in the community knows her.

At eighty-one years of age, she finds time to keep an enormous garden, volunteer at Big Cove Head Start, teach pottery at Smoky Mountain Elementary, make pottery for the Qualla Craft Cooperative in Cherokee, North Carolina, and maintain the social obligation of lunch every day at Tsali Manor, a community nursing home. When I asked people in Cherokee, "Could I please use your phone? I'm looking for Amanda Swimmer," they not only knew who she was but were not at all surprised that yet another interested interviewer was asking for Amanda.

We arranged to meet at the library in Cherokee, and from there, I would drive her home. We drove up Big Cove Road to the very end, and she told me how the cove used to look with corn planted all the way to the ridgelines when she was a girl. The ridgelines were covered with big poplar trees. I realized that the person sitting next to me had a greater depth of view than anyone I had spoken with in a very long time. I had a pillar of the Cherokee community right next to me, in my own car! I slowed down just a bit. When we arrived at her house, she began to tell me about Tom Hill.

—*Russell Bauman*

TOM HILL works with Melvina, my granddaughter. His grandma's my first cousin. Melvina was tellin' me about you's comin' and wantin' to interview me. She told me about that. I go up there at the school sometimes—at Smoky Mountain—and work with the kids. Then I always tell my story when I'm up there.

One thing about it I tell 'em, "Don't ask me about my medicine. Now, I'm not givin' it away." Yeah, if I knew any kind of medicine, I told 'em, "Don't ask me, 'cause I'm not supposed to give my medicine away." That's one thing I'll let you know first before you ask me 'cause my parents said we never give our medicine—what y' know—to other people. If you do, it ain't gon' be worth anything.

Just like the people goin' to the hospital, getting all kinds of pills and takin' the pills—I don't take no kinda pills from the hospital. Only thing I take is Tylenol. Whenever I got a cold, I use my own medicine. I don't take flu shots either. No, that's what I told 'em. I said, "I ain't gonna tell you what kind of medicine I use." I said, "And what I'm livin' on." I said, "The Lord furnished our Indian medicine." We ain't supposed to give it out. The old people was really particular on their medicine. They wouldn't even let

PLATE 176 Amanda in her living room in Big Cove
outside of Cherokee, North Carolina

y' know anything. I said, "Then if y' do, it ain't gonna be worth nothin'." And that's the way I believe in it. That's why I told them people . . . I said, "Now y' might want to ask what kinda medicine I use, but I'm not gonna give it to y'." I'll just tell you first before you ask me anything.

I can tell y' how I was growed up and what we done when I was growin' up. Now that's what I can tell y'. I was born right down there where that house is there. We had a log house made out of poplar logs, and they were about this wide [hands spread a foot and a half apart]. And that's where I was born. It was just like a tall house. It had an upstairs with it. It had a chimney to it from our farplace [fireplace]. They just used rock and dirt for that chimney.

My grandma bought this place right here—Old Man Chiltoskey built it. He must have been the one that built that house. Old Man Chiltoskey. Gosh, that's been a long time before I was born, and I'm eighty-one years old. My mother bought that one right after they got married, and I don't know what year it was. That's been *way* back. She bought that place. They lived on Big Cove side—way up on the hill. She said to my parents, "I bought that land over there on Straight Fork. Since you're married, you'uns can have that land over there. It's a hundred and ninety-nine acres."

They just called him Old Man Chiltoskey; that's how come they named that ridge Chiltoskey Ridge. That's what's they called it. [I then asked Mrs. Swimmer if she knew Goingback Chiltoskey.] This is Goin'back Chiltoskey you talkin' about, and Mary Chiltoskey. Yeah, they lived down here at Cherokee, North Carolina. G.B. lived a long time, but his brother died *way* back. This is another man: Old Man Chiltoskey. He was . . . they didn't have no kids. Just his wife lived there. So that's the one that had this land, and it was a hundred and ninety-nine acres. Now the park's got half of it. It's on the list as ninety-nine acres. They [the park service] just went ahead. They'd get anywhere, and they wouldn't do *nothin'* about it [giving land back to its owners]! They went across the mountain and over the Big Cove on Old Man Jess Swayney. They went on his side. Well, he went down there, and they told him they was on his side, and he got his land back. My mother told him, "The line's way above there." And they said, "We just makin' the line straight." It goes right straight from that ridge there on up that way, our land was. It was in the thirties or somethin' like that. My mother didn't like it. She told 'em, "You'uns comin' down too far." Said, "My land goes right up there where that curve is way above there." And they was comin' way up there. That gate was right above there where that fish place is [the Eastern Band's fish hatcheries]. Yeah, she told 'em about it.

I don't have no trouble at all. I don't see no animals around my place. They be so much animals like in Asheville or over in Hendersonville. They

PLATE 177 Amanda's mother, Molly Davis Sequoyah,
with Amanda's son Don

said they's a lot of bears comin' in their farms and stuff. "Well," I said, "I live right next to the mountains." Said, "I ain't seen no bear around my yard yet."

They had some of these old animals—what they call 'em—"elk-somethin' " out there. They came across Cattaloochee over here. They went way above there. There's a river up here. They went up on that side. They went on the Big Cove side. They didn't stay around here. No, I don't never see nothin' and nobody don't bother me up here and it's quiet. Well, there's tourists come from across the mountain, come down this way, and they come up and go up the road. They go about three and four miles up the road and go to the end of the river fishin'. Some people goes up there where it's cool when it gets hot—go up to the river and sit around. That's the only time we see 'em, but during the nighttime it's just as quiet as it can be.

So we lived in that house till Mother had all the twelve children. Most of them died and passed away. Just four of us livin' for a while, and then my two brothers passed away; so I just got one sister livin'. She's about eighty-seven. I'm the youngest. My two sisters who were the oldest, they've gone, and I have two older brothers and then three younger brothers between us.

Well, we had to use oil lamps way back. Well, we didn't have no lamps either. They just put th' oil in a jar or glass bottle, then put the rag in there and put th' lamp oil in there an' light it. That's the only light they had to use at that time. We didn't have no electricity.

I was just about maybe five or six years old, seven, somethin' like that, when we got 'lectricity. I can remember lightin' them old bottles, and then when we go on the road, we just carry that bottle and that light. It'll burn long as you carryin' it. Wouldn't go out 'cause of that lamp oil on the bottom. They just turned them rags over and make 'em round and roll 'em up and stick 'em in the bottle—let it soak a little.

Well, a lotta people was glad to get their lights put in there, and I never did hear anybody complain about it after they got their 'lectricity. They didn't have to buy no lamp oil. That's what they said. Yeah, we had to use lamp bottles keep our house lighted up, had each one in our bedroom for light.

Well, they had to cook over a farplace . . . didn't have no stove. And later on then, I guess I was about twelve years old when they started buyin' stoves for to cook with. They just had to cook on th' farplace. They put their pots on the farplace, and when we made bread, we just put it in the oven [dutch oven], put it by the farplace, and put yer coals down there and get your oven really hot; then put your dough in there to make th' bread. Yeah, and that's the way they cooked. Had a lid to it. Y' put the coals on top o' that, and you put 'em under till the bread gets done. Y' can check it after that when it gets really hot. That lid, they used to get it all red—you know how that stove gets red on top? They put the coals on there. [If the lid didn't get red hot,] they'd knock the coals off and put some more coals on there. Yeah, it just cooks as same as a 'lectricity stove. It was a lot of work. Well, y' didn't have to watch it. All y' had to do was put coals on there and keep it hot all the time. We had a big ol' far built, and then we cook somethin' and set it on 'em logs, y' know, till it's burnin' down, and y' put yer coals down there and set yer pot on it. And it'd cook. They had some big ol' pots they'd cook in set on top of that wood when it's burnin'. They can tell when it's 'bout burned down. Then they put some more wood on there so it can stay on that pot.

Well, it was hot in th' summertime, but in wintertime it was really good. But you couldn't keep warm when it got cold. Get cold one side and get hot one side—had to turn 'round to keep warm. They had ears to the pots and they'd put 'em on, and they had some hooks [so they could] pull the pots off the farplace. Yeah, even we done that to that oven for our bread. We had some hooks about that long and use that and pick up the lid and set it on the side. Yeah, and my mother cooked on that big farplace all that time. Then she got a cookstove, wood cookstove. Put it in the kitchen, and she used

PLATE 178 Amanda's father, Running Wolf Sequoyah,
with a blowgun resting on his shoulder

that. Mostly all the times when she want to cook somethin', like hominy corn, she used this big ol' pot . . . put it on the farplace to cook it.

**"We didn't have nothin' to worry about if you got hungry. Now-adays, them kids'd starve to death if they didn't have nothin' to eat."**

My dad was a farmer, and he didn't do nothin' but farm. He had a horse done all the work in the field. He tended that field down there and those trees up that mountain—filled with poplar trees. We had corn, and they raised potatoes. They raised everything we used to eat. Didn't buy no canned pinto beans, you know. He raised corn and cane, and he raised tobacco, too, part of it. Yeah, he'd plant corn on the steep hill up there. You wouldn't think corn will grow on a steep hill, but all these hills right here where all them poplar trees are . . . there was a big field there where they'd raise corn. Right up here, go 'round the curve; they's a hill up there where my daughter lives now with my grandson. [My dad] had to farm all that with corn. And when the fall comes—they had a crib right up on the ridge above this house over there—had that crib plumb full of corn. We always put everything up in the fall for th' winter. He had cane down in the bottom. He made syrup out of it. They used syrup instead of sugar. We didn't use much sugar. When they had to sweeten somethin', had to use that syrup. They made bread with it, sweet bread. They raised beans, and they killed hogs at Christmastime when it got cold. Then we had a milk cow—give a lot of milk. [In the wintertime,] they'd just set back and make blowguns and work 'round the house and cut wood all the time.

Well, we [grew] the food ourselves. We raised potatoes and we raised beans and we raised cabbage. We put our cabbage up and made kraut and all that stuff. We'd dry cabbage and beans. We didn't have nothin' to worry about if you got hungry. Nowadays, them kids'd starve to death if they didn't have nothin' to eat.

Yeah, my dad 'd hunt and fish, too. He made blowguns, and then he made bows and arrows. We didn't have to buy no chairs. He made chairs hisself just like that. His name was Running Wolf Sequoyah. My mama's name was Molly Davis Sequoyah. That's her standing right there [points to a picture of her mother on the wall].

They worked all their lives. Even my husband just overdone himself. He overworked too much, just got down sick, and when we got this house, well, he just stayed in here four months and he got sick on us and he passed on.

PLATE 179 Luke Swimmer, Amanda's late husband

My husband's name was Luke Swimmer. He's been gone a long time—thirty years. He worked on Fontana Dam and just worked all of his life.

Yeah, we had to work! We didn't raise up like these kids nowadays. They say no, no. They told us to get out there! We had to get out. Then our mother taught us how to cook, and we couldn't say, "After a while." She meant to do it right then. Well, we got it done. It was already done in the evenings. I had a little ol' hoe with a handle 'bout that long [indicates a short handle], and I'd go and hoe corn ever' time they went and hoed corn. When the corn gets that high, we still hoe it till it gets so far along; then they just let it go.

We didn't have to buy everything, but everything was cheap at that time. You could get a bag of flour of maybe twenty-five pounds for maybe two dollars. And then y' buy a box of crackers; that's a nickel. Now y' can pay 'bout fifteen dollars for a bag like that, I guess, if they had to sell it that high. I had to buy some shoes for my kids—paid a dollar a pair of shoes for a little baby.

When they got a little bigger, they'd be about six or seven dollars or somethin' like that. That's how cheap the shoes was. Now you pay sixty dollars for a pair of little kid's shoes, and they got the biggest feet I ever seen, these kids growin' up. They wear eight and nine size shoes.

We didn't have no fancy weddings. We just went down to the courthouse and got married. We didn't dress up like they do now, buying all those fancy clothes. I had me my own work dress on, and he had his own work clothes

PLATE 180 Amanda and Luke Swimmer

on: overalls. When we got married, he went back to his mother to cut logs, and I come home here. Then, 'bout a week after that, he come up here, and we stayed here with my mother awhile. Well, we went together about two or three years. After we got married, he just went on cuttin' logs, and I kept house.

He growed up on that side, and he was ten years older than I was. He was married before, but he lost his first wife and had two kids. He lost the other baby and had one girl. When we got married, she was four years old.

We lived way up on the hill with one small room, and then we got too crowded. Lived up there ten years; then I asked my daddy if we could build a little bigger [house]. He used to come up and sit breakfast with me when my mama 'as goin' to work. She used to go to work for the people up here at Round Bottom a lot. When she 'as gone, he come and eat supper with us or breakfast. So I told him, I said, "You want to come down here and live a little closer, right there close to the branch?" I said, "You gonna let us put a house there?" I said, "That way you don't have to go up the hill comin' to eat." Well, he said, "Yous can build anywhere you want to. That's your own land." So we built it right here, and we stayed ten years right here.

Well, when my daddy died, my mother came and stayed with me here when my house was right here. She let my brother move in there, and somehow, the kitchen was kindly old. The door wouldn't shut too good, and she let him stay. She said, "I'll just let Lloyd live in there." That was my oldest brother. Later, my brother and his wife moved over to the other Big Cove side and were gone.

This horse we had, he didn't like [for us] to make a far [fire] outside. They'd make a far out there to keep the bugs and gnats away. That horse would come and put his foot down and scatter that far out and put it out right then. He didn't like that smoke somehow. I woke up about one o'clock—bright outside. I told my husband, "What makes it so bright outside?" So he jumped up and said, "Your mama's house is on far." And it was goin' up to the top. Then we jumped up, went down, and got out on the porch. We stayed there. Now where's that horse? I knew that horse, and he went down that way. That horse was way down the road. He'd took off. He was lookin' up thisaway. We just believed he walked in that room—there was some far in that farplace that they left after they went to Big Cove. They had papers all over the floor, the kids did. Put them coals in there, and it started burnin'. He must've tried to put that far out.

They was nothin' we could do to keep that house from goin' down. It had already gone too far. It had way big logs, poplar logs, about that wide [holds her hands a foot and a half wide]. Had an upstairs, too.

"Yeah, boy, it's changed! . . . You could walk down the road after dark and nobody'd bother y' . . . And now y' can't walk the road with anybody not runnin' over y'."

Yeah, boy, it's changed! They always ask me, "You think it's better right now than what it was when you was growin' up?" One thing about it I'll say: It was better when I was growin' up. You could walk down the road after dark and nobody'd bother y'. Then y' could come home and nobody'd open yer door. We left our doors open, and nobody never bothered it. Now y' can't leave yer door unlocked without somebody gettin' in. And now y' can't walk the road with anybody not runnin' over y'. That's how mean these people are nowadays!

"We had just a box of candy, and that's all we'd get for Christmas. We were satisfied. Didn't have nothin' to ride, no wagons or nothin'."

We were happy way back when we was growin' up, but we didn't have all kinds of things to play with like the kids do now. The kids just pile up the toys and everything like that, spend all that money. We didn't have nothin' when we growed up. Christmastime, all we'd get is a pair a socks, and now kids'll get mad if they don't get a toy at Christmastime! If they knew hardly what we had to go through—we had just a box of candy, and that's all we'd get for Christmas. We were satisfied. Didn't have nothin' to ride, no wagons or nothin'.

My boys, when they got bigger, they made their own wagons. They cut down a poplar tree and cut the wheels about that thick [hands four inches apart], saw 'em up, and then they drill a hole in the middle and put 'em on a stick for their axle. Then they put a board on top and make a wagon and ride down the hill. That's what they was usin'. I just let 'em. They was just kids, you know. I'd just watch over 'em so they wouldn't get hurt. That's the way our boys was. When it snowed, they'd get their big coats on and get some tote sacks wrap around their legs and said, "We went over to Big Cove to see how deep the snow is over there." Then they made a sled, and at the hill right here, they'd slide off that snow. At midnight they be out there playin' in the snow. We didn't make 'em stop. They just had fun and played outside. They didn't go nowheres to homes, and when they growed up, they stayed around the house. They didn't go out with the different things and start drinkin' and somethin' like that. They just stayed right here at the house.

"I liked it way back, and I told 'em, I said, 'Nowadays, they's just too much weary.' "

We didn't have no place to play when I was growin' up. All we done is play around these trees and climb trees and swing on the grapevine. That's all we had to do. Yeah, I was happy. We didn't have nothin' to watch in the house—just go out and play outside, go swimmin' in the summertime. That's all we had to do. I liked it way back, and I told 'em, I said, "Nowadays, they's just too much weary." Too much things goin' on. You can't go to town without some-body tryin' to steal everything, grab your basket and everything like that.

We didn't have a big town in Cherokee. We just had one store down in Cherokee. That's the only one we had. It's way down there where we go around the curve there—where that mission church is. It's right by the road, and that's the only store we had. Me and my husband had to leave here by eight o'clock to go to Cherokee to get some groceries. This road wadn't nothin' but railroad track, and the train did run on this track. We just walked down to Cherokee and then on these other roads where we'd go. We had wagon roads. We'd cut off somewheres in the railroad track and get on the wagon road—then walk down, get on the railroad track again, and we'd get to Cherokee by eleven o'clock in the morning. We'd leave six, seven—some-thin' like that—in the summertime. We'd get down there by eleven o'clock.

Then we had to get a taxi; just one taxi was runnin' down Cherokee. He had to bring us there through the ford where we'd turn off this way. Then he had to go around that way, cross the river, and go 'cross that mountain there. That's just how far that car'd come, and so we had to carry our groceries up here to the house—about a mile and a half, two miles. It was just a railroad track. That's all we had. We didn't have no big roads like we have now.

Then they had some CCC [Civilian Conservation Corps] camp up there so they can build this road. It was mostly just gravel road first time. After they tore this railroad track out, the train stopped. That train went all the way to that mountain on the other side, made a switchback, and hauled some logs out and take 'em down.

They had them CCC boys up there; then they start buildin' this road up there till they finished. They was from different places.

There was some had a camp up at the Round Bottom—what they call Round Bottom—up there 'bout three miles, four miles up here. There was some mens cuttin' logs, and they went all the way.

They ain't nothin' but woods now; you can't tell. Well, you can tell a little bit where they got the horse stables up there now where they ride horses on the mountainside—every summer people up there leading. Some white people lived there. My mother went up there and worked for 'em.

It was all right. Anyway, I told 'em people were friendly, and they were willin' to help everybody. These peoples around here, these Indians, had rules. Anybody's sick in their home, the people . . . they'd cook somethin' and take it to that person. It's a bad sick woman, and they'll help 'em out with their food and take some stuff out there. That's the way they had.

We had free labors that'd come work for you. They'd get your wood if you didn't have no wood, haul it up on the porch, and saw it up in the yard. Then they could help you hoe corn for nothin'. All you had to do was just feed 'em for lunch. That was the free labors.

Then when somebody passed away, they used to just bring 'em home at that time. They didn't embalm 'em. They had two womens do the cookin' in the nighttime, coffee and stuff like that. Then they had two womens do the cookin' in the daytime. They had the grave diggers that's around there. That family, that's the way they used to have them things. Now the old people are all gone. These young kids don't know what free labors are. We've got a few of them, but they're a little older. They come around and cut our grasses. Just our boys here, they just gathered up and called theirselves free labors. You can call them, and they'll do the work for you. All you have to do is give them dinner. We've got some yet called free labors in the Big Cove community, about eight, I guess, right here. When somebody dies, they're the ones that cover the body up. The undertakers don't do much of anything up here. We use funeral homes, but when they bring the body up, the free labors close the grave and helps 'em cover up that person. Each community had free labors.

The communities in Cherokee are Big Cove, Wolf Town, Paint Town, Soco, Big Y, Bird Town, and Snowbird—that's way down Graham County— Robbinsville and Murphy. They all Indian mostly.

We went to school. All we had was geography, 'rithmetic, English—that's all they had that we'd study. I just went to fourth grade. It was hard work to walk to school. We didn't have no bus to ride. We walked from there: You know where that curve is where we came by that church down yonder—big, sharp curve? That's where our school was. We walked way down there, and we walked home—rain and snow. Ever' day, that's how we suffered going to school.

My grandchildren, they don't like to go to school, and I said, "Now you 'uns got a bus runnin' in your yard, and here I had to walk on the railroad tracks and I be the smallest one! I be *way* behind, and then sometimes they slap me around for bein' so slow." I had to get there by about eight o'clock. We had to go down there at eight, and we'd be there till three-thirty let out school. I would guess it takes about an hour, two hours. We just take our time. They's hard to walk on, railroad tracks.

Now they send 'em when they're three years old. We had to wait till we was about six years old when we went to school—or seven. I don't know what they do. They send these little babies to school—take 'em out of bed and send 'em on to school. [Mrs. Swimmer volunteers at the Head Start a few miles down the road.] They start 'em out at two, three years old, and some of 'em two months old. We got babies in there, too! They be two months old and a month old and a year old. They just bring them in—have to go to work and leave the babies there. We had one about two months old baby not too long ago. Her mama had to go to work.

> **"They had a person to come get you when you had to go to the hospital, and sometimes he was so slow to get there, them babies just beat him. I had two boys at home and one girl."**

I had nine kids. Seven are living. He's the youngest here [points toward her son Don, who was in the back of the house]. He lives in that house [points toward one of the neighboring houses]. There was a hospital we had to go to, but I had three of them at home. I just couldn't make it there in time. They come too fast. I had the rest of them in the hospital. Well, it was hard to get down there! They had a person to come get you when you had to go to the hospital, and sometimes he was so slow to get there, them babies just beat him. I had two boys at home and one girl.

I lost the oldest one. He was the oldest of all of them, but he was just eight months baby almost. He was supposed to be nine months baby, but he was born about eight months baby. Doctor told me eight months baby don't hardly live. So that's when I lost him. I guess it 'as about the sixth one, right between these two girls—I lost him. He was four years old when he died. So these other four here alive, one lives in Mexico, and one lives in Michigan. The one's in Mexico, he's next to the oldest that's living. Then there's another—we call him Virgil, the third one; the girls, two girls; and he's the last one, Don.

Well, Virgil's workin' for the road department. He gets 'em fixed workin' with the tribe. Herb, he's retired from General Motors. Don lives in that house down there. Then I got one more boy. He stays in Mexico; he takes care the motels over there: McKinley. I got three girls. Flora, Flora Mae Bradley, she works with women with the Cancer Society. They call it Wellness Women. Marilyn Swimmer works at the Indian village. She's a potter and crafts. The other'n that's livin', Merina, she just keeps house. She don't work nowhere. She's a wife. It's more work!

[We descended from] Axe and Standing Wolf. Standing Wolf had a big family, and that's where we came from. They buried up around here. I don't know where Standing Wolf's buried, but Old Man Axe's buried up Bunches Creek. They was here when it [the Trail of Tears] happened. My grandma's brother was Old Man Whippoorwill, and he died back *way* back. I guess he died before or right after I got married. He couldn't hear good, but he'd walk around and work and cut wood and cut trees and stayed down here at the yellow hill down Cherokee. I didn't know that was my grandmother's brother till just lately. We looked on the record, and that was her brother.

We always named our children in Indian names, so whenever they have to go somewhere's around these old people they'd know how to call these Indian names to my children. That's how come they name 'em these old names. I got my boys all named in Cherokee, but their English names is different. I had to have my Indian name for 'em on account of these old people couldn't even say those English words. I had to name 'em in Cherokee so they could call them who they are, and that's the way it goes. A lot of people don't tell you that, though. Yeah, and then some of 'em tell you, "It means like this; we just name 'em like this," but that's not truth. All you have to do is name 'em what you want to name 'em in Cherokee. So your people, your grandpa wouldn't know what English is. If you name 'em in English, they wouldn't know what that mean. All you had to do is tell 'em what their name is in Cherokee.

The old people had names. Way back, they had all different kind of Indian names. Nowadays, they name 'em the hardest name you ever seen. I can't even name some of my grandchildren's names. They don't name 'em in Cherokee no more. They all talk English, and that's why it's so hard to name 'em in Cherokee. I had one granddaughter . . . she wants to name her baby Standing Wolf. It was born fourth of July. She wants to name it Standing Wolf in Indian. She's the only one namin' her kids in the Cherokee language. That's why I get after my grandchildren. I say, "Why don't y'uns name 'em old names?" I said, "Y'uns name 'em some names I can't even say the words!" I said, "Don't know what they mean." We had some old people with old names. I said, "Name 'em that after 'em. Don't name these hard words like you get the word from overseas." [Laugh]

Well, it was a little bit pretty hard during the Depression but not really. You could get by with it. Well, we had it pretty good. We always had everything put away, and we didn't live without everything. We ate three times a day. That was pretty good! I fed my kids before they went to school, got 'em up in the morning; then, suppertime, they were ready to eat when they went home from school. They'd feed 'em down there at the school.

Well, I was about, let's see, about seventeen or something like that when I started pottery. I just went ahead and played with the clay down there to see if I could make somethin' [laugh]. Went to work in a motel awhile. Then, about a year after that, I went up to the village and worked—sat with some womens that knew how to make pottery, and I just learned more from that. I learned from Cora Wahnetah. Then when I'd set somethin' out, they'd finish it for me. So I just stayed there at the pottery. Well, I went around all over the place at the village relievin' 'em at lunchtime; and finally, they sit me in the pottery, and I sit there for thirty-five years. That lady up there in the pink shirt, she's a good potter [points to a picture of Mabel Bigmeat]. She married my son. She was the best pottery maker.

I don't go up there no more. I ain't been up there in a long time. They could use me up there, but I can't stand to sit still no more. It's too much sittin' down. I'd rather be movin'. I make pottery ever' now and then. I just know when to quit and rest. At the village they got all the craftsmen. They can go in there and watch what they're makin'. I guess I was there when you went through [previously I spoke with Mrs. Swimmer about my trip to the Oconaluftee Indian Village when I was a little boy]. There're a lot of people there.

When they like that, you ready to burn it [points toward some unfinished pots on the oven]. Then when you burn 'em, you have to preheat 'em first in the oven. That's before you put 'em into the fire. Then you put them in the fire pit. You put the wood to 'em. You just let 'em burn out till the fire goes out. I had a pit, but right now it's been so rainy, it messed it up. I have to fix it.

I use poplar, dried poplar mostly, and maple. Then if I want to make a light color, I just use hardwood. That's oak and locust. If you use locust, it give you an orange color. Hardwood uses more flame and less smoke, and the soft wood makes more smoke than flame. It's a difference. You can't cook in 'em, but they can hold water. My son had a broken vase and set it out there a week on the porch with water in it, and it didn't even mash up.

This is the way they turn out when they're done. You never know how they're gonna come out. One time I burned my son's pig. He made a pig, and when I burned it, it come out black like on its back, and then right on its nose it had a brown spot like that—like it's been diggin' in the mud! I said, "Look at that pig. It looks like it's been diggin' in the ground!" Right on its nose, that's the way it came out.

I use a stick and a seashell to make the designs. I can use a corncob to put a corncob design on it. I burn the cob and I just roll it up when it's wet like this and it gives a design. This is the stick I use to make the design, and here's the shinin' rock.

I had a place right there to get clay, but when the park made this road, they covered my clay up. It was right on the bank in there. That's where we used to get our clay, and now you can't get it. They piled all that dirt in there. You can't get it no more, and I had to buy this. After I quit diggin', I had to go to Asheville to a factory over there. We buy our clay from Asheville right now, the red clay. They sifted that clay, and we always buy the clay from them. The village bought many mounds of clay over there for us to work on when I was workin'. I think I made a thousand pots for 'em. They got some

PLATE 181 Two pots crafted and fired by Amanda
in the traditional Cherokee method
using a sharpened stick and sometimes
a dried corncob to make her designs;
afterwards, she smooths them
with a smooth river stone or shinin' rock.

in Washington and got some in New York and some in Chapel Hill and
Raleigh. I got a pot for everybody, I guess. They really price 'em, though.
They can't hardly sell 'em, puttin' too much price on them. They'd sell a pot
like this [points to the pot on the table] for forty dollars. My son made those
pots over there on the stove. He's had them over two weeks. He's supposed
to burn 'em, but he hadn't got to burn 'em yet. I guess he can fix my place to
burn 'em. I made those tiny wedding jugs. They's some womens down there
at Tsali Manor who wants 'em. I'll take 'em down there and give 'em to 'em.

The Western Indian used the wedding jug. [See Nola Campbell, *Foxfire*
*9*, pages 238–66.] They just brought a pattern for us to use at the village.
When they get married, the bride and groom drinks out of one side; then
they throw it over their shoulder. If they didn't break, the marriage would
stand. Well, I don't know if they do it or not. I haven't seen anybody doing it.
I told 'em that's the way they told us what they do up there. I ain't never
watched 'em do it.

When they call me, I go work at the school. Just whenever they get kids
that want to make pottery, they call me. They pay me for teachin' them kids.
I guess they send y' two hundred dollars for teachin', and I had to burn

them, too. Vina brought 'em home, and then she took 'em back. They really want to learn. They can make some things I can't make! One little boy had a little ol' flat thing then. He had something sittin' right in the middle then. On the handle right here and right in the middle, he had somethin' sharp—clay—stickin' out, and he said that was woodchopper. They had woodchopper machines, you know, that chop wood. I thought that's what he meant to make. He said, "That's woodchopper," and it turned out good. I don't never lose those kids' pottery when they burn. They all come out. I don't know. I guess the Lord works on the kids. Oh, they so proud of them! They take it home and show it to their mother. And they's askin' Vina, "When she comin' back to teach us?" They teach blowguns, and they teach beadwork, and all that stuff now, and they teach 'em how to sing in Cherokee. We had some kids down there . . . they can sing "God Bless America" in Cherokee.

My daddy didn't speak hardly English, and my grandfather didn't either. Well, I learned my English after I got around these white people's kids around here when I was about nine years old. I didn't speak English. They'd come down and play with me, and Mama would take us up there and play with them. So I learned how to speak while they was talkin'.

They owned their land up there, and when the park came in, they paid 'em off and got 'em out. We had *good* friends. We just talked to each other when they were around us. I picked it up and I started talkin' English every now and then. Then I went to school.

Well, they didn't get us in trouble for speakin' Cherokee in school that time. That was way back before when my oldest sister was going to school when we weren't allowed to speak in Cherokee, but after that, we could speak in Cherokee. That was way back when the other kids, old people, went to school; whenever they got 'em, put something in their mouth—keep 'em from talking in Cherokee. We talked both ways. They didn't say nothin' to us. They teach them Cherokee language, and they sang in Cherokee.

Yeah, there're a lot of 'em [elders] that speak in Cherokee. It's these young kids the ones don't know how to speak Cherokee but speak English all the time. I was tellin' them, "When I want to speak in Cherokee, yous have t' understand what I'm sayin', too." Yeah, Melvina understands me when I tell her in Cherokee, but she don't speak it. Well, I don't know, sometimes she'll say a few words. I tell 'em, "Speak the old language right now. It's gon' go away, and you'll never know." Now Robbinsville people . . . their kids talks Cherokee all the time. They talk more than our kids do. Here in Cherokee, they don't talk in Cherokee to each other. They talk English. So Robbinsville still got an old way of talkin' their own language. And you see them kids, they'll talk to you in Cherokee. They talk different than I do, but then they talkin' the right way, what's in the Cherokee alphabet. That's the way it supposed to be. They kindly talk like Oklahoma. Now Oklahoma people talk just like Robbinsville people.

**"And I don't like Oklahoma. It's too level! I couldn't see the mountains in just a level place like that."**

I went to Oklahoma one time, but they come out here a lot. You know, some of our people was driven to Oklahoma—was pushed over there to Oklahoma. Their children don't like to come back here. These mountains too different for them. They say they feel like they're in a hole when they come back here. And I don't like Oklahoma. It's too level! I couldn't see the mountains in just a level place like that.

I don't like to go to Florida. I don't like to see that water, and there's nothin' but water down there. That's one thing I said: "I don't like Florida. I'd rather go north than go to Florida." I don't like to go to the ocean neither. I don't like to hear that noise. I'd just rather see these little ol' springs, branches, than see that big river rollin' around. I don't know what they see out of it. They say it's purty, but I don't see nothin' purty out of that ocean. That's what I told 'em.

They took us to Jacksonville. We stayed there Thursday and we come back Friday and I was ready to come home and see these mountains. They said, "We're leavin' at six o'clock in the mornin'." I said, "Good. I want to get back to those ol' mountains." I get lonesome when I go to these level places. I miss these mountains here. No, I hadn't traveled too much either till I traveled with the senior citizens. I been to Massachusetts, Niagara Falls—then went to what-y'-call-it . . . the beach? Myrtle Beach? Then we went to Nashville and Chattanooga one time. That's the only places we've been. I enjoyed goin' to Niagara Falls.

Well, I went to Connecticut one time. I went there a long time ago. It's been about thirty years! Now that's the first time I ever rode a plane. I wasn't about to go, and my boss told me, "Go on. That'll be a nice trip for you."

Went down to Bird Town and goin' to take Juanita Wolf and Louise Maney. She's a potter. Louise Maney didn't want to go. She 'as afraid she might get fired from workin' at the school. So she asked me if I'd go. Come up here about this time, and I said, "I ain't *never* gon' ride up in a plane," and I wadn't goin' to. All these planes droppin' off and they wonder why I wouldn't go.

They said, "You can't even tell you movin'. You so *smooth*. Oh, you might feel a little bit where there's fog somewhere."

Well, that's what I said, "I don't like to ride 'em." Well, he begged, and he begged. I asked, "When you leavin'?"

"Next Sunday," he said.

I said, "I don't think I want to go."

"But you're the only one can go and make pottery for us," he said. We was gonna give to Save the Children over there in Connecticut. Said, "Louise couldn't go, so you can use her ticket."

So I said, "Let me think about it. I'll let you know by Thursday if I'm gonna travel on the plane or not." Well, Thursday night, he come 'bout seven o'clock.

"You still goin'?"

I still hadn't made up my mind yet. I said, "I don't know."

I talked to Virgil, and he said, "Why don't you just go, Mom? That'll be a nice trip. You may not see that place anymore. You enjoy your trip. Go on. They ain't nothin' to it."

I said, "Yous ain't been on a plane!"

"Nuh-uh," they said. "No, it's safe. It's all right. Y'll make it."

"Well," I said. "If I decided I'll come, I'll let you know Saturday night." Well, he come back Saturday night to see if I was goin'. "Well, I guess I give up. I'll go with you." We went on. We caught the plane and went on to Cincinnati.

Well, it about took my breath when they went up in the air! That's one thing I don't like! They sit me in the middle, and they wanted to put me on the side so I could look around. I said, "No, no, right here." I just had my head down.

We passed Washington, and they said, "I'll show you where Washington is."

I said, "I don't want to go look around at Washington—ain't lookin' around till I get off this plane!" No, we just got off the plane, and then peoples were already waitin' for pottery to sell.

They're havin' that national meetin', that National American Meeting [in Mexico]. My son, who takes care of the motel in Mexico, he's takin' me in September. I said, "Well, I'll go with you, yeah." He gets a discount: He rides so many planes all the time. He said, "We'll go to Atlanta and catch the plane from there and fly straight on through to Mexico so we don't have to change nothin'."

Well, I guess it's gettin' late now. Say, you want to put down?

# TOM HILL: A MODERN
# CHEROKEE STORYTELLER

*"That heritage has always been a part of who I am, and my family made sure that happened. I didn't have to go find it."*

Tom Hill tells stories. Although he is not sure if they are authentic Cherokee legends, the manner in which Tom applies them is certainly genuine. He is the program director for Cherokee Challenge, a local community-based adventure program designed to help at-risk boys and girls in the Cherokee community. Through camping, climbing and ropes courses, hiking, and woodcraft, Tom's students accomplish personal goals and learn valuable lessons about life.

Before Sequoyah created the Cherokee alphabet in 1820, the people passed down their legends and myths in an oral tradition. Each storyteller wove his story a little differently from those before him, while still keeping the soul of the tale intact. So when I visited Tom to hear some of his stories, I remembered that he was passing on something from his Native American ancestry. Tom told me in the beginning of the interview that he wasn't sure if his stories were Cherokee or not. Strong similarities exist in many Indian legends, and in most cases these legends do not come from one particular tribe.

On that day, Tom told me two legends: how the first stars were made and how earth was created in a world where only water existed. Also, Tom diverged into telling two funny bear anecdotes.

You might notice that Tom is younger and more contemporary than most of our Foxfire contacts, but he embodies the continuum of storytelling, an invaluable component of Cherokee heritage. Each time one of Tom's students experiences joy on the ropes course or awe around the campfire, he or she has gained something from Tom, a man who gives back to his community every day.

—*Russell Bauman*

HOW DID I become interested in my heritage? When I think about it, it's kinda strange how it worked out. My father, who was Cherokee, died when

I was two years old. He was in the Navy at the time. Then my mother married another man in the Navy who wasn't Indian, but she made a point that—and even my stepfather made a point that—me and my brother were in Cherokee [North Carolina] often. We moved around a lot, being Navy brats, but just about every summer we found ourselves in Cherokee with my grandmother. So my family made sure that I was part of that heritage. What's funny is, right after high school, me and my then girlfriend that is now my wife, we drove up here to visit my grandmother, and my girlfriend looked at me and said, "We're moving up here." So I said, "Okay, that's fine." She'd never been here, and when she saw the area, she said, "We're livin' here." So we've been here, gosh, since '80, '81, you know, so I'm a naturalized North Carolinian now. That heritage has always been a part of who I am, and my family made sure that happened. I didn't have to go find it.

I run the Cherokee Challenge. It's an adventure-based program for Cherokee. The largest population of the program is sixth-graders. At the beginning of the school year, we put groups of sixth-graders together. We get referrals from the schools and from parents. Then we start putting groups together. We have four staff here right now, and each one of them usually has two groups of kids. We put them together at the beginning of the year, and we meet with those groups throughout the school year and a lot of the way through the summer, based on what our schedules look like. The kids that have been through the program are ones we've selected who have leadership qualities, so the summer camp for them is actually the beginning of a training process. These kids that we're taking to New Mexico are gonna become peer leaders, coleaders with us, to help with these groups. [Tom left the following day for New Mexico.]

It's primarily a crime and substance abuse prevention program. We have a ropes course and an alpine tower, camping, and white-water paddling . . . those kinds of things. We also incorporate a lot of cultural stuff into what we do. Used to be, we'd try to do it directly, but as soon as you say anything about "so-and-so from the museum is coming next week to talk to us about history," they wouldn't show up. This is strictly a voluntary program.

### "If we're shooting arrows or blowguns, we talk about the Wolf Clan, who were the hunters for the tribe."

I'll use some examples; we build the seven clans of the Cherokee into what we do. If we're shooting arrows or blowguns, we talk about the Wolf Clan, who were the hunters for the tribe. The Wild Potato Clan were the gatherers of plants, so we do plant identification. The Long Hair Clan were the

PLATE 182  Tom and some campers attack the rapids on the Nantahala River.

peace chiefs, and I talk about them when I teach them how to facilitate on the ropes course.

One, the kids gain a lot of personal stuff, but then there's also the business end of it. These kids are developing real skills. I use my son as an example. He's one of the peer leaders in this program. I now contract with him because he's got so much experience belaying on the tower and working on the ropes course. I've got two young people that are in that position that we've brought up through training. The next step is to get them out there in the wider community with other programs. We're sending them out with those skills like basic first aid, CPR, and the harder skills for camping and hiking.

I see an immediate change. The real stuff is lowering a kid from the tower that you spent twenty minutes getting to the top and just looking at their face (that's what it's about for me—I mean, you see the change right there) or a kid getting off the van after a weekend of being out in the woods saying, "Thanks, Tom. That was fun."

We give these kids a lot of responsibility when we're out in the woods. I try to do as little as possible and give them the bulk of the responsibility. A lot of them are flabbergasted, especially parents. The kids are, you know, "We're doing what? We're rafting a river?" But the parents go, "Man! That's really cool that my kid gets to be involved in things like that." It's funny how people aren't aware of the places you can go and things you can do like rafting trips and camping trips. We provide that outlet for kids in this community because most of them are watching TV and playing their computer games.

> **"I have so much fun at this job. I talk about this job, and people look at me and say, 'You do *what* for a living? You get *paid* to do that?' "**

I've been with the Challenge program since '86, so about sixteen years. I've been here since '86, and actually before that. The Challenge program started in '79, '80. I was a volunteer in '80 and '81, and then went away for a couple of years. I was actually overseas in the Peace Corps when I got a letter from the then director of the Challenge program that said, "Would you be interested in a full-time job with the Challenge program?" Yeah, so I came back and been here ever since. I'm program director now. It's a wonderful job. I have so much fun at this job. I talk about this job, and people look at me and say, "You do *what* for a living? You get *paid* to do that?"

It's funny how storytelling started. I was actually on an outing. We were doing an outing with Outward Bound. We had a cooperative thing at that time, and we still do. We had five kids and two adults out in Pisgah Forest when one of the Outward Bound leaders came over to the fire and said, "Can I tell you guys a story?" He told a story, and it was great. It was great to listen to. Syd Culapher, he's the one that told me that first story around the campfire. I actually called Outward Bound to just find him and thank him.

> **"The animals have never seen darkness. It's a very different place, but it's a very nice place."**

After that outing, I came home, and my kids were probably three and five at the time. One night I looked at them, and I said, "Let me tell you this story." I told it to them, and they looked at me. You know, they were in awe! I went, "Hey, that was cool." Working with kids in the Challenge program, I started telling the story to some of the groups of kids that I worked with. Somehow the word got out that I was telling stories, so people started calling me and asking me if I could come to the schools to tell stories. So basically it grew from the storytelling at that fireplace, to telling my kids, to groups that I work with, then to school groups and groups of folks over here and groups of folks over there. Word just kind of spread and crept out there. I mean, it's like it wasn't anything I was seeking. It just happened. I love doing it, especially with young kids. After I tell stories, I'm on such a high. My blood's just pumping, and my adrenaline's going. It's just a really neat thing to do.

The first story is a story about the first stars. This is the story Syd Culapher told that night around the fireplace. When I go places and tell stories, it's always the first story I tell, and it goes like this. It's a story that takes place a very long time ago. It's so long ago that there are only animals on the earth, no people yet, just the animals. And it's so long ago that the sun's out all the time. There's no nighttime. There's no darkness. The animals have never seen darkness. It's a very different place, but it's a very nice place. It's warm all the time. It's easy to grow crops. The animals loved it.

There's a mischief-maker, and it's the mischief-maker that you'll hear about in a lot of Native American stories: That's Coyote. So Coyote's walking around one day, and he's getting bored. He decides he needs to do a practical joke on the animals just to get things hopping around and excited. So this is what Coyote does. He comes up with a plan. He goes and finds the biggest blanket that he can find, and he threw it as hard as he could up into the sky. When he did, he covered the sun, and everything went completely black. All the animals on the earth stopped what they were doing because they'd had no experience with darkness before. They stood there a minute, and nothing happened. Then panic started to creep into the animals. They didn't know what was going on. The sun was gone! Then the panic really started to creep in, and they started moving around. They were bumping into each other. They couldn't see each other, and they were scaring each other. They were bumping into trees and they were bumping into each other and soon they were just in a major panic, screaming and yelling and running around and bumping into things. This went on for two or three days.

On the third day, the Great Chief, who at the time was the bear, decided, "We've had enough of this. We need to find out what's going on." So he called a Grand Council. When the tribe calls a Grand Council, that means all the tribal members come together, which at that time were all the animals.

Word spread out that there was going to be a Grand Council. It took another three or four days for all the animals to make their way to the council site because they had to creep along—feel along as they went. Finally they were all in the council site, and they were all wailing and screaming about the sun disappearing. What were they going to do? Nobody knew what was going on, and somebody in the crowd said, "What we need to do is send somebody up to find out what has happened to the sun."

Someone else answered, "Well, that's a good idea, but who's that going to be?"

Well, up walked the most powerful bird that there is, and that is Eagle. Word spread that Eagle was going to go up to find out what had happened to the sun. The animals got excited: "Yeah, Eagle will be able to find out what happened." They couldn't see Eagle, but they could hear him when he spread his wings. His large wings opened up—whoosh, whoosh—and they heard him leave the earth. The animals stood there a long time as they listened to Eagle get further and further away from the earth—whoosh, whoosh [in a softer voice]. They stood there a long time, and they could just barely hear Eagle—whoosh, whoosh [softer still]. Then they heard . . . bump. Then they didn't hear anything, until soon they heard Eagle falling back to earth [softly makes a wind sound]. The animals started to panic, and they started bumping into each other and running into each other: "Eagle's falling to earth!"

Just before Eagle hit the earth, he spread his wings out. He alit on the earth and shrugged his shoulders and said, "I don't know what that was up there, but I bumped my head on something."

"Eagle went up there, and he couldn't find out what happened to the sun. What we gonna do?" They started to panic again and scream.

Well, up walked the wisest bird that there is, and that was Owl. The animals were excited again, "All right, Eagle couldn't find out what happened to the sun, but now we're gonna send up one of the smart birds." That was Owl. The same thing again. The animals stood there and listened as Owl got farther and farther away from the earth. They stood there a long time again. Just as they could barely hear Owl, they heard thump, thump, thump . . . thump, thump . . . thump, thump, thump, thump . . . thump.

Owl finally got tired and came back down to earth and said, "I don't know what that was up there, but I stayed up there as long as I could. I finally got tired. I don't know what that was."

The animals were really sad this time: "We sent Eagle up and we sent Owl up and neither one of them could figure out what happened to the sun!" They started to scream and yell, and it was loud.

Through all the noise a little voice said, "I'll go find out what happened to the sun."

Up walked the smallest bird that there is. It was Hummingbird. All the animals were laughing and crying at the same time. They pointed at Hummingbird: "We sent the largest, most powerful bird, and we sent the smartest bird, and Hummingbird thinks she's gonna go up and find out what happened to the sun?"

And the chief said, "Wait a minute. Give her a chance. Let's see what happens."

Well, Hummingbird left the earth, but you couldn't hear her and you couldn't see her. So the animals stood there to see what was going to happen. They stood there a long, long time, and then they stood there longer.

Finally the animals started to give up on her and said, "She must have gotten lost in the darkness." The animals started to wail and cry again.

Someone in the crowd said, "Wait! Look up there!"

And way up in the sky was a little prick of light, and then right next to that one was another prick of light and another one next to that and another one and another one. Hummingbird was sticking her beak through the blanket. She stayed up there a long time, and pretty soon there were lights all across the sky.

She flew back down to earth and said, "Somebody threw a blanket over the sun."

All the animals were relieved, "Oh, that's no problem. We can take care of that." Then the animals looked up in that sky and saw how beautiful it was. They decided during that council meeting, "Half the day we will have the sun, but this sky is so beautiful that we're gonna share it with the rest of the world." So the other half of the day, they share the night sky, and those were the first stars.

That was the first story, and after I heard it that night, I told that story to my two kids; they just went . . . [Tom gives an openmouthed, wide-eyed expression and laughs.] So it was cool, and getting around a campfire . . . there's a world of difference.

You want to hear another one? We were talking about a creation story earlier. It's funny. When I go tell stories, most of the groups are school groups. A lot of schools call me, and I'll look at the stories and decide which ones I'm gonna work with because of the age groups and things like that. I tell this story to older groups of kids, usually fifth grade and older just because of what's involved. Well, it's just that type of story, you know. I just like to take my time with it. Well, you'll see.

It's a story that takes place when the earth is totally covered by water, and the only animals living on earth are all water animals, including the birds, ducks, and swans. The water animals, like beavers and muskrats, are able to live there as well.

Way above the earth, there are people. They're called the Sky People. The wife of the chief of the Sky People wakes up one morning. She looks at her husband and says, "I had a very powerful dream last night. I dreamed about the large tree in the middle of our village. The tree was uprooted." Chief looked at her and said, "Sounds like it was a very powerful dream, and these dreams are important. I think we need to pull up the tree and see what happens." So the chief calls all the villagers together. A couple of the warriors come over, and he says, "We need to pull this tree up." The warriors try and try and can't get the tree out. Finally the chief just pushes them aside, wraps his arms around the tree, and in one big tug, pulls the tree out by its roots and lays it down. It created a hole. Sky Woman goes over, and she's lookin' down in the hole. Way far down, she sees earth, and it's covered with water. It's way down there. She grabs one of the tree branches and starts leaning out over the hole so she can get a better view. When she does, her hand slips off the branch, and she falls into the hole and begins falling to earth.

All the animals down on earth are swimming around when one of the birds flies down and starts raising an alarm that one of the Sky People is falling to earth. Some of the animals start collecting around and said, "Well, what's gonna happen to her? We need to send someone to get her. She's not gonna be able to live here." They call over two of the swans and say, "Go up and get Sky Woman. Help her come down to earth." The two swans go up and they grab Sky Woman. The animals are looking around: "There's nowhere for her to stand. This is all water. She's not a water animal." One of the animals said, "You know, I've heard that way far underneath the ocean, there's dirt down there. If we bring some of that dirt up, maybe it will give her a place to stand." The rest answered, "Okay, yeah, that sounds like a good plan."

Well, up swam Duck, and the animals said, "Well, Duck's a good swimmer. Why don't we send Duck down to get some of the dirt and bring it back up?" Duck dives under the water and starts to swim and swim and swim. He goes as deep as he possibly can, and his lungs start to just ache. He keeps going and keeps going, and finally he just can't take it anymore. He swims back to the top and says, "I'm sorry. That's too far for me."

Otter swam over and says, "I'll do it." Otter does the same thing—dives under the water and swims and swims and swims, gets deeper and deeper and deeper. The same thing again. His lungs start to ache; he keeps going and keeps going, really just pushes himself. He can't make it, so he finally gives in and he comes back up. "That's way too deep for me."

Up swims Muskrat. This is what I like about these stories: It's always the underdog. Up swims Muskrat, you know, and the animals say, "Muskrat's not gonna make it. He's not a very strong swimmer."

To this, Muskrat says, "Give me a chance."

So Muskrat dives under the water. He swims and swims and swims. The same thing starts happening to Muskrat. His lungs start to ache until he just can't take it anymore, but he keeps going. He swims and swims, and he passes out. Just when he passed out, he reached his hand out and grabbed the bottom. He floated back to the top of the ocean and pops up. He's unconscious, and the animals said, "Well, he didn't make it . . . Well, look, he's got something in his hand." Sure enough, he opens his hand, and they said, "That's great. We got some dirt, but what are we gonna do with it?"

Someone says, "Well, let's put it on Turtle's back. That will give a place for

PLATE 183 Muskrat, though not as strong a swimmer as others,
swims and swims until his lungs start to ache;
he reaches out his hand and grabs the bottom.
*(illustration by Jessica Wilson)*

the Sky Woman to stand." Turtle swims over, and they put the dirt on Turtle's back.

When they did that, the land started to spread and started to grow and started to cover the water. It became a great place for Sky Woman to stand. The swans brought Sky Woman down to the land that was still growing, and when they put her down, she opened her hands. When she had slid off of that branch, she grabbed a lot of the seeds and leaves. When she opened her hand, all those seeds dropped onto the ground, and as soon as they did, they started to grow, and those started to spread across the land. Those seeds were the first plants and the first trees on the earth. That's the story of how our first land developed and where our plants and trees came from.

I like telling them all. Because I have so much experience outside with kids, I have true stories that I tell. I've got a couple of experiences with animals included 'cause, you know, I'm the type of camper who sleeps outside. I usually don't take a tent, and if I do, it's usually a tarp for if it rains.

**"I decided I was gonna sit up and keep an eye out for the bear. One of the reasons was I had a kid in camp that had candy in his hair [laugh], and, I'm thinkin', to the bear this is gonna be a big ol' lollipop."**

Let me preface this with this real quick story because it's fairly new. It happened last year, not this last year but the school year before this. Actually, one of the kids that's going to New Mexico with us was with me the night that this happened. It was down in Standing Indian, below Franklin [North Carolina]. When we set up camp and things, I talk to the kids about controlling their food because the food is what attracts the animals. I had six boys from Smoky Mountain Elementary School. We were there at Hurricane Creek at the horse camp. I think it was the end of winter because there weren't a lot of people there, and it was gonna be cool that night. I looked at them and said, "Control your food. Don't drop it on the ground." Well, after we've been there a while, I'm noticing that there's soda cans everywhere, and they're spilling soda. Then one of the boys was lying outside of his tent. He had fallen asleep, and it wasn't dark yet. A couple of the other kids got together and poured liquid candy in his hair. I think I know who it was. As a matter of fact, he is going with us, too. I got two kids from this group going with us tomorrow.

So I'm sitting there: "Go wash it out as best you can." Well, as it starts getting dark, we've got our fire there, and I decided that I'm gonna go through the other firepits and see what other wood I can find. I walk across a field, look over, and about probably thirty feet from me, there's a black bear. My first thought was if I go back and tell the boys there's a bear in camp, we're gonna end up in the van headed home. I go back to camp and say, "Okay, get your food together. Get everything off the ground. We just need to put all the trash and all the food in the vans." I didn't tell them that there was a bear there, and what's funny is, every single one of them ended up sleeping outside their tents by the fireplace. I don't know how that happened, but here we were around the fireplace. I decided I was gonna sit up and keep an eye out for the bear. One of the reasons was I had a kid in camp that had candy in his hair [laugh], and I'm thinkin', to the bear this is gonna be a big ol' lollipop. I'm sitting there in a chair that one of the kids had brought, keeping the fire up most of the night. I nod off a couple of times during the night, and all through the night, I'd wake up and turn around; there'd be the bear lickin' the soda out of the ground. The coolest part of the night was at three o'clock in the morning: The fire is real low, and I wake up. I look across, and the bear wasn't even ten feet away. It was the coolest experience looking in that bear's eyes. I always say we shared a couple of seconds of an experience, that bear and I did. I was sitting there looking at him. It just created a warm, neat feeling in me sharing that time with that bear. He stood there and looked at me for a couple of seconds and then walked on out of camp. I thought it was really great.

I preface this next story with that because, about ten years ago, we had an experience with a bear that wasn't quite as friendly. I had a group of six boys, twelve to fourteen years old. One of the boys that was in that particular group came up through the program and actually worked with us as one of the employees for two years. He just recently graduated from Warren Wilson College with a degree in outdoor education. That's part of the reason I like telling the story.

PLATE 184 Right across the creek, the bear was standing there looking at him.
(*illustration by Jessica Wilson*)

## "When there's no cage, they look huge, and this was a big bear!"

This one happened in Slickrock Wilderness down below Robbinsville [North Carolina]. There's a great place down there, about a two-mile hike. The first mile is all downhill and then a mile along the creek to a place called Wildcat Falls. There's two waterfalls, and the upper waterfall drops into a pool. It's a great place to swim and things like that. Coming out's a killer 'cause you get that mile-shot uphill. I took those kids out there to Wildcat Falls, went in, and set up camp. I sent 'em down to the waterhole, and I said, "I'll be down there in a minute." I had to go up in the woods and take care of some stuff. As I was walking up, I looked, and right next to a tree there was a huge bear. He was standing on his hind legs, and you know, being out in the woods, they look bigger. When there's no cage, they look huge, and this was a big bear! I'm used to seeing bears in the park, and, you know, generally, they're smaller, but I bet you this was a 250-pound bear! He was big!

I slowly backed down and went back to camp. I told the kids, "There's a bear in the area. We got to get the food rounded up in the trees." So we did that, and then we went about our business the rest of the evening, had our dinner, and went down for bed. We had a thunderstorm coming through late in the evening, so I was in the tent.

About one o'clock in the morning, I heard the bear snuffling around out in the camp. My general rule is if I'm by myself and I hear an animal, I'll just leave it alone, but I had these six other boys with me. So I went out to see what was going on. I had one of those Mini Maglites where the light goes about a foot. I stuck my head out the tent, and I was looking around. I didn't see anything. So I crawled out of the tent, and I stood up. *Grrrrrrrrr!* It was a growl right in my ear! Scared the pooh out of me! [Laugh]

There were still some coals in the fire, and this was one of the fastest fires I have ever built in my life—apoof, apoof, apoof, apoof, apoofa! Throwing wood on there! I had the fire, and I looked over. There was a tree right outside my tent, and the bear was about three feet off the ground in the tree. So I'm sitting there, and I got the fire built up. I see where the bear is, and the boys start coming out of their tents. They said, "Tom, what'd you scream about?" I don't remember screaming! [Laugh] I said, "There's a bear here!" We grabbed up a big cookpot and a spoon, and I started banging on it— yelling at the bear. He finally came down out of the tree and went out the back side of the campsite.

Here's me and the six boys standing on one side of the fire, and we've got all our flashlights out there to see where the bear has gone. Well, the bear went out one side of the campsite, went around behind us, and then growled again and charged into camp! I swear, all seven of us *floated* across to the other side of the fire! It scared the pooh out of us! When he charged in, he went up a tree right outside the camp, so we spent the rest of the night . . . all the kids brought the sleeping bags out, and I stayed up all night long. It was the most aggressive bear I've ever dealt with in my life. I mean, he scared me initially because of that first charge, but the pot and the spoon was scaring him away. I stayed up all night long. He'd disappear, come back in, disappear, come back in. We got up when the sun finally came up. I said, "You know, we just need to get out of here." We started loading up our stuff. In almost a perfect circle around camp, the bear had been going out and eating leaves off of the bushes. It was almost every bush in a perfect circle in the campsite. I remember this was a drought year, and that's one of the theories. That bear was down where we were because there was just no food for them anywhere else.

### "Right across the creek the bear was standing there looking at him."

So we're getting ready to go, and Julian, the kid that I talked about that graduated from Warren Wilson College, went down to the creek to get some water. We're getting ready to go, throwing our packs on, and we hear Julian go, "*Tom!*" He's high-stepping through the woods, headed right toward us. When he went down to get the water out of the creek, he bent down, and he looked up. Right across the creek, the bear was standing there looking at him. We pulled our stuff together and finally just got out of there, and we were wired when we were walking out.

What's really cool about that night is probably about a year ago, one of the kids that was in that group walked up to me. He had his two daughters in tow; they were toddlers. He looked at me and said, "You remember that night that that bear harassed us all night long?" And I answered, "Yeah, I sure do." Every kid, whenever I see one of them—they're young adults now—they say, "Remember that night when that bear just wouldn't leave us alone?" Yeah, I do.

# SUMMER CAMPS

"Camp was a great place, a place that provided
and encouraged character-building."

—*Archie Griffin*

O ne of the toughest tasks in life is to hold a child's attention. All of us who are parents know exactly how trying and taxing this feat can be. Nowadays, children can pursue so many avenues to entertain themselves: video games, Little League sports, computer games, the Internet, television, movies. The list could go on and on. Forty or fifty years ago, times were different. Many children had to work, and work was just something to which folks in that generation were accustomed. In those times, money was hard to come by, and of course, some folks had no television until the 1960s. Little League baseball has been around, but many small, rural counties, such as Rabun, haven't always had it, and folks who lived in the cities wanted their children to experience the great outdoors.

One form of entertainment at the end of the school year was summer camps. Various kinds of camps—Boy and Girl Scout camps, YMCA camps, 4-H camps, church camps, sports camps—enabled youths to venture from home and participate in varied activities, learn new skills and crafts, and have fun. The camp experience also instilled in the participants a sense of independence and aided in the child's maturation. Many had never been away from home; now they would learn to make their beds, do laundry, and participate in cleanup detail. Children could also learn about the outdoors through canoeing, kayaking, and hiking.

With all its creeks, streams, and lakes, along with its mountains and trails, Rabun County was a perfect location for summer camp. A structured day, packed with activities, kept the camper busy—too busy to have idle hands or become homesick. Raymond Woodall elaborates: "When you're off doing things you like, you don't get homesick . . . I didn't know what homesickness was at camp."

This section profiles three camps that were in Rabun County: Camp Dixie, Red Barron's Camp, and Camp Pinnacle. Camp Dixie for Boys was located in southern Rabun County, in the community of Wiley. Jeff Davis explains that Camp Dixie "was not officially a Christian camp, but it was probably as much a Christian camp as they have now . . . It probably had more Christian values back in those days, more than they do now." Camp Dixie was also known for its outdoor activities. Campers hiked to Lake Rabun and Lake Burton and participated in many different competitive sports. They also completed crafts and performed skits. Sometimes cabins competed. Rutherford Ellis, a former camp participant, describes the competition: "In cabin competition you got points for winning basketball games, baseball games, and kickball games. If your cabin didn't pass inspection or if you had some misbehavin' with something, they would take points off . . . The cabin with the most points would win."

In Mountain City, just north of Clayton, Georgia, was Red Barron's Camp. Red Barron, an All-American football player at Georgia Tech, owned it, so naturally his camp focused on sports, but campers could participate in many other activities. Mike Hunter recalls, "Some people thought it was an all-sports camp, but it wasn't. We had periods like you have in high school. We could choose what we would do each day. They had a lot of activities: photography, crafts, taxidermy, swimming, canoeing, riflery, and archery." So Red Barron's Camp was much like Camp Dixie for Boys.

Camp Pinnacle, located off of Warwoman Road in Clayton, was initially Camp Sequoia, a Boy Scout camp. When I originally began an article on Camp Pinnacle years ago, I did not know that a Boy Scout camp was there first. Today, the Georgia Baptist Women's Missionary Union supports the camp, Christian in nature and philosophy. The cinder-block cabins, now refurbished, and the small, white, steepled church nestled in the pines edge a placid lake and provide an atmosphere of peacefulness. Many Camp Pinnacle participants speak of a closeness to each other and to God.

Many of these camps underwent a metamorphosis. Camp Dixie for Boys later combined with Camp Dixie for Girls on Germany Mountain in Rabun County. The original Camp Dixie for Boys camp was abandoned, but years later, the Atlanta Braves bought it and used it as a training camp. I don't know how many years they used it, nor do I know who owns that property now. Red Barron's Camp later became Camp Come-Be-Gay. When I was a child, growing up in the 1980s and early 1990s, it was known as Blue Ridge Camp. Although several summer camps operate in Rabun County today, these, here since the early 1950s, have a part in our earlier history.

Some campers' lives underwent a change as a result of their summer experiences. As adults, a few even moved here because of their discovering Rabun County when they were at camp. Mike Hunter explains why he came back to Rabun County: "I was a city boy, so I learned to love the outdoors, hiking, fishing, and animals. I learned all of that up here. Atlanta didn't have too much of that. A lot of the guys that came were city guys that really learned a lot about the mountains. I liked it so well that I knew one day I wanted to live here, and now I do. It's beautiful. It had a big impact on my life."

—*Robbie Bailey*

# CAMP DIXIE

*"Camp Dixie was a great place, a place that provided*
*and encouraged character-building in boys."*
— Archie Griffin

I nterviewing Mr. Rutherford (Ruddy) Ellis and Mr. Jeff Davis for my article on Camp Dixie for Boys was an experience I will not soon forget. I have always been curious about Rabun County's historic camps and houses. When I heard about this interview opportunity, I did not hesitate to start making phone calls. This is only the second article I had done for *The Foxfire Magazine*, and I had never interviewed two people at one time before. I was quite nervous. As soon as I met them, my nerves were immediately calmed. Both gentlemen greeted me with a smile. They were extremely friendly and seemed comfortable with being interviewed. I've known people to run from cameras and tape recorders, but Mr. Ellis and Mr. Davis just smiled and spoke in their naturally strong voices. Suddenly I was really looking forward to this interview.

When they entered the room laughing and joking with each other, I could tell that Mr. Ellis and Mr. Davis had been friends for a long time. They both seemed excited to talk about old memories of Camp Dixie. One of the years they attended camp together was an interesting year for all. It was the summer of 1942—right before the beginning of World War II.

It was an exceptional interview! The only statement I had to make was "Tell me about Camp Dixie for Boys." They started at the beginning, and by the time they had finished, I had a full sixty-minute tape of interesting stories. Every question I had prepared to ask, they had answered.

Their stories were about everything from getting hit in the mouth with a baseball to picking up cow pies in the pasture. Stories of the past have always intrigued me, and the story of Camp Dixie is no exception. Camp Dixie for Boys no longer exists. It has combined with Camp Dixie for Girls on Germany Mountain in Rabun County, where it is presently located. Though the original camp is gone, the memories of others who spent summers there will endure.

— *Emili Davis*

An interview with Ernest Jones from one of the earlier *Foxfire Magazine* articles also helped portray the life of Camp Dixie for Boys. Mr. Jones provided information about working at Camp Dixie and about the dining hall there that was named after him. Also, Mr. Archie Griffin sent us a letter describing what he did at Camp Dixie and how it really impacted his life. Camp Dixie was a special place for both the campers and the workers that were there.

*—Robbie Bailey*

**Jeff Davis:** Camp Dixie for Boys is located in Wiley, Georgia.

**Archie Griffin:** When I was five years old, my father died, and my mother felt that my older brother and I should be under the direction of men and [be] with boys. A family friend had sent their son to Camp Dixie and highly recommended it. In the summer of 1940, my brother and I went to Camp Dixie for two months.

Pop J., one of the authors of *The Boy Scout Handbook,* was the head of the camp when I went there in 1940. He was A. A. Jameson. Although [he was] very stern but fair, all the campers learned a lot from his leadership. He died about 1945.

Dr. Alfred Scott, Pop J.'s longtime assistant, then ran the camp. He was head of the Chemistry Department at the University of Georgia. What Camp Dixie stood for didn't change under Scottie. He was still running the camp my last year in 1951.

**Ernest Jones:** W. A. Sutton, Ed Jameson, and P. H. Quenshaw [started Camp Dixie for Boys]. I reckon they named it Camp Dixie at the start. Now old man Jameson, he was a scout man before they built this camp. That's how come he built it. Never knew how much the camp cost to build, but it wasn't like it is now. When they started off there was 635 acres. But now there's been a little corner sold off. First I ever knowed, Spark Ramey owned the land the camp was built on. Spark, now he was named something else, but I think Spark was his nickname. Before that, though, I believe all that country back in yonder belonged to the Worleys. I believe they owned three or four large land lots in there. But how Spark got ahold of it, I don't know. I reckon the land was bought for the camp in 1912 or 1913. I'd say Ed Jameson didn't give over five or six dollars an acre. I don't know how much the camp paid for it altogether.

Ed Jameson was the first owner. Before he died, he willed the whole thing to Scotty and his three boys. Scotty was his first name, and I don't know what

PLATE 185 Assistant camp director Alfred Scott Sr.

his last name was. He wasn't related to Jameson that I know of, but he came here with Jameson when Jameson first took the camp and stayed with him. Well, then Carlos Kotilla bought the camp; he also ran Camp Dixie for Girls in Clayton, until he sold it to Ann Taylor. She's been there five or six or seven years, somewhere along in there. Then Kotilla sold Camp Dixie for Boys to Sonny Mayor, but later Kotilla had to take the whole thing back. The Atlanta Braves baseball team bought it for a training camp, but I don't know what year they did. All the papers were drawed up and fixed right there on my dining room table. Well, the Braves recently sold it. I ain't got into that yet.

**Rutherford (Ruddy) Ellis:** Yeah, it's in Wiley, Georgia. You go up the old highway, say, coming from Lakemont. You go past the little community of Wiley, and then you kind of go down a road a little way. On the right was the big Wiley Scott's Trestle on the Tallulah Falls Railroad. Right there, there's a little road comin' in on the side, and I believe that road's paved now. It was dirt then. There was a sign there that said CAMP DIXIE FOR BOYS. You'd go down that dirt road a mile or so, and you'd pass by some farmhouses. That road led on up into areas farther in the little valley there where there were people living. You'd go down that road and you'd kind of bear to the left and you'd go down to Worley Creek. The camp was located in the bottomlands of Worley Creek, although the mountain behind the cabins went straight up.

**Mr. Davis:** The Chattahoochee National Forest was on one side of us, I recall.

**Mr. Ellis:** It was north and west of the camp. If you follow the creek, you'll end up in Lakemont—if you go downstream. If you go past there, you'll go on to Tiger. But it's located in really a beautiful place. [Wiley, Lakemont, and Tiger are towns on the south side of Rabun County in Northeast Georgia.]

**Mr. Jones:** I think most of the people in Wiley liked the camp, all right. Back when it started up there, why they bought all the vegetables from people in the settlement. We used to sell vegetables right out of the gardens. But, in later years, the camp didn't buy stuff from the people here. The camp was a help to the people.

**Mr. Davis:** I went to Camp Dixie before the war, and they would take us places on school buses then, but in '42, when Ruddy was up there, I don't remember ever going anywhere because the gasoline was rationed during World War II. Anywhere we couldn't walk, I don't think we went.

**Mr. Ellis:** The big thing about the years we're mainly talking about, which was 1942 and so forth, was it was wartime, so you couldn't travel a lot. Gas was rationed, you couldn't get tires, you couldn't get new cars, and trains were real crowded with troops and all. Also, we didn't have any interaction with anybody outside the camp because we were quarantined for polio. The airline traffic was not much in those days. There wasn't a whole lot of people traveling by air. What parents would do is send their children off to camp, I guess, 'cause there really wasn't much else for them to do. You couldn't take a vacation and go anywhere. I got sent up to Camp Dixie, and my sister went to Camp Laurel Falls up in Clayton [the county seat of Rabun County]. It was exciting times for us. They sent a bunch of old coaches down to Atlanta to pick us up. They were from the Atlanta Terminal Station, I think. They brought us up to Cornelia on one of the Southern Railroad trains, and then they switched those cars over onto the Tallulah Falls Railroad, which took us up to Wiley. Somebody said they thought it might have been Lakemont.

PLATE 186  Leader Jack Hook instructs members of
cabin 10 on the proper stance for a dash.

**Mr. Davis:** I think it was Lakemont.

**Mr. Ellis:** It was either Lakemont or Wiley. It was someplace where the
school buses could meet us. We loaded all our gear on these school buses,
and they took us to the camp. I think my folks came and picked me up at the
end of camp that year. They probably could've scrounged up enough gas
and tires to get up there once during the summer. Until then, for about
eight weeks, we were away from our folks. We didn't have much in the way
of visitors. People just didn't travel then. Of course we did get a little
wartime news. We weren't all that interested in the war. There was one little
kid who was from Cairo, Georgia, and one time, when the newspaper came
out, Cairo, Egypt, had been bombed. We showed this newspaper to him and
said, "Hey, look, your home's been bombed!" He went for it for a few minutes, but he eventually figured out it was Cairo, Egypt, not Georgia. I don't
remember playing with war toys either. We didn't get a bit obsessed with the
war going on.

Camp Dixie was owned and run by A. A. Jameson, who we called Pop J.
He was sort of the father figure 'cause he was much older than us, and that's
probably why we called him that. He insisted on everything being done his
way. So when it came to building a fire, we had to build it his way; singing
the songs, he made us sing *his* songs.

**Mr. Griffin:** We left Valdosta at midnight on the train arriving in Atlanta at 8:00 A.M. We were met by Dixie officials at the station. A big deal for a little boy was being taken to downtown Atlanta to the S&W Cafeteria. Around noon, we boarded a train for Cornelia, where we changed to the Tallulah Falls train to go to Wiley.

On the trip from Cornelia, the leaders rounded up their campers. From Wiley, a "yellow dog" bus took us to camp. The only sign at the camp entrance was 441. It was about two miles from the highway into camp. The first thing you saw was Sweet Pea Cabin, home of Pop J. while he was at camp. Following that were ballfields, the Cow Pen, Chapel Island, tennis courts, dining hall, business office, infirmary, and staff cabins. The Cow Pen was our place for skits, storytelling, etc.

**Mr. Davis:** We had to sing Camp Dixie songs. You didn't sing all the songs that were popular; he didn't want 'em. For example, you couldn't sing other camp-type songs like you'd sing on retreats and things like that. He always wanted Camp Dixie songs.

**Mr. Ellis:** Most of the Camp Dixie tunes were old World War I tunes. He was getting fairly old in the forties. When he died, he was buried in Jameson Cemetery, which is up Worley Creek near Wiley. I think George Scott, Sr., from the University of Georgia, was second in command. His son, George, was about our age, so we got to know George pretty well. He was a very good athlete. He looked like he had a little Indian blood in him. There were some other older people on the staff, too, but we had more contact with the leaders, who were mostly college students. When we first got to Camp Dixie, we were given a sheet of rules like you've got in school. You know, "You don't do this and this." It was cleverly done with just keepin' you busy all the time. You didn't have time to think of other things to do.

**Mr. Davis:** Actually, George Scott, Sr., was a very famous basketball player in Georgia. He was known as the Georgia Peach, somewhere long before my time. I think Pop J. just had a knack for making friends with people and then getting them to come to his camp and help. He got outstanding people. Some were from the University of Georgia, some of them were athletes there, and some were just people who liked camp.

**Mr. Ellis:** I think Jeff said about nine to fourteen years old was the age span. I went there when I was twelve and thirteen years old. My family has a real tradition in camps. My grandparents were associated with a camp in Maine. Two of my nephews went there. I did go to a camp in North Carolina when

I was ten. That camp was sponsored by the Episcopal church. Camp Dixie sent out a lot of brochures. I don't know whether they sent them out to schools or other groups, but they were well known. I went to New England the next year, and then the next two years I went to Camp Dixie. Jeff and I learned to walk together. We lived right next to each other. We had old 16-millimeter black-and-white movies of us and our dads learning how to walk together.

**Mr. Davis:** I went from '38 to '42. I was a leader in 1941. As a leader I supervised the cabin. You just had to entertain them. You made sure they got fed. We had devotions every night in the cabin. You just had to take care of the boys. I think I got paid twenty-five dollars. We didn't get paid much but I liked it and it was fun. I started when I was nine years old and went until I was fourteen 'cause I really enjoyed it up there. My brother went to Athens Y Camp. Camp Dixie and Athens Y Camp were the big camps in Georgia at that time. You got to see some of the people who came back every year. You had some old friends. It was just a good thing to do in the summertime. My parents had to work in the summertime, so I really liked Camp Dixie.

PLATE 187 Jeff Davis

**Mr. Griffin:** I was a leader at Dixie for two years. It was a great experience working with young boys to reach the common goal of being the best you can be. We never won Honor Cabin, but we surely worked hard on it.

I met a lot of boys during my twelve years at camp. They came mostly from the South—even as far away as Texas. I have not kept up with any specifically, but I am always running into someone I knew at camp. A large number of boys from Valdosta attended.

**Mr. Ellis:** Most of the boys were from medium-sized towns like Valdosta and Athens, and of course, the only city was Atlanta. I don't think that we had any farmer-type people. I think it was more of the city boys that needed to get out.

**Mr. Davis:** A lot of people were from Athens because Dr. Scott was at the University of Georgia.

Luther Turpin built this whole camp. I say he did, but he supervised it. He did a lot of it by himself. This was a big official-size gym, and they even had ten feet on each side. He put the top on it, and, you know, he didn't have any formal engineer training or anything like that. He finished it, and Pop J. had some structural engineer come from Atlanta to see if it would stay up there. The man said, "That will stay up forever because Mr. Turpin used twice as much wood as needed. It will never come down."

## DESCRIPTION

**"We called the privy 'the lighthouse' because it was the only place you had lights at night. The lantern would burn all night."**
*—Rutherford (Ruddy) Ellis*

**Mr. Ellis:** The cabins were very rustic. They were connected by a covered walkway all the way from the lake up to the big gym. The gym, all the cabins, and the dining hall were connected by covered walkways with tin roofs so that on a rainy day you could go to all different areas without gettin' outdoors. We had tin roofs but no screens. Of course the back of the cabin was solid. The front was open to the walkway that came by. There was one little place where you could walk in right off the walkway, and then the bunks were nothing more than just a set of springs, which were mounted on wood. There were not any beds per se. You just had these bunks. I think there

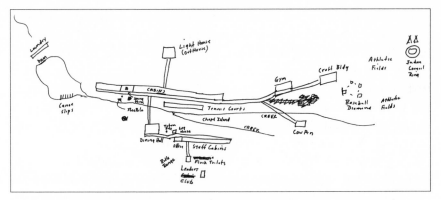

PLATE 188  Map of Camp Dixie, drawn by Rutherford Ellis and Jeff Davis

were two in the front, two on each side, two in the back; and then there was kind of a crow's nest up high in the back. Those beds, they just sat up there, and if you pushed one over a little ways, it would drop off. At night they would hang a kerosene lantern on the stairs going up to the eight-holer [bathroom] outside. We called the privy "the lighthouse" because it was the only place you had lights at night. The lantern would burn all night, so if you had to go in the middle of the night, you could go up there to that area.

**Mr. Griffin:** The campers' cabins were in a long line with a covered board-walk in front that ran from cabin 1 to cabin 25. The walk also went to the gym and the Cow Pen, as well as the springhouse.

All the cabins were alike. The leader's bunk was always on the right of the opening. There were two bunks on each side and three in the back. [In] my early years [I] saw no electricity: Only kerosene lamps were used. Each cabin held eight boys and one leader. The cabins were open in the front and on both sides with tin roofs. When it rained, canvas tarps were rolled down to keep out the rain.

**Mr. Jones:** The camp's buildings were built out of rough mountain lum-ber—mostly pine and a little oak. Oh, Lord, there's a lot of wood in the camp—guess there's 200,000 board feet. There's lots of buildings over there and lots of lumber in 'em. We cut the logs off of the camp property and had them sawed right over there at E. B. Lovell's in Wiley. The gym up there alone has 22,000 board feet in it. For foundation pillars we used some rock, but most of 'em was made of locust poles. For flooring we used nothing but rough pine lumber—whatever length of board that we could get. Practically every bit of wood was pine. For the roofs, at first we used roll roofing. It gave out, and we put tin across it when we rebuilt the cabins.

The sleeping cabins had curtains for walls when they were first built; then, after we put up walls, we used screening on the windows and rough pine doors. There's only one office. It's got paneling on the inside, but all the framing and everything is made from pine boards—but it has or did have a hardwood floor in it. Each cabin slept about five or six children, but they could put eight in them after they rebuilt the cabins. The cabin used to be open around the sides; in the summertime, they would put curtains on them, and you could roll up the curtains on poles. The campers were "scrouged" up too much, and we tore all of the cabins down to the floor and added four feet to 'em and roofed 'em all up a different way. Every one [of them] has been remodeled—but that's been done several years ago. There are some other cabins up above the dining hall that were built for boys, but they kept getting less and less campers—didn't have enough boys to fill them up. So they put the cooks up there, and the cooks stayed up there several years. If they needed the cabins for boys, they would put boys up there. The coaches stayed here and yonder—they didn't all stay together. Plenty of the sleeping cabins have bathrooms, but there's not one for every cabin. On the back side of the sleeping cabin line, there's two bathhouses. Each one of 'em has got four commodes in it. The buildings up there in the holler had a bathroom apiece, and another bathhouse had three commodes and two showers.

They had one cabin, and we rounded up about fourteen bunks in there. That's where Jameson whipped the boys at. He would make them go to bed and make them stay in bed all day long if they done something he had to punish them for. 'Course, now, on some things, he wouldn't make them stay that long. But for some things he would make them stay all day long. And of course, they had to have somebody in there with them—one of their coaches had to stay in there with them. In one sense he was punishing the coach, too!

**Mr. Davis:** We didn't have any electricity on that side of the camp. All the electricity was on the other side for the dining hall, the office, the infirmary, and places like that. Since then, they've modernized the cabins with screens and electricity and things.

**Mr. Ellis:** Staff quarters had electricity. Everything was kerosene lanterns over on the campers' side. Like I said, the cabins were very rustic. The only water we had was one pipe that ran down behind the cabins, and each cabin had a faucet. It was just one long pipe, so by the time it got down to the end, if all the faucets were on, you didn't have any water. It just kind of dripped out. Yet you had to brush your teeth, and later, you had to meet the inspection requirements with clean fingernails, hands, face, and hair and all. So a lot of the time, what we'd have to do is, we'd have to store up a little water. We'd get a bucket or something, and in the middle of the night, we'd fill up the bucket so we'd have water, 'cause you really couldn't depend on having any water at all in the morning. You could go down to the creek. Creeks in those days were pretty pollution-free. You could go down to the creek and wash your face and brush your teeth. There were no flush toilets in the cabins either.

The lake was just a simple dam on Worley Creek. The water was ice cold, so you didn't stay in there very long. You'd come out of the water with your lips blue.

**Mr. Jones:** The lake was just a creek at first; then we built the dam and made it a lake. When we built it, we got the sand to make the concrete out of the creek—dished it out with a shovel. And . . . one man, all he done was, when they were pouring the concrete, was roll the sand over to the mixer. And they had one man on the rock pile and he'd beat the rock and roll 'em down to the mixer. There was five of us workin', and five of us built that dam. Then we built the dock after the dam was built. The bridges across the creek are made of hickory. Bridges aren't hard to build. I built the ones up by the dining hall, then built a roof over it. It's a footbridge. You can't cross it with a car. It's not wide enough.

**Mr. Davis:** Let me tell you 'bout the dining hall. The dining hall was just this big screened-in building. It had tables in it, and every cabin had an assigned table. Back in those days, money would buy a lot of things.

PLATE 189 The lake at Camp Dixie

The story was that Pop J. wanted to decorate the dining hall, and he sent word out all over Rabun County: He'd pay ten cents a hornets' nest to anybody who could bring one in. He probably thought he wouldn't get too many, but I guess there were a hundred hornets' nests hanging from the ceiling. They were just tied on a string to the rafters. It was just decoration. He just wanted to decorate the dining hall with hornets' nests. That was a pretty interesting place.

**Mr. Jones:** I didn't build the Ernest Jones Dining Hall by myself, but I worked lots on it by myself. It's made just like all the other buildings, made out of pine. When the camp first started to run, for, God knows, fifty years, we had wood tables. We built the tables and benches and had four benches to a table: two small ones to go at the end, and two long ones for the sides. They've got metal tables in there now. They didn't have no refrigerator in the beginning. They kept stuff cool in the spring box. The spring box was made of concrete, and fresh water was coming into it. It's awful cold water and awful hard water, hardest water I know of anywhere. I guess the spring would hold several hundred gallons of water, and they had places fixed so they could put pots of food and things in there to keep it cool.

**Mr. Ellis:** One of the outstanding features of the camp was the huge gymnasium. That was probably the best built, loveliest building in the whole camp. There was a local builder, and he reinforced that roof like you wouldn't believe! It was reinforced to withstand two feet of snow.

**Mr. Griffin:** The gym was a magnificent structure. I believe it was built by Luther Turpin, the camp handyman, and some of his helpers. It was used constantly: basketball, volleyball, and badminton. I doubt if any camp had a better gym.

**Mr. Davis:** There was a fellow up there, just an old mountain fellow, and he's the one that built all the cabins and everything. His name was Luther Turpin, I remember. Anyway, Luther Turpin, he did all the major repairs around the camp, and he built his gymnasium, and [it] didn't have any posts. It was freestanding, and it must have been a hundred feet long.

**Mr. Ellis:** It was bigger than a basketball court!

**Mr. Davis:** Yeah, it was bigger than a basketball court. He built this roof with no plans. In other words, Pop J. just said, "Luther, I want you to build a gym-thing yourself." I think he probably told him to build it and the dimensions. Other than that, he built it with no plans or anything. He built this freestanding building with no posts in the center or no posts on the sides, but it did have walls.

**Mr. Ellis:** There were great big tree trunks for posts. The trusses that held the roof up were just elaborate. They were really much stronger than they needed to be.

**Mr. Davis:** A lot of the trusses were just a lot of triangles up there. So Pop J. got to worryin' about it—that, you know, maybe this roof might fall down. I mean, it really was a work of art. So he got some architect from Atlanta to come to the camp and look at it and see if it was safe. The architect, all he said was, "That roof will be there a long time after you're gone." He said, "He used so much wood up there with all those trusses that it's never gonna fall down."

Back in those days, people were a lot more independent. Up in this part of Georgia, they're still more independent. Up in the mountains, people are a lot more independent than they are in Atlanta. If people in Atlanta want something done, well, call a plumber—call someone else to do it. Up here, especially back in those days, because there wasn't many roads up here and there wasn't many stores for supplies, you just kind of had to fix everything yourself. Mr. Turpin was just one of those mountain people who didn't have any formal training in how to build stuff. He just had enough common sense, or he had built enough stuff, that he was able to build this huge gymnasium with no posts. That was pretty amazin'.

**Mr. Ellis:** It was very impressive! You'd look up at that structure and say, "Wow!" He's so typical of local craftsmen.

**Mr. Jones:** The gym is built of pine. We put a basket for basketball up at each end; then the Atlanta Braves, I think it was, put some baskets up crossways. And there is outside tennis courts and some soccer fields on the upper end. And they had some baseball fields to play on.

**Mr. Davis:** I think Mr. Turpin built a concrete dam for one of the lakes. It was originally a wooden dam out of logs; one spring or something, there was a huge rain, and it got washed out. I think he had also built the original dam out of logs. Then he built another one out of concrete. So he was just one of those people that anything you wanted, he could figure out a way to get it built. He lived over here in Wiley.

**Mr. Jones:** The camp brought in most of the boys and most of the staff members. They weren't all from the same state now. They were from different states. There were three of the staff from Houston, Texas, and one that I remember from Dallas, Texas. When the camp first started, the biggest majority of the whole outfit came from Texas.

There were a few Rabun County kids that went there. In the beginning, kids were there from every state in the union, and from some foreign countries. Now seven boys came up there one time that had to have a translator with them, because you couldn't understand nary a word they said. But he stayed right with them, and that's all he done. I won't say for some, but I believe they was from Italy. They'd talk to their translator and he'd talk to you.

**Mr. Ellis:** When we went to the camp, it was pretty rigidly run, and Jeff and I were just talking about it the other day. It was pretty well scheduled: We had some free time, but they had a whistle to wake you up, and then you had your calisthenics; then you had to rush back and freshen up, brush your teeth, clean the cabin, and go over to the mess hall to eat, or the dining hall, I guess I should say.

**Mr. Davis:** As Ruddy said, the typical day would be, after you get up, I think probably seven o'clock. I'm not sure. You just went by the whistle. They kind of whistled and told you what to do, but anyway, everybody got up at a certain time and went down. You had calisthenics, and [because it was] boy's camp, nobody wore clothes to calisthenics. You might have had a towel around your neck or something like that. So we'd go down and pledge allegiance to the flag and had calisthenics. Afterwards, the brave boys took a morning dip. You could imagine one of these mountain creeks and how cold that water was. Ruddy and I took a few, but some of the other boys took 'em every day. That would really wake you up! Then you'd go back to your cabin, get dressed, and you'd have personal inspection. You had to brush your teeth, comb your hair, and clean under your fingernails. If those fingernails were not clean, they would take points off. After personal inspection, you went to eat breakfast. After breakfast, you'd have cabin inspections. We would have to sweep out from under our bunks and clean the lanterns. That was always the hardest to clean 'cause the lanterns were run on kerosene and smoke came out of it. Cleaning those always took the most time.

**Mr. Griffin:** A day at Camp Dixie—up at seven-thirty, assemble at the flag-pole, where we raised the flag; a dip in the stream that ran into Dixie Lake (at the end of camp, ice cream at Lakemont if you never missed a dip); get dressed and have personal inspection; breakfast. Everyone gathered outside the dining hall and waited for the whistle to blow. Every camper stopped talking and waited for the second whistle. No one talked until after the blessing was said.

After breakfast, we went back to our cabins to clean up for inspection. There was a lot to do at camp. We had cabin competition and played each cabin in all sports: softball, football, basketball, tennis, swim meets, canoe races, horseshoes, badminton, and volleyball. We also made crafts: leather, metal, and bows and arrows. There also was instruction in archery, boating, tennis, and various other sports. There was not an idle time at Camp Dixie.

On Mondays, Wednesdays, and Fridays, we had cabin competition in sports. On Tuesdays, Thursdays, and Saturdays, we either did crafts or had sports instruction. After morning activities, we went swimming in Dixie Lake. Lunch followed and an hour's rest and then cabin competition and afternoon swims. There was free time for canoeing, horseshoes, etc. After dinner was Cow Pen time with skits, stories, and sing-alongs—then back to our cabins for devotionals and bed.

Sunday was a very special day at Camp Dixie. Up at seven-thirty, raise the flag, calisthenics, morning dip. Then we dressed in white and went to Chapel Island, where we had a devotional and communion.

Breakfast, cabin inspection, then back to Chapel Island, where Dr. Sutton, superintendent of the Atlanta schools, talked to us. He had a wonderful way of telling Bible stories and using the camp staff in the stories. All the kids loved him!

After morning services, we had lunch and rest time. Afternoons were on your own. Kids went hiking, canoeing, played tennis, or worked on their crafts. After supper, we returned to Chapel Island, where we had cabin sings, a short devotional, and award time. The first award was a red-felt triangle. After two weeks, a camper could get a green triangle; and after six weeks, a Dixie honor emblem. Awards were earned for good attitude, trying to better yourself, and getting along with fellow campers. Just being a good athlete did not earn [you] an award. The camper had to have the Dixie Spirit! The Dixie Spirit—it was something all the campers worked hard to obtain. The spirit of doing your best, trying to improve, helping your fellow camper, pitching in, not complaining. [These were] the criteria a camper was judged by. The felt triangle was as important to a young camper as any award could be.

**Mr. Jones:** The campers wore plain clothes—regular clothes, not uniforms. They wore short pants and often no shirt at all, except when they'd go to the dining hall. They all had to put on their clothes at mealtime. When they went to the dining hall, they wouldn't let them go like children do now. There was no boys up at Camp Dixie for Girls, and no girls down here at

Camp Dixie for Boys. Of course they had visiting days: Every two or three weeks they would take them backwards and forwards. Last time I was up there on visiting day, they had the boys on one side of the creek and the girls on the other side and a bridge separating them.

**Mr. Davis:** We had to wear shoes all the time. In other words, nobody walked around camp barefooted because, I guess, that kept you from gettin' your feet hurt. Everybody wore tennis shoes—shoes and socks. You could have no money in camp. If you bought something in camp, you had this little chip, and you would sign your name to the chip. If you bought some craft supplies or something like that, you'd sign the chip, and they'd put down the amount, whether it was a dollar or fifty cents or whatever it was.

**Mr. Ellis:** No candy.

**Mr. Davis:** And no candy. You couldn't have any candy in camp. It was so regimented that everything was kind of run by a whistle. You didn't really appreciate that at nine, ten, or twelve years old. You were busy all the time; you had something to do all the time. You got up, had calisthenics, personal inspection, eat, cabin clean, some sort of sport, and then maybe eat again. Then you had a rest siesta, a rest period, after lunch for about an hour, and then you had more competition with sports; then you'd swim, eat supper, go to the Cow Pen at night, and then you went to bed. Well, you had devotions in the cabin, and then you'd go to bed. That was just the routine. Twice a week you could write letters home, and when your cabin turned in the letters, they did get a plate of candy, which was just chocolate and peppermints. That's the only candy, so it was a big deal to get that box of candy at the end of camp. We read comic books. That summer the war hadn't started yet.

**Mr. Jones:** There's a place up at the top of the springhouse that they didn't box up, and the boys got to going in there and getting into the food and stuff. Of course boys will be boys. I don't care where they're at. The camp kept candy in there, and the boys would get into the springhouse and take it out of there. The camp gave each cabin a box of candy for the ride home. They didn't ride home, they didn't get any candy. The leaders of the cabins were pretty particular about giving the candy out. Well, the candy would usually give out before they got to give it all away. The parents would bring bubblegum to the kids when they came to visit, and then there was so much bubblegum you couldn't walk. Scotty came down there one morning and stepped up on the walk, and he had so much gum stuck to his shoes he could hardly pick his feet up. He said, "Well, I'm going to put a stop to that." I reckon he went through every cabin, and all the boys had bubblegum in their trunks . . . why, I reckon he took it and gave it back to them the day before camp closed. If the parents came around and he saw them, he told them, "No bubblegum!" You take about 200 or 300 children and them all using chewing gum . . . Of course when they'd start to the dining hall, they would just throw it out on the ground.

**Mr. Ellis:** Yeah, I guess it was routine more than rules. We followed the routine. I don't recall any forbidden things. I'm sure there were some after lights out. No noise after lights out and stuff like that, but I don't recall any big, rigid set of rules. If you followed the schedule, you were pretty much followin' the rules, so to speak. Mostly, breaking rules was tied in with cabin competition. So if you broke a rule, your cabin got penalized. You had a lot of peer pressure to behave.

**Mr. Davis:** I remember that the campers' cabins were on one side of the creek and the staff's cabins were on the other. If the boys talked after lights out, they'd hear somebody say, "All right, cut that noise out down there." That was about it. There were things like, well, you couldn't wander off camp by yourself, but you were always busy with one of those routines that you didn't have much of an opportunity to wander off by yourself. Actually, your counselor kind of took care of you. For example, if you didn't have shoes on, he'd just tell you to go put shoes on. Each leader was responsible for his cabin. The kids back in those days just followed what their mothers, fathers, and cabin leaders said. I can't recall anybody really breakin' any rules.

**Mr. Ellis:** We were used to following orders. I can't remember any time that there wasn't some older person keepin' an eye out for you.

## JOBS

"When I started out working at the camp, I got twenty cents an hour, then thirty cents an hour, and it went up until it was $1.25 an hour."

—*Ernest Jones*

The camp was for youths, but to maintain the camp and to keep it running smoothly necessitated cooks, counselors, camp managers, staff, and maintenance people. Sometimes these jobs were stressful, but the adults who worked there talk of touching lives and of giving young people experiences in the outdoors that those young folks would remember for a lifetime.

**Mr. Jones:** The main work I had was working at Camp Dixie, but of course I worked in the wintertime back then for somebody else. Back when the camp first started, I just worked there three or four months a year.

When I started out working at the camp, I got twenty cents an hour, then thirty cents an hour, and it went up until it was $1.25 an hour. Now part of the time when they paid me twenty cents an hour, sometimes they wanted something special done, and they would pay me thirty cents an hour. Most of the time there was just one worker, just me, but there were five other men who cut most of the logs. Outside of the staff during the camp season, I reckon they hired all Rabun County men. It took about two months to build the whole camp. They had several hands there when they first started. Of course there were not as many buildings as there are now. Five or six weeks before camp opening time, there were six or eight men besides me to get the camp ready, but I didn't work with them much. Most of the time I was doing one thing and they were doing something else. At the first when I started work at the camp, I just worked two months in the spring and one month in the fall, along in the last of August. Camp used to close the twenty-eighth of August. Later on, I was the only one that was there all the time, and it kept me busy in the wintertime getting prepared for the next season—had to keep everything in shape. They kept horses there all year 'round, and I had to feed the horses—ten, twelve horses—and I fed the hogs. But when Carlos was there, he took care of them. During my later years at the camp, I was the caretaker. And the last two years, they give me $200 a month, and I would eat one meal a day with them—that was lunch. And once in a while, they would give me a bonus check for $100 or $50. Well, after Carlos sold the camp—he'd been gone four or five years—I had to retire. I worked there fifty-four years.

# FOOD

"Scrambled eggs were not good at all . . . So they said, 'Rah, rah, rah, rah, rah, eggs, eggs, eggs!' Of course the cooks and Pop J. didn't appreciate that too much. I don't think anybody ever lost weight."
—*Rutherford (Ruddy) Ellis*

With a group of youths, one of the most important aspects of life is food. The campers had to eat properly to maintain their stamina for the many activities planned for them. Some campers liked the food, while others did not. Nevertheless, the campers ate because they knew that was the only food they were going to get until care packages arrived from home.

**Mr. Ellis:** The food was acceptable. A lot of us came from pretty nice homes, and we were used to eating pretty good food. There was a tradition. Anytime somebody would do something important, maybe somebody fired a real high score on the rifle range, then his cabin sittin' at the table would get up and say, "All right, we've got to have fifteen rahs!" So they'd say, "Rah, rah, rah, rah, rah! Rah, rah, rah, rah, rah! Rah, rah, rah, rah, rah!" Then everybody would clap. So it was supposed to be for something good that somebody had done or some award that they'd gotten. But sometimes we'd get a little tired of the food—like scrambled eggs were not good at all. So one morning, one of the cabins said, "All right, we're going to have fifteen rahs!" So they said, "Rah, rah, rah, rah, rah, eggs, eggs, eggs!" Of course, the cooks and Pop J. didn't appreciate that too much. I don't think anybody ever lost weight. We probably gained weight. That was one of the few screened-in rooms, of course, was the dining hall, and the kitchen was right adjacent to it.

**Mr. Davis:** The cooks were black men. Pop J. got the cooks out of Atlanta. They cooked it well. I think a lot of cooks just came for two weeks' vacation or somethin'. I don't even know if they stayed the whole summer. I think that another shift of cooks came in. He had good kitchen facilities. He had a place to make that homemade bread: rolls and all those things. I think the stoves were wood. I could be wrong, but I know that they were big stoves.

## ACTIVITIES

"They ain't no girls in the camp, so you'd just run down and swim nude. You know, that's great swimmin'—swimmin' nude."
                                                                —*Jeff Davis*

The campers had many activities while they were at camp. The staff structured the day's events so the children didn't have much idle time on their hands. Also, the activities were varied so the campers had an opportunity to take part in a vast array of games and crafts and participate in friendly competitions for a summer of companionship and fun. These activities often gave campers, many of them from large cities, opportunities to try new things.

**Mr. Ellis:** The whole day was scheduled around cabin competition. That was the big thing. They divided the campers up by age groups. We had four divisions. In cabin competition you got points for winning basketball games, baseball games, and kickball games. If your cabin didn't pass inspection, or if you had some misbehavin' with something, they would take points off. Then, at the end of a period of time, the cabin with the most points would win. Athletic competition was scheduled throughout the day, and in addition to that, you had other opportunities to earn points. One of the jobs I had was to go over to Chapel Island, which was the outdoor chapel. It just had a tent that was covered and fit over the chimes. You would take the big cover off and polish the chimes.

**Mr. Davis:** They had some cows in the athletic fields. Some of the boys would go across the bridge that crossed the creek and pick the cow pies up and take 'em off the athletic field. You could police the camp to get points, too. You'd have to clean out the kerosene lantern in your cabin, which would

PLATE 190  A camper plays tetherball.

smoke up at night; and the inspection was if the leader could rub their finger up in the top of the lantern and get any soot out, that was so many points off. At the end of the camping season, when you had the big banquet, they'd say, "Okay, cabin ten in division one won the competition," and everybody would get a box of candy, which was a big deal because we couldn't have any candy. They didn't give you any back then.

Nine- and ten-year-olds were in division one; and divisions two, three, and four was for the [older] boys. Each division had an activity planned for the mornin', whether it was basketball or baseball or crafts. We had a lot of crafts. We had the silversmith craft activity. I made a little sterling silver pin for my mother. That was a big thing back in those days—to make something for your mother. Anyway, I made that, but you could make other things, too. You could work with beads.

**Mr. Ellis:** I did model trains. Model trains were my favorite.

**Mr. Davis:** They had a lot of crafts that you could do. You probably did crafts for about two hours. Then they might have had swimmin'. You didn't wear your clothes to go swimmin' either. They ain't no girls in the camp, so you'd just run down and swim nude. You know, that's great swimmin'—swimmin' nude.

**Mr. Ellis:** We did have bathin' suits, but the only time we wore them was if we knew there were gonna be visitors in camp—like the parents would

PLATE 191  Cabin leader Jeff Davis
with his cabin members in 1941

come; occasionally, the girls from Camp Dixie for Girls would come down. At least once during the summer we had a dance in the gym or something, and we'd wear suits then. Occasionally, there'd be some unannounced [female] visitors that would come into camp. The first person that saw one would holler out, "WIC!" for "women in camp." The next guy would pass it down: "WIC!"; it'd go all the way up and down the camp 'cause the cabins were open. If anybody walked by the cabin, there's no privacy, and if you heard "WIC," you'd put clothes on. I didn't like swimmin' too much 'cause the water was too cold.

**Mr. Griffin:** We hated to hear "WIC," and we would have to wear bathing suits. Nude was the way to go! We carried soap to the afternoon swim for our bath. There were real showers if we wanted to use them.

**Mr. Ellis:** Back then, most of the time we stayed right there at the camp, but we would have hikes out in all directions. We went up Worley Creek, and we could go all the way to Lake Burton for an overnight camp. We also had overnight hikes where we went over the mountain to Lake Rabun down to Rabun Beach. We also had hikes down to Lakemont to Alley's Store, which is still open. That was a big deal because you had maybe a nickel or a dime you could spend there, and then we had other hikes that went off in different directions, sometimes an overnight hike. We went up one creek, which I think is all covered up by the new highway now. It was up near Wiley, and we camped by a creek there. Then we had hikes, nature hikes, where they would take us out, and we'd look for snakes. We would climb up the mountain above the camp, and we would take one of the leaders or staff members who was the naturalist. I think his name was Lee Richmond. We would turn over the logs and rocks. We had a forked stick with a rope on it. You could slip it over the snake and pull it tight. I remember carrying a backpack with a snake in it. I was very apprehensive about that, but we had snake cages. Down by the creek, there was kind of a meadow. We had these cages, and they had all kinds of rocks and laurels and greenery in there—sort of a habitat. We'd put the different snakes in the different cages, and we were supposed to learn to recognize the different snakes. Then we always had that fight between the copperhead and the king snake. That was the highlight of the season. Copperheads, as you know, are pretty common in the mountains. The whole camp would gather around. They put the king snake in the copperhead's cage, and they'd bite a little bit; then the king snake would get a good bite on the copperhead. They would take them out and put them down on the ground so that everybody could see them. Of course, the king snake, being a constrictor, would wrap around the copperhead and just choke him to death. The king snake always won, and then he would eat him.

**Mr. Davis:** It was so quick and fast. You can't believe that he could get his mouth open that far. As a kid, I had never seen that—watching that king snake killing that copperhead. It would take him an hour to eat him. You see, he would eat his head first and then just keep on going. It would take him maybe an hour to eat the whole snake.

**Mr. Ellis:** He'd swallow him whole, and, over a number of days, he would digest the whole thing. That's the way they eat. They swallow animals whole. These were some of the things that we learned at camp. I don't remember anybody getting snakebit. In fact, in my hiking explorations in the mountains, I very seldom saw a snake.

**Mr. Davis:** The snake is more scared of you than you are scared of the snake. The only time you happen to get bit by a snake is when you step on a snake bed or a mother with a little snake. If you walked in the leaves as you went along, that snake is going to go the other way.

**Mr. Griffin:** Overnight hikes were big at Camp Dixie. The second, third, and fourth divisions hiked over the mountains to Lake Rabun. We usually spent two nights. The fourth division, older boys, also hiked to Lake Seed and Lake Burton. The Burton hike was a long, hard hike. The campers were brought back in buses.

We also went to Hall's Boathouse by bus and went on powerboat rides on Lake Rabun. That was well received, as well as the hike to Lakemont for ice cream at the country store.

**Mr. Ellis:** Of course, we learned a lot of sports and crafts, and Jeff was just reminding me that we had Indian lore.

**Mr. Davis:** The camp had an Indian tepee with logs around it. They would teach maybe two or three cabins Indian dances, and they would get a program together. At nighttime around the campfire, whoever took the Indian lore program that week dressed up in headgear and did the Indian dances. Some of the leaders who were interested in Indian lore would end up telling stories, too. For [those of us who had never] heard Indian stories, that was pretty interesting.

**Mr. Ellis:** We did have some horseback riding, and that was one of the activities. There was a range you could ride on. I guess there were some trail rides. I don't remember going very far on horseback.

**Mr. Davis:** You'd mostly ride down the road. I don't recall going on too many trails.

**Mr. Ellis:** The big thing we enjoyed was that we would have some sort of activity in the Cow Pen. The Cow Pen was a building that was an open area with a roof over it and was full of straw. The campers would come in. You would step down into the Cow Pen, and you'd just sit in the straw. There was a stage. One of the things, as part of cabin competition, was that each cabin would put on a skit. They had some judges to judge and give out points. The younger kids would put on some simple skits, and the older ones would put on more sophisticated plays. You'd sit around and enjoy the skits, and then there would be singing. The camp songs were a big thing. Everybody was supposed to learn all the camp songs, and we'd sing those often. That was fun! There wasn't much else to do at night because you didn't have any lit places. You just had a kerosene lantern for light, so we had to go to the Cow Pen pretty early. There were not many activities you could have after dark, but the Cow Pen had a piano. It also, incidentally, had a room back behind the stage with Ping-Pong tables. That was also connected by the covered walkway, so even if it was raining, we could walk down to the Cow Pen. Almost every night, there was some kind of activity going on there for entertainment. I don't think we ever had any movies, and I don't think they ever took us anywhere, 'cause again, there was a lot of travel restrictions.

**Mr. Davis:** The thing I remember most was a skit where some wires [were placed] under the sheet that were connected to one of those old generators. Each cabin had to do some sort of entertainment—it didn't have to be a skit. One cabin had this bench about three feet long with a sheet on top of it and wires underneath, and I think it was hooked up to an old Ford generator. But anyway, somebody would sit on the bench, and a guy backstage would crank this thing. Whoever was sitting on the bench would get an electric shock, and he'd jump off. Nobody knew why you couldn't sit on the bench. So everybody wanted to try to sit on it, and of course, all of the older boys thought, "Well, I can sit up there." And then they'd shoot that juice, and he'd jump up. It ended up, some little boy about eight years old came up and tried; the guy backstage didn't crank the generator, so the little boy ended up winning. That was great! Some little fifty-pound boy who was up there ended up winning a candy bar or something. They had some interesting programs. One time, they had a schoolteacher from Augusta whose name was P. D. Watkins. He was a great storyteller. He would tell all these stories like Dracula and Frankenstein. He was really good! He'd kind of lull you, and you'd relax in that straw; then suddenly he'd come out with this exciting part or this bloodcurdling scream! Everybody would just jump.

**Mr. Ellis:** We had other activities on the lake, too. We had the usual canoe jousting where one person stands up on the canoe with a long pole that had a pad on the end of it. One guy paddles while the other guy stands up there and tries to knock the other guy in the other canoe off. It was real tricky because you didn't have too much balance. So we had the canoe jousting, and we had the other regular canoeing activities. Then we had the submarine races, which were what I liked. You'd take two canoes, turn them upside down, and put two or three guys underneath. You'd start out just swimming and pushing the canoe. Eventually one of the canoes would start to go off in another direction 'cause they couldn't see where they were going. Every now and then, one of the guys would have to come up and stick his head outside the canoe to see where they were going, get back under there, and push real hard again. We'd see which canoe would reach the finish line first. We also did some frog gigging.

**Mr. Davis:** There were lots of frogs around the lake.

**Mr. Ellis:** We were able to go out at night with flashlights and frog gigs in the canoes. The gig was about three or four feet long, with three sharp prongs on the end of it. We'd silently glide around the shore looking for these great big bullfrogs. I don't think I remember ever catching one. Sometimes we would be out frog gigging, and a snake would come up and get the frog before we did.

**Mr. Davis:** Naw, I don't think we ever got one, but I remember you would shine the light in the frogs' eyes, and that would kind of freeze 'em. Then you would gig the frog. Those frogs were pretty smart, though. Some of the boys did end up catching frogs. I don't think I ever got one. It is harder than you think—maybe not if you're older and quieter, but, I mean, ten- and twelve-year-old boys aren't going to be quiet.

**Mr. Ellis:** They usually jumped in the lake as soon as they saw you coming. The other activity we had on the lake . . . of course we had swimming and diving off a platform. We also had a genuine Turkish bath. We had a low shed, which had two bench seats in it, and you'd get in there with no clothes on. Outside, they had a fire where they'd heat these big rocks. They'd open this back door and put these rocks in a little depression. Then you'd sprinkle the rocks with some water from a bucket. This created steam. You'd get in there, and it got so super humid that you'd get to the point where you felt like you almost couldn't breathe. The steam was so heavy in there; you'd get real hot, and you would just sweat profusely. The whole idea in a Turkish bath, of course, is to clean your pores. So you'd get to sweating all over; then they'd open the door, and you'd run down and dive into that cold lake. Wow! What a shock!

**Mr. Davis:** Down at the dock—they had a dock with a swimming tower, a diving board tower—there was this log that went through the dock. You would walk out on the log, and then somebody would challenge you on it. Then you'd go out there and try to knock the other fellow off with your hands and be king of the log. That was lots of fun! It was just a lot of fun swimmin', too, because most of us had never swam with our clothes off. It was great! It's a lot easier to swim without a bathin' suit. Now they've got these new bathin' suits that are so tight you don't even know they're there. In those days there were just loose trunks.

**Mr. Ellis:** That's right, we had the old-fashioned stuff. We didn't have anything like what they have now.

**Mr. Davis:** Like on the Olympics, they had those tight . . .

**Mr. Ellis:** . . . Speedos! The camp had what they called an honor emblem. It was round, and it had a Camp Dixie design on it.

**Mr. Davis:** There was a canoe in the middle of it.

**Mr. Ellis:** Campers had to earn an honor emblem and, before you got one of those, you got little felt triangles. You had a red triangle and a green triangle. You had to earn those, too. The triangles were awarded at the campfires. You'd sing songs and all, and then they'd give awards. I was not a very good camper. I was a little smart aleck. I got a red triangle the first year and a green triangle the second year, and I never did get an honor emblem.

**Mr. Davis:** They were made of felt. Division one got little red triangles. Divisions two, three, and four got the honor emblems. You earned them by just being a good camper—I mean, for just gettin' in the spirit of things and cleanin' the cabin up and just bein' cooperative. You earned a triangle by just getting along with the other boys in the cabin and things like that. They gave them out once a week.

**Mr. Ellis:** My attitude was not very good. I guess I didn't like the leader. I'm not sure how you individually would earn it other than your attitude and your sportsmanship. I was a real poor sport. When my team was losin', I was a poor loser. I remember being real sad when we didn't do well in the athletics.

**Mr. Davis:** [You received awards for] just getting along with other boys in the cabin—the other boys in the camp, too. Really, just bein' a good guy, I guess you'd say.

**Mr. Ellis:** Just bein' a model camper—what they expected out of you.

**Mr. Davis:** They also had an honor camper who was the best camper in the whole camp, and that was usually one of the older boys who was twelve, thirteen, or fourteen years old. Then they had merit camper, which was right under the honor camper. Then they had these honor emblems that you could earn. That was another way that everything was kind of a subtle competition up there.

**Mr. Ellis:** That was a way of making you behave. Everybody wanted to earn those honor emblems.

**Mr. Davis:** I've got one somewhere. They'd give you an honor emblem one year, and then if you earned one another year, you would get a star. I went about five or six years. I think I've got an emblem with three stars if I'm not mistaken.

We had an awards banquet where the people got their emblems. It was a good meal, and everyone dressed up. The honored campers were always recognized there. I don't recall any speaker, but we decorated the dining hall. We got lemons and put them in the hornets' nests. We also decorated the screens in the dining hall.

**Mr. Ellis:** Also, in cabin competition, they recognized the cabin with the highest score.

**Mr. Davis:** Each division had a winner.

**Mr. Ellis:** Yeah, we had four divisions.

**Mr. Davis:** There were four competitions. They had the younger boys, and then they got the ones that were a little older, and on up. So each division they had—divisions one, two, three, and four—would be in competition.

Whoever got the most points in each division would win. I can't think of any
way of gettin' points except in sports and doin' chores. I won the first year I
was there. I can't remember if we got anything. Of course, back in those
days, it wasn't much. It was just prestige—something to write home about.

**Mr. Ellis:** Every time you'd get something done, you could get points.

**Mr. Davis:** I can think of ways you could get them taken off: you know, personal inspection, cabin inspection, and things like that. It was real competitive. It's probably not as big as Little League baseball, but just kind of subtle.
You wanted to win. You wanted to be the cabin to have the most points in
your division.


## GENERAL


"He had some chemicals in a tin can, and the can blowed up and
blew the whole dang end off the stove in the kitchen!"

—*Ernest Jones*

Many campers and workers have special memories of camp life. The memories may be related to pranks, games, hidden dangers, or camp competitions. Camp capers are in fact part of any camp experience: short-sheeting a
fellow camper, blowing up a stove, getting teeth knocked out, unexpectedly
coming up on a copperhead or a rattlesnake. Mr. Davis and Mr. Ellis aver
that none of their seemingly hazardous experiences were particularly dangerous! Several people we interviewed shared special stories describing different events that occurred at camp.

**Mr. Jones:** Lots of things happened there. One time they had a boy there. He
had some chemicals in a tin can, and the can blowed up and blew the whole
dang end off the stove in the kitchen! They had a gas stove, and it blowed two
eyes off of that! One woman got hurt but not too bad. But dang wonder it
hadn't cut her awful. It happened before dinnertime. There was nothing
funny about that. I don't know what he had in the can, but it sounded like a
case of dynamite going off. I was up at the office when it went off.

**Mr. Ellis:** I had an unfortunate accident. We were gettin' ready to play some
baseball, and there was one fellow that was throwin' the ball up in the air
and hittin' it out to the field. Whoever was leading the group at the time

said, "Okay, everybody come over here, and we'll choose our teams." I followed instructions. I walked toward the leader, and that punk threw up the baseball and hit it one more time. The bat hit me right in the mouth and knocked out two teeth immediately, and I lost another one later—split my lip open, too. So I spent a lot of time in the infirmary. As far as dangers go, there were the usual falls 'cause of the rocky terrain. You could fall and get bruises; and then, naturally, when we played sports, boys always had a certain amount of accidents. But as far as dangers go, we had to be a little bit on the lookout for copperheads in the woods. I don't recall any dangerous snakes being in the lake, though.

**Mr. Davis:** One time, my cabin was goin' on a hike, and there was a rattlesnake right in the middle of the path. We had to get the rattlesnake out of the way before we could keep going. In fact we weren't too far from camp, so we just ran back. When Ruddy was talking about snakes, we never caught any poisonous snakes. On a nature hike, the leader usually had a forked stick. He would put it over the snake's head, and he knew how to pick up the snake. Of course, poisonous snakes—we didn't mess with poisonous snakes.

**Mr. Ellis:** There were dangers just like there are today. We had to watch out for hornets, yellow jackets, and wasps. I don't remember anything that was particularly hazardous.

**Mr. Davis:** They were mostly just sports accidents.

**Mr. Ellis:** Even on the hikes, I don't remember anybody having any problems. We had battles with spitwads. We would fold up paper and put 'em on a rubber band. Sometimes we'd drive two nails into a board, and we'd get all these huge rubber bands like you would use with model airplanes. We'd stretch 'em across the board, and boy, you could really pop somebody with those things! 'Course, the leader frowned on all this. So what we'd do is we'd have our metal can with tennis balls in [it]—you'd buy these cans, and they had three tennis balls in them. You'd take the tennis balls out, and you'd fill 'em up with all your ammunition and your rubber bands and everything, and you'd just put one tennis ball on the top so everybody would think it was nothing but tennis balls. Then, when the battles would start, like after dark, we would get the ammunition out, and we'd usually bombard the next cabin 'cause the cabins were real close together. In fact, between cabins 18 and 19, where I was, there was just a walkway. There was just that short distance between each of those cabins, so you could easily bombard the guy in the next cabin with things. One of our favorite pranks was to make what we called a coat hanger bed. We would sneak some coat hangers in under the mattress and prop the end of it so that it was just barely supported by the coat hanger. So when somebody jumped up on it, the coat hangers would bend, and the bed would collapse. Another thing we had was short-sheeting, which you probably have heard about. I think everybody over the many years has done that before. You take one sheet and fold it around the bed so when the person climbs in the bed, his feet go in about halfway and hit the end of the sheet—can't go down any further. 'Course it was a big deal to short-sheet the leader 'cause they were pretty smart. They were older, wiser campers than we were. The leader was usually an older boy that slept in each cabin.

Jeff and I went back about ten years ago. We went over to the camp, and there were screens on all the windows of the cabins, and they had flush toilets. It was a far cry from what we thought was real campin'.

Red Barron had his camp in Mountain City [in northern Rabun County]. Somehow, he and Pop J. were big rivals. I don't know the full story behind it, but if Red Barron did somethin' one way, Pop J. would do it the other way, particularly in building fires. The Indian way, I think, was to build kind of a tepee out of sticks. That's the way Red Barron taught it, so Pop J. wouldn't let us build a tepee out of sticks. We had to lay ours in a little square sort of thing. There was a lot more people that I knew from Atlanta that went to Red Barron's camp than went to Camp Dixie. I don't know much about it. We never went up there.

PLATE 192  Rutherford (Ruddy) Ellis

Mr. Davis: No, I don't know much about it either. The rivalry was the only thing we knew. Actually, I didn't know much about that. Ruddy was the one, or maybe it was one of my other friends, who told me about that. It's funny, you know; I didn't know there was two different ways to build a fire.

Mr. Ellis: I thought the tepee was the best, logical way.

Mr. Davis: Yeah, that's probably the best way 'cause, as the fire burns, the ashes fall down to the middle.

Mr. Ellis: As best I know, that camp was very similar to what we had.

Mr. Davis: You know, I think it was just a natural rivalry between Red Barron and Pop J. I think it's just like the rivalry that different baseball teams and different football teams have with each other. You know, a "my camp is better than your camp" kind of situation.

## IMPACT OF CAMP LIFE

"Camp Dixie meant a lot to me. I learned a lot about life there."
—*Archie Griffin*

Camp was a very special time—so special, in fact, that former campers often reminisce about events that took place and lessons they learned there. Many tell of the impact the camp had on their lives. Because of the wonderful experiences they had at these local camps, some now call Rabun County their home.

Mr. Ellis: The chapel programs had a big influence on me as a young boy. We had a wonderful sermon with Dr. Sutton, the superintendent of the Atlanta school system. He was a fine speaker, and I can still remember some of the things he told us.

Mr. Davis: "Daniel and the Lion's Den" and things like that.

Mr. Ellis: I had started to learn the old favorite hymns of the Christian church at camp two years before that. We sang the hymns there, and now I'm in the church choir. So it has carried on the love of singing the hymns. The messages were very impressive on a young boy.

**Mr. Davis:** It was not officially a Christian camp, but it was probably as much a Christian camp as they have now. It probably had more Christian values back in those days, more than they do now. It wasn't affiliated with any church, but a lot of Christian principles.

**Mr. Ellis:** The services were nondenominational, but we sang Christian hymns. Denomination wasn't stressed in any way.

**Mr. Davis:** We always had a blessing before the meal. We always had devotion in the cabin. Sometimes the older boys would have to read a Bible verse, and then we would have a prayer. It was pretty Christian, even though it was not advertised as a Christian camp.

**Mr. Ellis:** Some of the things I learned there were sportsmanship, living in close quarters with other people, and learning to do your share.

**Mr. Davis:** Right. You would do that when you cleaned the cabins up. You would go on hikes, and everybody would have to carry something. I didn't know I was learning all that. When you're a kid, you're pretty spoiled, and that was my first taste of having to get along with other people. I believe that everybody should go to camp. The United States would be a better place if everybody had to serve for one year. I don't think you would have much crime and everything else.

**Mr. Ellis:** I was not a big horseback rider, and the things you learned in camp sticks in—like archery, rifle marching, horseback riding, swimming, canoeing. In the sports, not all of the boys knew how to play baseball or basketball and other sports. Those are the things you learn. You learned a little bit of creativity through singing songs and puttin' on the skits. We also learned about nature: snakes, frogs, birds, and things.

**Mr. Davis:** Everybody didn't know how to play every game. So we played a lot of different games like baseball. You might know part of it, and I did, but you learn the finer points of the game. You learned how to hold a bat and the best way to throw a ball, things like that. You learned to play, but they have sports camps now.

**Mr. Ellis:** The Braves eventually bought the camp. They tried to make a baseball camp out of it by improving the ballfields, and I think they made an extra ballfield in a pasture. Apparently they gave that up, and it was only opened for band camp or church camp or whoever wanted to rent it. The last time that Jeff and I went over there, it was a band camp. Last I heard, it was going to be developed over there. We haven't been over there in about ten years.

**Mr. Griffin:** Camp Dixie meant a lot to me. I learned a lot about life there. As a camper, being under men who had the well-being of the campers and who established rules we had to follow helped me grow and understand the meaning of discipline. Because of the positive experience I had at camp, both of my children went to camp. They each went for four years and had a positive experience also.

I have been back to Camp Dixie several times since it closed. Every time I was there, I had wonderful memories that I will never forget. Camp was a great place, a place that provided and encouraged character-building in boys.

# RED BARRON'S CAMP

*"It had a big impact on my life."*
—Mike Hunter

M ike Hunter relates his camp experiences for us:

Red Barron's Camp got its name from the owner of the camp: Red Barron. He was a football player at Georgia Tech, and he made All-American there. I understand that it was his and his wife's camp.

We stayed at the camp most of the summer; they had different sessions, though. You could go two weeks, four weeks, six weeks, or eight weeks. I was eleven and twelve when I went, and I think I stayed three to four weeks.

Red Barron was involved with the camp. I remember him and his wife coming to the dining hall and eating with us. He didn't go on every hike. He would always give us pep talks. He wasn't usually there a lot of times, but when we played baseball, he was the umpire. I got to know him pretty good as an eleven-year-old.

There were some guys there that were younger than me. I would say that the campers didn't get much younger than ten. You could become a junior counselor when you were thirteen or fourteen. I don't remember any sixteen-year-old campers, so it must have been campers as young as ten and as old as twelve to fourteen.

We came to camp on a bus. The bus would pick us up at a certain place. Everybody that was coming from Atlanta or anywhere around would be on that bus. We'd drive up what is now called Old 441. Trains were there. I remember the trestles. I remember I knew we were getting close to the camp when I started seeing those trestles. I remember those real well. It probably took me around three hours to get to camp from where I lived in Atlanta.

The camp wasn't much different from some of the camps today. There were a lot of sports, obviously, because Red Barron was a football player. You knew that there would be baseball, football, softball, swimming, archery, tennis, riflery, horseback riding, canoeing; in addition they had photography, crafts, and taxidermy. Some people thought it was an all-sports camp, but it wasn't. We had periods like you have in high school. We probably had about six a day, as I recall. We could choose what we would do each day. Basically, each day we'd spend about an hour at each one. At lunch, we would go eat in the dining hall, which was on the campus. We would have three more periods in the afternoon. There were a lot of extracurricular activities. We had swimming as an activity also.

The layout of the camp is still there, as far as I know. I've been back several times to go to the cabin that I was in when I was eleven, which was fifty-five years ago. When you came into the camp, you came by a couple of lakes and arrived at the dining hall. Behind the dining hall, to the left, were 250 or 260 steps that go up the mountain. They put the older boys up on the mountain because you had to go up all those steps. They would put the younger guys in cabins that were down on the lake so that it was easier for them to get to. Up on the mountain, there were at least four cabins. The cabins would probably hold twenty to twenty-five boys each. We all had cots to sleep on in our cabin.

The cabins were rectangular in shape, and each one of them had a bathroom [potty] only at one end of it. As I recall, there were ten or twelve cots on each side, then an open space right down the middle. It was like chicken houses, so to speak—just a long rectangle. I'm not sure if the cabins have

PLATE 193  Mike Hunter

been refurbished since I was there or not. They were pretty well built. They might still be there. They were wood all the way up. I know a lot of camp cabins are screened from the middle up, but ours weren't like that. There was a screen door at each end. There was no heat and no air. There wasn't even air-conditioning back then. The thing that I remember the most, I guess, is that all the water that went through the camp came out of the streams. They were pure then, and you could drink out of the streams around here in those days. They were real nice and cold. They had a long concrete basin that the water from the stream came into. That's where we brushed our teeth and washed our hands and faces. It might still be there this very day. We didn't have a sink and all that inside. There was a water fountain outside the dining hall that ran all the time. If you followed the pipe all the way back, the water came out of the stream. You didn't have showers up there at the cabins. We would have showers down by the bath-house near the dining hall.

We had an infirmary. I remember that well. I had to use it one time. I was crawling under a barbwire fence and came up too soon. That fence caught me and cut me right down my back. The scar is still there, if you know where to look. I had to stay in the infirmary a couple of days. They put me on my stomach and started putting iodine or something on it. I would say there were some situations where they had to take kids to the hospital. I don't ever remember anyone drowning or anyone getting shot, and I don't ever remember anything . . . maybe the breaking of an arm. I don't remember, but I'm sure there had to have been some snakebites. They were pretty careful about that, but gosh, we were walking right through the creeks among water moccasins.

Ninety-five percent of the time, we usually wore jeans or shorts, and a T-shirt. You had to have a different shirt on when you went to church. You had to have a collar on it. We never dressed up. There was no such thing as coats and ties at camp. I wouldn't have come to camp if I had to do that. It was just typical camp and its gear. We probably wore tennis shoes, too. We never went barefooted. I never remember wanting to go barefooted. There are too many things on the ground: rocks and all that stuff.

There was a whole bunch of camp rules. One of them is that you had to have a shower, a hot shower, at least once a week. They had a bathhouse down near the dining hall. They had a steam boiler for heating the water. You'd get the water hot, and you'd just march in. There were showers every-where. Another rule, I remember, is that once a week when we came down for supper, you had to have a letter you had written to your parents to get in to eat. If you didn't write a letter, they wouldn't let you in to eat. That way they forced us to write to our parents. Most of them were postcards. That was the smallest thing you could get by with where you didn't have to write a lot. Guys don't like to write much.

Discipline was pretty good. There were a lot of rules and regulations, things you could do and things you couldn't do. You just kind of learned them. It wasn't like you went into a classroom and said, "Okay, boys, now this is what you can do, and this is what you can't do." I remember one in particular: It was when we went swimming in a lake or anywhere. We had the buddy system. I don't know if you even know what that is. They probably still have it. We had to be within a count of ten of our buddy. If we were in a lake or anywhere that was halfway dangerous, the counselors started saying "Buddies, one, two . . . ," and at ten, if you weren't with your partner, you'd have to get out of the pool or wherever you were. You just didn't swim the rest of the day. I remember that rule. We also had a certain time we were supposed to go to bed. When the lights went out was when the fun began. That's when campers would sneak around, have pillow battles, shaving cream battles, short-sheet somebody, put frogs in beds, and all that stuff. I don't remember any particular discipline problem. They just kept us so busy you didn't have time to get in trouble. There was always something goin' on, and there were always counselors around. I'm sure they had problems, but I was so naive and having so much fun that I didn't look for people getting in trouble.

Some people got along; some people didn't. Everybody's got a different personality, and you have to try to get along with everybody. You had people you really liked to get along with and people that's just not your type that you would stay away from. I don't remember anybody in particular that was a bully, though.

I'm not 100 percent sure what time we were supposed to be in bed, but it wasn't eleven or twelve o'clock. It was early. I was tired, and late at night, most of the time, you were ready to go to bed. You had so much goin' on in the daytime. I would guess ten o'clock was when lights-out happened. That's not when everybody went to sleep, but that's what time the lights went out.

Another thing I remember . . . everybody looked forward to mail from home. Even though you didn't feel like writing, you looked forward to mail because your parents would send you stuff. I know at some of the camps nowadays, your parents can't send you stuff through the mail, but in those days you could. My mother would ask me what I wanted, and I'd say, "Vienna sausage (everything had to be nonrefrigerated), potted meat, Ritz crackers, and candy of some kind or another." Guys would cheer when you would get big packages from home. For those guys that didn't like vegetables or good ol' home cooking, you stuck to junk food from home. I do believe we had a camp store with candy.

The job we had to do at camp was keep our own stuff clean and neat—take care of our own bed and our footlocker. I don't remember doing any laundry, but I remember I had clean clothes, so you must have had to have your laundry ready on a certain day and they did it for you. As far as the dining hall was concerned, they had people that set the table and that did all that stuff. I know there are a lot of camps where you actually cook food, get up early in the morning and set the table, do the dishes, and stuff like that, but I don't ever remember having to do that. I guess they had people to do it. It was not an inexpensive camp in those days. It was pretty expensive. Looking back, I didn't notice at the time, but my parents sacrificed for me to go to that camp. We weren't affluent at all. Maybe some of the other boys' parents were, but I know my parents had to sacrifice.

All the food was excellent. Most of it was grown right here in Rabun County. A lot of the people that worked at the camp, that kept the camp in repair, that worked in the dining hall, were all people that lived in Rabun County. They had some good cooks. We had great food. It was kind of like the Dillard House. They had these big long tables, and you would eat with your cabin. You would go in, and they would bring food like corn, fresh tomatoes, and green beans in these big bowls. All of our parents, when they came for visitations, always wanted to eat at the camp.

I can remember many different things we did outside the camp. One of the things we did was hike up Black Rock Mountain. That was before the road was paved. In fact it wasn't a state park then. We would just walk up the trail following the same road that is there today. We would go by some of the same houses. I can go there and show you some of the apple trees that I got apples off of as we walked by. Many times the senior counselors, usually college-age guys from Georgia Tech and other colleges, would take rifles because there were a lot of snakes. I don't ever remember killing anything and actually stuffing it, but they would show us how it was done when we were in taxidermy class.

We had a lot of great trips. One was when we'd go to Tallulah Gorge. In those days there wasn't as many people goin' down in the gorge as there is today. They didn't have steps. It was just a narrow, dangerous trail. We went swimming down in the gorge at that sliding rock dressed only in our birthday suits. The water was real cold, and there were a lot of trout then. You could see the trout in the water. We took another trip to Cherokee, North Carolina. We'd camp out up there somewhere in the woods and go fishin'. That was a nice trip. We would also go to Warwoman Dell, but one of the most interesting things we did was go on a canoe trip. First, before you could go, you had to be a certain age, and you had to pass a lot of swimming tests. One of them, you had to be able to tread water for [a while] without touching anything. You had to be able to turn over a canoe and fill it up with water, and then, in deep water, you had to be able to turn it back over, get the water out, and get back in. I forget how far you had to be able to swim, but I guess it was a pretty good ways. After you passed the entire test, they would have a certain part of the summer that we would canoe all the way up Lake Rabun from Hall's Boathouse. When we got to Seed Dam, we would take the canoes out, and we would have to portage [carry] them around Seed Dam. We would then go the length of Seed, portage again, go around Burton Dam and then out onto Billy Goat Island. We would camp there three, four, or five days, almost a week out there. That was fun. I remember, in those days, the only boats on Rabun were all wooden Chris-Crafts. The local people that had boats, when they'd see a bunch of kids in canoes, they would come flying right by us and try to get the water in our canoes to make us sink. That was interesting to have a Chris-Craft come flying by you and water come over in the canoe.

Other things we did away from the camp were usually on Saturdays. We would walk from Red Barron's Camp into [Clayton, Georgia]. In those days, there was a theater downtown. If you're looking at Reeves' Hardware, it's in there probably where Reeves' Gift Shop is now—somewhere in that area— and we would go to the show. That's also when we would get haircuts.

We would visit a different church every Sunday. As I recall, they were all Baptist churches. I remember one of them being the church that when you're going south on 441 outside of Clayton, you turn right before you get to the Tiger connector. There's a little church back in there on the right, a little Baptist church—they now have a boat out there. I think it's called Bethel Baptist Church. I remember goin' to that one. We'd take the whole camp there. There'd be all these kids, fifty to one hundred kids. It just over-whelmed the churches that we went to.

I remember something that the senior counselors got to do. It wasn't something I got to do since I wasn't old enough, but the senior counselors on Saturday night would all get to leave and go to the Mountain City Play-house to meet all the local girls. That was a big deal to them. All we would ever hear about is "Can't wait till Saturday—get to go to the Mountain City Playhouse and dance with all of the local Rabun County girls." So that was a big deal to the counselors. The counselors were pretty nice, but when you are eleven, eighteen and nineteen seems really old. Most of them were probably freshmen, sophomores, or juniors in college. They had a great time at camp.

We had many swimming competitions. I remember, in one, Frank New-man beat me on swimming the farthest underwater. He was a year or two older than me, but I was second. We went a long ways. I don't remember

PLATE 194  The lake at Red Barron's Camp

how far; it was a pretty good ways. In a lake, you can't see how far you have gone like a swimming pool. Lakes also have a gooey bottom. Red Barron knew other sports people, so I remember one time he invited a swimmer. He was a young German guy about my age or a little older at the time. I mean he might have been fourteen or fifteen. I don't understand what it was, but he had his coach with him who was also from Germany. He put on a swimming exhibition in the lake, showing us his strokes and stuff like that. He was like a machine. He used his feet just like motors.

I wasn't much on crafts at camp. I liked photography. That's one thing I carried through with. I learned to love photography. It wasn't just taking pictures; I actually developed my own pictures. Of course everything back then was just black and white. You didn't have color film then. I remember after that, getting into high school, I bought my own darkroom equipment and actually developed my own black-and-white film. I would have probably never done that if I hadn't gone to camp. That was the one thing I kept. Of course I like swimming still. I have a canoe. I like to canoe. It's real quiet. I have a pontoon boat on Lake Burton. Photography is what stuck with me. That's my hobby. I do a lot of photography. I love wildflowers, which at the time I didn't even know existed. I do a lot of wildflower photography around Rabun County. I have learned Rabun County pretty good since moving here in 1996. I know where to go to see the wildflowers. I've also been to all the waterfalls in the area.

The camp had all kinds of achievement awards. They had merits. They had things you could do to earn different things. The big thing that everybody wanted to get to was Little Chief. They had campfires. It kind of went along with the Indian motif. We would walk through the woods at night with flashlights and little torches, way up in the woods where there was this big area that had been cleared out and build campfires. Senior counselors would be in charge. If you did real good in a particular area of camping, the counselors voted, and you could earn awards. I remember Little Chief was the biggest thing you could get.

You got Little Chief by being good in your sports, getting along with other campers, and being rated: on how well you did in photography, how well you did in archery, how well you did when you played baseball. I'm not bragging, but I was pretty good at most of the sports. I liked archery and riflery. I was a good swimmer because I learned to swim real young in my life at the YMCA. I don't ever recall anything that I didn't like—maybe crafts. I'm not really good with my fingers. I remember making rings, plastic things, and weaving bracelets. That was not my thing. They kept up with all that stuff. I remember they had an awards ceremony at the end of the year. They would hand out the awards for best archery, best rifle, best all-around camper, and I won that when I was twelve. I thought it was the biggest thing in the world. I had the trophy for a long time. Your cabins became a part of the awards, too. You got awards for best cabin. We did have cabin inspections. You had to know how to make your bed and keep your footlocker nice and clean. We would get different points for different things that we did. For the most part, everyone tried to get that. Most people tried hard to win.

A lot of crazy things went on around those cabins at night. We'd have pillow battles where one cabin would come into the other one. Everybody had a nickname; mine was Monk because I could climb up in the rafters like a monkey, where the big guys couldn't go. They were too big. I could get up there and smash all of them. We had a guy in our cabin, a real good friend of mine, and his nickname was Yellow Shirt. He just died recently, about a month ago. He also had a place in Rabun County. His name was Frank Newman. Frank got his nickname because, when he went to camp, he kept on the same T-shirt the whole time. It was so dirty that it turned yellow. It was that bad, so they nicknamed him Yellow Shirt. I remember one summer when I went, his parents actually got him shirts that were yellow and had Yellow Shirt written all over them. Everybody knew Frank as Yellow Shirt.

I made a lot of friends at camp. A lot of them lived in Atlanta. Back in those days, Atlanta might have had 300,000 people. That was back in the forties. We had nine or ten high schools. A lot of the guys I met were from other places in Georgia. They came in from all over the state. Some were

PLATE 195  A cabin at Red Barron's Camp

from South Georgia and some from North Georgia. I met a lot of people
that lived in Atlanta but went to a different school. Red Barron had a lot of
his kinfolk that came to his camp. I think he had a nephew named Pat Barron that came. I haven't seen a lot of these people since then, but I still
remember some of their names.

Other than Frank Newman, Yellow Shirt, who went to the same high
school I went to, I really didn't keep in touch with any of the other campers.
I think I knew two or three of them because their fathers owned businesses
in Atlanta. I think if I went to those businesses, if they are still there, the
sons who are my age would be running those businesses. Keeping in touch
with them over the years wasn't like high school, where you got to see them
every day. You see someone three or four weeks for two years; then you're
gone. You're eleven; you're getting older and getting ready to go into high
school. I keep up with a lot of my high school friends, but not too many from
Red Barron's Camp.

I don't ever remember us doing anything where girls were around, except
hearing about senior counselors going to the Mountain City Playhouse
every Saturday night. They couldn't wait. The junior counselors had to stay,
of course, and watch us, but the senior counselors got to go.

They kept us pretty busy. Our parents would come on the weekends and
you'd start thinking a little and you would get a little homesick. Like any
other camp, there are some people that are just not cut out for camp. Some

people just don't like that kind of thing. I just liked the outdoors, and I didn't think about it too much. In fact, my mother was all the time saying, "Don't you want to come home?" And I'd say, "No, I'm having too much fun." I remember kids that didn't make camp for four weeks. After a week or two, they just mysteriously disappeared. I'm sure they wanted to go home. If the counselors saw anybody that was that way, they would stick pretty close to them and keep them busy.

When your parents came for visitations, they could take you off the camp-grounds if they wanted, and most of the time my parents did. I remember staying at the York House when my parents would come up and visit on the weekend. I remember going down to a small stream and playing. I also remember eating at the Green Shutters. Green Shutters was here then. It was just one room at that time. They didn't have the porch. The ladies who ran it had one long table solid with food. You could go in, go down those steps, and you could eat upstairs then, or downstairs. The food was down-stairs. I had never been to this part of Georgia before camp. I had never even heard of it.

That's why I remember eating at all these places and staying at the York House. I actually stayed there. I guess they picked me up Friday afternoon and stayed Saturday and Sunday and then took me back. We looked around. We would drive to some places. I do remember all those places, though; they are still here, and that was fifty-five years ago that I ate at and I stayed at those places.

I'm sure at that time that Camp Dixie was probably here. I don't know if it was, but I guess it would be. Both my girls and my son went to Camp Dixie. At that time it was coed. I understand in the beginning there was girls' camp and boys' camp. I didn't know about any other camp at the time. My son hated camp. I couldn't believe it. I just couldn't wait to send him to camp because I had had all these wonderful experiences, but everybody's different. He just really didn't like camp. My daughters cried when we went to get them. They didn't want to come home. Everybody's different.

They had a lot of stuff that I don't think you could do today. One of them that I remember is called a sham battle. We were in the mountains, and in those days it wasn't as developed as it is today. We were just out there in Mountain City, Georgia, up in the mountains—not many people around. Sham battles would always be at night. You would have two sides. One was the handkerchief side, and the other one was the non-handkerchief side. You would try to get to where the headquarters of the other one was, and they would try to get to yours. I remember running through the woods out in the middle of nowhere by myself, just running through the woods to try not to get captured. We would run through gullies and creeks. It's a wonder we didn't get snakebit and everything else. We also had a watermelon thing where they bought a lot of watermelons and put them in the creek. They would get real cold, and then everybody would have a watermelon cutting. We did the same things you all do. You try and see how much you can get by with at night. I had a good time.

I never remember being scared. There were so many people around, you weren't ever by yourself very much. You had twenty guys in your cabin when they turned the lights out. There was one three feet to your right and one three feet to your left. I remember sometimes running through the woods in those sham battles when I just got to thinking, what if I get lost?

I'm not sure how I even heard about camp. It might have been from Frank Newman. It might have been through him. When I was growing up in Atlanta, they had electric streetcars, and when I was in grammar school, they'd have different programs for kids in the neighborhood. I was in the YMCA. They were in full force back then, just like they are now. I remember on Saturdays I would get on the streetcar by myself. I wasn't nine or ten, and I'd go to downtown Atlanta by myself and get off the streetcar and walk to the YMCA building. That's where I learned to swim, tumble, and other things like that. Schools didn't really have big athletic programs, not particularly sports in grammar schools. So that's how I learned to swim. They had pools around, but they were too far for me to get to. So it might have been through already liking stuff like that, but I could have learned about the camp from Frank.

I only went to camp two different years. When I was twelve, they asked me to be a junior counselor. When you were a junior counselor, they paid half your way. I think they still have camps like that that pay half your tuition at the camp if you will be a junior counselor. I wanted to be one, but back in those days when you were thirteen, sometimes before, you went to work. I went to work, so I didn't get to go back. I had two wonderful years there, though.

The last time I was over there was probably three, four, or five years ago. The last time I remember going, it was a church camp. I think it might still be there, but they changed owners. I would guess that if we went over there right now, it might still be there. I mean it was there four or five years ago, and over the years, I've gone back. The steps and the cabins were still there, and the water fountain was still there. I went in and there was where Frank Newman had written YELLOW SHIRT on his locker, and it was still there. A lot of stuff was still there. The thing that really got me about that was the first time I went back, many years after I went, everything seemed so small compared to what my mind remembers. I remember that lake being so far you couldn't hardly see across it. I could swim across it and swim back, yet I went there and saw that lake and I said, "Gosh, that's a little ol' lake." You have these vivid imaginations of how big things are.

A similar incident I had was when I went back to the grammar school that I went to. I remember how big the halls were. You couldn't get hardly three people shoulder to shoulder in those halls of that school when I went back. In my eyes, when I was young, it was big. I think that's true about a lot of things when you're a kid. When you're little, everything looks so big; then, when you go back, you say, "Gosh, nothing to this lake. I could throw a rock across it."

I don't remember being hot. In fact, compared to Atlanta, it was cool. Since we were young, we didn't know what air-conditioning was and there wasn't a fan. You went swimming a lot. That's about the only way they kept us cool. You would also go in creeks and everything. You'd run out the cabin and go over there in the creek and sit down and do whatever you wanted to do. I don't remember it being hot that much, but there were certainly times. I remember it raining a little. It didn't stop the activity too much because a lot of the classes were indoors. We had a gymnasium. You played basketball and indoor games. I remember photography, taxidermy, and crafts all had a classroom. You'd go inside a building, so you'd just go through the rain and keep on goin'.

Another thing I remember that's kind of different: I had a good friend of mine in Atlanta whose family couldn't afford to come to Red Barron, so they never could send him. But one year, he wanted to enter the soapbox derby in Atlanta. That's where you build your own race car and all that stuff. He built the race car; he named it the Red Barron Special, but he didn't win. I told Red Barron about it, and he let him come up for a free week of camp. So he got to come. I loved the camp. There is no question about it. If I could have gone again, I would have.

I was a city boy, so I learned to love the outdoors, hiking, fishing, and animals. I learned all of that up here. Atlanta didn't have too much of that. A lot of the guys that came were city guys that really learned a lot about the mountains. I liked it so well that I knew one day I wanted to live here, and now I do. It's beautiful. Camp had a big impact on my life.

# CAMP PINNACLE

*"There's a kind of calmness about Camp Pinnacle. It seems like if I have a problem . . . I can drive over there and sit by the lake, and whatever problem I had seems to just evaporate."*
—Mary Beth Brundage

As you are riding down a narrow little road called Pinnacle Trail, you will come upon a sign that reads DEDICATED TO GOD FOR THE DEVELOPING OF CHRISTIAN CHARACTER AND TO PROMOTE A BETTER KNOWLEDGE OF WORLD MISSIONS AMONG THE BAPTIST YOUTH OF GEORGIA . . . WELCOME TO CAMP PINNACLE.

When I was a young child, my grandmother, Mabel Garner, would talk of working at Camp Pinnacle. She talked of the hard work, and I thought the job was just one you hate but have to do. Later on, I discovered that she loved her work and thought it was a delight to cook for the campers at Camp Pinnacle.

Chris Nix and I did several interviews for this article, and in every interview—with campers, workers, counselors, and directors—was a sense of family. Camp Pinnacle and the people involved with it formed a bond that has been going strong for over forty years. Pinnacle, after being a Boy Scout camp (Camp Sequoia) prior to 1947, became a Baptist camp that brought in youths from all over the state of Georgia and gave them the opportunity to intermingle with different personalities and share the fellowship of God. It also enabled the campers to make lifelong friends.

Camp Pinnacle, opened in 1947, is a beautiful place. At the foot of Pinnacle Mountain, the camp is a playground for God's children. Campers not only have recreation but also learn about missions and missionaries, have Bible study, and share the fellowship of God with others who will soon become friends. Camp Pinnacle has fourteen cabins, a dining hall, a gymnasium, a swimming pool, a chapel, a prayer garden, and a beautiful lake. Recently, workers renovated buildings and cabins and added new facilities and a swimming pool.

Every summer, Camp Pinnacle's cabins wait to be filled with exuberant campers. In this beautiful, peaceful setting, the early-morning sunlight still glistens on the lake, and campers still awaken to learn from the day's activities. The young people still make discoveries about different cultures, foreign missionaries, and themselves. The towering trees, the lake, the prayer garden, and Pinnacle Mountain provide a setting where campers can talk to God and "grow and mature in the love of the Lord," as well as "build bonds . . . that will travel with them always."

*—Robbie Bailey*

**Raymond Woodall:** Before Camp Pinnacle was called Camp Pinnacle, it was called Camp Sequoia. It was a Boy Scout camp. I imagine the Scouts named it that when they built the camp. I belonged to a Boy Scout troop in Gainesville. In the summer, we used to come to Clayton to that camp for a week. That was a Boy Scout camp for the Northeast Georgia Council.

Camp Sequoia was in that same location as Camp Pinnacle. If you're familiar with Camp Pinnacle, you know what a beautiful place it is—the lake and the mountain view—but it was very rustic. Actually, what we did, our troop went to camp right at the end of the regular camp season, so we would have the whole camp to ourselves. We could have stayed as long as we wanted to, but we just stayed the one week.

I was there the first time in 1939. I was twelve years old. As soon as I got old enough to join the Scouts, I came. I had two brothers that were older than I, and they had come. Of course we didn't get to use that camp very long—I guess about three years after I started coming. They said there was a cloud-burst up on the mountain, and this surge of water came down and broke the dam. It was an earth and concrete dam; [the water] broke it and the lake was washed away. The last time we came here, the lake was not there, but the cabins and everything else was there. We slung down the ragweeds that had come up in the belly of the lake, and we dammed up the creek and made a wash hole. There's about three small streams that feed that lake that drain off from Courthouse Gap and Hogback. They're not large. They're just spring-fed right out of the mountain. So we had something to play around in that was cold and wet. After that, they kind of abandoned it as far as we were concerned. I think around 1942 was when they stopped using it because of the dam breaking.

**Mary Beth Brundage:** I went to camp every summer from the time I was nine years old (way back in the early 1950s) until I graduated from high school. Then I came back as a junior counselor, and then I went to college. I went to Camp Pinnacle because it was fun. I got to meet people from all over Georgia and missionaries that had been all over the world. I learned the best lessons in geography and social studies in camp from missionaries. They told you what life was really like. One could not get such information from a textbook.

Camp Pinnacle is sponsored by the Georgia Baptist Women, and it is owned and operated by the Georgia Baptist Women's Missionary Union [WMU]. We were active in our church in WMU, and they sponsored Girls In Action, which is what it is called now. When I was growing up, it was called Girls' Auxiliary, the GAs.

I was trying to think when I first started going. Mr. Harmon Deal was the camp manager at that time. Miss Sarah Stephens was over all the camp and the program of the camp. She was from Atlanta. It's been in existence close to forty-five years.

Camp was one week at the time that I was there. It was because there were so many girls all over the state that came. The camp didn't have time for more than a one-week stay, but when I first started going, it was also a boys' camp. The boys came to camp the first part of the summer, and the girls came the second part of the summer. I always came for one week until I was a junior counselor, and then I was here all summer. By that time the boys were not here, so I stayed the whole summer.

My mother and daddy paid the camp cost. I was not aware of the cost. I don't think it was more than twenty dollars. I'm sure it's a lot more than that now. I had grown up in GAs, in the love of the GA work, learning the Forward Steps, and just being around the other GAs and the people who knew what was going on in the organization. That was fun. Camp Pinnacle was something that I looked forward to every year. I wanted to go. My mother was a GA director in my church. The GAs was something that I had contact with all through my life from the time I was nine. You don't get to go to camp until you are a GA.

**Jane Donahue:** The year I attended Camp Pinnacle, I went to GA camp. This was a program for young girls in the Baptist denomination and was intended to keep us on the straight-and-narrow path in living our lives and to teach us altruism. Pisgah Baptist Church in Floyd County [West Georgia], where my family were third-generation members, received notification of the camp. They decided to send my best friend, Mary Ann Green, and me to the camp. Mrs. Jessie Dean, an older woman and a leader at Pisgah Church, drove Mary Ann and me to the camp. Mary Ann's parents picked us up at the end of camp. The ride from Rome to Clayton seemed to take forever. We rode for miles alongside a mountain stream. I was at camp one week.

I think we were probably from ages ten to twenty, but I'm not sure. Of course, the younger girls were separate from the older ones. If the ages went as high as twenty, that would mean the YWA [Young Women's Auxiliary] were there as well as the GAs. That was likely the case. It was an all-female camp at that time.

**Sonny Cannon:** I was at Camp Pinnacle in 1954. That is getting on back there! I am Baptist by faith, and I was brought up in the church by my mama and daddy. They offered young people the opportunity to go to camp at Clayton Baptist Church. Most children that came to Camp Pinnacle were away from Rabun County, and they would come for a week. Evidently, it was unusual for Rabun County kids to go, because me and Jerry Carnes were the only two that went that time. They did not have any place for us to sleep. We had to commute. They knew we were commuters because you were assigned to a little barracks. His daddy would take us over there at about six in the morning, and my daddy would come pick us up at nine that night. We did everything they did. When we got there, the other campers were still getting up out of the bunks. When lights were out, we would go home.

**Woody Woodfin:** Camp Pinnacle is set up to have an eight-week program for girls during the summer. It used to be four weeks for the boys and four weeks for the girls. Now it is strictly eight weeks for the girls.

The Georgia Baptist Women's Missionary Union's mission is to teach young people Christian values. Not only do they get Christian experience and are taught about different cultures, but they have the experience of just being out in the mountains like this. A lot of them just do not get that kind of experience living in the big cities.

**Eula Deal:** Camp Pinnacle was just a summer camp because it was too cold for anyone to be there in the wintertime. My family lived at Camp Pinnacle. My husband built and took care of the buildings at the camp. I didn't start working there until the summertime when the campers came. We really did a lot of good work then. I mainly prepared and cooked the food at the camp.

**Robert (Bob) Deal:** Daddy started work in 1946. We all moved there in 1952. He was the caretaker and manager from 1952 to 1972. Camp Pinnacle was originally a Boy Scout camp. By the time the war was over, the Baptist Women's Missionary Union was hunting a place for a camp. They made a trade with the Boy Scouts for the land to create a camp. Originally, most of the camp was funded by donations. I think Mother cared for up to 200 to 250 people at a time. It was originally a seven-day camp. Campers would leave out Monday morning, and the new campers would come in Monday at noon.

There was a man named Tommy Jones who was the first minister, caretaker, and manager at the camp when it initially started. He was there until we moved there in 1952. It was quite a place.

"They had a big day of it. There was dinner and singing on the grounds all day."

—*Robert (Bob) Deal*

**Robert (Bob) Deal:** I remember when they put the steeple on the chapel. They had a big day of it. There was dinner and singing on the grounds all day. They were going to do the cornerstone and the steeple the same day. They also had a festivity day when they did the time capsule. They made it out of copper, and Daddy had made it to put behind the cornerstone. For whatever reason, the capsule would not fit in there. They had to redo the whole thing. There's a coin in there from the year it was done, some pictures, and names in the cornerstone of that chapel.

The first six weeks of summer camp was always the boys. We'd then have the Women's Baptist Union for two weeks, and then the rest of the summer was spent on the girls' camp. Children ranged from seven years old to sixteen years old. There were no coed camps. This was a Baptist camp.

The first week school was out until the week before school started, we had campers. Sometimes we were overloaded. There was always at least 200 campers there. As time went on, they narrowed it down to only six weeks of campers. Little children don't go to the camps like they used to. However, back then, it was real full. The campers would sign up, and also a representative from that church would come as a counselor. I was there for twenty years, and I don't remember a problem of any kind. If there was a problem, the counselors would handle it, but I surely don't remember any kind of major discipline problems at Camp Pinnacle.

**Earl Ann Deal McConnell:** I think there were around twelve children for every counselor. A large part of the children came from a Baptist Home in Hapeville and also in Baxley. Those children were orphan children.

## DESCRIPTION

Pinnacle Mountain, a three-mile hike away from the camp, is reflected in the placid waters of the lake, which is surrounded by cabins that edge the wooded property. The white, steepled chapel nestles invitingly in the pines; the sounds of children's voices raised to the Lord in song emanate from within the front doors, seemingly seeping through the walls, and wafting up into the trees. To definitively describe the camp's pastoral and serene setting is impossible.

"It was really rustic, just a really nice place to visit. I looked forward to it from one year to the next."

—*Raymond Woodall*


**Raymond Woodall:** Before, the cabins were low-sided and the sides went up only so far, and then they sloped up so you didn't have a full height all the way inside. They had a screened area and then the canvas door. We didn't have a lot of ventilation inside. The best I remember, they had tin roofs because it was noisy when it rained. But that's part of it; you enjoyed that. The harder the rain, the louder the noise.

About six or eight boys stayed in the cabins. As you get older, things get smaller. You remember things as being large because you were smaller. You go back and see it when you're older, and it looks small. The cabins were just strung along on the south side of the lake. Where the buildings are now, on the north side of the lake, that was just a wilderness over there then. As you go in the gate, there was, up on a little slope on the left, a mess hall and a kitchen. I believe they had a wood-burning stove. The mess hall was screened in, and you could just sit there and look at the lake. On that south side of the lake, where the cabins were, there was a swimming dock. It went out about fifty or sixty feet out into the lake. The north side was just kind of grown up over there. Most of the bullfrogs stayed there. You knew they were there at night. It was really rustic, just a really nice place to visit. I looked forward to it from one year to the next. I'd save my money for Boy Scout camp. I looked forward to coming to Camp Sequoia.

There was no telephone, and we didn't get mail. If somebody needed to get in touch, I'm sure they had a number, but I wouldn't have known about that. I'm sure the scoutmaster and the assistants had some way of contacting. In fact, they may have even called somebody each day.

**Jane Donahue:** My mind's picture says there were eight to ten of us in a cabin. We had single cots—no bunk beds, as I recall. I don't remember any specific counselors, but I have memories of warm feelings of security and being treated with respect. I probably did make some new friends, but no friendships that lasted. I didn't keep in touch with anyone I met at camp. I attended camp with my best friend, Mary Ann Green, and we hung together.

**Leona Carver:** We had ten big tables in the dining hall, and those tables were really full.

**Mabel Garner:** The cooks stayed in a room on the weekends. We had a room off from the kitchen. We went out of the kitchen through one end of the dining room and then into our room. See, we had to be in there so early in the morning that my sister and I had to stay close to the kitchen. The rest of them had cabins up above the kitchen. Mr. and Mrs. Baskins had a cabin up there above the kitchen, too. I do not remember if it was two of them or four of them to a cabin. I do not know because I never went to their cabins.

We had a big walk-in cooler at the back of the kitchen. You did not even know it was there. You could not see it. It's completely separate from the kitchen. It was made onto the building, but it was separate. That is where we kept all the fresh vegetables. I know we had one great big deep freeze because everything I had to get out of there would be on the bottom. I would just freeze my hands off, and that convinced me never to buy a chest freezer! We had one big upright freezer also. We had plenty of room for everything, but on a certain day of the week—seemed like it was Thursday—it was my and Ola Hamby's job to clean that walk-in. Every week we had to clean those shelves, scrub the floors, and everything.

**Raymond Woodall:** We didn't have water in the cabins naturally, so between the cabins there was a spigot. It was a pipe coming out of the ground with a valve, and then there was another pipe running out here to support it on the other end. They had holes bored in at an angle in this pipe; so you'd open the valve and the pressure would come up and you'd have a bunch of little fountains coming out. So guys could line up like at a trough, line up in front of the water, and you could wash up, brush your teeth, and things like that. That was the extent of your running water, was that pipe out there, and we had an outhouse toilet. We didn't have electric lights. We had lanterns and flashlights.

**Robert (Bob) Deal:** A lot of times we had to put extra cots in each cabin. Each cabin had a bathroom, showers, and commodes. There were seventeen cabins and one guesthouse. The guesthouse was for the missionaries, just an overflow area. A lot of the kitchen help stayed in the guesthouse. It was about ten or fifteen dollars for a week of camp. I'm sure the churches paid for the ones that couldn't afford it. That was just to meet the overhead. The porch on the dining hall was screened in. There was a Ping-Pong table on the front and back porch of the dining hall.

**Earl Ann Deal McConnell:** Sometimes they'd start to eat, and a Ping-Pong ball would fly in and go in the milk pitcher.

PLATE 196  Cabins at Camp Pinnacle

**Robert (Bob) Deal:** We had a company store where they could establish credit. For a nickel or a dime, you could go to the little store and get a bar of candy or a Coke. I don't remember anybody ever losing anything or anything being stolen. The children were honest. Today you'd have to have a pistol with you!

**Earl Ann Deal McConnell:** They had shirts and stuff with the camp's name on it for sale.

## JOBS

The camp was in business for the campers' enjoyment and education, but in order to run a camp smoothly, behind-the-scenes people had much to do. Cooks, counselors, camp managers, staff, and maintenance folks worked hard to create an atmosphere of love and learning so as to minimize homesickness and instill in campers a new worldview. Running the camp was not always easy, but the hard work was fulfilling when those workers knew they had made a positive impact on a young person's life.

**Mary Beth Brundage:** As a junior counselor, I didn't have the full responsibility of a regular counselor. It is very much like an internship. I was in college at that time, so the responsibility was there, but still, you knew that you had those that were over you. You had the camp director, the assistant camp director, the counselors, and the missionaries. There were a lot of adults around. I don't know that I felt that much pressure, except possibly around the lake. I was not one of the lifeguards. I am sure I didn't feel as much pressure as a lifeguard felt. When you have kids swimming in a lake, that's a different kind of responsibility than the ordinary. There was also some pressure on the hikes to be sure that the kids didn't get hurt going up the mountain. If you have ever hiked up Pinnacle, you know that in some places it is almost straight up! When you start back down, you practically come down in a run. That's an easy place to get hurt. I worried more about kids' getting stung when grabbing a tree to pull up on. That was the main worry that I had.

When I came back as an assistant camp director, I was there for the full summer. They called me from the office in Atlanta and asked me if I would be interested in doing it. I said yes. At that time I was teaching at Rabun Gap-Nacoochee School, so I was already up here. It was convenient for me and for them, so I did it. I was already teaching, and I really didn't have to have the extra money like I did when I was going to college.

I really don't remember the wages. However, I do know that it wasn't much because you got your room and board. You got your food and all that provided.

At that time, as assistant camp director, I had to see to it that the books balanced in the camp store, to make sure that the money in the kids' accounts worked. They've done it several different ways. At that time we had a bank account, so the kids could put spending money in it. So anything they bought at the store, we had to subtract it from their bank account, then refund what was left over at the end of the week. That is a lot of paperwork to do.

I also helped with the schedule. I didn't plan the schedule. The camp director and the office people in Atlanta had already planned the schedule for camp before camp opened. Anyway, I had to help see to it that the schedule went along. I helped with the counselors, assisting in anything that required it. If a counselor got sick, I filled in. Those were my primary duties.

As far as the job at Pinnacle, I wanted to be there so much that it didn't matter whether I made a lot of money or not. That was not the point of being at Pinnacle. As a camper, the point of me being there was to learn more about Christ; then as a counselor and an assistant camp director, to share my beliefs with others, to help others grow and mature in the love of the Lord.

**Leona Carver:** I worked at Camp Pinnacle for two years. My job was to cook. Two of us had that job together. I would get up early in the morning, and Joe Hamby and I would fix the bacon. I would also scramble the eggs.

The first year I worked, I cooked the meat. The next year I worked, I made the bread and the cakes. I worked with Lola Hamby, Mabel Garner, May and Bonnie King, and Margie Kelly. I got paid fifty dollars a week. It wasn't too hard. You just get your breakfast over with, and then you get your lunch started. All we did was cook.

I had kinfolks that were at the camp one time. We each had one truck to unload. When the truck would come in, we would have to come in and show them where to unload it. This one boy would come every time and help me unload my truck.

Every Wednesday night, we would fix the campers a picnic lunch or supper, and they would go up on the hiking trail and have their picnic lunch. So we didn't have to cook lunch or supper on Wednesday nights. I stayed at the camp during the week, but I came home on the weekends. I stayed next to the dining hall.

I went in at six o'clock for breakfast, and I helped cook supper at six o'clock in the afternoon. We had church every night. It would be around nine when we got done. We had girls. They were Evelyn King, Mary Jane Carver, Jo Ann Carver, and they washed all the dishes. The cooks didn't have to do all that. The girls would also set up the tables.

"Nobody got sick from the food that I know of. I mean, none of them ever got ptomaine poisoning."
—*Mabel Garner*

**Mabel Garner:** I worked at Camp Pinnacle in 1958 and 1959 during the summer. I cooked and cleaned the kitchen. We cooked whatever was on the menu, which was a lot of different things. We cleaned the kitchen every night before we went to bed. I worked with my sister, Margie Kelly. We got that kitchen a grade A rating the first summer I worked there. We kept everything real clean. The kitchen had guidelines, which was supposed to be according to the Health Department, but people know how to keep things clean anyway.

I was not ever supposed to tell how much I got paid because I made more than any of them in the kitchen. Of course I did not make a fortune, but I made good money back in those times. I was glad to get the work. We all worked good together. There was eight of us that worked in the kitchen during the week. The ones that did not live here went home with some of the others. Some of the workers were from Tennessee, and some of them were from here in Rabun County.

We did a lot of hard work. We didn't have any time to fool around. We had two ten-minute breaks during the day. We had a break in the morning and a break in the afternoon. We could sit down for ten minutes. We usually got through with the kitchen cleaning and dishwashing at least by seven o'clock. Sometimes Margie and I stayed in there and worked on the kitchen cleaning before we went to bed, which would generally be about eleven o'clock. We would have to be in the kitchen by five o'clock in the morning.

Well, the first summer I worked, others in the kitchen included Evelyn King and her mama from Tennessee, Bonnie King from Tennessee, and Carolyn Caldwell from Tennessee. The next summer, Carolyn Caldwell did not come back. Her mama had surgery for cancer, and she needed to stay at home. So Evelyn King and her mama came back. The best I remember, Bonnie did not come that second summer. However, she could have. Eula Deal, Ola Hamby, Leona Carver, and usually one of her girls worked in the kitchen with me. Her children changed about, working in the kitchen. Sometimes it would be Mary Jane, Hilda—and I believe Jo Ann worked sometimes. I reckon that is all that worked besides Margie and me. Margie was the dietitian of that kitchen, but she worked just as hard as any of the rest of us did. That is the reason we kept that kitchen as clean as we did . . . because she knew the rules. She had worked at a good many camps before. She knew the health rules. She stayed there all the time because she was the dietitian. She just did not come in and write out the menu and go on about her business.

We never had the same two meals at a time. People here say *dinner* and *supper*. People away from here say *lunch* and *dinner*. We had to cook three meals a day. That is why I say it was hard work because it was a gang to cook for. We also had dishes and pots and pans to wash. We had these big ol' colanders, huge ones. We had to sterilize everything. We washed the dishes in a tub and then scalded them in another tub. We then put them in a tub of Clorox water. We had these big baskets that the plates and things like that fit in, and they had handles. We would dip them down in the tub of scalding water. Then we would dip them in the tub of Clorox water. They had to stay in there at least a minute. We were not allowed to touch the silverware with our hands after it was put through that Clorox water. There would be a colander full of the silverware. When it drained, we had these clean towels spread out on other drainboards. We would take the silverware and pour it out on those towels, and we would take another towel and rub over them until they were dry. We were not allowed to pick them up. When we went to put them in the silverware bags, we had to pick them up by the end of the handle. It was no fun, but still I liked it. I learned a lot of things there that I did not know before I went there. Of course, I had cooked at a lot of different places, but I had never cooked at a place that had to meet Board of Health specifications. I had cooked in homes and places like that. We met the specifications at camp because we had a grade A kitchen.

I don't know exactly how many people we cooked for, but there was a gang of them. That camp was supposed to hold 250, I think. I don't know if we had that many or not, but we sure did have a bunch of them to feed.

Mr. Deal and his son Robert saw over the disposal of the leftovers. We had these big garbage cans with lids on them. When we got through with a meal, they took those cans, emptied them, washed them out good, and scalded them. There were no filthy garbage cans in our kitchen. Back then, there was no such thing as plastic liners like there are now. If there was, we had never heard of them. There were water spigots down the hill below the dining room. They would take those garbage cans after they emptied them, and wash them with brushes and scald them good. It was a nice place to work, I can tell you that. Nobody got sick from the food that I know of. I mean, none of them ever got ptomaine poisoning.

They changed campers every week. They brought different crowds in from different churches all over Georgia. The camp staff stayed there during the weekend, and two from the kitchen staff had to stay to cook for them. There was usually about thirty-five counselors. Sometimes they would invite Preacher Marchman or Preacher Dillard, different preachers from the area, to come and have Sunday dinner. Margie and I stayed there on the weekends and cooked for them. It was hard work, as hard a work as I ever done. It was a beautiful place, and it had a big kitchen. We had all kinds of room. I just loved the place.

The campers always had supervisors with them from the churches where they came from. I remember one preacher, his son, and another boy that was there. I remember them better than anything. The boy was about sixteen years old, and I think his last name was McCall. This preacher and his son were from Calhoun, Georgia. His son was partially retarded. He was a Baptist preacher. He was a real nice man, and he was nice to everybody. I was kind of partial to that little boy, and his daddy did not want me to do that. He felt like it was not right, but I just felt for the boy. I loved that place better than anywhere I ever worked. It was the hardest work I ever done in my life.

**Joyce Woodfin:** I am the dietitian. I make sure everybody eats, and that is real important. I do all the menu planning, and that is real hard to do sometimes. You have to make sure you have food that kids will eat. I do all the buying and ordering, and I make sure it is on the table to be served. I do not do all the cooking. I could not do that by any means. We have three full-time staff and two part-time that help get it all ready.

**Woody Woodfin:** I'm the manager. My main job is to keep up the facilities. I am in charge of repair, remodeling, and any other such additions. The rest of the year, I work the weekend retreats. This year makes my fourth camping season. I have never had any prior experience as camp manager. Over the years, I have worked as a counselor at boys' camps. I served as camp pastor for about three different years with the RA [Royal Ambassadors] Camp.

**Earl Ann Deal McConnell:** Fourteen and a half dollars a week is what I worked there for. When I worked there, I had some of the best boyfriends ever.

**Robert (Bob) Deal:** I made forty cents an hour when I started at Camp Pinnacle. That was sixteen dollars a week. I worked in the kitchen. For sixteen dollars they would end up taking out a dollar or two. From the time we were five, we had to buy our own clothes.

There was a signal bell. My father's signal bell was three rings. One ring was for the camp director, and two was for the nurse. When the bell rang three times, Father knew to check into headquarters. We had a bugler to play in between sessions. He would play and let us know when to change.

Daddy was the head builder. He built the house and everything that was over there at camp. Most jobs have their good days and their bad. They furnished us a place to live, and they paid the utilities.

**Earl Ann Deal McConnell:** Daddy built it from the ground up. There wasn't much anything that he didn't build there.

We were paid every Friday by check. The money wasn't a lot, but it would buy all our school clothes. You could buy a lot with a little bit of money then.

**Jane Donahue:** The only jobs we [campers] had were keeping the area around our beds clean and making the beds. Our counselor taught us to make the beds using the hospital corner technique with the sheets.


## FOOD

In order for the campers to remain healthy and energetic, they needed nutritious—and wanted delicious—meals. Over two hundred hungry, chatty girls probably made mealtime hectic. Cooks report that, although the girls could be picky about food, the boys would eat anything. Planning and preparing these meals could be a difficult task.

**Raymond Woodall:** Our troop had a young black man who was the cook, and he could really prepare food well. That's why we had our own cook. He came with us. We had our own menu. It was great. It really was. I can't imagine cooking in there where he was because he didn't have very good ventilation. It was on a wood-burning stove, and it was hot. It was really hot. The mess hall was screened in and was open to the air. There was no air-conditioning. Like I said, you could really hear the bullfrogs croaking around the lake at night: *burra, burra,* you know. The assistant scoutmaster and all the leaders would get out at night in those boats and gig those frogs, and we'd have frog legs to eat. They'd get a bunch of them, and it quietened it down, too.

**Mabel Garner:** We cooked all kinds of good food. There was good country cookin', and we always had desserts. Every day we had a different kind of dessert. You know what kinds of food people have for their meals in the country. Well, we cooked stuff that way. The kind of bread depended on whatever we were having to eat. I made the biscuits if it was biscuits. If it was cornbread, I made the cornbread. We had iced tea or water to drink, even coffee for anybody that wanted coffee. Some of the older people wanted coffee.

Big trucks brought the food in there. My sister had to order all the food and keep up with it. She had to keep up with all the bills and turn them in to the Missionary Union. Earl Gillespie had a produce place in town back then. She ordered the vegetables from him, and they delivered them over here. Altogether, food she ordered from City Ice, Fleming Wholesale, and different companies; they delivered also. She would have to order from them for a week at a time because they made just one trip a week, but Gillespie's could come every day with fresh vegetables. She would call them and tell them when to come.

**Jane Donahue:** I don't remember the food, but I'm sure I enjoyed it. My generation was taught to be grateful for food and to enjoy what was prepared for us. I direct a young people's camp in the summer now, and I find that today's children can be very picky and wasteful eaters.

**Robert (Bob) Deal:** There would be a meal prepared that was unique to a country. Each country was represented. I remember I was only six or seven when I was a guest there. The night I was there was China night. We all had to eat with chopsticks. We also had to dress the little part. It was a fun camp, a good, plain-fun Christian camp. My father's farm was there.

**Earl Ann Deal McConnell:** The food back then was delicious because our food was not canned like it is today. Everything we had would be fresh: corn on the cob and green beans. We would have to come in at six in the morning and work until nine at night. They'd have homemade lemon pies in a big pan as well.

**Robert (Bob) Deal:** The chief cook that cooked there probably made fifty dollars a week, and again, that was from six o'clock in the morning until eight-thirty or nine at night, if you were lucky. There wasn't any jobs back then. I remember when minimum wage went to sixty cents an hour. I was probably workin' at Camp Pinnacle, and I got a raise. Then they were feeding between 200 and 250 campers three times a day. We probably had nine or ten working in the kitchen. I was there two or three years ago, and there were three people operating the kitchen. The difference is that we always had three dishwashers. One washed pots and pans, and two washed dishes. Now everything is eaten out of cans. All they do now is open the cans.

**Earl Ann Deal McConnell:** We never did have pizza or that sorta thing.

**Robert (Bob) Deal:** The chicken was fried. The sausage, ham, and bacon was fried for breakfast. Egg was scrambled by hand. It was nothing to break twenty dozen eggs a morning to scramble. All the potatoes were hand-peeled.

At one time they had some girls that worked the dining room, putting food on the tables. As time went on, due to labor shortages, counselors or some of the other staff members put it on the tables. We'd pass the food out a big window to them.

Everything was family style. One or two campers would bring the plates back to the window. They drank milk in the morning and lemonade or tea for lunch and supper.

**Earl Ann Deal McConnell:** We always served milk out of ten-gallon cans. We would have to drag those things out of the cooler and pour that milk.

**Robert (Bob) Deal:** We had lemonade or tea, but I don't ever remember having Kool-Aid. I worked there from 1954 until 1960.

I don't remember us making homemade ice cream. We had ice cream there that maybe we'd give them one ice cream a week or something like that. We kept it in the storage room in a little ice cream freezer on the right.

Luckily, we could get watermelon once a week. We'd put them in the creek on around the road from the camp and leave them to cool. Sometimes we would plug the watermelon to make sure they were ripe.

**Earl Ann Deal McConnell:** One night a week, each group would go out and build a little campfire and cook. We'd fix their food for the cookout together: hamburger patties in foil, etc.

Joyce Woodfin: I guess about the only thing that we have on the menu that was grown around here now would be the cabbage. Last year, we had an African village set up down in the woods area, and they cooked an African meal for all the girls every day. So we had to have a lot of cabbage for this particular meal, and we got it from here. We have so many things that are frozen, ready to eat. We use that to save time and labor. You really come out cheaper in the long run to do that. We have had watermelon cuttings in the evenings. We have had people interested in the camp from South Georgia, and they would send watermelon and cantaloupe. As far as the camp itself, we have never tried to do homemade ice cream. That would take a lot of freezers. Of course we do have ice cream, but it is commercial. I do have homemade ice cream quite often for the staff. The staff is here on weekends most of the time, and we make sure they are fed, especially on Sunday nights. They have their staff meetings on Sunday nights. We feed them their evening meal before the meeting. On Monday, at lunch, we try to have a real nice meal for them that day, something that they have not had or will not have during the week.

We really get more compliments on the food than criticism. I am sure the staff gets tired of having the same thing to eat all the time. We have a two-week menu that we go by. Of course the girls who attend the camp do not know that because they only come through one week.


## ACTIVITIES

The camps had structured activities so the children didn't have much idle time on their hands. Idle time meant campers could get into mischief or have time to think about home and become homesick. The activities were varied so the campers had an opportunity to learn many different skills and their minds and bodies were kept busy. "Idle hands are the devil's work!"


**"You would just be in prayer or in your own thoughts about life the rest of the way to the Vesper Garden."**
                                        —*Mary Beth Brundage*


Mary Beth Brundage: Some of the best experiences I had were at the prayer garden. We had different group leaders who would do the vesper service after supper at night. At that time, when we got to the last of the Glenview Cabins, everyone would stop talking, and you would just be in prayer or in your own thoughts about life the rest of the way to the Vesper Garden. You did not talk to anybody again until you got back to the cabins. I don't know if they still do this or not, but it sure helped make that time meaningful. During vespers, there would be times when we could quote Scriptures or sing a song or something like that. It was kind of a rule that you didn't say anything or talk to anyone but God. It's a very special time.

I don't ever remember being homesick. I missed my parents, but I didn't classify that as being homesick. It was just the fact that I was so busy that I didn't have time to think about being homesick. That was one thing that I enjoyed so much. You would get up in the morning, have breakfast; then you would have your cleanup duties. You had your own cabin, and the people who were running the camp inspected the cabins at that time. I don't know if they still do, but at that time they did. You would get a certain grade, and you got an honor camper if you had a good cabin at the end of the week. There was an honor badge that you took home. After cleanup, we had our Bible study and our quiet time. Then we had a learning time where we memorized Scriptures and worked on what we called Forward Steps at the time. It was like you have badges that you earn when you were in Scouts. We at Camp Pinnacle had Forward Steps that we earned. There were different levels.

We always swam in the lake. Camp Pinnacle didn't have a pool when I was there like they do now. It was fun to laugh and giggle about the fish nib-

PLATE 197  Pinnacle Lake

bling on you. They had canoes out there. We would go canoeing. We had games and hikes up to the top of Pinnacle Mountain. There were cookouts. We always camped out one night. I don't remember camping out when I first started going to Camp Pinnacle, but later on when I went to high school was when I remember us having the overnights. I remember us hiking the Bartram Trail several times. It was a real interesting experience. I experienced things at Camp Pinnacle that there was no way I could have in the city of Atlanta. You didn't have things like that.

**Sonny Cannon:** I remember one or two different trips we climbed to the top of Pinnacle Mountain. That was a pretty big deal. I guess there was probably one hundred or more people over there, at least. It was packed, and it was not easy to get in over there.

Of course you would get to swim a couple times a day, and they would have some kind of crafts shop with different crafts. The routine each day was pretty near the same, but they had different programs for you to do. Later on in the evening, everybody would crowd around and have a big bonfire. Different groups of the barracks would put on little plays.

**Jane Donahue:** I was a farm girl. Of course I got homesick! I was one of six children in a farm family. I missed all the rowdy activity that exists in such a situation, but I got through my homesickness. We didn't take trips. We had all our activities on the campgrounds. We swam, listened to missionary speakers, sang, and heard stories. We probably did handicrafts, but I don't remember them.

**Robert (Bob) Deal:** They'd have retreats for parents throughout the year. There would be a weekend retreat where different ones would come up.

Some of the staff would make up tales and tell the youngsters. There was not much leisure time, period. We had an activities time, but there were certain crafts they had to do.

On Friday morning you didn't have an activities time. They'd go to the chapel and visit. They would start leaving out just about lunchtime on Friday. Back then, there was a bus schedule, and we had a lot of campers come by bus.

They would take the older children to Cherokee to see *Unto These Hills*, and some they have taken to the Hiawassee Fair. Mr. Coleman would take two school buses of campers that wanted to go.

**Woody Woodfin:** We have got a swimming pool for the campers to swim in. There is the lake for boating. We also have paddleboats.

PLATE 198  The chapel at Camp Pinnacle

The camp is divided up basically into thirds. Either Tuesday, Wednesday, or Thursday, they will hike to Pinnacle Point, which is three miles up from the camp. They will have a home missionary, foreign missionary, and a mission leader/worship program every week. They have a service at night, and they will learn during the day about life in faraway places from the missionaries. They learn how to be clowns and other activities like that during the day.

We have camp for eight weeks with kids coming from all over the state. Then we have four weekends for girls that are too young to come to camp. They come with their mothers. They will come in on Friday afternoon and stay until Saturday afternoon for a mini-camp.

The campers usually get up at seven, have breakfast at seven-thirty, and then go back and have forty-five minutes for cabin cleaning. Their cabins are judged each day. A prize is awarded for the best cabin each day. From that, the program is divided up into hour-long programs: Bible study, mission study, and recreation time throughout the day. There are also night services. They usually go back to the cabin at ten o'clock at night. So the campers have a full day.

In the past there was a bugler who played to wake everyone. The counselors just wake the campers up now. The kitchen staff has four employees. We hire one lifeguard. There are fourteen counselors who are college students. There is one counselor for each cabin. This year we had two assistants to the camp director. That gave us sixteen counselors altogether.

**Robert (Bob) Deal:** There were activities all day for the children. At seven o'clock everybody was up. There would be a short devotion and then breakfast at seven-thirty. At eight o'clock we'd go to maybe a Bible study and have Bible study for an hour. At nine o'clock we'd go to crafts. There would be all different kinds of crafts set up. There was stuff from basket weaving to lariat weaving. They had activities such as horseshoes, archery, tennis, volleyball, basketball, and softball. At ten o'clock we'd usually go swimming until maybe eleven-thirty. There would be lunch until one and a rest period between one and two. Then we'd do some other activity until four o'clock. We'd have supper at five or six. Then at seven, we'd have church again. When we got out of church, there would be letter writing for the children to write home. At ten there would be lights out. Some of the older groups, we'd take to Rabun Bald to see the sunrise. We'd leave at four o'clock in the morning and drive up there. We would also take the older groups to hike through Tallulah Gorge.

**Raymond Woodall:** We hiked, and we each took different groups, like different patrols, and you know, Boy Scouts has patrols. We would take a group and hike up on top of Pinnacle. Another day we would hike through Courthouse Gap and down through Finney Creek. Now you would drive out Warwoman, past Warwoman Dell, turn left and go up Finney Creek Falls. We used to hike to the falls by coming in from Courthouse Gap. We also hiked up on Hogback. Hogback wasn't a big thrill because you didn't have a good look-off to see things. You just stood up there and it was all grown up. You need open space like that on Pinnacle. Pinnacle was good for mountain views because you had that knob, and you could get up on the knob and look west, especially if you looked down in the valley toward Hiawassee and Lake Burton. Every once in a while you'd find a snake or two on some of those hikes. In fact, one trip, we went over on Finney Creek Falls, and two rattlesnakes were found together. I guess they were family.

We did hiking, swimming, and rowing. We had those canvas-type canoes with slats in them. We had kayaks. That was my first experience with kayaks in the lake there, and we had some flat-bottom boats. Well, I learned how to get back into a canoe after turning over. It's not easy getting back into a canoe. Ever try it? It wants to turn back over with you. So you get ahold of it, and then you kind of kick your feet up on top of the water, reach across and scoot yourself up across it, and then work yourself around into it. You just don't get ahold of the sides and pull yourself in it because it will come right over with you.

We would work on merit badges there, especially swimming merit badges. Camp was a good place for that. I had thought about getting my camping merit badge by hiking up and spending the night on Pinnacle, but

I never got around to doing that, spending the night by myself. We did earn merit badges while there.

We got into some mischief. Well, if you're familiar with the camp, as you go in between the rock pillars, before you get to the gate going into the camp, across the road where the manager's house is now, there was a knoll, and you didn't have that road there. You had a couple of cabins across from the ones along the lake. So one night, I and one of my buddies that was in the cabin with me decided to go to town. Now, Warwoman Road was a big gravel road all the way to town. After lights-out, we slipped out of the cabin and walked. That's a good walk. We walked to town and walked up and down Main Street. That was in early August, but it wasn't like it is now. Now if you go to town at night, it's dead. At night, I mean, everybody's going home, and there's nothing going on. Well, people that were there didn't have air-conditioning like you have now. A lot of people came to the mountains to get cool. So Clayton Hotel was where it is now. Across the street, next to the Methodist Church, there's some concrete steps. There used to be the Green Hotel there. There was another house next door. I can remember us walking up and down Main Street and seeing all the activities. People were out sitting on the porch at the Green Hotel, and they had a canopy from the porch out to the sidewalk. It was a resort-type atmosphere. I thought it was fairly unique. That's when I said, "When I grow up, I wanna live in Clayton." At a very young age, I wanted to live in Clayton, and I never gave up on that dream. I don't know if anybody knew we did it. I know the leaders didn't know we did it. We'd have been in serious trouble. I guess lights-out was probably nine o'clock because if it'd been too late, there wouldn't have been anybody out on the street in Clayton.

I've only got homesick one time in my life. When you're off doing things you like, you don't get homesick, not at Boy Scout camp. I didn't know what homesickness was at camp.

**Earl Ann Deal McConnell:** One of the main activities they did was climb Pinnacle Mountain. We'd line up in a group, go, and come back. Now that's when we'd have problems. People would get yellow jacket stung, or they'd see snakes. I remember I'd go up that mountain and run all the way back down.

**Robert (Bob) Deal:** It was a two-and-a-half- or three-hour climb to get to the top. Sometimes we would take lunch with us and eat it on the way up. Sometimes we'd go that morning and try to get back by lunchtime.

**Earl Ann Deal McConnell:** If you were down the mountain, you could see the ones up there walking around. You could holler at them, and they could hear your voice. Some of the kids wouldn't want to climb, but most of them would. We had a lot of repeat campers. We would do all our swimming in the lake. We always had the lake. We never had any drowning accidents.

**Robert (Bob) Deal:** We always had two lifeguards watching, and the children always swam on the buddy system. [Each camper had a buddy anytime he or she was in the water. The buddies had to stay within ten feet of each other so that when the lifeguard blew a whistle, the buddies could hold hands and raise them in the air to be counted.]

Camp is where I learned to short-sheet somebody. You fold the top sheet back under, and when you open up your cover to get in the bed, you only got half a sheet. Your feet would only go down so far.

## GENERAL

The narrow, winding road to the camp led to new adventures, new friends, and new learning experiences. Every camper had special memories of Camp Pinnacle, memories that remained with him or her throughout the years.

**Mary Beth Brundage:** They chartered Trailways buses for us to travel to the camp from where we lived. All the churches in the Atlanta area that had kids coming to camp met at the Trailways station. That was real exciting, too, because I have never been on a road as narrow as that road going out to Camp Pinnacle. When you are on a big Trailways bus going out there, and you're as young as I was, you don't think there is enough room to get through there. As a child, you think you aren't going to make it!

The mischief was always trying to keep the counselor from hearing you talk during quiet time in the afternoon. We had our quiet time—our rest time—after lunch before we went swimming, or after lights-out at night. All these times, we were not allowed to talk to one another, but I don't remember anybody ever sneaking out of the cabins or anything like that. It probably happened. It does with all children. I don't remember being involved with any of that.

**Raymond Woodall:** We brought our own counselors. I do remember one of our assistant scoutmasters had a movie camera, and he would get ahead of you and make pictures of us coming up the trail. We would get those pictures developed and show them at our meetings to relive the trip.

"Do unto others," I guess, was our rules. I guess, like any other camp you've been to, don't disturb people after certain hours. You were controlled because you had a leader during the day and at night also. They just told you what to expect, and they'd expect you to do it. As far as discipline, I don't remember us having a problem. We didn't need any discipline [laugh]. I don't remember any fights, and everybody got along fine. Sometimes you do have someone who wants to cause trouble, but we didn't have any. Sometimes, you know, kids have to be sent home, but all my group wanted to be there so badly they'd do whatever they were told.

There were no snakebites, but there were chigger bites and mosquito bites. I don't remember any problems with mosquitoes. In fact, I remember one time I was leading my patrol, and we were going up Pinnacle. The trail zigzags back and forth. Instead of going straight up, which would be a lot shorter, I told the boys, I said, "Hey, let's take a shortcut" (instead of going way out yonder winding around). "Let's just cut up right through this laurel thicket," I said. Laurel is heavy overhead, but down underneath it's pretty open where the leaves fall off. So I got down on my knees, crawling right through the laurel thicket. The kids were behind me. I was the only one in

PLATE 199   Raymond Woodall

front of the group. I crawled right up on a copperhead, right in front of it, and I said, "Whoa!" I tried to back up 'cause I didn't have anything to get rid of it, and I wasn't going to fight it with my bare hands. So we backed up and got on the trail and took the long way [laugh]. The snake kinda straightened us out on that.

> "They would be squalling and crying because they were homesick, and I would just lay right there with 'em!"
>
> —*Sonny Cannon*

**Sonny Cannon:** I was comin' home every day from camp, but it was a rule to write your parents back home. The other campers would do it right before the campfire, after the evening meal, so I would write my parents just like they would write theirs. They would be squalling and crying because they were homesick, and I would just lay right there with 'em! My daddy was coming to get us in about thirty minutes! Thank goodness me and Jerry were coming home every night!

There was a lot of cryin' going on over there whenever it was time for the campers to go home. It was mournful. It was an experience that I never did forget. I guess it meant a lot to me. It must be hard, even back then, to get into this camp.

**Mabel Garner:** I did not ever have time to go anywhere, except at night. When we would get through at night, maybe two or three times a week, we would go and see how my mama was. It would be late when we got up there, and it would be later when we got back. They always had the gate locked. They locked that gate when it got late in the evening. There was a back road that we could take. It went right to the kitchen. That is the way we went back in there at night. The caretaker, Mr. Harmon Deal, knew about my mama, and he had known her for years and years. He knew that she was not well, and he knew that we went to see about her. It was all right with him for us to go through that back road to get to the kitchen. There would not be anybody there to unlock the gate. It would be ten o'clock when we would go to see her, and it would be sometimes ten-thirty or later when we would get back. They locked that gate just before dark. The campers did not get to go out of there. Of course they did not have any way to go anyhow. They brought them there by the busloads from the churches. They did not have any way to go unless they walked. They did not know where to go anyway because all of them were strange to this part of Georgia.

When the boys were at camp, we had a great long table at the front of the dining room between the door to the kitchen and the wall. The door that came into the dining room was further down. We carried that food out of the steam tables and put it on the table. We served those boys from the pans there at the table. They lined up, and we served them as they came down the line. Those boys would eat everything you handed to them. That little McCall boy would tell me, "Make me a great big biscuit like Grandma used to make." We had regular biscuit cutters, but he wanted some bigger than that. I took a good-sized juice can, cut both ends out of it, washed it good, and cut his biscuits with that. His biscuits would be about three inches across. He would go to town on them! He reminded me of my own son. A young man would come to me and say, "Make us some good ol' cornbread like Grandma used to make." He did not say, "Like Mama used to make." He said, "Like Grandma used to make."

**Woody Woodfin:** I met a man who is a pastor and also a counselor. He spent a couple summers up here as a camper and then as staff. He talked about how it really made a difference in his life, and he answered the call to preach here. We met another couple that met here and fell in love here and ended up marrying at camp. That is just an example. Even my wife's doctor in Atlanta, Dr. Davis, found out that we were serving here at Camp Pinnacle, and he was surprised. His wife came here as a little girl. Her father had died, and her mother always made a point to make sure she got to come to camp. The camp meant a whole lot to them. We have met different people like that throughout the state who came to camp as young people. They always tell how much camp meant to them.

**Joyce Woodfin:** One story that has stayed with me happened the second or third year Woody and I were here. One night, a Monday night, one of the counselors brought a little girl in to me. They said she could not eat anything we had that night. We had spaghetti and salad, and usually that is one of their favorite meals. So I told them I would talk to her. We try to keep chicken noodle soup and things like that for girls who get sick because they do have fevers and upset stomachs. This little girl said she was allergic to tomatoes. Of course tomato sauce is in spaghetti sauce. So I asked her if she wanted me to fix her some soup; she said no, and I said, "What about a peanut butter and jelly sandwich?" (We always have that available on the table for the girls.) Then big tears started running down her face, and she said, "What I really want is my mother. I have been away at camp for two weeks, and my parents are getting a divorce. I've not seen my mother all summer. I need my mother." So I tried to comfort her a little bit and let her talk. All week long, every time she would see me, she would make sure I saw her, too. We have a lot of things such as that, but that was my first encounter. It stuck with me. It helped me realize that we have a lot of little girls like this every week.

**Robert (Bob) Deal:** We've had campers who would grow up and become counselors. Mary Beth Brundage was a camper, came back as a counselor, and then became camp director. A lot of them, we'd see year after year and watch them grow up.

**Earl Ann Deal McConnell:** Sometimes we'd go to the campfires. Each week they'd have a candlelight service down there.

**Eula Deal:** If they were in trouble, I'd cry with them. The sad part was when the children would leave. There was the dining room across from the office; a bunch of them were crying, and I cried with them. I felt attached to the children. I loved every one of them.

Sadly enough, they write me letters. Some campers still send me Christmas cards.

**Robert (Bob) Deal:** We've had a lot of people to come back and visit Mother. Still, occasionally, we'll have a camper who was at camp forty years ago come and see Mother. It was a lot of fun. Every member of my family was there. Once you got big enough to work, whether you got paid or not, you worked.

**Eula Deal:** Sometimes the campers would sneak out and come to my house, just outside the camp. They'd get a piece of cake. We were all like a big family.

**Earl Ann Deal McConnell:** Mother made everyone feel special. They'd come to get a little motherly petting!

**Robert (Bob) Deal:** Sometimes we would go to church over there. We would go some, but there wasn't many times that the camp would run seven days a week. Sometimes they would put together a little choir. Over a period of years, there was a lot of people who worked there.

**Earl Ann Deal McConnell:** The best part of the whole thing was every year after it closed, we would go over there, our whole family, and move in for a weekend at the camp. There were ten children in our family. Everyone had beds, and there was room for everybody. We would cook and go swimming. In fact, Bill Conner videotaped with an old-fashioned video camera where Daddy was jumping on one of those bouncing balls. It was always so much fun.

**Robert (Bob) Deal:** We spent our life there. We had to walk to the Legion Hall to catch the bus—about a mile or a mile and a half. While we lived there, there was seven of Mother's children in school at once. She had to work from daylight until dark.

We had a big lady that worked there at the kitchen. She was a honey. She could sure play a piano. She never took a music lesson in her life, but she could make the keys ride along the piano. Some of us boys came up with a little ground snake about six inches long. She was working in the kitchen one day, and we turned the little snake loose in the kitchen. The snake took off after her. We had a big table there in the kitchen, and she tried to get up on the table. She could only get one leg on the table. She tried to lift the rest of her body off the floor. She never could make it. She was hollering and screaming, *"Snake!"*

A man was hired as the cook one time, and he was pretty bad to drink whiskey. A lot of mornings he didn't act exactly right, so finally, Daddy or some of them figured out what was going on. He stayed in the little room in the dining hall. He had whiskey hidden in there, and he mysteriously disappeared.

## IMPACT OF CAMP LIFE

Camp was a very special time. Making new friends, learning new skills, and testing your own abilities were all a part of camp life. The following are some small glimpses into camp life and the impact it had on the people we interviewed.

"It's a place where I still go today, when nobody is around, for quiet time."

—*Mary Beth Brundage*

**Mary Beth Brundage:** It was sad leaving because most of the time I didn't want to go. I wanted to stay. You were going to miss seeing your friends. The girls in each cabin had gotten so close together in a week's time that they were crying that they didn't want to leave. Some kids I saw again when I went to college. We remembered that we had been together at camp.

Probably the happiest days of my life were spent at Camp Pinnacle. I don't remember a single bad time there. I do not. It's a place where I still go today, when nobody is around, for quiet time. I can go sit over there by the lake, or I can go out to the prayer garden. Those places are quiet. As long as the gates are open, I can go.

There's a kind of calmness about Camp Pinnacle. That feeling may come from the past experiences. It seems like if I have a problem or something that is weighting me down, I can drive over there and sit by the lake, and whatever problem I had seems to just evaporate.

My times at Pinnacle are summed up in three ways: primarily, fellowship with God; next, fellowship with other Christians; and then learning new friends who loved the Lord and helped me grow and strengthen my love in the Lord. Without that, I wouldn't have the happy times in my life.

**Sonny Cannon:** It is a Christian camp. They always touched on that. There was not any talk of drinking or drugs at all back then. When a little crisis arose, you were taught to handle it in a Christian manner. It gives you training that you will remember in the back of your head all your life. Camp Pinnacle was a good thing in life that I remember.

**Jane Donahue:** As an adult, I love traveling and meeting people from all over the world. I attribute this in part to Camp Pinnacle's having missionaries at the camp. The missionaries brought people from exotic lands such as China with them. I loved hearing the guests talk about their countries and how life was there. These early exposures to people from different countries sparked interests in me that haven't diminished.

I know that Camp Pinnacle is still very much as it was when I went. My husband, my middle daughter, and her family and I visited Rabun County this summer [2002]. We happened to see a sign for Camp Pinnacle and followed directions to the camp. Seeing it again after all these years was a very emotional experience for me. The lake looks just as I remembered it; the small cinder-block cabins are the same except the color; the crescent of benches between the road and the lake, where we had vespers, is decrepit but still there. Of course Mount Pinnacle in all its splendor still rises above the camp and is reflected in the lake.

**Leona Carver:** I had some good times talking and laughing with my coworkers. I didn't get too attached to the campers because I was a cook. I never really did see them. But I did hate to see them go because they were having such a good time.

> "Camp Pinnacle was beautiful, especially when the campers would get in canoes with lights and be out on the lake at night."
> —*Mabel Garner*

**Mabel Garner:** I loved that place better than anywhere I ever worked. Camp Pinnacle was beautiful, especially when the campers would get in canoes with lights and be out on the lake at night. It was a pretty scene. Sometimes they would have singings. When I could, I would get out there and watch them. I saw them a lot of times, but I could not watch them all the time.

Sometimes we were glad to see the campers go and get a little break during the weekends. A lot of them, I missed. I got attached to some of those girls and boys. I had much rather had the boys there. The girls were picky about what they ate. The boys would eat anything and everything we give them. They would not say a word. The girls did not want potatoes. They did not want bread and this, that, and another. They were afraid they would get fat. The boys came during the first part of the summer, and we all hated to see them leave and know the girls would be there next.

I think it is a wonderful place. At least it was when I was there. It has been so long ago, and I have not been back but one or two times since I left there. Mr. Harmon Deal was the caretaker as long as I was there.

**Woody Woodfin:** I always thought I would enjoy doing this kind of work. Of course I pastored before I came here, and I had been involved with young people. The summer program is a very good program here at Camp Pinnacle. A lot of the children are coming from some of the bigger churches, bigger towns, and broken homes. Camp gives them the opportunity to have Christian fellowship together. It shows that somebody loves and cares for them.

Camp offers the unique experience of the mountains. We have a little fifteen-acre pasture over here that we rent to Herman Beck, and he has pigs that he is raising over there. Some of the children went over there to see those pigs, and they had no idea what a hog looked like or how they were raised. It is a unique experience for the children, and they build bonds with a lifetime experience that will travel with them always.

I see Camp Pinnacle as something that society needs more of. We are having more and more divided families, and the children need something to be a positive influence in their life. Children need to have the opportunity to be out in the outside because more and more of our homes and everything are in towns and subdivisions. They do not have this outside activity and the close bonding to Christ and one another.

We have had a lot of joys working at Camp Pinnacle. However, there have been some heartaches and hard times. We have enjoyed working with the different people from all over the state. Not only does it bring us in contact with the children, but it brings us in contact with a lot of the adults.

**Joyce Woodfin:** What has really been surprising to me is that some of the little girls are sent from camp to camp. They do this all summer because their parents work or their parents are going through a divorce. Camp would be their home for the summer. It is very important for me, and even my staff, to always try to encourage them and be a positive influence.

**Raymond Woodall:** I was from Gainesville; I went to work for the power company, and there wasn't a job up here for me to do because I was on the line crew. All they had here was a serviceman, a meter reader, one lady that worked in the office, and a local manager, but things worked out after a while. I came as a serviceman when the meter reader died. I suggested, and I don't know if it had anything to do with it or not, I said what they ought to do instead of replacing the meter reader is they ought to make a serviceman's job, serviceman B job, out of that; and I said, "I'll go up there, and I'll read the meters. I'll catch the trouble. I'll help deliver appliances and service them and do whatever needs to be done." It would be more valuable than just a meter reader. So they set up that classification; I bid on it and got the job. I got here and somebody down the road died and the guy in front of me, the serviceman A, was promoted to the local manager; and for the first time with the company, I got promoted without having to move. I'd moved five times, and I was where I wanted to be when I wanted to be. So whenever they would ask me about moving somewhere and taking a promotion, I'd just turn them down because I was where I wanted to be. A lot of people retire and move to the mountains, but I was already here when I retired. I didn't have to move. It worked out, and it was a dream come true. All those wishes and desires came from going to Camp Sequoia and getting me introduced to the area. We've lived here forty-nine years and still love it. I went to Camp Sequoia, and my children went to Camp Pinnacle.

I don't know of anyone around here that went to Camp Sequoia. In fact, a lot of the guys that went to that camp aren't here at all. I was twelve then, and now I'm seventy-six. My knowledge of the camp is very limited because it [Camp Sequoia] was there just a short time, but I did enjoy it. Nobody that ever went to camp there enjoyed it more than I did. Where the dam is now, I don't know if you are familiar with Camp Pinnacle, but on the dam you can look across the lake at Pinnacle, and you just have a beautiful view. Of course they're starting to build houses up there now. It's not the same view, but it has always been such a beautiful view. When you're looking across the lake, especially in the evenings, when the shadows get in on the lake and the reflections of the trees and the mountain, it's just a gorgeous view.

# CONTRIBUTORS

## CONTACTS

Sallie Beaty

Mrs. Rachel Page
Berheim

Jay Bland

Mrs. E. H. Brown

Tubby Brown

Mary Beth
Brundage

Brett Burrell

Thad Byers

Becky Cannon

Edith Cannon

J. H. Cannon

Larry Cannon

Sonny Cannon

Leona Carver

Ruby Cheek

Goingback Chiltoskey

Mary Chiltoskey

Bob Daniel

Jeff Davis

Eula Deal

Robert (Bob) Deal

Mack Dickerson

Jane Donahue

Earl Dotson

Carl Dover

Rutherford Ellis

Lewis Free

Preacher John Freeman

Mabel Garner

Regina Galloway

Archie Griffin

Tom Hill

Teenie Howell

Fred Huff

Mike Hunter

John Huron

Gene Jackson

Ernest Jones

Bob Justus

John Kelley

Lillie Lovell

Bill Martin

Fannie Ruth
Martin

Ches McCartney

Earl Ann Deal
McConnell

Mort Meadors

Harvey J. Miller

Lindsey Moore

Margaret Norton

Richard Norton

Darryl Patton

Harley Penland

Icie Rickman

Kenny Runion

Janet Shepherd

Arleen Snow

Arthur Speed

Mack Suttles

Amanda Swimmer

Duncan Taylor

Melvin Taylor

Harley Thomas

Dwayne Thompson

Steve Turpin

Frank Vinson

Lester J. Wall

Willard Watson

Lori Wilbanks

Raymond Woodall

Joyce Woodfin

Woody Woodfin

**STUDENTS**

Robbie Bailey
Austin Bauman
Russell Bauman
Cary Brown
Lynn Butler
Diana Carpenter
Kaye Carver
Eddie Conner
Phil Conner
Kenny Crumley
Emili Davis
Stephanie Dollar
Greg Doughty
Candi Forester
Lacy Forester
Ivy Garland
Kandi Gay

Teresia Gravley
Keith Head
Kasie Hicks
Shane Holcomb
Kari Hughes
Lacy Hunter
Stephanie Jobbitt
Andrea Johnson
Rachel Koch
Andrew Lampros
Patrick Marcellino
Phillip Marsengill
Alicia Nicholson
Chris Nix
Suzanne Nixon
Max Norton
Al Oakes
Johnny Pearce

Anthony Stalcup
Cheryl Stocky
Cary Suttles
Teresa Thurmond
Lynn Tyler
Cheryl Wall
Dee Jay Wall
Sarah Wallace
Missy Watts
Jared Weber
Maggie Whitmire
Adam Wilburn
DeeDee Wilburn
Jessica Wilson
Lori Wofford
Heather Woods
Amy York

# EDITORS

PLATE 200  Foxfire editors (left to right): front row,
Stephanie Jobbitt and Angie Cheek;
back row, Kaye Carver Collins and Teresia Thomason
(not pictured: Robbie Bailey and Russell Bauman)

Angie Cheek teaches Advanced Placement English and is a *Foxfire Magazine* facilitator at Rabun County High School. Former Foxfire student Kaye Carver Collins, after serving for thirteen years as the community and teacher liaison at Foxfire, recently accepted a teaching position with the Rabun County Board of Education. The other editors are former students of the *Foxfire Magazine* classroom at Rabun County High School. Current and former students involved in Rabun County High School and Rabun Gap-Nacoochee School's *Foxfire Magazine* class conducted the interviews featured in this book.

# INDEX

Boldface numerals 10, 11, and 12 refer to *Foxfire 10, Foxfire 11,* and *Foxfire 12,* respectively. *Page numbers in italics indicate illustrations or their captions.*

Harvey, J. E., **10**:164–66
  Blalock on, **10**:169–70
  Burton Dam and, **10**:177
  Craig on, **10**:175
Harvey, John, **10**:11, **10**:75
Haskell Institute, **12**:384–85
Hauntings, **12**:66
Hawks, **12**:67, **12**:113
Hawthorn *(Crataegus)*, **11**:153
Hay, **11**:298
  in beekeeping, **11**:171
  Justus on, **12**:99
  livestock and, **11**:206, **11**:211
  storage of, **11**:18
Hayrides, **10**:102, **10**:113
Hazel Creek trestle, **10**:11, **10**:75–76, **10**:*76*
Head, Keith, **12**:295
Headaches, **11**:130, **11**:136–38, **11**:140,
  **11**:151, **12**:56
Head Start, **12**:394, **12**:405–6
Heart problems, **11**:120, **11**:131
Heaton, William, **10**:333, **10**:338–39
Hemlock *(Tsuga canadensis)*, **11**:133, **11**:*133*
Henning, Ernest J., **11**:54, **11**:201–2
Henry, Bill, **10**:394, **10**:402, **11**:200
Henry, Billie, **10**:394
Henry Grady Hotel, **10**:122
Henslee, Belle Wilburn:
  on hogs, **11**:235, **11**:*235*
  on making hominy, **11**:107–8
Henslee, Buck, **11**:233–34, **11**:*233–34*
Henson, Bill and Louise, **12**:144
Henson, Claude, **10**:27
Herbs, *see* Wild plants
Hermit stories, **10**:205
Hewell, Caleb, **10**:440, **10**:442
Hewell, Mark, **10**:440, **10**:442
Hiawassee, **12**:375
Hiccups, **11**:140–41
Hicks, Roberta, **11**:57, **11**:99–101
Hicks, Stanley,, **12**:234, **12**:250
Hides:
  in banjo-building, **10**:420–22, **10**:425,
    **12**:235, **12**:240, **12**:243, **12**:247–49,
    **12**:*248*
  hunting and, **11**:238–39
  Miller on, **12**:63
  TF and, **10**:18
High Harbor Camp, **12**:253
Hiking, **12**:429
  Hill and, **12**:413
  at summer camps, **12**:452–53, **12**:459,
    **12**:462, **12**:468, **12**:475, **12**:484,
    **12**:493–99
  Tallulah Falls and, **10**:102

Hill, Louise Parker, **12**:104, **12**:109
Hill, Sally, **10**:382
Hill, Tom, **12**:361–62, **12**:413–25
  at-risk children and, **12**:413–16
  childhood of, **12**:361, **12**:414
  heritage of, **12**:361, **12**:413–14, **12**:417
  storytelling of, **12**:361, **12**:413, **12**:416–25,
    **12**:*421*, **12**:*423*
  Swimmer on, **12**:394–95
Hill, Wilson Lumpkin, **10**:309
*History of Rabun County and Its People, A,*
  **12**:xii, **12**:98
Hitler, Adolf, **10**:365, **12**:317–18
Hives, **11**:128
Hodgins, Edd, **11**:245–46
Hoedown music, **12**:246–47
Hogs, **11**:213–14, **11**:*215*, **11**:231–37, **11**:*231*,
  **12**:55, **12**:57, **12**:504
  branding and marking, **11**:214
  at Camp Dixie, **12**:448
  Chastain on, **11**:289, **11**:291
  feeding, **11**:201
  Justus on, **12**:97
  killing, **11**:232–34
  Nix on, **11**:302, **11**:304
  preparing meat of, **11**:234–36, **11**:*234–35*
  remedy for, **11**:123
  of Thompson, **12**:253–54
  wild, **11**:231–32, **11**:248–50, **11**:*249*, **11**:302
  *see also* Pork
Hog scalders, **11**:13, **11**:20–21, **11**:*20–21*
Hogsed, Ernest, **10**:11
Holbrooks, Will, **12**:46
Holcomb, Hugh, **11**:*86*
  apple growing and, **11**:86–93
  CCC and, **10**:274, **11**:88
Holcomb, Jeff, **11**:86, **11**:91
Holcomb, Ruth, **11**:115–16, **11**:118
Holidays, **11**:39, **11**:45–46
Hollifield, Coyle, **10**:84–85, **10**:*85*
Hollifield, Eric, **10**:239, **10**:355, **10**:*356*
Hollifield, Mary Ann, **10**:190–92, **10**:*191*
Holloway, Dixie, **10**:337
Homeplaces, **10**:xx, **11**:11–27
  barns, **11**:13, **11**:18–20, **11**:*18–19*, **11**:27
  of Beaty, **11**:13–14, **11**:16
  of Bleckley, **11**:13, **11**:*14*, **11**:25
  of Buchanan, **11**:27, **11**:*27*
  of Carpenter, **11**:*15*
  of Carver, **11**:12
  chicken houses, **11**:13–14, **11**:*14*
  cornhouses, **11**:21, **11**:*21*
  definitions of, **11**:11–12, **11**:27
  hog scalders, **11**:13, **11**:20–21, **11**:*20–21*
  of Justice, **11**:26